PENGUIN

ON SLAVERY AND

SARAH GRIMKÉ was born in 1792, followed by her sister, ANGELINA, in 1805. The Grimké sisters were born into Southern aristocracy, bonded at a young age, and grew up surrounded by slaves. However, both sisters also witnessed the cruelty of slavery early on and developed a strong aversion to the system. Sarah even defied her father early on by teaching a beloved slave, Hetty, to read. In 1819, Sarah made her first visit to Philadelphia and decided to move there two years later, followed by Angelina in 1829. Both sisters became Quakers and began attending abolitionist meetings. When abolitionist leader William Lloyd Garrison published an appeal for support in his newspaper *The Liberator* after proslavery riots shook Boston in 1835, Angelina wrote a letter intended for a private audience. However, Garrison published it, and the sisters quickly rose to prominence within the abolitionist movement. They became the first female agents for the American Anti-Slavery Society, touring as lecturers and continuing to write powerful antislavery tracts. In 1838, Angelina made history as the first woman to speak before an American legislative body. Though their speaking careers eventually tailed off as the result of backlash within the movement and dangerous riots, the Grimké sisters remained active abolitionists and women's rights advocates while working as teachers. Sarah Grimké died in 1873, and Angelina died in 1879.

MARK PERRY is the critically acclaimed author of nine books on American history, military history, and foreign affairs, including *Lift Up Thy Voice: The Sarah and Angelina Grimké Family's Journey from Slaveholders to Civil Rights Leaders*. He is former codirector of the internationally–based Conflicts Forum and recipient of the 1995 National Jewish Book Award. He writes for *Al-Jazeera* and *Foreign Policy*, among other publications. He currently resides in Arlington, Virginia.

SARAH AND
ANGELINA GRIMKÉ

On Slavery and Abolitionism

Introduction by
MARK PERRY

PENGUIN BOOKS

PENGUIN BOOKS

Published by the Penguin Group
Penguin Group (USA) LLC
375 Hudson Street
New York, New York 10014

USA | Canada | UK | Ireland | Australia | New Zealand | India | South Africa | China
penguin.com
A Penguin Random House Company

First published in Penguin Books 2014

LIBRARY OF CONGRESS CATALOGING-IN-PUBLICATION DATA
Grimké, Sarah Moore, 1792–1873.
[Works. Selections]
On slavery and abolitionism / Sarah and Angelina Grimké; introduction by Mark Perry.
pages cm. — (Penguin classics)
ISBN 978-0-14-310751-4
1. Antislavery movements—United States—History—19th century—Sources. 2. Slavery—Moral and ethical aspects—United States—History—19th century—Sources. 3. Women's rights—United States—History—19th century—Sources. 4. Grimké, Sarah Moore, 1792–1873—Archives. 5. Grimké, Angelina Emily, 1805–1879—Archives. 6. Women abolitionists—United States—Archives. 7. Abolitionists—United States—Archives. 8. Quakers—United States—Archives. I. Grimké, Angelina Emily, 1805–1879. II. Title.
E449.G872 2014
326'.8—dc23
2014016168

Printed in the United States of America
1 3 5 7 9 10 8 6 4 2

Set in Sabon LT Std

Contents

Introduction

"We Defied The Law Of South Carolina"
The Grimké Sisters in American History

February 21, 1838, was a bright and sunny day in Boston, though the burgeoning metropolis remained gripped by a winter chill. Such frigid temperatures were hardly unknown to the city's residents, who had endured a heavy snowfall just weeks before, and they weren't enough to keep the city's most important families, as well as the merely curious, from gathering at the Massachusetts Statehouse. There, during an afternoon session, a *woman* was scheduled to address a committee of the State Legislature, an event so unusual as to be unprecedented.[1]

Many of our century would be surprised to learn that the women of our early republic were confined to their own spheres of home and family, but this was the tradition in nineteenth-century America, and had been so for as long as anyone could remember. Then, too, not only were women expected to remain silent in public, it was considered inappropriate for them to speak out on any political issue, and particularly on slavery—the most contentious issue of the era.

But that is precisely what Angelina Grimké, not only a woman but a Southerner, planned to do on that sunny Wednesday. Which explains why so many of the good citizens of Boston, and others from as far away as Springfield and Worcester, crowded the pavement in front of the statehouse, packed themselves into the legislative hearing room and even, several hours before Grimké's appearance, clung to the railings of the legislature's stairwells.

"The attendance of so many people at a legislative hearing

was quite out of the ordinary," historian Gerda Lerner tells us, "especially since no public notice had been given, but news of this kind could be trusted to travel speedily by word of mouth."[2] And so it did: By two o'clock the statehouse, and the courtyard and steps leading to it, were so packed with onlookers that arriving legislators had to fight their ways through the crowd to take the seats reserved for them in the hearing room.

Angelina Grimké knew that her appearance would draw attention, but when she alighted from her carriage just minutes before she was scheduled to appear, she was shocked by the sheer number of people who'd come to hear her. For a moment she felt unequal to the task. "I never was so near fainting under the tremendous pressure of the feeling," she later remembered. "My heart almost died within me. The novelty of the scene, the weight of the responsibility, the ceaseless exercise of the mind thro' which I had passed for more than a week—all together sunk me to the earth. I well nigh despaired."

Fortunately, Angelina was escorted to the statehouse by Maria Weston Chapman, a native Bostonian, wife of a well-known New England merchant, and an uncompromising abolitionist. Chapman was that most unusual of nineteenth-century women: She refused to be silenced—enduring catcalls during abolitionist rallies attended by the smattering of men who not only loathed the abolitionist movement but were equally scandalized by the fact that women had founded and led it. Maria was on Angelina's arm as the two climbed the statehouse steps, reassuring her that her appearance before the legislature would be a triumph. "God strengthen you, my sister," Chapman said.[3]

A hush fell as the two entered the hearing room, and soon thereafter the committee chairman called on Angelina to speak. Whatever rustling there was in the gallery ceased then, and a hush fell on the hearing room as the Charleston, South Carolina, woman stood to face the legislators. At first her voice was so soft that many in the room had to lean forward to hear her, but then it took on a surprising strength, so that her words rang out for all to hear.

> I stand before you as a southerner, exiled from the land of my birth by the sound of the lash, and the piteous cry of the

> slave. . . . I stand before you as a moral being . . . and as a moral being I feel that I owe it to the suffering slave, and to the deluded master, to my country and the world, to do all that I can to overturn a system of complicated crimes, built up upon the broken hearts and prostrate bodies of my countrymen in chains, and cemented by the blood and sweat and tears of my sisters in bonds.[4]

Angelina Grimké spoke for two hours on that February day in 1838. A silence greeted her last words as she defiantly eyed the legislators seated before her. But then, and much to her own surprise, those in the seats behind her, and in the galleries, rose in a thunderous applause.

Angelina Grimké's speech to the Massachusetts legislature made headlines across the nation and was a turning point for the abolitionist movement, the moment from which we can date the remarkable growth that culminated, more than two decades later, in the election of Abraham Lincoln to the presidency. But as important as Angelina's Boston appearance was, it would not have been possible without the support of her older sister, Sarah. Born in 1792, the third year of George Washington's first term as president, Sarah was Angelina's lifelong teacher, guide, and intellectual mentor.

Sarah and Angelina spent their formative years in South Carolina, the daughters of Judge John Faucheraud Grimké and his wife, Mary, who were the owners of a large plantation in South Carolina's up-country, called Belmont, and a spacious home in Charleston. When John wasn't managing Belmont, he and his family spent their time in the city, then the nation's fourth largest, where "the Judge" and Mary, known affectionately as "Polly" to her husband, could be seen, every Sunday, leading their fourteen children (Sarah was the eighth child, Angelina the last) to St. Philip's Episcopal Church.

John Grimké, a devout Episcopalian, supported his family through the sale of cotton, sea rice, beef, and vegetables, and led them in prayers each afternoon and evening. The Grimkés owned hundreds of slaves, housing them under the stairway of their Charleston house and in the extensive slave quarters at Belmont. One of these slaves was Hetty, an eleven-year-old house servant who was Sarah's playmate and (or so Sarah believed) her equal. That belief lasted until the day that her father discovered that Sarah had been teaching Hetty to read, in violation of South Carolina's strict slave codes—which he'd helped write. Hetty was punished, and the two were separated, with the Judge's daughter given a strict lecture.

The incident marked a turning point in Sarah's development. Her father had been angrier than she'd ever seen, and his discipline nearly as harsh. He threatened to beat Hetty if he ever found her reading. Sarah was enraged and, in defiance of her father, vowed to continue her instruction of the Grimké slaves, albeit in secret. Years later she identified the event as planting the seeds of her antislavery activism. "I took an almost malicious satisfaction in teaching my little waiting-maid at night, when she was supposed to be occupied in combing and brushing my locks," she later wrote. "The light was put out, the keyhole screened, and flat on our stomachs before the fire, with the spelling-book under our eyes, we defied the law of South Carolina."[5]

The relationship with Hetty transformed Sarah's thinking on slavery, as did the books in her father's library. In addition to scolding her for teaching Hetty how to read, Sarah's father also barred her from his library when he caught her reading one of his law books. Even so, it didn't take long for John Grimké to conclude that Sarah was a different kind of a child. Bookish, reflective, inquisitive, and uncomfortable in social settings, he grew to admire his daughter's rebellion, and so, eventually, he began to purposefully overlook her indiscretions, steering himself away from his library when he knew she was in there. If she had been born a man, he once remarked, "she would have made the greatest jurist in the country."

The law books, and Sarah's religious views, had an impact. She became an abolitionist before the movement got its name, openly questioning her father on the state's slave codes, confronting her religious teachers on their defense of the institution, and regularly condemning her mother's harsh treatment of the family's servants. And so it was that on Sunday afternoons Sarah gathered the slave children, with Hetty in the lead, to read from the Bible. The Judge was disturbed by this practice, but he felt powerless to discipline his daughter. What Sarah was doing was a secret subversion of all that he and his family stood for. Yet how could he punish a child for teaching others about God?

Sadly, the year that Sarah turned twelve, Hetty died of an identified childhood ailment and was laid to rest in the slave cemetery of Charleston. Sarah was nearly inconsolable; it was for this reason that she celebrated the birth, in 1805, of Angelina, convincing her parents that she be named the child's godmother. She stood proudly before the font in St. Philips as her "precious Nina" was baptized. As she later wrote: "I had been taught to believe in the efficacy of prayer, and I will remember, after the ceremony was over, slipping out and shutting myself up in my own room, where, with tears streaming down my cheeks, I prayed that God would make me worthy of the task I had assumed, and help me to aid and direct my precious child."[6]

The two Grimké girls were inseparable. Sarah took charge of Angelina's religious training, monitored her daily chores, and proselytized her about the evils of slavery. But the two were also markedly different. Round-faced, short, and painfully shy, Sarah was obsessed by religious questions, while Angelina, angular and outspoken, focused on politics. Over the years that followed, as both converted to Quakerism and then made their way north, the differences between the two grew more distinct—while becoming more intellectually compatible. Sarah searched for ways to reform herself, while Angelina was interested in reforming society. Sarah sought personal salvation, but Angelina sought justice.

After traveling to Philadelphia for medical treatment, with Sarah as his lone companion, John Grimké died in Long Branch, New Jersey, in August 1819.[7] Three months later Sarah finally made her way back to Charleston, meeting Quaker Israel Morris on the way. Several months later she became a Quaker convert and returned to Philadelphia, attending meetings of the Society of Friends at their Arch Street Meeting House. Sarah spent the next ten years in study and contemplation, overcoming her innate shyness about speaking in public and pledging her life to being "a protector of the helpless" and a "pleader for the poor and unfortunate."

Inevitably, Angelina followed in her wake, having also adopted Quakerism. But while Sarah left Charleston to search for God, Angelina left Charleston in a search for social justice—and to remove herself from the stench of slavery. "Sometimes I think that the children of Israel could not have looked towards the land of Canaan with keener longing than I do to the North," she wrote at the time. "I do not expect to go there and be exempt from trial, far from it; and yet it looks like a promised land, a pleasant land, because it is a land of freedom."[8]

It didn't take long for either woman, however, to become as disenchanted with the North as they were with the South, for while there were no slaves in Philadelphia, racial prejudice remained prominent. While it was Sarah who first commented on it, in her diary and letters, it was Angelina who first protested it, disagreeing openly with the Quaker admonition that its followers abstain from political activities. When, in the summer of 1835, the abolitionist newspaper editor William Lloyd Garrison was attacked by a Boston mob, Angelina penned a letter for his newspaper, *The Liberator.* "If persecution is the means which God has ordained for the accomplishment of this great end, EMANCIPATION," she wrote, "I feel as if I could say, LET IT COME; for it is my deep, solemn, deliberate conviction, that *this is a cause worth dying for.*"[9]

When Garrison reprinted the letter, to Angelina's surprise, Sarah worried that Philadelphia's Quaker leaders would repudiate them, cutting them loose not simply from a set of beliefs that Sarah practiced and admired, but from her second family. But when threatened with expulsion by the Society of Friends, Angelina refused to renounce what she'd written. It was then, in the summer of 1835, the famous "abolition summer" of American history, that Sarah and Angelina's relationship changed. Before the publication of Angelina's letter, Sarah had been her intellectual mentor; now it was Angelina who took the lead, guiding Sarah into a career of antislavery activism.

When, after the publication of Angelina's letter, the two were exiled from Philadelphia's Quaker community, Angelina found a new home for her and Sarah among the leaders of the Philadelphia Female Anti-Slavery Society. By 1836, Sarah and Angelina Grimké had befriended Lucretia Mott, the society's founder. It was under Mott's guidance that the sisters were able to escape the suffocating conservatism of the Arch Meeting and strike out on their own. In 1836 they lectured at Quaker meetings in Rhode Island, and the next summer Angelina agreed to conduct an antislavery lecture tour in Massachusetts. Sarah, still pursuing her religious calling, was skeptical, but now Angelina led the way.

It was in preparation for that tour—in the summer of 1836—that Angelina wrote "An Appeal to the Christian Women of the South," perhaps the most eloquent and emotional argument against slavery made by any abolitionist. "Oh that it could be rained down into every parlor in our land," Elizur Wright, who published it, wrote. Eventually, Angelina Grimké's "Appeal" acquired a notoriety that few other antislavery publications achieved. Cut off now from her Quaker family, Sarah quietly followed Angelina's lead—though not for long.

In the fall of 1836, after attending an organizing meeting of the American Anti-Slavery Society in New York, Sarah once again found her voice. While "An Epistle to the Clergy of the Southern States" did not have the emotional power of Angelina's "Appeal," its attack on Christian orthodoxy sparked a fiery reaction: It was confiscated by state agents at the Charleston customs house and copies of the "Epistle" that eluded their cordon were burned on the city's piers. Sarah's writing was not only learned and detailed, it struck at the heart of the "peculiar institution." The "Epistle" was meant to undermine and embarrass Southern ministers who used the Bible to defend the indefensible, and it did.

As important, however, Angelina's "Appeal" and Sarah's "Epistle" evidenced a new and powerful current inside the abolitionist movement that highlighted the importance women had in developing the movement's ideas. While William Lloyd Garrison, Theodore Weld (who would marry Angelina in 1838), Theodore Wright, Gerrit Smith, Lewis Tappan, and Wendell Phillips played crucial leadership roles in the welter of groups that shaped Northern antislavery opinion, the great organizers of the abolitionist crusade, as well as its most important intellectual figures, were women.

In 1837, in her "Letters on the Equality of the Sexes, and the Condition of Women" (eleven years before a meeting at Seneca Falls officially established the women's rights movement), Sarah repudiated the notion that God had reserved a special "domestic sphere" for females. Her message was unmistakable and aimed not simply at slaveholders but at men who believed that women should be seen at church and heard only at the dinner table: "Our powers of mind have been crushed, as far as man could do it, our sense of morality has been impaired by his interpretation of our duties; but no where does God say that he made any distinction between us, as moral and intelligent beings."[10]

Students and scholars will find in this volume the most important writings of Sarah and Angelina Grimké. But their words are not simply a part of the past; they are as accessible now to the general public as they were at a time when black Americans were held in chains. The Grimké sisters did not write simply for clergymen or women but for everyone—and their appeals and epistles are a part of the foundation of our republic. So it is that this introduction cannot be concluded without mentioning the obvious: The election of America's first African American president has sparked a renewed interest in a part of our history that many would rather forget.

So, too, the reader is urged to focus renewed attention on the careers of Sarah and Angelina after the war that began in their hometown of Charleston was concluded at Appomattox—some twenty-five years after their most important written work. For the simple truth is that both women knew that the crusade they led was not complete. In February 1868, while reading through a short article in the *National Anti-Slavery Standard*, Angelina noted that two Grimkés unknown to her and Sarah, Archibald and Francis, were then attending Lincoln University, outside of Philadelphia. She was stunned but sensed immediately that the two young men were her nephews, the children of her and Sarah's brother Henry Grimké. Their mother, as Angelina would soon learn, was Nancy Weston, who had been Henry's slave, nurse—and wife.

There was never any question of what Angelina, and Sarah, would do. They supported Archibald and Francis and brought them proudly into their lives. Ironically, though perhaps not surprisingly, the two, the Grimké brothers, spent their adult years in the same crusade their two aunts, the Grimké sisters, had founded—working not for the emancipation of the slave but for equal rights. Like Angelina and Sarah, they were both crusaders and intellectuals, putting in place the paving stones of the civil rights movement.

It is the fashion among historians to dismiss fictional treatments of history, blithely commenting that the truth is much less romantic. Most recently, Ain Gordon's drama "If She Stood," with Angelina and Sarah as its main characters, was staged during the Philadelphia Arts Festival in 2013 and Sue Monk Kidd's novel *The Invention of Wings*, imspired in part by Sarah Grimké, became a number one *New York Times* bestseller.

These two works demonstrate that such extraordinary lives can inspire a broad and modern audience through the power of fiction.

These women, Sarah and Angelina, were, in fact, larger than life. And the words that they spoke and the essays and letters they wrote—greeted with trepidation in their own time—speak to us now as examples of triumph and hope.

And so it is, in reading the works of Angelina and Sarah Grimké contained in this volume, we extol their work and beliefs, though not simply because they were southerners and women. But because they were Americans.

NOTES

1. Angelina Grimké's Massachusetts Statehouse appearance is the centerpiece of Gerda Lerner's biography of the Grimké Sisters. See Gerda Lerner, *The Grimké Sisters from South Carolina* (Boston: Houghton Mifflin, 1967).
2. Ibid., p. 5.
3. Ibid., p. 5.
4. The events leading up to and following Angelina's statehouse appearance and its place in abolitionist history is discussed at length in my own work, *Lift Up Thy Voice* (New York: Viking, 2001). For her speech, see page 329.
5. Ibid., p. 2.
6. Ibid., p. 27.
7. John Grimké's journey north is filled with mystery, as is his death. Aged seventy, he sought expert medical opinion on his failing health, but Philadelphia doctors could not identify his ailment. But it also seems likely that Judge Grimké made the journey at least in

part, to escape Polly, his increasingly unstable wife—and may well have been seeded by his own doubts about slavery. It is very likely he passed these on to his daughter, Sarah, his favorite child. [From text above, it seems Sarah had doubts about slavery before he did, and she seeded his.]

8. Mark Perry, *Lift Up Thy Voice*, pp. 83–84. Angelina's decision to follow her sister Sarah to Philadelphia marked a final break with her mother, with whom she argued endlessly. Mary spent extravagantly and lectured Angelina endlessly, disapproving of her religion and her ideas.
9. See page 125.
10. See page 41.
11. Sue Monk Kidd, *The Invention of Wings* (New York: Viking, 2014).

Note on the Text

The pieces in this collection were selected under the guidance of Grimké sisters biographer Mark Perry to represent the major works of Sarah and Angelina Grimké. All writings are printed verbatim from first editions. The transcript of Angelina Grimké's "Address to the Massachusetts Legislature" is found in the March 2, 1838, edition of *The Liberator.* Obvious misspellings and typographical errors have been silently corrected.

Sarah and Angelina Grimké's great grandparents were Germans from the French borderlands. The acute accent in the family surname denotes that Huguenot background, but over time, it was dropped from the name. When signing her letters, Sarah omits the accent, however, Angelina retains it, perhaps to indicate that her ancestry was Catholic rather than Protestant (though this is purely speculation). In this volume, we have employed the accented surname throughout to conform to popular usage in modern scholarship and culture.

On Slavery and Abolitionism

SARAH M. GRIMKÉ

AN EPISTLE TO THE CLERGY OF THE SOUTHERN STATES

"And when he was come near, he beheld the city and wept over it, saying—If thou hadst known, even thou, at least in this thy day, the things which belong unto thy peace." Luke xix, 41–42.

BRETHREN BELOVED IN THE LORD:

It is because I feel a portion of that love glowing in my heart towards you, which is infused into every bosom by the cordial reception of the gospel of Jesus Christ, that I am induced to address you as fellow professors of his holy religion. To my dear native land, to the beloved relatives who are still breathing her tainted air, to the ministers of Christ, from some of whom I have received the emblems of a Saviour's love; my heart turns with feelings of intense solicitude, even with such feelings, may I presume to say, as brought the gushing tears of compassion from the Redeemer of the world, when he wept over the city which he loved, when with ineffable pathos he exclaimed, "O Jerusalem! Jerusalem! thou that killest the prophets, and stonest them which are sent unto thee, how often would I have gathered thy children together, even as a hen gathereth her chickens under her wings, and ye would not." Nay, these are the feelings which fill the hearts of Northern Abolitionists towards Southern slave-holders. Yes, my brethren, notwithstanding the bon fire at Charleston—the outrages at Nashville on the person of Dresser—the banishment of Birney and Nelson—the arrest and imprisonment of our colored citizens—we can still weep over you with unfeigned tenderness and anxiety, and exclaim, O that ye would even now listen to the christian remonstrances of those who feel that the principle they advocate "is not a vain thing for YOU, because it is YOUR LIFE." For you the midnight tear is shed, for you the daily and the nightly prayer ascends, that God in his unbounded mercy may open your hearts to believe his awful denunciations against those who "rob the poor because he is poor." And will you still disregard the supplications of those, who are lifting up their voices like the prophets of old, and reiterating the soul-touching enquiry. "Why will ye die, O house of Israel?" Oh, that I could clothe my feelings in eloquence that would be irresistible, in tones of melting tenderness that would soften the hearts of all, who hold their fellow men in bondage.

A solemn sense of the duty which I owe as a Southerner to every class of the community of which *I* was once a part, likewise impels me to address *you*, especially, who are filling the important and responsible station of ministers of Jehovah, expounders of the lively oracles of God. It is because you sway the minds of a vast proportion of the Christian community, who regard you as the channel through which divine knowledge must flow. Nor does the fact that you are voluntarily invested by the people with this high prerogative, lessen the fearful weight of responsibility which attaches to you as watchmen on the walls of Zion. It adds rather a tenfold weight of guilt, because the very first duty which devolves upon you is to teach them not to trust in man.—Oh my brethren, is this duty faithfully performed? Is not the idea inculcated that to you they must look for the right understanding of the sacred volume, and has not your interpretation of the Word of God induced thousands and tens of thousands to receive as truth, sanctioned by the authority of Heaven, the oft repeated declaration that slavery, American slavery, stamped as it is with all its infinity of horrors, bears upon it the signet of that God whose name is LOVE?

Let us contemplate the magnificent scene of creation, when God looked upon chaos and said, "Let there be light, and there was light." The dark abyss was instantaneously illuminated, and a flood of splendor poured upon the face of the deep, and "God saw the light that it was good." Behold the work of creation carried on and perfected—the azure sky and verdant grass, the trees, the beasts, the fowls of the air, and whatsoever passeth through the paths of the sea, the greater light to rule the day, the lesser light to rule the night, and all the starry host of heaven, brought into existence by the simple command, Let them be.

But was man, the lord of this creation, thus ushered into being? No, the Almighty, clothed as he is with all power in heaven and in earth, paused when he had thus far completed his glorious work—"Omnipotence retired, if I may so speak, and held a counsel when he was about to place upon the earth the sceptered monarch of the universe." He did not say let man be, but "Let us make man in OUR IMAGE, after our likeness, and let them have dominion over the fish of the sea, and over the fowl of the air, and over the cattle, and over all the earth, and over every creeping thing, that creepeth upon the earth." Here is written in characters of fire continually blazing before the eyes of every man who holds his fellow man in bondage—In the image of God created he man. Here is marked a distinction which can never be effaced between a man and *a thing*, and we are fighting against God's unchangeable decree by depriving this rational and immortal being of those inalienable rights which have been conferred upon him. He was created a little lower than the angels, crowned with glory and honor, and designed to be God's vicegerent upon earth—but slavery has wrested the sceptre of dominion from his hand, slavery has seized with an iron grasp this God-like being, and torn the crown from his head. Slavery has disrobed him of royalty, put on him the collar and the chain, and trampled the image of God in the dust.

Eternal God! when from thy giant hand,
Thou heaved the floods, and fixed the trembling land:
When life sprung startling at thy plastic call;
Endless her forms, and man the Lord of all—
Say, was that lordly form, inspired by thee,
To wear eternal chains and bow the knee?
Was man ordained the slave of man to toil,
Yoked with the brutes and fettered to the soil?

This, my brethren, is slavery—this is what sublimates the atrocity of that act, which virtually says, I will as far as I am able destroy the image of God, blot him from creation as a man, and convert him into a thing—"a chattel personal." Can any crime, tremendous as is the history of human wickedness, compare in turpitude with this?—No, the immutable difference, the *heaven-wide distinction* which God has established between *that* being, whom he has made a little lower than the angels, and all the other works of this wonderful creation, cannot be annihilated without incurring a weight of guilt beyond expression terrible.

And after God had destroyed the world by a flood because of the wickedness of man, every imagination of whose heart was evil, and had preserved Noah because he was righteous before him, He renewed man's delegated authority over the whole animate and inanimate creation, and again delivered into his hand every beast of the earth and every fowl of the air, and added to his former grant of power, "Every moving thing that liveth shall be meat for you, even as the green herb have I given you all things." Then, as if to impress indelibly upon the mind of man the eternal distinction between his rational and immortal creatures and the lower orders of beings, he guards the life of this most precious jewel, with a decree which would have proved all-sufficient to protect it, had not Satan infused into man his own reckless spirit.

Permission ample was given to shed the blood of all inferior creatures, but of this *being, bearing the impress of divinity*, God said, "And surely your blood of your lives will I require, at the hand of every beast will I require it, and at the hand of man, at the hand of every man's brother will I require the life of man. Whoso sheddeth man's blood, by man shall his blood be shed, for in the IMAGE OF GOD made he man." Let us pause and examine this passage.—Man may shed the blood of the inferior animals, he may use them as *mere means*—he may convert them into food to sustain existence—but if the top-stone of creation, the *image of God* had his blood shed by a beast, that blood was required even of this irrational brute: as if Deity had said, over *my likeness* I will spread a panoply divine that all creation may instinctively feel that he is precious to his Maker—so precious, that if his life be taken by his fellow man—if man degrades himself to the level of a beast by destroying his brother—"by man shall his blood be shed."

This distinction between *men and things* is marked with equal care and solemnity under the Jewish dispensation. "If a man steal an ox, or a sheep, and kill it, or sell it, he shall restore five oxen for an ox, and four sheep for a sheep." But "he that stealeth a man and selleth him or if he be found in his hand, he shall surely be put to death." If this law were carried into effect now, what must be the inevitable doom of all those who now hold man as property? If Jehovah were to exact the execution of this penalty upon the more enlightened and more spiritually minded men who live under the Christian dispensation, would he not instantly commission his most tremendous thunderbolts to strike from existence those who are thus trampling upon his laws, thus defacing his image?

I pass now to the eighth Psalm, which is a sublime anthem of praise to our Almighty Father for his unbounded goodness to the children of men. This Psalm alone affords irrefragable proof that God never gave to man dominion over his own image, that he never commissioned the Israelites to enslave their fellow men. This was

> Authority usurped from God not given—
> . . . . Man over men
> *He* made not Lord, such title to *himself*
> Reserving, human left, from human free.

This beautiful song of glory to God was composed three thousand years after the creation, and David who says of himself, "The spirit of the Lord spake by me, and his word was in my tongue," gives us the following exquisite description of the creation of man and of the power with which he was intrusted. "Thou hast made him a little lower than the angels, and crowned him with glory and honor. Thou madest him to have dominion over the works of thy hands: thou hast put all things under his feet: all sheep and oxen, yea, and all the beasts of the field, the fowl of the air and the fish of the sea, and whatsoever passeth through the paths of the sea."

David was living under that dispensation to which slaveholders triumphantly point as the charter of their right to hold men as PROPERTY; but he does not even intimate that any extension of prerogative had been granted. He specifies precisely the same things which are specified at the creation and after the flood. He had been eminently instrumental in bringing into captivity the nations round about, but he does not so much as hint that Jehovah had transferred the sceptre of dominion over his immortal creatures to the hand of man. How could God create man in his own image and then invest his fellow worms with power to blot him from the world of spirits and place him on a level with the brutes that perish!

The same Psalm is quoted by the Apostle Paul, as if our heavenly Father designed to teach us through all the dispensations of his mercy to a fallen world, that man was but a little lower than the angels, God's vicegerent upon earth over the inferior creatures. St. Paul quotes it in connection with that stupendous event whereby we are saved from eternal death. "But we see Jesus who was made a little lower than the angels for the suffering of death, crowned with glory and honor; that he by the grace of God should taste death for every man." Here side by side the apostle places "God manifest in the flesh" and his accredited representative man. He calls us to view the master-piece of God's creation, and then the master-piece of his mercy—Christ Jesus, wearing our form and dying for our sins, thus conferring everlasting honor upon man by declaring "both he that sanctifieth and they who are sanctified are all of one: for which cause he is not ashamed to call them brethren." It is then, the Lord's brethren whom we have enslaved; the Lord's brethren of whom we say "slaves shall be deemed, taken, reputed, and adjudged, chattels personal in the hands of their owners and possessors to all intents and purposes whatever."—*Laws of South Carolina.*

And here I cannot but advert to a most important distinction which God has made between immortal beings and the beasts that perish.—No one can doubt that by the fall of man the whole creation underwent a change. The apostle says, "We know that the whole creation groaneth and travaileth in pain together." But it was for *man* alone that the Lord Jesus "made himself of no reputation and took upon him the form of a servant." When he came before his incarnation to cheer his servants with his blessed presence, when he visited Abraham and Manoah, he took upon himself a human form. Manoah's wife says, "a man of God came unto me." And when he came and exhibited on the theatre of our world, that miracle of grace

"God in Christ reconciling the world unto himself," what form did he wear? "Verily," says the apostle, "he took not on him the nature of angels; but he took on him the seed of Abraham:" Oh, my brethren, he has stamped with high and holy dignity the form we wear, he has forever exalted our nature by condescending to assume it, and by investing man with the high and holy privilege of being "the temple of the holy Ghost." Where then is our title deed for enslaving our equal brother?

Mr. Chandler of Norfolk, in a speech in the House of Delegates of Virginia, on the subject of negro slavery in 1832, speaking of our right to hold our colored brethren in bondage, says:

> As a Virginian, I do not question the master's title to his slave; but I put it to that gentleman, as a man, as a moral man, as a Christian man, whether he has not some doubts of his claim to his slaves, being as absolute and unqualified as that to other property. Let us in the investigation of this title go back to its origin—Whence came slaves into this country?—From Africa. Were they free men there? At one time they were. How came they to be converted into slaves?—By the stratagem of war and the strong arm of the conqueror; they were vanquished in battle, sold by the victorious party to the slave trader; who brought them to our shores, and disposed of them to the planters of Virginia.............The truth is, our ancestors had *no title* to this property, and we have acquired it only by legislative enactments.

But can "legislative enactments" annul the laws of Jehovah, or sanctify the crimes of theft and oppression? "Wo unto them that decree unrighteous decrees . . . . . to take away the *right* from the poor of my people." Suppose the Saviour of the world were to visit our guilty country and behold the Christianity of our slave holding states, would not his language be, "Ye have heard that it hath been said by them of old time, enslave your fellow men, but I say unto you "Do unto others as ye would they should do unto you," and set your captives free!

The sentiment—

> Man over man
> He made not lord—

is the sentiment of human nature. It is written, by the Almighty, on the soul, as a part of its very being. So that, urge on the work of death as we may, in the mad attempt to convert a free agent into a machine, a man into a thing, and *nature* will still cry out for freedom. Hear the testimony of James McDowell, in the House of Delegates, in Virginia in 1832.

> As to the idea that the slave in any considerable number of cases can be so attached to his master and his servitude, as to be indifferent to freedom, it is wholly unnatural, rejected by the *conscious testimony* of every man's heart, and the *written testimony of the world's experience*.................You may place the slave where you please, you may oppress him as you please, you may dry up to the uttermost the fountain of his feelings, the springs of his thought, you may close upon his mind every avenue of knowledge, and cloud it over with artificial night, you may yoke him to your labors as the ox which liveth only to work, you may put him under any process, which without destroying his value as a slave, will debase and crush him as a rational being, and the idea that *he was born to be free* will survive it all. It is allied to his hope of immortality—it is the ethereal part of his being, which oppression cannot reach; it is a torch lit up in his soul by the hand of Deity, and never meant to be extinguished by the hand of man.

I need not enter into an elaborate proof that Jewish servitude, as permitted by God, was as different from American slavery, as Christianity is from heathenism. The limitation laws respecting strangers and servants, entirely prohibited cruelty and oppression, whereas in our slave states, "THE MASTER MAY, AT HIS DISCRETION, INFLICT ANY SPECIES OF PUNISHMENT UPON THE PERSON OF HIS SLAVE,"* and the law throws her protecting ægis over the master, by refusing to receive under any circumstances, the testimony of a colored man against a white, except to subserve the interests of the owner.—"It is manifest," says the author (a Christian Minister) of "A calm enquiry into the countenance afforded by the Scriptures to the system of British Colonial

*Sketch of the Laws relating to slavery, in the United States of America, by George M. Stroud.

Slavery" "that the Hebrews had no word in their language equivalent to slave in the West Indian use of that term. The word עבד obed, is applied to both bond servants and hired, to kings and prophets, and even to the Saviour of the world. It was a general designation for any person who rendered service of any kind to God or man. But the term SLAVE, in the Colonial sense, could not be at all applied to a freeman." The same word in the Septuagint which is translated servant, is also translated child, and as the Hebrew language is remarkable for its minute shades of distinction in things, had there been, as is asserted, slaves in Judea, there would undoubtedly have been some term to designate such a condition. Our language recognizes the difference between a slave and a servant, because those two classes actually exist in our country. The Burmese language has no word to express ETERNITY, hence a missionary remarked that it was almost impossible to convey to them any conception of it. So likewise among the ancient Greeks and Romans there was no word equivalent to humility, because they acknowledged no such virtue. The want of any term therefore in the Hebrew, to mark the distinction between a slave in the proper sense of the term and other servants, is proof presumptive to say the least, that no such condition as that of slave was known among the Jews of that day.

To assert that Abraham held slaves is a mere slander. The phrase, translated "souls that they had gotten in Haran," Gen. 12: 5, has no possible reference to slaves, and was never supposed to have any allusion to slavery until the commencement of the slave trade in England, in 1563. From that time commentators endeavored to cast upon Abraham the obloquy of holding his fellow creatures in bondage, in order to excuse this nefarious traffic. The Targum of Onkelos thus paraphrases this passage "souls gotten, i. e. those whom they had caused to obey the law." The Targum of Jonathan calls them "Proselytes." Jarchi, "Those whom they had brought under the wings of Shekinah." Menochius, "Those whom they converted from idolatry." Luke Franke, a Latin commentator, "Those whom they subjected to the law." Jerome calls them "Proselytes." Here is a mass of evidence which is incontrovertible. Abraham's business as "the friend of God" was to get souls as the seals of his ministry. Would he have been called from a heathen land to be the father of the faithful in all generations, that he might enslave the converts he made from idolatry? As soon might we suspect our missionaries of riveting the chains of servitude on souls that they may have gotten, as seals of their ministry, from among those to whom they proclaim the unsearchable riches of Christ. Would heathen then, any more than now, be attracted to a standard which bore on it the inscription SLAVERY? No, my brethren; and if our downtrodden slaves did not distinguish between Christianity, and the Christians who hold them in bondage, they could never embrace a religion, which is exhibited to them from the pulpit, in the prayer-meeting, and at the domestic altar, embodied in the form of masters, utterly regardless of the divine command, "Render unto your servants that which is just." From the confidence which Abraham reposed in his servants we cannot avoid the inference that they clustered voluntarily around him as the benefactor of their souls, the patriarch of that little community which his ministry had gathered.

Again, it is often peremptorily asserted that "the Africans are a divinely condemned and proscribed race." If they are, has God constituted the slave holders the ministers of his vengeance? This question can only be answered in the negative, and until it can be otherwise answered, it is vain to appeal to the curse on Canaan, or to Hebrew servitude, in support of American slavery. As well might the bloodstained Emperor of France appeal to the conquest of Canaan by the Israelites, and challenge the Almighty to reward him for the work of death which he wrought on the fields of Marengo and Leipsic, because God invested his peculiar people, with authority to destroy the nations which had filled up the measure of their iniquity. The express grant to the Jews to reduce to subjection some of the Canaanitish nations and to exterminate others, at once condemns American slavery, because those who derive their sanction to hold their fellow men in bondage from the Bible, admit that a specific grant was necessary to empower the Israelites to make bond-men of the heathen; and unless this permission had been given, they would not have been justified in doing it. It is therefore self-evident that as *we* have never been commanded to enslave the Africans, *we* can derive no sanction for our slave system from the history of the Jews.

Another plea by which we endeavor to silence the voice of conscience is, "that the child is invariably born to the condition of the parent." Hence the law of South Carolina, says "ALL THEIR (THE SLAVES) ISSUE AND OFFSPRING, BORN, OR TO BE BORN, SHALL BE, AND THEY ARE HEREBY DECLARED TO BE, AND REMAIN FOREVER HEREAFTER ABSOLUTE SLAVES, AND SHALL FOREVER FOLLOW THE CONDITION OF THE MOTHER." To support this assumption, recourse is had to the page of inspiration. Our colored brethren are said to be the descendants of Ham who was cursed with all his posterity, and their condition only in accordance with the declaration of Jehovah, that he visits the iniquities of the fathers upon the children.—I need only remark that Canaan, not Ham, was the object of Noah's prophecy, and that upon his descendants it has been amply fulfilled.

But we appeal to prophecy in order to excuse or palliate the sin of slavery, and we regard ourselves as guiltless because we are fulfilling the designs of Omnipotence. Let us read our sentence in the word of God: "And he said unto Abraham, Know of a surety that thy seed shall be a stranger in a land that is not theirs and shall serve them, and I will afflict them four hundred years, and also that nation whom they shall serve, I WILL JUDGE." That nation literally drank the blood of the wrath of Almighty God. The whole land of Egypt was a house of mourning, a scene of consternation and horror. What did it avail the Egyptians that they had been the instruments permitted in the inscrutable counsels of Jehovah to accomplish every iota of the prophecy concerning the seed of Abraham?

Appeal to prophecy! As well might the Jews who by wicked hands crucified the Messiah claim to themselves the sanction of prophecy. As well might *they* shield themselves from the scathing lightning of the Almighty under the plea that the tragedy they acted on Calvary's mount, had been foretold by the inspired penman a thousand years before. Read in the 22d Psalm an exact description of the crucifixion of Christ. Hear the words of the dying Redeemer from the lips of the Psalmist: "My God! my God! why hast thou forsaken me?" At that awful day when the dead, small and great, stand before God, and the books are opened, and another book is opened, which is the book of life, and the dead are judged out of those things which are written in the book ACCORDING TO THEIR WORKS—think you, my brethren, that the betrayer and the crucifiers of the Son of God will find their names inscribed in the book of life "*because they* fulfilled prophecy in killing the Prince of Peace? Think you that they will claim, or receive on this ground, exemption from the torments of the damned? Will it not add to their guilt and woe that "To Him bare all the prophets witness," and render more intense the anguish and horror with which they will call upon "the rocks and the mountains to fall upon them and hide them from the face of Him that sitteth upon the throne and from the wrath of the Lamb?"

Contemplate the history of the Jews since the crucifixion of Christ! Behold even in this world the awfully retributive justice which is so accurately pourtrayed by the pen of Moses. "And the Lord shall scatter thee among all people from the one end of the earth even unto the other, and among those nations shalt thou find no ease." And can we believe that those nations who with satanic ingenuity have fulfilled to a tittle these prophecies against this guilty people, will stand acquitted at the bar of God for their own cruelty and injustice, in the matter? Prophecy is a mirror on whose surface is inscribed in characters of light, that sentence of deep, immitigable woe which the Almighty has pronounced and executed on transgressors. Let me beseech you then, my dear, though guilty brethren, to pause, and learn from the tremendour past what must be the inevitable destiny of those who are adding year after year, to the amount of crime which is treasuring up "wrath against the day of wrath." "A wonderful and horrible thing is committed in the land! The *prophets prophecy falsely*, and the priests bear rule by their means, and my people love to have it so, and what will ye do in the end thereof?" "Thus saith the Lord of hosts concerning the prophets, Behold, I will feed them with wormwood, and make them drink the water of gall."

The present position of my country and of the church is one of deep and solemn interest. The times of our ignorance on the subject of slavery which God may have winked at, *have passed away*. We are no longer standing unconsciously and carelessly on the brink of a burning volcano. The strong arm of Almighty power has rolled back the dense cloud which hung over the terrific crater, and has exposed it to our view, and although no human eye can penetrate the abyss, yet enough is seen to warn us of the consequences of trifling with Omnipotence. Jehovah is calling to us as he did to Job out of the whirlwind, and every blast bears on its wings the sound, Repent! Repent! God, if I may so speak, is waiting to see whether we will hearken unto his voice. He has sent out his light and his truth, and as regards us it may perhaps be said—there is now silence in heaven. The commissioned messengers of grace to this guilty nation are rapidly traversing our country, through the medium of the Anti-Slavery Society, through its agents and its presses, whilst the "ministering spirits" are marking with breathless interest the influence produced by these means of knowledge thus mercifully furnished to our land. Oh! if there be joy in heaven over one sinner that repenteth, what hallelujahs of angelic praise will arise, when the slave-holder and the defender of slavery bow before the footstool of mercy, and with broken spirits and contrite hearts surrender unto God that dominion over his immortal creatures which he alone can rightly exercise.

What an appalling spectacle do we now present! With one hand we clasp the cross of Christ, and with the other grasp the neck of the down-trodden slave! With one eye we are gazing imploringly on the bleeding sacrifice of Calvary, as if we expected redemption though the blood which was shed there, and with the other we cast the glance of indignation and contempt at the representative of Him who there made his soul an offering for sin! My Christian brethren, if there is any truth in the Bible, and in the God of the Bible, *our hearts bear us witness* that he can no more acknowledge us as his disciples, if we wilfully persist in this sin, than he did the Pharisees formerly, who were strict and punctilious in the observance of the ceremonial law, and yet devoured widows' houses. *We have added a deeper shade to their guilt*, we make widows by tearing from the victims of a cruel bondage, the husbands of their bosoms, and then devour the widow herself by robbing her of her freedom, and reducing her to the level of a brute. I solemnly appeal to your own consciences. Does not the rebuke of Christ to the Pharisees apply to some of those who are exercising the office of Gospel ministers, "Wo unto you, Scribes and Pharisees, hypocrites! for ye devour widow's houses, and for a pretence make long prayers, therefore ye shall receive the greater damnation."

How long the space now granted for repentance may continue, is among the secret things which belong unto God, and my soul ardently desires that all those who are enlisted in the ranks of abolition may regard every day as possibly the last, and may pray without ceasing to God, to grant this nation repentance and forgiveness of the sin of slavery. The time is precious, unspeakably precious, and every encouragement is offered to us to supplicate the God of the master and of the slave to make a "right way" "for us, and for our little ones, and for all our substance." Ezra says, "so we fasted and besought the Lord, and he was entreated for us." Look at the marvellous effects of prayer when Peter was imprisoned. What did the church in that crisis? She felt that her weapons were not carnal, but spiritual, and "prayer was made without ceasing." These petitions offered in humble faith were mighty through God to the emancipation of Peter. "Is the Lord's arm shortened that it cannot save, or his ear grown heavy that it cannot hear?" If he condescended to work a miracle in answer to prayer when *one* of his servants was imprisoned, will he not graciously hear our supplications when two millions of his immortal creatures are in bondage? We entreat the Christian ministry to co-operate with us to unite in our petitions to Almighty God to deliver our land from blood guiltiness; to enable us to see the abominations of American slavery by the light of the gospel. "This is the condemnation, that light is come into the world, but men loved darkness rather than light, because their deeds were evil." Then may we expect a glorious consummation to our united labors of love. Then may the Lord Jesus unto whom belongeth all power in heaven and in earth condescend to answer our prayers, and by the softening influence of his holy spirit induce our brethren and sisters of the South "to undo the heavy burdens, to break every yoke and let the oppressed go free."

My mind has been deeply impressed whilst reading the account of the anniversaries held last spring in the city of New York, with the belief that there is in America a degree of light, knowledge and intelligence which leaves us without excuse before God for upholding the system of slavery. Nay, we not only sustain this temple of Moloch; but with impious lips consecrate it to the Most High God; and call upon Jehovah himself to sanctify our sins by the presence of his Shekinah. Now mark, the unholy combination that has been entered into between the North and the South to shut out the light on this all important subject. I copy from a speech before the "General Assembly's Board of Education." As an illustration of his position, Dr. Breckenridge referred to the influence of the Education Board in the Southern States. "Jealous as those States were, and not without reason, of all that came to them in the shape of benevolent enterprise from the North, and ready as they were to take fire in a moment at whatever threatened *their own peculiar institutions*, the plans of this Board had *conciliated* their fullest confidence: in proof of which they had placed nearly two hundred of their sons under its care, that they might be *trained and fitted to preach to their own population*." The inference is unavoidable that the "*peculiar institution*" spoken of is domestic slavery in all its bearings and relations; and it is equally clear that the ministry educated for the South are to be thoroughly imbued with the slave-holding spirit, that they may be "*fitted to preach to their own population*," *not* the gospel of Jesus Christ, which proclaims LIBERTY TO THE CAPTIVE, but a religion which grants to man the privilege of sinning with impunity, and stamps with the signet of the King of heaven a system that embraces every possible enormity. Surely if ye are ambassadors for Christ, ye are bound to promulgate the *whole* counsel of God. But can ye preach from the language of James, "Behold the hire of your laborers which is of you kept back by fraud crieth, and the cries of them which have reaped, are entered into the ears of the Lord of Sabaoth." Multitudes of other texts must be virtually expunged from the Bible of the slave holding minister; every denunciation against oppression strikes at the root of slavery. God is in a peculiar manner the God of the poor and the needy, the despised and the oppressed. "The Lord said I have surely seen the affliction of my people, and have heard their cry by reason of their task-masters, for I know their sorrows." And he knows the sorrows of the American slave, and he will come down in mercy, or in judgment to deliver them.

In a speech before the "American Seamen's Friend Society," by Rev. William S. Plumer of Virginia, it is said, "The resolution spoke of weighty considerations, why we should care for seamen, and one of these certainly was, because *as a class, they had been long and criminally neglected.* Another weighty consideration was that seamen were a suffering race."......... "And who was the cause of this? Was it not the Church who withheld from these her suffering brethren, those blessed truths of God, so well calculated to comfort those who suffer?" Oh my brother! while drawing to the life a picture of a class of our fellow beings, who have been "long and criminally neglected," of "a suffering race," was there no cord of sympathy in thy heart to vibrate to the groans of the slave? Did no seraph's voice whisper in thine ear "Remember them which are in bonds?" Did memory present no scenes of cruelty and oppression? And did not conscience say, thou art one who withholds from thy suffering colored brethren those blessed truths of God so well calculated to comfort those who suffer? Can we believe that the God of Christianity will bless the people who are thus dispensing their gifts to all, save to those by whose *unrequited* toil, we and our ancestors for generations past have subsisted?

Let us examine the testimony of Charles C. Jones, Professor in the Theological Seminary, Columbia, S. C. relative to the condition of our slaves, and then judge whether they have not at least as great a claim as seamen to the sympathy and benevolent effort of Christian Ministers. In a sermon preached before two associations of planters in Georgia in 1831, he says: "Generally speaking, they (the slaves) appear to us to be without God and without hope in the world, a nation of HEATHEN in our very midst. We cannot cry out against the Papists for withholding the scriptures from the common people, and keeping them in ignorance of the way of life, for we *withhold the Bible* from our servants, and *keep them* in ignorance of it, while we *will not* use the means to have it read and explained to them. The cry of our perishing servants comes up to us from the sultry plains as they bend at their toil; it comes up to us from their humble cottages when they return at evening, to rest their weary limbs; it comes up to us from the midst of their ignorance and superstition, and adultery and lewdness. We have manifested *no emotions* of horror at abandoning the souls of our servants to the adversary, the "roaring lion, that walketh about, seeking whom he may devour."

On the 5th of December, 1833, a committee of the synod of South Carolina and Georgia, to whom was referred the subject of the religious instruction of the colored population, made a report in which this language was used.

> Who would credit it that in these years of revival and benevolent effort, in this Christian republic, there are over TWO MILLIONS of human beings in the condition of HEATHEN, and in some respects in a *worse* condition. From long continued and close observation, we believe that their moral and religious condition is such that they may be justly considered the HEATHEN of this Christian country, and will bear comparison with heathens in *any country in the world*. The negroes are destitute of the gospel, and *ever will be* under the present state of things.

In a number of the Charleston Observer (in 1834,) a correspondent remarked: "Let us establish missionaries among our own negroes, who, in view of religious knowledge, are as debasingly ignorant as any one on the coast of Africa; for I hazard the assertion that throughout the bounds of our Synod, there are at least ONE HUNDRED THOUSAND SLAVES, speaking the same language as ourselves, who never heard of the plan of salvation by a Redeemer."

The Editor, Rev. Benjamin Gildersleeve, who has resided at least ten years at the South, so far from contradicting this broad assertion, adds, "We fully concur with what our correspondent has said, respecting the benighted heathen among ourselves."

As Southerners, can we deny these things? As Christians, can we ask the blessing of the Redeemer of men on the system of American slavery? Can we carry it to the footstool of a God whose "compassions fail not," and pray for holy help to rivet the chains of interminable bondage on TWO MILLIONS of our fellow men, the accredited representatives of Jesus Christ? If we cannot ask in faith that the blessing of God may rest on this work of cruelty to the bodies, and destruction of the souls of men, we may be assured that his controversy is against it. Try it, my brethren, when you are kneeling around the family altar with the wife of your bosom, with the children of your love, when you are supplicating Him who hath made of one blood all nations, to sanctify these precious souls and prepare them for an inheritance with Jesus—then pray, *if you can* that God will grant you power to degrade to the level of brutes your colored brethren. Try it, when your little ones are twining their arms around your necks, and lisping the first fond accents of affection in your ears; when the petition arises from the fulness of a parent's heart for a blessing on your children. At such a moment, look in upon your slave. He too is a father, and *we know* that he is susceptible of all the tender sensibilities of a father's love. He folds his cherished infant in his arms, he feels its life-pulse throb against his own, and he rejoices that he is a parent; but soon the withering thought rushes to his mind—I am a slave, and tomorrow my master may tear my darling from my arms. Contemplate this scene, while your cheeks are yet warm with the kisses of your children, and then try if you can mingle with a parent's prayer and a parent's blessing, the petition that God may enable you and your posterity to perpetuate a system which to the slave denies—

> To live together, or together die.
> By felon hands at one relentless stroke
> See the fond links of feeling nature broke;
> The fibres twisting roused a parent's heart,
> Torn from their grasp and bleeding as they part.

A southern minister, Rev. Mr. Atkinson of Virginia, in a speech before the Bible society last spring, says: "The facts which have been told respecting the destitution of some portions of our country are but samples of thousands more. Could we but feel what we owed to him who gave the Bible, we would at the same time feel that we owed it to a fallen and perishing world not merely to pass *fine resolutions*, or listen to *eloquent speeches*, but to exhibitit a life devoted to the conversion of the world."

Let us now turn to the heart-sickening picture of the "destitution" of our slaves drawn by those who had the living original continually before their eyes. I extract from the report of the Synod of South Carolina and Georgia before referred to.

> We may now enquire if they (the slaves) enjoy the privileges of the gospel in their own houses, and on our plantations? Again we return a negative answer—They have no Bibles to read by their own fire-sides—they have no family altars; and when in affliction, sickness, or death, they have no minister to address to them the consolations of the gospel, nor to bury them with solemn and appropriate services.

This state of things, is the result of laws enacted in a free and enlightened republic. In North Carolina, to teach a slave to read or write, or to sell or give him any book, (the Bible not excepted) or pamphlet, is punished with thirty-nine lashes, or imprisonment, if the offender be a free negro, but if a white then with a fine of two hundred dollars. The reason for this law assigned in the preamble is, that "teaching slaves to read and write tends to excite dissatisfaction in their minds, and to produce insurrection and rebellion."

In Georgia, if a white teach a free negro, or slave, to read or write, he is fined $500, and imprisoned at the discretion of the court. If the offender be a colored man, bond or free, he is to be fined, or whipt at the discretion of the court. By this barbarous law, which was enacted in 1829, a white man may be fined and imprisoned for teaching his own child if he happens to be colored, and if colored, whether bond or free, he may be fined or whipped.

> "We have," says Mr. Berry, in a speech in the House of Delegates of Virginia in 1832, "as far as possible closed every avenue by which light might enter their (the slaves) minds. If we could extinguish the capacity to see the light, our work would be completed; they would then be on a level with the beasts of the field, and we should be safe. I am not certain that we would not do it, if we could find out the necessary process, and that on the plea of necessity."

Oh, my brethren! when you are telling to an admiring audience that through your instrumentality nearly two millions of Bibles and Testaments have been disseminated throughout the world, does not the voice of the slave vibrate on your ear, as it floats over the sultry plains of the South, and utters forth his lamentation, "Hast thou but one blessing, my father? *bless me, even me also,* O my father!" Does no wail of torment interrupt the eloquent harrangue?—And from the bottomless pit does no accusing voice arise to charge you with the perdition of those souls from whom you wrested, as far as you were able, the power of working out their own salvation?

Our country, I believe, has arrived at an awful crisis. God has in infinite mercy raised up those who have moral courage and religion enough to obey the divine command, "Cry aloud and spare not, lift up thy voice like a trumpet, and show my people their transgressions."—Our sins are set in order before us, and we are now hesitating whether we shall choose the curse pronounced by Jehovah, "Cursed be he that perverteth the judgment of the stranger, fatherless and widow," or the blessing recorded in the 41st Psl. "Blessed is the man that considereth the poor (or the weak,) the Lord will deliver him in the time of trouble."

And is there no help? Shall we be dismayed because our mistaken countrymen burned our messengers of Truth in Charleston, S. C.? No, my brethren, *I am not dismayed!* I do not intend to stamp the anti-slavery publications as inspired writings, but the principles they promulgate are the principles of the holy Scriptures, and I derive encouragement from the recollection that Tindal suffered martyrdom for translating and printing the New Testament—and that Tonstal, Archbishop of London, purchased every copy which he could obtain and had them burnt by the common hangman. Now Great Britain is doing more than any other people to scatter the Bible to every nation under heaven. Shall we be alarmed as though some new thing had happened unto us because our printing press has been destroyed at Cincinnati, Ohio? The devoted Carey was compelled to place his establishment for the translation of the sacred volume beyond the boundary line of the British authorities. And now England would gladly have the Bible translated into every tongue.

If then there be, as I humbly trust there are among my Christian brethren some who like the prophet of old are ready to exclaim! "Wo is me! for I am undone; because I am a man of unclean lips; for mine eyes have seen the King, the Lord of Hosts"—If to some of you Jehovah has unvailed the abominations of American Slavery, the guilt of yourselves and of your brethren! Oh remember the prophet of Israel and be encouraged. Your lips like his will be touched with a live coal from off the altar. The Lord will be your light and your salvation: He will go before you and the God of Israel will be your reward.

If ever there was a time when the Church of Christ was called upon to make an *aggressive* movement on the kingdom of darkness, *this is the time.* The subject of slavery is fairly before the American public.—The consciences of the slave-holders at the South and of their coadjutors at the North are aroused, notwithstanding all the opiates which are so abundantly administered under the plea of necessity, and expediency, and the duty of obedience to man, rather than to God. In regard to slavery, Satan has transformed himself into an angel of light, and under the false pretence of consulting the good of the slaves, pleads for retaining them in bondage, until they are prepared to enjoy the blessings of liberty. Full well he knows that if he can but gain time, he gains every thing. When he stood beside Felix and saw that he trembled before his fettered captive, as Paul reasoned of righteousness, temperance, and judgment to come, he summoned to his aid this masterpiece of satanic ingenuity, and whispered, say to this Apostle, "Go thy way for this time, at a more convenient season, I will call for thee." The heart of Felix responded to this intimation, and his lips uttered the fatal words—fatal, because, for aught that appears, they sealed his death warrant for eternity. Let me appeal to every Christian minister, who has known what it is to repent and forsake his sins: Have you not all found that prospective repentance and future amendment are destruction to the soul? The truth is, to postpone present duty, to get ready for the discharge of future, is just putting yourselves into the hands of Satan to prepare you for the service of God. Just so, gradualism puts the slave into the hands of his master, whose interest it is to keep him enslaved, to prepare him for freedom, because that master says at a convenient season I will liberate my captive. So says the adversary of all good, serve me to-day and to-morrow thou mayest serve God. Oh lay not this flattering unction to your souls, ye that are teachers in Israel. God is not mocked, and ye may as well expect indulgence in sin to purify the heart and prepare the soul for an inheritance with the saints in light, as to suppose that slavery can fit men for freedom. That which debases and brutualizes can never fit for freedom. The chains of the slave must be sundered; he must be taught that he is "heaven-born and destined to the skies again;" he must be restored to his dignified station in the scale of creation, he must be crowned again with the diadem of glory, again ranked amongst the sons of God and invested with lordly prerogative over every living creature. If you would aid in this mighty, this glorious achievement—"Preach the word" of IMMEDIATE EMANCIPATION. "Be instant in season and out of season." "If they persecute you in one city, flee ye unto another," that your sound may go out through all our land; and you may not incur the awful charge,

"YE KNEW YOUR DUTY, BUT YE DID IT NOT."

It is now twenty years since a beloved friend with whom I often mingled my tears, related to me the following circumstance, when helpless and hopeless we deplored the horrors of slavery, and I believe many are now doing what we did then, weeping and praying and interceding, "but secretly, for fear of the Jews." On the plantation adjoining her husband's, there was a slave of pre-eminent piety. His master was not a professor of religion, but the superior excellence of this disciple of Christ was not unmarked by him, and I believe he was so sensible of the good influence of his piety that he did not deprive him of the few religious privileges within his reach. A planter was one day dining with the owner of this slave, and in the course of conversation observed that all profession of religion among slaves was mere hypocricy. The other asserted a contrary opinion, adding, I have a slave who I believe would rather die than deny his Saviour. This was ridiculed, and the master urged to prove his assertion. He accordingly sent for this man of God, and peremptorily ordered him to deny his belief in the Lord Jesus Christ. The slave pleaded to be excused, constantly affirming that he would rather die than deny the Redeemer, whose blood was shed for him. His master, after vainly trying to induce obedience by threats, had him severely whipped. The fortitude of the sufferer was not to be shaken; he nobly rejected the offer of exemption from further chastisement at the expense of destroying his soul, and this blessed martyr died in consequence of this severe infliction. Oh, how bright a gem will this victim of irresponsible power be, in that crown which sparkles on the Redeemer's brow; and that many such will cluster there, I have not the shadow of a doubt.*

Brethren, you are invested with immense power over those to whom you minister in holy things—commensurate with your power is your responsibility, and if you abuse, or neglect to use it aright, great will be your condemnation. Mr. Moore, in a speech in the House of Delegates in Virginia, in 1832, says:

> It is utterly impossible to avoid the consideration of the subject of slavery. As well might the Apostle have attempted to close his eyes against the light which shone upon him from heaven, or to turn a deaf ear to the name which reached him from on high as for us to try to stifle the spirit of enquiry which is abroad in the land...... The MONSTROUS CONSEQUENCES which arise from the existence of slavery have been exposed to open day; the DANGERS arising from it stare us in the face, and it becomes us as men to meet and overcome them, rather than attempt to escape by evading them. Slavery, as it exists among us, may be regarded as the heaviest calamity which has ever befallen any portion of the human race. (If we look back at the long course of time which has elapsed from the creation to the present moment, we shall scarcely be able to point out a people whose situation was not in many respects preferable to our own, and that of the other states in which slavery exists. True, we shall see nations which have groaned under the yoke of despotism for hundreds and thousands of years, but the individuals composing those nations have enjoyed a degree of happiness, peace and freedom from apprehension which the holders of slaves in this country can never know.)

*Since writing the above, I have received information that "the perpetrators of the foul deed were in a state of inebriation," and that this martyr was an aged slave. Drunkenness instead of palliating crime aggravates it even according to human laws. But such are the men in whose hands slavery often places absolute power.

The daughters of Virginia have borne their testimony to the evils of slavery, and have pleaded for its extinction. Will this nation continue deaf to the voice of reason, humanity, and religion? In the memorial of the female citizens of Fluvanna Co., Va. to the General Assembly of that Commonwealth in 1832, they say:

> We cannot conceal from ourselves that an evil (slavery) is amongst us, which threatens to outgrow the growth, and dim the brightness of our national blessings. A shadow deepens over the land and casts its thickest gloom upon the sacred shrine of domestic bliss, darkening over us as time advances.
>
> We can only aid by ardent outpourings of the spirit of supplication at a throne of grace..... We conjure you by the sacred charities of kindred, by the solemn obligations of justice, by every consideration of domestic affection and patriotic duty, to nerve every faculty of your minds to the investigation of this important subject, and let not the united voices of your mothers, wives, daughters and kindred have sounded in your ears in vain.

We are cheered with the belief that many knees at the South are bent in prayer for the success of the Abolitionists. We believe, and we rejoice in the belief that the statement made by a Southern Minister of the Methodist Episcopal Church, at the session of the New York Annual Conference, in June of this year, is true: "Don't give up Abolitionism—don't bow down to slavery. You have thousands at the South who are secretly praying for you."—In a subsequent conversation with the same individual, he stated, That the South is not that unit of which the pro-slavery party boast—there is a diversity of opinion among them in reference to slavery, and the REIGN OF TERROR alone suppresses the free expression of sentiment. That there are thousands who believe slaveholding to be sinful, who secretly wish the abolitionists success, and believe God will bless their efforts. That the ministers of the gospel and ecclesiastical bodies who indiscriminately denounce the abolitionists, without doing any thing themselves to remove slavery, have not the thanks of thousands at the South, but on the contrary are viewed as taking sides with slaveholders and recreant to the principles of their own profession. *Zion's Watchman, November*, 1836.

The system of slavery is necessarily cruel. The lust of dominion inevitably produces hardness of heart, because the state of mind which craves unlimited power, such as slavery confers, involves a desire to use that power, and although I know there are exceptions to the exercise of barbarity on the bodies of slaves, I maintain that there *can be no exceptions* to the exercise of the most soul-withering cruelty on the *minds* of the enslaved. All around is the mighty ruin of intellect, the appalling spectacle of the down-trodden image of God. What has caused this mighty wreck? A voice deep as hell and loud as the thunders of heaven replies, SLAVERY! Both worlds of spirits echo and re-echo, SLAVERY! And yet American slavery is palliated, is defended by slave-holding ministers at the South and their coadjutors at the North. Perhaps all of you would shrink with horror from a proposal to revive the Inquisition and give to Catholic superstition the power to enforce in this country its wicked system of bigotry and despotism. But I believe if all the horrors of the Inquisition and all the cruelty and oppression exercised by the Church of Rome, could be fully and fairly brought to view and compared with the details of slavery in the United States, the abominations of Catholicism would not surpass those of slavery, while the victims of the latter are ten fold more numerous.

But it is urged again and again, that slavery has been entailed upon us by our ancestors. We speak of this with a degree of self-complacency, which seems to intimate that we would not do the deeds of our fathers. So to speak, argues an utter want of principle, as well as an utter ignorance of duty, because as soon as we perceive the iniquity of that act by which we inherit PROPERTY IN MAN, we should surrender to the rightful owner, viz. the slave himself, a right which although legally vested in us, by the "unrighteous decrees" of our country, is vested in the slave *himself* by the laws of God. We talk as if the guilt of slavery from its first introduction to the present time, rested on our progenitors, and as it we were innocent because we had not imported slaves originally from Africa. The prophet Ezekiel furnishes a clear and comprehensive answer to this sophistry. "What mean ye, that ye use this proverb saying: The fathers have eaten sour grapes, and the children's teeth are set on edge..... Behold all souls are mine, as the soul of the father, so also the soul of the son is mine. THE SOUL THAT SINNETH IT SHALL DIE. If a man be just and doeth that which is lawful and right, he shall surely live. If he beget a son that hath opprest the poor and needy, he shall surely die; his blood shall be upon him. Now, lo! if he beget a son that seeth all his father's sins which he hath done, and doeth not such like, that hath not opprest any, neither hath spoiled by violence; that hath taken off his hand from the poor, he shall not die for the iniquity of his father. THE SOUL THAT SINNETH IT SHALL DIE. The son shall not bear the iniquity of the father, neither shall the father bear the iniquity of the son. The righteousness of the righteous shall be upon him—and the wickedness of the wicked shall be upon him."

Upon the present generation, rests, I believe, an accumulated weight of guilt. They have the experience of more than two centuries to profit by—they have witnessed the evils and the crimes of slavery, and they know that sin and misery are its legitimate fruits. They behold every where, inscribed upon the face of nature, the withering curse of slavery, as if the land mourned over the iniquity and wretchedness of its inhabitants. They contemplate in their domestic circles the living examples of that description given by Jefferson, in his "Notes on Virginia," of the influence of slavery, on the temper and morals of the master, and they know that there is not one redeeming quality, in the system of American slavery.

And now we have the most undeniable evidence of the safety of Immediate Emancipation, in the British West Indies. Every official account from these colonies, especially such as have rejected the apprenticeship system, comes fraught with encouragement to this country to deliver the poor and needy out of the hand of the oppressor.

To my brethren of the Methodist connection, with some of whom I have taken sweet counsel, and whose influence is probably more extensive than that of any other class of ministers at the South, it may avail something to the cause of humanity, which I am pleading, to quote the sentiments of John Wesley and Adam Clarke. Speaking of slavery the former says, "The blood of thy brother crieth against thee from the earth: oh, whatever it costs, put a stop to its cry before it is too late—instantly, at any price, were it the half of thy goods, deliver thyself from blood guiltiness. Thy hands, thy bed, thy furniture, thy house and thy lands, at present are stained with blood. Surely it is enough—accumulate no more guilt, spill no more blood of the innocent. Whether thou art a Christian or not, show thyself A MAN." Adam Clarke says, "In heathen countries, slavery was in some sort excusable. Among Christians it is an enormity and crime, for which perdition has scarcely an adequate punishment."

Yet this is the crime of which the Synod of Virginia, convened for the purpose of deliberating on the state of the Church in November last, speaks thus: "The Synod solemnly affirm, that the General Assembly of the Presbyterian Church have *no right* to declare that relation (viz. the relation between master and slave) sinful, which Christ and his apostles teach to be consistent with the most unquestionable piety. And that any act of the General Assembly which would impeach the *Christian* character of any man because he is a slave holder, would be a palpable violation of the just principles on which the union of our Church was founded—as well as a daring usurpation of authority granted by the Lord Jesus."

And this is the sin which the Church is fostering in her bosom—This is the leprosy over which she is casting the mantle of charity, to hide, if possible, the "putrefying sores"—This is the monster around which she is twining her maternal arms, and before which she is placing her anointed shield inscribed "holiness to the Lord"—Oh, ye ministers of Him who so loved the slave that he gave his precious blood to redeem him from sin, can ye any longer with your eyes fixed upon the Cross of Christ, plant your foot on his injured representative, and sanction and sanctify this heart-breaking, this soul destroying system?

> Wo to those whose hire is with the price of blood
> Perverting, darkening, changing as they go
> The sacred truths of the Eternal God.

Brethren, farewell! I have written under a solemn sense of my responsibility to God for the truths I have uttered: I know that all who nobly dare to speak the truth will come up to the help of the Lord, and add testimony to testimony until time would fail to hear them. To Him who has promised that "the expectation of the needy shall not perish forever"—who "hath chosen the weak things of the world to confound the things that are mighty, and the foolish things of the world to confound the wise, and base things of the world, and things which are despised, hath God chosen, yea and things which are not, to bring to nought things that are, that no flesh should glory in his presence," I commend this offering of Christian affection, humbly beseeching him so to influence the ministers of his sanctuary, and the people committed to their charge by his Holy Spirit, that from every Christian temple may arise the glorious anthem,

Blow ye the trumpet blow,
The gladly solemn sound!
Let all the nations know,
To earth's remotest bound,
The year of jubilee is come.

Yours in gospel love,

SARAH M. GRIMKÉ.

New-York, 12th Mo. 1836.

LETTERS ON THE EQUALITY OF THE SEXES, AND THE CONDITION OF WOMAN

Addressed to Mary S. Parker, President of the Boston Female Anti-Slavery Society

LETTER I.

The Original Equality of Woman.

Amesbury, 7th Mo. 11th, 1837.

My Dear Friend,—In attempting to comply with thy request to give my views on the Province of Woman, I feel that I am venturing on nearly untrodden ground, and that I shall advance arguments in opposition to a corrupt public opinion, and to the perverted interpretation of Holy Writ, which has so universally obtained. But I am in search of truth; and no obstacle shall prevent my prosecuting that search, because I believe the welfare of the world will be materially advanced by every new discovery we make of the designs of Jehovah in the creation of woman. It is impossible that we can answer the purpose of our being, unless we understand that purpose. It is impossible that we should fulfil our duties, unless we comprehend them; or live up to our privileges, unless we know what they are.

In examining this important subject, I shall depend solely on the Bible to designate the sphere of woman, because I believe almost every thing that has been written on this subject, has been the result of a misconception of the simple truths revealed in the Scriptures, in consequence of the false translation of many passages of Holy Writ. My mind is entirely delivered from the superstitious reverence which is attached to the English version of the Bible. King James's translators certainly were not inspired. I therefore claim the original as my standard, *believing that to have been inspired,* and I also claim to judge for myself what is the meaning of the inspired writers, because I believe it to be the solemn duty of every individual to search the Scriptures for themselves, with the aid of the Holy Spirit, and not be governed by the views of any man, or set of men.

We must first view woman at the period of her creation. "And God said, Let us make man in our own image, after our likeness; and let them have dominion over the fish of the sea, and over the fowl of the air, and over the cattle, and over all the earth, and over every creeping thing that creepeth upon the earth. So God created man in his own image, in the image of God created he him, male and female created he them." In all this sublime description of the creation of man, (which is a generic term including man and woman,) there is not one particle of difference intimated as existing between them. They were both made in the image of God; dominion was given to both over every other creature, but not over each other. Created in perfect equality, they were expected to exercise the vicegerence intrusted to them by their Maker, in harmony and love.

Let us pass on now to the recapitulation of the creation of man:—"The Lord God formed man of the dust of the ground, and breathed into his nostrils the breath of life; and man became a living soul. And the Lord God said, it is not good that man should be alone, I will make him an help meet for him." All creation swarmed with animated beings capable of natural affection, as we know they still are; it was not, therefore, merely to give man a creature susceptible of loving, obeying, and looking up to him, for all that the animals could do and did do. It was to give him a companion, *in all respects* his equal; one who was like himself *a free agent,* gifted with intellect and endowed with immortality; not a partaker merely of his animal gratifications, but able to enter into all his feelings as a moral and responsible being. If this had not been the case, how could she have been an help meet for him? I understand this as applying not only to the parties entering into the marriage contract, but to all men and women, because I believe God designed woman to be an help meet for man in every good and perfect work. She was a part of himself, as if Jehovah designed to make the oneness and identity of man and woman perfect and complete; and when the glorious work of their creation was finished, "the morning stars sang together, and all the sons of God shouted for joy."

This blissful condition was not long enjoyed by our first parents. Eve, it would seem from the history, was wandering alone amid the bowers of Paradise, when the serpent met with her. From her reply to Satan, it is evident that the command not to eat "of the tree that is in the midst of the garden," was given to both, although the term man was used when the prohibition was issued by God. "And the woman said unto the serpent, WE may eat of the fruit of the trees of the garden, but of the fruit of the tree which is in the midst of the garden, God hath said, YE shall not eat of it, neither shall YE touch it, lest YE die." Here the woman was exposed to temptation from a being with whom she was unacquainted. She had been accustomed to associate with her beloved partner, and to hold communion with God and with angels; but of satanic intelligence, she was in all probability entirely ignorant. Through the subtlety of the serpent, she was beguiled. And "when she saw that the tree was good for food, and that it was pleasant to the eyes, and a tree to be desired to make one wise, she took of the fruit thereof and did eat."

We next find Adam involved in the same sin, not through the instrumentality of a supernatural agent, but through that of his equal, a being whom he must have known was liable to transgress the divine command, because he must have felt that he was himself a free agent, and that he was restrained from disobedience only by the exercise of faith and love towards his Creator. Had Adam tenderly reproved his wife, and endeavored to lead her to repentance instead of sharing in her guilt, I should be much more ready to accord to man that superiority which he claims; but as the facts stand disclosed by the sacred historian, it appears to me that to say the least, there was as much weakness exhibited by Adam as by Eve. They both fell from innocence, and consequently from happiness, *but not from equality.*

Let us next examine the conduct of this fallen pair, when Jehovah interrogated them respecting their fault. The both frankly confessed their guilt. "The man said, the woman whom thou gavest to be with me, she gave me of the tree and I did eat. And the woman said, the serpent beguiled me and I did eat." And the Lord God said unto the woman, "Thou wilt be subject unto thy husband, and he will rule over thee." That this did not allude to the subjection of woman to man is manifest, because the same mode of expression is used in speaking to Cain of Abel. The truth is that the curse, as it is termed, which was pronounced by Jehovah upon woman, is a simple prophecy. The Hebrew, like the French language, uses the same word to express shall and will. Our translators having been accustomed to exercise lordship over their wives, and seeing only through the medium of a perverted judgement, very naturally, though I think not very learnedly or very kindly, translated it *shall* instead of *will,* and thus converted a prediction to Eve into a command to Adam; for observe, it is addressed to the woman and not to the man. The consequence of the fall was an immediate struggle for dominion, and Jehovah foretold which would gain the ascendency; but as he created them in his image, as that image manifestly was not lost by the fall, because it is urged in Gen. 9:6, as an argument why the life of man should not be taken by his fellow man, there is no reason to suppose that sin produced any distinction between them as moral, intellectual and responsible beings. Man might just as well have endeavored by hard labor to fulfil the prophecy, thorns and thistles will the earth bring forth to thee, as to pretend to accomplish the other, "he will rule over thee," by asserting dominion over his wife.

> Authority usurped from God, not given.
> He gave him only over beast, flesh, fowl,
> Dominion absolute: that right he holds
> By God's donation: but man o'er woman
> He made not Lord, such title to himself
> Reserving, human left from human free.

Here than I plant myself. God created us equal;—he created us free agents;—he is our Lawgiver, our King and our Judge, and to him alone is woman bound to be in subjection, and to him alone is she accountable for the use of those talents with which her Heavenly Father has entrusted her. One is her Master even Christ.

Thine for the oppressed in the bonds of womanhood,

SARAH M. GRIMKÉ.

LETTER II.

Woman Subject Only to God.

Newburyport, 7th mo. 17, 1837.

MY DEAR SISTER,—In my last, I traced the creation and the fall of man and woman from that state of purity and happiness which their beneficent Creator designed them to enjoy. As they were one in transgression, their chastisement was the same. "So God drove out *the man,* and he placed at the East of the garden of Eden a cherubim and a flaming sword, which turned every way to keep the way of the tree of life." We now behold them expelled from Paradise, fallen from their original loveliness, but still bearing on their foreheads the image and superscription of Jehovah; still invested with high moral responsibilites, intellectual powers, and immortal souls. They had incurred the penalty of sin, they were shorn of their innocence, but they stood on the same platform side by side, acknowledging *no superior* but their God. Notwithstanding what has been urged, woman I am aware stands charged to the present day with having brought sin into the world. I shall not repel the charge by any counter assertions, although, as was before hinted, Adam's ready acquiescence with his wife's proposal, does not savor much of that superiority *in strength of mind,* which is arrogated by man. Even admitting that Eve was the greater sinner, it seems to me man might be satisfied with the dominion he has claimed and exercised for nearly six thousand years, and that more true nobility would be manifested by endeavoring to raise the fallen and invigorate the weak, than by keeping woman in subjection. But I ask no favors for my sex. I surrender not our claim to equality. All I ask of our brethren is, that they will take their feet from off our necks, and permit us to stand upright on that ground which God designed us to occupy. If he has not given us the rights which have, as I conceive, been wrested from us, we shall soon give evidence of our inferiority, and shrink back into that obscurity, which the high souled magnanimity of man has assigned us as our appropriate sphere.

As I am unable to learn from sacred writ when woman was deprived by God of her equality with man, I shall touch upon a few points in the Scriptures, which demonstrate that no supremacy was granted to man. When God had destroyed the world, except Noah and his family, by the deluge, he renewed the grant formerly made to man, and again gave him dominion over every beast of the earth, every fowl of the air, over all that moveth upon the earth, and over all the fishes of the sea; into his hands they were delivered. But was woman, bearing the image of her God, placed under the dominion of her fellow man? Never! Jehovah could not surrender his authority to govern his own immortal creatures into the hands of a being, whom he knew, and whom his whole history proved, to be unworthy of a trust so sacred and important. God could not do it, because it is a direct contravention of his law. "Thou shalt worship the Lord thy God, and *him only* shalt thou serve." If Jehovah had appointed man as the guardian, or teacher of woman, he would certainly have given some intimation of this surrender of his own prerogative. But so far from it, we find the commands of God invariably the same to man and woman; and not the slightest intimation is given in a single passage of the Bible, that God designed to point woman to man as her instructor. The tenor of his language always is, "Look unto ME, and be ye saved, all the ends of the earth, for I am God, and there is none else."

The lust of dominion was probably the first effect of the fall; and as there was no other intelligent being over whom to exercise it, woman was the first victim of this unhallowed passion. We afterwards see it exhibited by Cain in the murder of his brother, by Nimrod in his becoming a mighty hunter of men, and setting up a kingdom over which to reign. Here we see the origin of that Upas of slavery, which sprang up immediately after the fall, and has spread its pestilential branches over the whole face of the known world. All history attests that man has subjected woman to his will, used her as a means to promote his selfish gratification, to minister to his sensual pleasures, to be instrumental in promoting his comfort; but never has he desired to elevate her to that rank she was created to fill. He has done all he could to debase and enslave her mind; and now he looks triumphantly on the ruin he has wrought, and says, the being he has thus deeply injured is his inferior.

Woman has been placed by John Quincy Adams, side by side with the slave, whilst he was contending for the right side of petition. I thank him for ranking us with the oppressed; for I shall not find it difficult to show, that in all ages and countries, not even excepting enlightened republican America, woman has more or less been made a *means* to promote the welfare of man, without due regard to her own happiness, and the glory of God as the end of her creation.

During the *patriarchal* ages, we find men and women engaged in the same employments. Abraham and Sarah both assisted in preparing the food which was to be set before the three men, who visited them in the plains of Mamre; but although their occupations were similar, Sarah was not permitted to enjoy the society of the holy visitant; and as we learn from Peter, that she "obeyed Abraham, calling him Lord," we may presume he exercised dominion over her. We shall pass on now to Rebecca. In her history, we find another striking illustration of the low estimation in which woman was held. Eleazur is sent to seek a wife for Isaac. He finds Rebecca going down to the well to fill her pitcher. He accosts her; and she replies with all humility, "Drink, my lord." How does he endeavor to gain her favor and confidence? Does he approach her as a dignified creature, whom he was about to invite to fill an important station in his master's family, as the wife of his only son? No. He offered incense to her vanity, and "he took a golden ear-ring of half a shekel weight, and two bracelets for her hands of ten shekels weight of gold," and gave them to Rebecca.

The cupidity of man soon led him to regard woman as property, and hence we find them sold to those, who wished to marry them, as far as appears, without any regard to those sacred rights which belong to woman, as well as to man in the choice of a companion. That women were a profitable kind of property, we may gather from the description of a virtuous woman in the last chapter of Proverbs. To work willingly with her hands, to open her hands to the poor, to clothe herself with silk and purple, to look well to her household, to make fine linen and sell it, to deliver girdles to the merchant, and not to eat the bread of idleness, seems to have constituted in the view of Solomon, the perfection of a woman's character and achievements. "The spirit of that age was not favorable to intellectual improvement; but as there were wise men who formed exceptions to the general ignorance, and were destined to guide the world into more advanced states, so there was a corresponding proportion of wise women; and among the Jews, as well as other nations, we find a strong tendency to believe that women were in more immediate connection with heaven than men."—L. M. Child's Con. of Woman. If there be any truth in this tradition, I am at a loss to imagine in what the superiority of man consists.

Thine in the bonds of womanhood,

SARAH M. GRIMKÉ.

LETTER III.

The Pastoral Letter of the General Association of Congregational Ministers of Massachusetts.

Haverhill, 7th Mo. 1837.

DEAR FRIEND,—When I last addressed thee, I had not seen the Pastoral Letter of the General Association. It has since fallen into my hands, and I must digress from my intention of exhibiting the condition of women in different parts of the world, in order to make some remarks on this extraordinary document. I am persuaded that when the minds of men and women become emancipated from the thraldom of superstition and "traditions of men," the sentiments contained in the Pastoral Letter will be recurred to with as much astonishment as the opinions of Cotton Mather and other distinguished men of his day, on the subject of witchcraft; nor will it be deemed less wonderful, that a body of divines should gravely assemble and endeavor to prove that woman has no right to "open her mouth for the dumb," than it now is that judges should have sat on the trials of witches, and solemnly condemned nineteen persons and one dog to death for witchcraft.

But to the letter. It says, "We invite your attention to the dangers which at present seem to threaten the FEMALE CHARACTER with wide-spread and permanent injury." I rejoice that they have called the attention of my sex to this subject, because I believe if woman investigates it, she will soon discover that danger is impending, though from a totally different source from that which the Association apprehends,—danger from those who, having long held the reins of *usurped* authority, are unwilling to permit us to fill that sphere which God created us to move in, and who have entered into league to crush the immortal mind of woman. I rejoice, because I am persuaded that the rights of woman, like the rights of slaves, need only be examined to be understood and asserted, even by some of those, who are now endeavoring to smother the irrepressible desire for mental and spiritual freedom which glows in the breast of many, who hardly dare to speak their sentiments.

"The appropriate duties and influence of women are clearly stated in the New Testament. Those duties are unobtrusive and private, but the sources of *mighty power*. When the mild, *dependent*, softening influence of woman upon the sternness of man's opinions is fully exercised, society feels the effects of it in a thousand ways." No one can desire more earnestly than I do, that woman may move exactly in the sphere which her Creator has assigned her; and I believe her having been displaced from that sphere has introduced confusion into the world. It is, therefore, of vast importance to herself and to all the rational creation, that she should ascertain what are her duties and her privileges as a responsible and immortal being.

The New Testament has been referred to, and I am willing to abide by its decisions, but must enter my protest against the false translation of some passages by the MEN who did that work, and against the perverted interpretation by the MEN who undertook to write commentaries thereon. I am inclined to think, when we are admitted to the honor of studying Greek and Hebrew, we shall produce some various readings of the Bible a little different from those we now have.

The Lord Jesus defines the duties of his followers in his Sermon on the Mount. He lays down grand principles by which they should be governed, without any reference to sex or condition.—"Ye are the light of the world. A city that is set on a hill cannot be hid. Neither do men light a candle and put it under a bushel, but on a candlestick, and it giveth light unto all that are in the house. Let your light so shine before men, that they may see your good works, and glorify your Father which is in Heaven." I follow him through all his precepts, and find him giving the same directions to women as to men, never even referring to the distinction now so strenuously insisted upon between masculine and feminine virtues: this is one of the anti-christian "traditions of men" which are taught instead of the "commandments of God." Men and women were CREATED EQUAL; they are both moral and accountable beings, and whatever is *right* for man to do, is *right* for woman.

But the influence of woman, says the Association, is to be private and unobtrusive; her light is not to shine before man like that of her brethren; but she is passively to let the lords of the creation, as they call themselves, put the bushel over it, lest peradventure it might appear that the world has been benefitted by the rays of *her* candle. So that her quenched light, according to their judgment, will be of more use than if it were set on the candlestick. "Her influence is the source of mighty power." This has ever been the flattering language of man since he laid aside the whip as a means to keep woman in subjection. He spares her body; but the war he has waged against her mind, her heart, and her soul, has been no less destructive to her as a moral being. How monstrous, how anti-christian, is the doctrine that woman is to be dependent on man! Where, in all the sacred Scriptures, is this taught? Alas! she has too well learned the lesson which MAN has labored to teach her. She has surrendered her dearest RIGHTS, and been satisfied with the privileges which man has assumed to grant her; she has been amused with the show of power, whilst man has absorbed all the reality into himself. He has adorned the creature whom God gave him as a companion, with baubles and gewgaws, turned her attention to personal attractions, offered incense to her vanity, and made her the instrument of his selfish gratification, a plaything to please his eye and amuse his hours of leisure. "Rule by obedience and by submission sway," or in other words, study to be a hypocrite, pretend to submit, but gain your point, has been the code of household morality which woman has been taught. The poet has sung, in sickly strains, the loveliness of woman's dependence upon man, and now we find it re-echoed by those who profess to teach the religion of the Bible. God says, "Cease ye from man whose breath is in his nostrils, for wherein is he to be accounted of?" Man says, depend upon me. God says, "HE will teach us of his ways." Man says, believe it not, I am to be your teacher. This doctrine of dependence upon man is utterly at variance with the doctrine of the Bible. In that book I find nothing like the softness of woman, nor the sternness of man: both are equally commanded to bring forth the fruits of the Spirit, love, meekness, gentleness, &c.

But we are told, "the power of woman is in her dependence, flowing from a consciousness of that weakness which God has given her for her protection." If physical weakness is alluded to, I cheerfully concede the superiority; if brute force is what my brethren are claiming, I am willing to let them have all the honor they desire; but if they mean to intimate, that mental or moral weakness belongs to woman, more than to man, I utterly disclaim the charge. Our powers of mind have been crushed, as far as man could do it, our sense of morality has been impaired by his interpretation of our duties; but no where does God say that he made any distinction between us, as moral and intelligent beings.

"We appreciate," say the Association, "the *unostentatious* prayers and efforts of woman in advancing the cause of religion at home and abroad, in leading religious inquirers TO THE PASTOR for instruction." Several points here demand attention. If public prayers and public efforts are necessarily ostentatious, then "Anna the prophetess, (or preacher,) who departed not from the temple, but served God with fastings and prayers night and day," "and spake of Christ to all them that looked for redemption in Israel," was ostentatious in her efforts. Then, the apostle Paul encourages women to be ostentatious in their efforts to spread the gospel, when he gives them directions how they should appear, when engaged in praying, or preaching in the public assemblies. Then, the whole association of Congregational ministers are ostentatious, in the efforts they are making in preaching and praying to convert souls.

But woman may be permitted to lead religious inquirers to the PASTORS for instruction. Now this is assuming that all pastors are better qualified to give instruction than woman. This I utterly deny. I have suffered too keenly from the teaching of man, to lead any one to him for instruction. The Lord Jesus says,—"Come unto me and learn of me." He points his followers to no man; and when woman is made the favored instrument of rousing a sinner to his lost and helpless condition, she has no right to substitute any teacher for Christ; all she has to do is, to turn the contrite inquirer to the "Lamb of God which taketh away the sins of the world." More souls have probably been lost by going down to Egypt for help, and by trusting in man in the early stages of religious experience, than by any other error. Instead of the petition being offered to God,—"Lead me in thy truth, and TEACH me, for thou art the God of my salvation,"—instead of relying on the precious promises—"What man is he that feareth the Lord? him shall HE TEACH in the way that he shall choose"—"I will instruct thee and TEACH thee in the way which thou shalt go—I will guide thee with mine eye"—the young convert is directed to go to man, as if he were in the place of God, and his instructions essential to an advancement in the path of righteousness. That woman can have but a poor conception of the privilege of being taught of God, what he alone can teach, who would turn the "religious inquirer aside" from the fountain of living waters, where he might slake his thirst for spiritual instruction, to those broken cisterns which can hold no water, and therefore cannot satisfy the panting spirit. The business of men and women, who are ORDAINED OF GOD to preach the unsearchable riches of Christ to a lost and perishing world, is to lead souls to Christ, and not to Pastors for instruction.

The General Association say, that "when woman assumes the place and tone of man as a public reformer, our care and protection of her seem unnecessary; we put ourselves in self-defence against her, and her character becomes unnatural." Here again the unscriptural notion is held up, that there is a distinction between the duties of men and women as moral beings; that what is virtue in man, is vice in woman; and women who dare to obey the command of Jehovah, "Cry aloud, spare not, lift up thy voice like a trumpet, and show my people their transgression," are threatened with having the protection of the brethren withdrawn. If this is all they do, we shall not even know the time when our chastisement is inflicted; our trust is in the Lord Jehovah, and in him is everlasting strength. The motto of woman, when she is engaged in the great work of public reformation should be,—"The Lord is my light and my salvation; whom shall I fear? The Lord is the strength of my life; of whom shall I be afraid?" She must feel, if she feels rightly, that she is fulfilling one of the important duties laid upon her as an accountable being, and that her character, instead of being "unnatural," is in exact accordance with the will of Him to whom, and to no other, she is responsible for the talents and the gifts confided to her. As to the pretty simile, introduced into the "Pastoral Lerter," "If the vine whose strength and beauty is to lean upon the trellis work, and half conceal its clusters, thinks to assume the independence and the overshadowing nature of the elm," &c. I shall only remark that it might well suit the poet's fancy, who sings of sparkling eyes and coral lips, and knights in armor clad; but it seems to me utterly inconsistent with the dignity of a Christian body, to endeavor to draw such an anti-scriptural distinction between men and women. Ah! how many of my sex feel in the dominion, thus unrighteously exercised over them, under the gentle appellation of *protection*, that what they have leaned upon has proved a broken reed at best, and oft a spear.

Thine in the bonds of womanhood,

SARAH M. GRIMKÉ.

LETTER IV.

Social Intercourse of the Sexes.

Andover, 7th Mo. 27th, 1837.

My Dear Friend,—Before I proceed with the account of that oppression which woman has suffered in every age and country from her *protector,* man, permit me to offer for your consideration, some views relative to the social intercourse of the sexes. Nearly the whole of this intercourse is, in my apprehension, derogatory to man and woman, as moral and intellectual beings. We approach each other, and mingle with each other, under the constant pressure of a feeling that we are of different sexes; and, instead of regarding each other only in the light of immortal creatures, the mind is fettered by the idea which is early and industriously infused into it, that we must never forget the distinction between male and female. Hence our intercourse, instead of being elevated and refined, is generally calculated to excite and keep alive the lowest propensities of our nature. Nothing, I believe, has tended more to destroy the true dignity of woman, than the fact that she is approached by man in the character of a female. The idea that she is sought as an intelligent and heaven-born creature, whose society will cheer, refine and elevate her companion, and that she will receive the same blessings she confers, is rarely held up to her view. On the contrary, man almost always addresses himself to the weakness of woman. By flattery, by an appeal to her passions, he seeks access to her heart; and when he has gained her affections, he uses her as the instrument of his pleasure—the minister of his temporal comfort. He furnishes himself with a housekeeper, whose chief business is in the kitchen, or the nursery. And whilst he goes abroad and enjoys the means of improvement afforded by collision of intellect with cultivated minds, his wife is condemned to draw nearly all her instruction from books, if she has time to peruse them; and if not, from her meditations, whilst engaged in those domestic duties, which are necessary for the comfort of her lord and master.

Surely no one who contemplates, with the eye of a Christian philosopher, the design of God in the creation of woman, can believe that she is now fulfilling that design. The literal translation of the word "help-meet" is a helper like unto himself; it is so rendered in the Septuagint, and manifestly signifies a companion. Now I believe it will be impossible for woman to fill the station assigned her by God, until her brethren mingle with her as an equal, as a moral being; and lose, in the dignity of her immortal nature, and in the fact of her bearing like himself the image and superscription of her God, the idea of her being a female. The apostle beautifully remarks, "As many of you as have been baptized into Christ, have put on Christ. There is neither Jew nor Greek, there is neither bond nor free, there is neither *male* nor *female;* for ye are all one in Christ Jesus." Until our intercourse is purified by the forgetfulness of sex,—until we rise above the present low and sordid views which entwine themselves around our social and domestic interchange of sentiment and feelings, we never can derive that benefit from each other's society which it is the design of our Creator that we should. Man has inflicted an unspeakable injury upon woman, by holding up to her view her animal nature, and placing in the back ground her moral and intellectual being. Woman has inflicted an injury upon herself by submitting to be thus regarded; and she is now called upon to rise from the station where *man,* not God, has placed her, and claim those sacred and inalienable rights, as a moral and responsible being, with which her Creator has invested her.

What but these views, so derogatory to the character of woman, could have called forth the remark contained in the Pastoral Letter? "We especially deplore the intimate acquaintance and promiscuous conversation of *females* with regard to things 'which ought not to be named,' by which that modesty and delicacy, which is the charm of domestic life, and which constitutes the true influence of woman, is consumed." How wonderful that the conceptions of man relative to woman are so low, that he cannot perceive that she may converse on any subject connected with the improvement of her species, without swerving in the least from that modesty which is one of her greatest virtues! Is it designed to insinuate that woman should possess a greater degree of modesty than man? This idea I utterly reprobate. Or is it supposed that woman cannot go into scenes of misery, the necessary result of those very things, which the Pastoral Letter says ought not to be named, for the purpose of moral reform, without becoming contaminated by those with whom she thus mingles?

This is a false position; and I presume has grown out of the never-forgotten distinction of male and female. The woman who goes forth, clad in the panoply of God, to stem the tide of iniquity and misery, which she beholds rolling through our land, goes not forth to her labor of love as a female. She goes as the dignified messenger of Jehovah, and all she does and says must be done and said irrespective of sex. She is in duty bound to communicate with all, who are able and willing to aid her in saving her fellow creatures, both men and women, from that destruction which awaits them.

So far from woman losing any thing of the purity of her mind, by visiting the wretched victims of vice in their miserable abodes, by talking with them, or of them, she becomes more and more elevated and refined in her feelings and views. While laboring to cleanse the minds of others from the malaria of moral pollution, her own heart becomes purified, and her soul rises to nearer communion with her God. Such a woman is infinitely better qualified to fulfil the duties of a wife and a mother, than the woman whose *false delicacy* leads her to shun her fallen sister and brother, and shrink from *naming those sins* which she knows exist, but which she is too fastidious to labor by deed and by word to exterminate. Such a woman feels, when she enters upon the marriage relation, that God designed that relation not to debase her to a level with the animal creation, but to increase the happiness and dignity of his creatures. Such a woman comes to the important task of training her children in the nurture and admonition of the Lord, with a soul filled with the greatness of the beings committed to her charge. She sees in her children, creatures bearing the image of God; and she approaches them with reverence, and treats them at all times as moral and accountable beings. Her own mind being purified and elevated, she instils into her children that genuine religion which induces them to keep the commandments of God. Instead of ministering with ceaseless care to their sensual appetites, she teaches them to be temperate in all things. She can converse with her children on any subject relating to their duty to God, can point their attention to those vices which degrade and brutify human nature, without in the least defiling her own mind or theirs. She views herself, and teaches her children to regard themselves as moral beings; and in all their intercourse with their fellow men, to lose the animal nature of man and woman, in the recognition of that immortal mind wherewith Jehovah has blessed and enriched them.

Thine in the bonds of womanhood,

SARAH M. GRIMKÉ.

LETTER V.

Condition in Asia and Africa.

Groton, 8th Mo. 4th, 1837.

My Dear Sister,—I design to devote this letter to a brief examination of the condition of women in Asia and Africa. I believe it will be found that men, in the exercise of their usurped dominion over woman, have almost invariably done one of two things. They have either made slaves of the creatures whom God designed to be their companions and their coadjutors in every moral and intellectual improvement, or they have dressed them like dolls, and used them as toys to amuse their hours of recreation.

I shall commence by stating the degrading practice of SELLING WOMEN, which we find prevalent in almost all the Eastern nations.

Among the Jews,—

> Whoever wished for a wife must pay the parents for her, or perform a stipulated period of service; sometimes the parties were solemnly betrothed in childhood, and the price of the bride stipulated.

In Babylon, they had a yearly custom of a peculiar kind.

> In every district, three men, respectable for their virtue, were chosen to conduct all the marriageable girls to the public assembly. Here they were put up at auction by the public crier, while the magistrate presided over the sales. The most beautiful were sold first, and the rich contended eagerly for a choice. The most ugly, or deformed girl was sold next in succession to the handsomest, and assigned to any person who would take her with the least sum of money. The price given for the beautiful was divided into dowries for the homely.

Two things may here be noticed; first, the value set upon personal charms, just as a handsome horse commands a high price;

and second, the utter disregard which is manifested towards the feelings of woman.

> In no part of the world does the condition of women appear more dreary than in Hindostan. The arbitrary power of a father disposes of them in childhood. When they are married, their husbands have despotic control over them; if unable to support them, they can lend or sell them to a neighbor, and in the Hindoo rage for gambling, wives and children are frequently staked and lost. If they survive their husbands, they must pay implicit obedience to the oldest son; if they have no sons, the nearest male relation holds them in subjection; and if there happen to be no kinsmen, they must be dependent on the chief of the tribe.

Even the English, who are numerous in Hindostan, have traded in women.

> India has been a great marriage market, on account of the emigration of young enterprising Englishmen, without a corresponding number of women. Some persons actually imported women to the British settlements, in order to sell them to rich Europeans, or nabobs, who would give a good price for them. How the importers acquired a right thus to dispose of them is not mentioned; it is probable that the women themselves, from extreme poverty, or some other cause, consented to become articles of speculation upon consideration of receiving a certain remuneration. In September, 1818, the following advertisement appeared in the Calcutta Advertiser:
>
> FEMALES RAFFLED FOR.
>
> Be it known, that six fair pretty young ladies, with two sweet engaging children, lately imported from Europe, having the roses of health blooming on their cheeks, and joy sparkling in their eyes, possessing amiable tempers and highly accomplished, whom the most indifferent cannot behold without rapture, are to be raffled for next door to the British gallery.

The enemy of all good could not have devised a better means of debasing an immortal creature, than by turning her into a saleable commodity; and hence we find that wherever this custom prevails, woman is regarded as a mere machine to answer the purposes of domestic combat or sensual indulgence, or to gratify the taste of her oppressor by a display of personal attractions.

> Weighed in the balance with a tyrant's gold,
> Though nature cast her in a heavenly mould.

I shall now take a brief survey of the EMPLOYMENTS of women in Asia and Africa. In doing this, I have two objects in view; first to show, that women are capable of acquiring as great physical power as men, and secondly to show, that they have been more or less the victims of oppression and contempt.

> The occupations of the ancient Jewish women were laborious. They spent their time in spinning and weaving cloth for garments, and for the covering of the tents, in cooking the food, tending the flocks, grinding the corn, and drawing water from the wells.

Of Trojan women we know little, but we find that—

> Andromache, though a princess and well beloved by her husband, fed and took care of the horses of Hector.

So in Persia, women of the middling class see that proper care is taken of the horses. They likewise do all the laborious part of the house work.

> The Hindoo women are engaged in every variety of occupation, according to the caste of their husbands. They cultivate the land, make baskets and mats, bring water in jars, carry manure and various other articles to market in baskets on their heads, cook food, tend children, weave cloth, reel thread and wind cocoons.
>
> The Thibetian women of the laboring classes are inured to a great deal of toil. They plant, weed, reap, and thresh grain, and are exposed to the roughest weather, while their indolent husbands are perhaps living at their ease.
>
> Females of the lower classes among the Chinese endure as much labor and fatigue as the men. A wife sometimes drags the

plough in rice fields with an infant tied upon her back, while her husband performs the less arduous task of holding the plough.

The Tartar women in general perform a greater share of labor than the men; for it is a prevalent opinion that they were sent into the world for no other purpose, but to be useful and convenient SLAVES to the stronger sex. Among some of the Tartar tribes of the present day, females manage a horse. hurl a javelin, hunt wild animals, and fight an enemy as well as the men.

In the island of Sumatra, the women do all the work, while their husbands lounge in idleness, playing on the flute, with wreaths of globe amaranth on their heads, or racing with each other, without saddle or stirrup, or hunting deer, or gambling away their wives, their children, or themselves. The Battas consider their wives and children as slaves, and sell them whenever they choose.

The Moors are indolent to excess. They lie whole days upon their mats, sleeping and smoking, while the women and slaves perform all the labor. Owing to their uncleanly habits, they are much infested with vermin; and as they consider it beneath their dignity to remove this annoyance, the task is imposed on the women. They are very impatient and tyrannical, and for the slightest offence beat their wives most cruelly.

In looking over the condition of woman as delineated in this letter, how amply do we find the prophecy of Jehovah to Eve fulfilled, "Thy husband will rule over thee." And yet we perceive that where the physical strength of woman is called into exercise, there is no inferiority even in this respect; she performs the labor, while man enjoys what are termed the pleasures of life.

I have thought it necessary to adduce various proofs of my assertion, that men have always in some way regarded women as mere instruments of selfish gratification; and hope this sorrowful detail of the wrongs of woman will not be tedious to thee.

Thine in the bonds of womanhood,

SARAH M. GRIMKÉ.

LETTER VI.

Women in Asia and Africa.

Groton, 8th Mo. 15th, 1837.

Dear Friend,—In pursuing the history of woman in different ages and countries, it will be necessary to exhibit her in all the various situations in which she has been placed.

We find her sometimes *filling the throne*, and exercising the functions of royalty. The name of Semiramis is familiar to every reader of ancient history. She succeeded Ninus in the government of the Assyrian empire; and to render her name immortal, built the city of Babylon. Two millions of men were constantly employed upon it. Certain dykes built by order of this queen, to defend the city from inundations, are spoken of as admirable.

Nicotris, wife of Nabonadius, the Evil-Merodach of Scripture, was a woman of great endowments. While her husband indulged in a life of ease and pleasure, she managed the affairs of state with wisdom and prudence.

Zenobia queen of Palmyra and the East, is the most remarkable among Asiatic women. Her genius struggled with and overcame all the obstacles presented by oriental laws and customs. She knew the Latin, Greek, Syriac, and Egyptian languages; and had drawn up for her own use an abridgement of oriental history. She was the companion and friend of her husband, and accompanied him on his hunting excursions with eagerness and courage equal to his own. She despised the effeminacy of a covered carriage, and often appeared on horseback in military costume. Sometimes she marched several miles on foot, at the head of the troops. Having revenged the murder of her husband, she ascended the throne, and for five years governed Palmyra, Syria, and the East, with wonderful steadiness and wisdom.

Previous to the introduction of Mohammedism into Java, women often held the highest offices of government; and when the chief of a district dies, it is even now not uncommon for the widow to retain the authority that belonged to her deceased husband.

Other instances might be adduced to prove that there is no natural inferiority in woman. Not that I approve of woman's holding the reins of government over man. I maintain that they are equal, and that God never invested fallen man with unlimited power over his fellow man; and I rejoice that circumstances have prevented woman from being more deeply involved in the guilt which appears to be inseparable from political affairs. The few instances which I have mentioned prove that intellect is not sexed; and doubtless if woman had not almost universally been depressed and degraded, the page of history would have exhibited as many eminent statesmen and politicians among women as men. We are much in the situation of the slave. Man has asserted and assumed authority over us. He has, by virtue of his power, deprived us of the advantages of improvement which he has lavishly bestowed upon himself, and then, after having done all he can to take from us the means of proving our equality, and our capability of mental cultivation, he throws upon us the burden of proof that God created man and woman equal, and endowed them, without any reference to sex, with intelligence and responsibilities, as rational and accountable beings. Hence in Hindostan, even women of the higher classes are forbidden to read or write; because the Hindoos think it would inevitably spoil them for domestic life, and assuredly bring some great misfortune upon them. May we not trace to the same feeling, the disadvantages under which women labor even in this country, for want of an education, which would call into exercise the powers of her mind, and fortify her soul with those great moral principles by which she would be qualified to fill *every* department in *social, domestic* and *religious* life with dignity?

In Hindostan, the evidence of women is not received in a court of justice.

In Burmah, their testimony is not deemed equal to that of a man, and they are not allowed to ascend the steps of a court of justice, but are obliged to give their testimony outside of the building.

In Siberia, women are not allowed to step across the footprints of men, or reindeer; they are not allowed to eat with men, or to partake of particular dainties. Among many tribes, they seem to be regarded as impure, unholy beings.

> The Mohammedan law forbids pigs, dogs, women and other impure animals to enter a mosque; and the hour of prayers must not be proclaimed by a female, a madman, a drunkard, or a decrepit person.

Here I am reminded of the resemblance between the situation of women in heathen and Mohammedan countries, and our brethren and sisters of color in this Christian land, where they are despised and cast out as though they were unclean. And on precisely the same ground, because they are said to be inferior.

The treatment of women as wives is almost uniformly the same in all heathen countries.

The ancient Lydians are the only exception that I have met with, and the origin of their peculiar customs is so much obscured by fable, that it is difficult to ascertain the truth. Probably they arose from some great benefit conferred on the state by women.

Among the Druses who reside in the mountains of the Anti Libanus, a wife is often divorced on the slightest pretext. If she ask her husband's permission to go out, and he says,—"Go," without adding "but come back again," she is divorced.

In Siberia, it is considered a wife's duty to obey the most capricious and unreasonable demands of her husband, without one word of expostulation or inquiry. If her master be dissatisfied with the most trifling particular in her conduct, he tears the cap or veil from her head, and this constitutes a divorce.

A Persian woman, under the dominion of the kindest master, is treated much in the same manner as a favorite animal. To vary her personal graces for his pleasure, is the sole end and aim of her existence. As moral or intellectual beings, it would be better for them to be among the dead than the living. The mother instructs her daughter in all the voluptuous coquetry, by which she herself acquired precarious ascendency over her absolute master; but all that is truly estimable in female character is utterly neglected.

Hence we find women extravagantly fond of adorning their persons. Regarded as instruments of pleasure, they have been degraded into mere animals, and have found their own gratification principally in the indulgence of personal vanity, because their external charms procured for them, at least a temporary ascendency over those, who held in their hands the reins of government. A few instances must suffice, or I shall exceed the limits I have prescribed to myself in this letter.

During the magnificent prosperity of Israel, marriages were conducted with great pomp; and with the progress of luxury and refinement, women became expensive, rather than profitable in a pecuniary point of view. Hence probably arose the custom of wealthy parents giving a handsome dowry with their daughters. On the day of the nuptials, the bride was conducted by her female relations to the bath, where she was anointed with the choicest perfumes, her hair perfumed and braided, her eyebrows deepened with black powder, and the tips of her fingers tinged with rose color. She was then arrayed in a marriage robe of brilliant color; the girdle and bracelets were more or less costly.

Notwithstanding the Chinese women have no opportunity to rival each other in the conquest of hearts, they are nevertheless very fond of ornaments. Bunches of silver or gilt flowers are always interspersed among their ringlets, and sometimes they wear the Chinese phoenix made of silver gilt. It moves with the slightest motion of the wearer, and the spreading tail forms a glittering aigrette on the middle of the head, and the wings wave over the front. Yet a Chinese ballad says,—The pearls and precious stones, the silk and gold with which a coquette so studiously bedecks herself, are a transparent varnish which makes all her defects the more apparent.

The Moorish women have generally a great passion for ornament. They decorate their persons with heavy gold ear-rings, necklaces of amber, coral and gold; gold bracelets; gold chains and silver bells for the ankles; rings on the fingers, &c. &c. The poorer class wear glass beads around the head, and curl the hair in large ringlets. Men are proud of having their wives handsomely dressed.

The Moors are not peculiar in this fancy. Christian men still admire women who adorn their persons to gratify the lust of the eye and the pride of life. Women, says a Brahminical expositor, are characterized by an inordinate love of jewels, fine clothes, &c. &c. I cannot deny this charge, but it is only one among many instances, wherein men have reproached us with those very faults and vices which their own treatment has engendered. Is it any matter of surprise that women, when unnaturally deprived of the means of cultivating their minds, of objects which would elevate and refine their passions and affections, should seek gratification in the toys and the trifles which now too generally engage their attention?

I cannot close this, without acknowledging the assistance and information I have derived, and shall continue to derive on this part of my subject, from a valuable work entitled "Condition of Women, by Lydia M Child." It is worth the perusal of every one who is interested in the subject.

Thine in the bonds of womanhood,

SARAH M. GRIMKÉ.

LETTER VII.

Condition in Some Parts of Europe and America.

Brookline, 8th Mo., 22d, 1837.

DEAR SISTER,—I now come to the consideration of the condition of woman in Europe.—In this portion of the world, she does not appear to have been as uniformly or as deeply debased, as in Eastern countries; yet we shall find little in her history which can yield us satisfaction, when we regard the high station she was designed to occupy as a *moral and intellectual* being.

In Greece, if we may judge from what Eustathius says, "women should keep within doors, and there talk,"—we may conclude, that in general their occupations were chiefly domestic. Thucydides also declares, that "she was the best woman, of whom the least was said, either of good or of harm." The heathen philosophers doubtless wished to keep woman in her "*appropriate sphere;*" and we find our clerical brethren of the present day re-echoing these pagan sentiments, and endeavoring to drive woman from the field of moral labor and intellectual culture, to occupy her talents in the pursuit of those employments which will enable her to regale the palate of her lord with the delicacies of the table, and in every possible way minister to his animal comfort and gratification. In my humble opinion, woman has long enough subserved the interests of man; and in the spirit of self-sacrifice, submitted almost without remonstrance to his oppression; and now that her attention is solicited to the subject of her rights, her privileges and her duties, I would entreat her to double her diligence in the performance of all her obligations as a *wife*, a *mother*, a *sister*, and a *daughter*. Let us remember that our claim to stand on perfect equality with our brethren, can only be substantiated by a scrupulous attention to our domestic duties, as well as by aiding in the great work of moral reformation—a work which is now calling for the energies and consecrated powers of every man and woman who desires to see the Redeemer's kingdom established on earth. That man must indeed be narrow minded, and can have but a poor conception of the power of moral truth on the female heart, who supposes that a correct view of her own rights can make woman *less solicitous to fill up every department of duty*. If it should have this effect, it must be because she has not taken a comprehensive view of the whole subject.

In the history of Rome, we find a little spot of sunshine in the valley where woman has been destined to live, unable from her lowly situation to take an expansive view of that field of moral and mental improvement, which she should have been busy in cultivating.

> In the earliest and best days of Rome, the first magistrates and generals of armies ploughed their own fields, and threshed their own grain. Integrity, industry and simplicity, were the prevailing virtues of the times; and the character of woman was, as it always must be, graduated in a degree by that of man. Columella says, Roman husbands, having completed the labors of the day, entered their houses free from all care, and there enjoyed perfect repose. There reigned union and concord and industry, supported by mutual affections. The most beautiful woman depended for distinction on her economy and endeavors to assist in crowning her husband's diligence with prosperity. All was in common between them; nothing was thought to belong more to one than another.

> The wife by her assiduity and activity within doors, equalled and seconded the industry and labor of her husband.

In the then state of the world, we may conclude from this description, that woman enjoyed as much happiness as was consistent with that comparatively unimproved condition of our species; but now a new and vast sphere of usefulness is opened to her, and she is pressed by surrounding circumstances to come up to the help of the Lord against the giant sins which desolate our beloved country. Shall woman shrink from duty in this exigency, and retiring within her own domestic circle, delight herself in the abundance of her own selfish enjoyments. Shall she rejoice in her home, her husband, her children, and forget her brethren and sisters in bondage, who know not what it is to call a spot of earth their own, whose husbands and wives are torn from them by relentless tyrants, and whose children are snatched from their arms by their unfeeling task-masters, whenever interest, or convenience, tempts them to this sacrilegious act? Shall woman disregard the situation of thousands of her fellow creatures, who are the victims of intemperance and licentiousness, and retreating to the privacy of her own comfortable home, be satisfied that her whole duty is performed, when she can exhibit "her children well clad and smiling, and her table neatly spread with wholesome provisions?" Shall she, because "her house is her *home*," refuse her aid and her sympathy to the down trodden slave, to the poor unhappy outcasts who are deprived of those blessings which she so highly prizes? Did God give her those blessings to steel her heart to the sufferings of her fellow creatures? Did he grant her the possession of husband and children, to dry up the fountains of feeling for those who know not the consolations of tenderness and reciprocal affection? Ah no! for every such blessing, God demands a grateful heart; and woman must be recreant to her duty, if she can quietly sit down in the enjoyments of her own domestic circle, and not exert herself to procure the same happiness for others.

But it is said woman has a mighty weapon in secret prayer. She has, I acknowledge, *in common with man;* but the woman who prays in sincerity for the regeneration of this guilty world, will accompany her prayers by her labors. A friend of mine remarked—"I was sitting in my chamber, weeping over the miseries of the slave, and putting up my petitions for his deliverance from bondage; when in the midst of my meditations, it occurred to me that my tears, unaided by effort, could never melt the chain of the slave. I must be up and doing." She is now an active abolitionist—her prayers and her works go hand in hand.

I am here reminded of what a slave once said to his master, a Methodist minister. The slaveholder inquired, "How did you like my sermon to-day?" "Very good, master, but it did not preach me free."

Oh, my sisters, suffer me to entreat you to assert your privileges, and to perform your duties as moral beings. Be not dismayed at the ridicule of man; it is a weapon worthy only of little minds, and is employed by those who feel that they cannot convince our judgment. Be not alarmed at contumely, or scorn; we must expect this. I pray that we may meet it with forbearance and love; and that nothing may drive us from the performance of our high and holy duties. Let us "cease from man, whose breath is in his nostrils, for wherein is he to be accounted of?" and press forward in all the great moral enterprises of the age, leaning *only* on the arm of our Beloved.

But I must return to the subject I commenced with, viz. the condition of woman in Europe.

> The northern nations bore a general resemblance to each other. War and hunting were considered the only honorable occupations for men, and all other employments were left to women and slaves. Even the Visigoths, on the coasts of Spain, left their fields and flocks to the care of women. The people who inhabit the vast extent of country between the Black sea and the North sea, are divided into various distinct races. The women are generally very industrious; even in their walks, they carry a portable distaff, and spin every step of the way. Both Croatian and Walachian women perform all the agricultural operations in addition to their own domestic concerns.

Speaking of the Morlachian women, M. Fortis says, "Being treated like beasts of burden, and expected to endure submissively every species of hardship, they naturally become very dirty and careless in their habits."

The Cossack women afford a contrast to this disgusting picture. They are very cleanly and industrious, and in the absence of their husbands, supply their places by taking charge of all their usual occupations, in addition to their own. It is rare for a Cossack woman not to know some trade, such as dyeing cloth, tanning leather, &c.

The condition of Polish and Russian serfs in modern times is about the same. The Polish women have scarcely clothing enough for decency, and they are subjected to great hardships and privations. "In Russia, women have been seen paving the streets, and performing other similar drudgery. In Finland, they work like beasts of burden, and may be seen for hours in snow water, up to the middle, tugging at boats and sledges."

In Flanders and in France, women are engaged in performing laborious tasks; and even in England, it is not unusual to see them scraping up manure from the streets with their hands, and gathering it into baskets.

In Greece, even now the women plough and carry heavy burdens, while the lordly master of the family may be seen walking before them without any incumbrance.*

*Since the preceding letters were in type, I have met with the following account in a French work entitled "De l' education des meres de famille on de la civilization du Genre Humain par les femmes," printed at Brussels in 1837. "The periodicals have lately published the following circumstance from the journal of an English physician, who travelled in the East. He visited a slave market, where he saw about twenty Greek women half naked, lying on the ground waiting for a purchaser. One of them attracted the attention of an old Turk. The barbarian examined her shoulders, her legs, her ears, her mouth, her neck, with the minutest care, just as a horse is examined, and during the inspection, the merchant praised the beauty of her eyes, the elegance of her shape, and other perfections; he protested that the poor girl was but thirteen years of age, &c. After a severe scrutiny and some dispute about the price, she was sold body and soul for 1375 francs. The soul, it is true, was accounted of little value in the bargain. The unfortunate creature, half fainting in the arms of her mother, implored help in the most touching accents, but it availed nothing—This infernal scene passed in Europe in 1829, only 600 leagues from Paris and London, the two capitals of the human species, and at the time in which I write, it is the living history of two thirds of the inhabitants of the earth."

Generally speaking, however, there is much more comparative equality of labor between the sexes in Europe than among the Orientals.

I shall close this letter with a brief survey of the condition of women among the Aborigines of America.

> Before America was settled by Europeans, it was inhabited by Indian tribes, which greatly resembled each other in the treatment of their women. Every thing, except war and hunting, was considered beneath the dignity of man.—During long and wearisome marches, women were obliged to carry children, provisions and hammocks on their shoulders; they had the sole care of the horses and dogs, cut wood, pitched the tents, raised the corn, and made the clothing. When the husband killed game, he left it by a tree in the forest, returned home, and sent his wife several miles in search of it. In most of the tribes, women were not allowed to eat and drink with men, but stood and served them, and then ate what they left.

The following affecting anecdote may give some idea of the sufferings of these women:

> Father Joseph reproved a female savage for destroying her infant danghter. She replied, "I wish my mother had thus prevented the manifold sufferings I have endured. Consider, father, our deplorable situation. Our husbands go out to hunt; we are dragged along with one infant at our breast, and another in a basket. Though tired with long walking, we are not allowed to sleep when we return, but must labor all night in grinding maize and making chica for them.—They get drunk and beat us, draw us by the hair of the head, and tread us under foot. Would to God my mother had put me under ground the moment I was born."

In Greenland, the situation of woman is equally deplorable. The men hunt bears and catch seals; but when they have towed their booty to land, they would consider it a disgrace to help the women drag it home, or skin and dress it. They often stand and look idly on, while their wives are staggering beneath the load that almost bends them to the earth. The women are cooks, butchers, masons, curriers, shoemakers and tailors. They will manage a boat in the roughest seas, and will often push off from the shore in the midst of a storm, that would make the hardiest European sailor tremble.

The page of history teems with woman's wrongs, and it is wet with woman's tears.—For the sake of my degraded sex every where, and for the sake of my brethren, who suffer just in proportion as they place woman lower in the scale of creation than man, lower than her Creator placed her, I entreat my sisters to arise in all the majesty of moral power, in all the dignity of immortal beings, and plant themselves, side by side, on the platform of human rights, with man, to whom they were designed to be companions, equals and helpers in every good word and work.

Thine in the bonds of womanhood,

SARAH M. GRIMKÉ.

LETTER VIII.

On the Condition of Women in the United States.

Brookline, 1837.

My dear Sister,—I have now taken a brief survey of the condition of woman in various parts of the world. I regret that my time has been so much occupied by other things, that I have been unable to bestow that attention upon the subject which it merits, and that my constant change of place has prevented me from having access to books, which might probably have assisted me in this part of my work. I hope that the principles I have asserted will claim the attention of some of my sex, who may be able to bring into view, more thoroughly than I have done, the situation and degradation of woman. I shall now proceed to make a few remarks on the condition of women in my own country.

During the early part of my life, my lot was cast among the butterflies of the *fashionable* world; and of this class of women,

I am constrained to say, both from experience and observation, that their education is miserably deficient; that they are taught to regard marriage as the one thing needful, the only avenue to distinction; hence to attract the notice and win the attentions of men, by their external charms, is the chief business of fashionable girls. They seldom think that men will be allured by intellectual acquirements, because they find, that where any mental superiority exists, a woman is generally shunned and regarded as stepping out of her "appropriate sphere," which, in their view, is to dress, to dance, to set out to the best possible advantage her person, to read the novels which inundate the press, and which do more to destroy her character as a rational creature, than any thing else. Fashionable women regard themselves, and are regarded by men, as pretty toys or as mere instruments of pleasure; and the vacuity of mind, the heartlessness, the frivolity which is the necessary result of this false and debasing estimate of women, can only be fully understood by those who have mingled in the folly and wickedness of fashionable life; and who have been called from such pursuits by the voice of the Lord Jesus, inviting their weary and heavy laden souls to come unto Him and learn of Him, that they may find something worthy of their immortal spirit, and their intellectual powers; that they may learn the high and holy purposes of their creation, and consecrate themselves unto the service of God; and not, as is now the case, to the pleasure of man.

There is another and much more numerous class in this country, who are withdrawn by education or circumstances from the circle of fashionable amusements, but who are brought up with the dangerous and absurd idea, that *marriage* is a kind of preferment; and that to be able to keep their husband's house, and render his situation comfortable, is the end of her being. Much that she does and says and thinks is done in reference to this situation; and to be married is too often held up to the view of girls as the sine qua non of human happiness and human existence. For this purpose more than for any other, I verily believe the majority of girls are trained. This is demonstrated by the imperfect education which is bestowed upon them, and the little pains taken to cultivate their minds, after they leave school, by the little time allowed them for reading, and by the idea being constantly inculcated, that although all household concerns should be attended to with scrupulous punctuality at particular seasons, the improvement of their intellectual capacities is only a secondary consideration, and may serve as an occupation to fill up the odds and ends of time. In most families, it is considered a matter of far more consequence to call a girl off from making a pie, or a pudding, than to interrupt her whilst engaged in her studies. This mode of training necessarily exalts, in their view, the animal above the intellectual and spiritual nature, and teaches women to regard themselves as a kind of machinery, necessary to keep the domestic engine in order, but of little value as the *intelligent* companions of men.

Let no one think, from these remarks, that I regard a knowledge of housewifery as beneath the acquisition of women. Far from it: I believe that a complete knowledge of household affairs is an indispensable requisite in a woman's education,—that by the mistress of a family, whether married or single, doing her duty thoroughly and *understandingly*, the happiness of the family is increased to an incalculable degree, as well as a vast amount of time and money saved. All I complain of is, that our education consists so almost exclusively in culinary and other manual operations. I do long to see the time, when it will no longer be necessary for women to expend so many precious hours in furnishing "a well spread table," but that their husbands will forego some of their accustomed indulgences in this way, and encourage their wives to devote some portion of their time to mental cultivation, even at the expense of having to dine sometimes on baked potatoes, or bread and butter.

I believe the sentiment expressed by the author of "Live and let Live," is true:

> Other things being equal, a woman of the highest mental endowments will always be the best housekeeper, for domestic economy, is a science that brings into action the qualities of the mind, as well as the graces of the heart. A quick perception, judgment, discrimination, decision and order are high attributes of mind, and are all in daily exercise in the well ordering of a family. If a sensible woman, an intellectual woman, a woman of genius, is not a good housewife, it is not because she is either, or all of those, but

because there is some deficiency in her character, or some omission of duty which should make her very humble, instead of her indulging in any secret self-complacency on account of a certain superiority, which only aggravates her fault.

The influence of women over the minds and character of *children* of both sexes, is allowed to be far greater than that of men. This being the case by the very ordering of nature, women should be prepared by education for the performance of their sacred duties as mothers and as sisters. A late American writer,* speaking on this subject, says in reference to an article in the Westminster Review:

> I agree entirely with the writer in the high estimate which he places on female education, and have long since been satisfied, that the subject not only merits, but *imperiously demands* a thorough reconsideration. The whole scheme must, in my opinion, be reconstructed. The great elements of usefulness and duty are too little attended to. Women ought, in my view of the subject, to approach to the best education now given to men, (I except mathematics and the classics,) far more I believe than has ever yet been attempted. Give me a host of educated, pious mothers and sisters, and I will do more to revolutionize a country, in moral and religious taste, in manners and in social virtues and intellectual cultivation, than I can possibly do in double or treble the time, with a similar host of educated men. I cannot but think that the miserable condition of the great body of the people in all ancient communities, is to be ascribed in a very great degree to the degradation of women.

There is another way in which the general opinion, that women are inferior to men, is manifested, that bears with tremendous effect on the laboring class, and indeed on almost all who are obliged to earn a subsistence, whether it be by mental or physical exertion—I allude to the disproportionate value set on the time and labor of men and of women. A man who is engaged in teaching, can always, I believe, command a higher

*Thomas S. Grimké.

price for tuition than a woman—even when he teaches the same branches, and is not in any respect superior to the woman. This I know is the case in boarding and other schools with which I have been acquainted, and it is so in every occupation in which the sexes engage indiscriminately. As for example, in tailoring, a man has twice, or three times as much for making a waist-coast or pantaloons as a woman, although the work done by each may be equally good. In those employments which are peculiar to women, their time is estimated at only half the value of that of men. A woman who goes out to wash, works as hard in proportion as a wood sawyer, or a coal heaver, but she is not generally able to make more than half as much by a day's work. The low remuneration which women receive for their work, has claimed the attention of a few philanthropists, and I hope it will continue to do so until some remedy is applied for this enormous evil. I have known a widow, left with four or five children, to provide for, unable to leave home because her helpless babes demand her attention, compelled to earn a scanty subsistence, by making coarse shirts at 12 1-2 cents a piece, or by taking in washing, for which she was paid by some wealthy persons 12 1-2 cents per dozen. All these things evince the low estimation in which woman is held. There is yet another and more disastrous consequence arising from this unscriptural notion—women being educated, from earliest childhood, to regard themselves as inferior creatures, have not that self-respect which conscious equality would engender, and hence when their virtue is assailed, they yield to temptation with facility, under the idea that it rather exalts than debases them, to be connected with a superior being.

There is another class of women in this country, to whom I cannot refer, without feelings of the deepest shame and sorrow. I allude to our female slaves. Our southern cities are whelmed beneath a tide of pollution; the virtue of female slaves is wholly at the mercy of irresponsible tyrants, and women are bought and sold in our slave markets, to gratify the brutal lust of those who bear the name of Christians. In our slave States, if amid all her degradation and ignorance, a woman desires to preserve her virtue unsullied, she is either bribed or whipped into compliance, or if she dares resist her seducer, her life by the laws of some of the slave States may be, and has actually been sacrificed to the fury of disappointed passion. Where such laws do not exist, the power which is necessarily vested in the master over his property, leaves the defenceless slave entirely at his mercy, and the sufferings of some females on this account, both physical and mental, are intense. Mr. Gholson, in the House of Delegates of Virginia, in 1832, said, "He really had been under the impression that he owned his slaves. He had lately purchased four women and ten children, in whom he thought he had obtained a great bargain; for he supposed they were his own property, *as were his brood mares.*" But even if any laws existed in the United States, as in Athens formerly, for the protection of female slaves, they would be null and void, because the evidence of a colored person is not admitted against a white, in any of our Courts of Justice in the slave States. "In Athens, if a female slave had cause to complain of any want of respect to the laws of modesty, she could seek the protection of the temple, and demand a change of owners; and such appeals were never discountenanced, or neglected by the magistrate." In Christian America, the slave has no refuge from unbridled cruelty and lust.

S. A. Forrall, speaking of the state of morals at the South, says, "Negresses when young and likely, are often employed by the planter, or his friends, to administer to their sensual desires. This frequently is a matter of speculation, for if the offspring, a mulatto, be a handsome female, 800 or 1000 dollars may be obtained for her in the New Orleans market. It is an occurrence of no uncommon nature to see a Christian father sell his own daughter, and the brother his own sister." The following is copied by the N. Y. Evening Star from the Picayune, a paper published in New Orleans. "A very beautiful girl, belonging to the estate of John French, a deceased gambler at New Orleans, was sold a few days since for the round sum of $7,000. An ugly-looking bachelor named Gouch, a member of the Council of one of the Principalities, was the purchaser. The girl is a brunette; remarkable for her beauty and intelligence, and there was considerable contention, who should be the purchaser. She was, however, persuaded to accept Gouch, he having made her princely promises." I will add but one more from the numerous testimonies respecting the degradation of female slaves, and the licentiousness of the South. It is from the Circular of the Kentucky Union, for the moral and religious improvement of the colored race. "To the female character among our black population, we cannot allude but with feelings of the bitterest shame. A similar condition of moral pollution and utter disregard of a pure and virtuous reputation, is to be found *only without the pale of Christendom.* That such a state of society should exist in a Christian nation, claiming to be the most enlightened upon earth, without calling forth any *particular attention* to its existence, though ever before our eyes and *in our* families, is a moral phenomenon at once unaccountable and disgraceful." Nor does the colored woman suffer alone: the moral purity of the white woman is deeply contaminated. In the daily habit of seeing the virtue of her enslaved sister sacrificed without hesitancy or remorse, she looks upon the crimes of seduction and illicit intercourse without horror, and although not personally involved in the guilt, she loses that value for innocence in her own, as well as the other sex, which is one of the strongest safeguards to virtue. She lives in habitual intercourse with men, whom she knows to be polluted by licentiousness, and often is she compelled to witness in her own domestic circle, those disgusting and heart-sickening jealousies and strifes which disgraced and distracted the family of Abraham. In addition to all this, the female slaves suffer every species of degradation and cruelty, which the most wanton barbarity can inflict; they are indecently divested of their clothing, sometimes tied up and severely whipped, sometimes prostrated on the earth, while their naked bodies are torn by the scorpion lash.

> The whip on WOMAN's shrinking flesh!
> Our soil yet reddening with the stains
> Caught from her scourging warm and fresh.

Can any American woman look at these scenes of shocking licentiousness and cruelty, and fold her hands in apathy, and say, "I have nothing to do with slavery"? *She cannot and be guiltless.*

I cannot close this letter, without saying a few words on the benefits to be derived by men, as well as women, from the opinions I advocate relative to the equality of the sexes. Many women are now supported, in idleness and extravagance, by the industry of their husbands, fathers, or brothers, who are compelled to toil out their existence, at the counting house, or in the printing office, or some other laborious occupation, while the wife and daughters and sisters take no part in the support of the family, and appear to think that their sole business is to spend the hard bought earnings of their male friends. I deeply regret such a state of things, because I believe that if women felt their responsibility, for the support of themselves, or their families it would add strength and dignity to their characters, and teach them more true sympathy for their husbands, than is now generally manifested,—a sympathy which would be exhibited by actions as well as words. Our brethren may reject my doctrine, because it runs counter to common opinions, and because it wounds their pride; but I believe they would be "partakers of the benefit" resulting from the Equality of the Sexes, and would find that woman, as their equal, was unspeakably more valuable than woman as their inferior, both as a moral and an intellectual being.

Thine in the bonds of womanhood,

SARAH M. GRIMKÉ.

LETTER IX.

Heroism Of Women—Women In Authority.

Brookline, 8th Mo. 25th, 1837.

My Dear Sister,—It seems necessary to glance at the conduct of women under circumstances which place them in juxtaposition with men, although I regard it as entirely unimportant in proving the moral equality of the sexes; because I condemn, in both, the exercise of that brute force which is as contrary to the law of God in men as in women; still, as a part of our history, I shall notice some instances of courage exhibited by females.

"Philippa, wife of Edward III., was the principal cause of the victory gained over the Scots at Neville Cross. In the absence of her husband, she rode among the troops, and exhorted them to 'be of good courage.'" Jane, Countess of Mountfort, and a contemporary of Philippa, likewise possessed a great share of physical courage. The history of Joan of Arc is too familiar to need repetition. During the reign of James II. a singular instance of female intrepidity occurred in Scotland. Sir John Cochrane being condemned to be hung, his daughter twice disguised herself, and robbed the mail that brought his death warrant. In the mean time, his pardon was obtained from the King. Instances might be multiplied, but it is unnecessary. I shall therefore close these proofs of female courage with one more fact. "During the revolutionary war, the women shared in the patriotism and bravery of the men. Several individuals carried their enthusiasm so far as to enter the army, where they faced all the perils and fatigues of the camp, until the close of the war."

When I view my countrywomen in the character of soldiers, or even behold them loading fire arms and moulding bullets for their brethren to destroy men's lives, I cannot refrain a sigh. I cannot but contrast their conduct at that solemn crisis with the conduct of those women who followed their Lord and Master with unresisting submission, to Calvary's Mount. With the precepts and example of a crucified Redeemer, who, in that sublime precept, "Resist not evil," has interdicted to his disciples all war and all violence, and taught us that the spirit of retaliation for injuries, whether in the camp, or at the fire-side, is wholly at variance with the peaceful religion he came to promulgate. How little do we comprehend that simple truth, "By this shall all men know that ye are my disciples, if ye have *love one to another.*"

Women have sometimes distinguished themselves in a way more consistent with their duties as moral beings. During the war between the Romans and the Sabines, the Sabine women who had been carried off by the Romans, repaired to the Sabine camp, dressed in deep mourning, with their little ones in their arms, to soften, if possible, the feelings of their parents. They knelt at the feet of their relatives; and when Hersilia, the wife of Romulus, described the kindness of their husbands, and their unwillingness to be separated from them, their fathers yielded to their entreaties, and an alliance was soon agreed upon. In consequence of this important service, peculiar privileges were conferred on women by the Romans. Brutus said of his wife, "I must not answer Portia in the words of Hector, 'Mind your wheel, and to your maids give law,' for in courage, activity and concern for her country's freedom, she is inferior to none of us." After the fatal battle of Cannæ, the Roman women consecrated all their ornaments to the service of the state. But when the triumvirs attempted to tax them for the expenses of carrying on a civil war, they resisted the innovation. They chose Hortensia for their speaker, and went in a body to the market-place to expostulate with the magistrates. The triumvirs wished to drive them away, but they were compelled to yield to the wishes of the people, and give the women a hearing. Hortensia pleaded so well the cause of her sisters, who resolved that they would not voluntarily aid in a *civil war*, that the number of women taxed was reduced from 1400 to 400.

In the wars of the Guelphs and the Ghibbelines, the emperor Conrad refused all terms of capitulation to the garrison of Winisberg, but he granted the request of the women to pass out in safety with such of their effects as they could carry themselves. Accordingly, they issued from the besieged city, each bearing on her shoulders a husband, son, father, or brother. They passed unmolested through the enemy's camp, which rung with acclamations of applause.

During our struggle for independence, the women were as exemplary as the men in various instances of self-denial: they refused every article of decoration for their persons; foreign elegances were laid aside, and they cheerfully abstained from luxuries for their tables.

English history presents many instances of women exercising prerogatives now denied them. In an action at law, it has been determined that an unmarried woman, having a freehold, might vote for members of Parliament; and it is recorded that lady Packington returned two. Lady Broughton was keeper of the gatehouse prison. And in a much later period, a woman was appointed governor of the house of correction at Chelmsford, by order of the court. In the reign of George II. the minister of Clerkenwell was chosen by a majority of women. The office of grand chamberlain in 1822 was filled by two women; and that of clerk of the crown, in the court of king's bench, has been granted to a female. The celebrated Anne, countess of Pembroke, held the hereditary office of sheriff of Westmoreland, and exercised it in person, sitting on the bench with the judges.

I need hardly advert to the names of Elizabeth of England, Maria Theresa of Germany, Catharine of Russia, and Isabella of Spain, to prove that women are capable of swaying the sceptre of royalty. The page of history proves incontestibly, not only that they are as well qualified to do so as men, but that there has been a comparatively greater proportion of good queens, than of good kings; women who have purchased their celebrity by individual strength of character.

I mention these women only to prove that intellect is not sexed; that strength of mind is not sexed; and that our views about the duties of men and the duties of women, the sphere of man and the sphere of woman, are mere arbitrary opinions, differing in different ages and countries, and dependant solely on the will and judgment of erring mortals.

As moral and responsible beings, men and women have the same sphere of action, and the same duties devolve upon both; but no one can doubt that the duties of each vary according to circumstances; that a father and a mother, a husband and a wife, have sacred obligations resting on them, which cannot possibly belong to those who do not sustain these relations. But these duties and responsibilities do not attach to them as men and as women, but as parents, husbands, and wives.

Thine in the bonds of womanhood.

SARAH M. GRIMKÉ.

LETTER X.

Intellect Of Woman.

Brookline, 8th Mo. 1837.

MY DEAR SISTER,—It will scarcely be denied, I presume, that, as a general rule, men do not desire the improvement of women. There are few instances of men who are magnanimous enough to be entirely willing that women should know more than themselves, on any subjects except dress and cookery; and, indeed, this necessarily flows from their assumption of superiority. As *they* have determined that Jehovah has placed woman on a lower platform than man, they of course wish to keep her there; and hence the noble faculties of our minds are crushed, and our reasoning powers are almost wholly uncultivated.

A writer in the time of Charles I. says—"She that knoweth how to compound a pudding, is more desirable than she who skilfully compounded a poem. A female poet I mislike at all times." Within the last century, it has been gravely asserted that, "chemistry enough to keep the pot boiling, and geography enough to know the location of the different rooms in her house, is learning sufficient for a woman." Byron, who was too sensual to conceive of a pure and perfect companionship between the sexes, would limit a woman's library to a Bible and cookery book. I have myself heard men, who knew for themselves the value of intellectual culture, say they cared very little for a wife who could not make a pudding, and smile with contempt at the ardent thirst for knowledge exhibited by some women.

But all this is miserable wit and worse philosophy. It exhibits that passion for the gratification of a pampered appetite, which is beneath those who claim to be so far above us, and may justly be placed on a par with the policy of the slaveholder, who says that men will be better slaves, if they are not permitted to learn to read.

In spite, however, of the obstacles which impede the progress of women towards that state of high mental cultivation for which her Creator prepared her, the tendency towards the universal dissemination of knowledge has had its influence on their destinies; and in all ages, a few have surmounted every hindrance, and proved, beyond dispute, that they have talents equal to their brethren.

Cornelia, the daughter of Scipio Africanus, was distinguished for virtue, learning and good sense. She wrote and spoke with uncommon elegance and purity. Cicero and Quinctilian bestow high praise upon her letters, and the eloquence of her children was attributed to her careful superintendence. This reminds me of a remark made by my brother, Thomas S. Grimké, when speaking of the importance of women being well educated, that "educated men would never make educated women, but educated women would make educated men."

I believe the sentiment is correct, because if the wealth of latent intellect among women was fully evolved and improved, they would rejoice to communicate to their sons all their own knowledge, and inspire them with desires to drink from the fountain of literature.

I pass over many interesting proofs of the intellectual powers of women; but I must not omit glancing at the age of chivalry, which has been compared to a golden thread running through the dark ages. During this remarkable era, women who, before this period, had been subject to every species of oppression and neglect, were suddenly elevated into deities, and worshipped with a mad fanaticism. It is not improbable, however, that even the absurdities of chivalry were beneficial to women, as it raised them from that extreme degradation to which they had been condemned, and prepared the way for them to be permitted to enjoy some scattered rays from the sun of science and literature. As the age of knight-errantry declined, men began to take pride in learning, and women shared the advantages which this change produced. "Women preached in public, supported controversies, published and defended theses, filled the chairs of philosophy and law, harangued the popes in Latin, wrote Greek and read Hebrew. Nuns wrote poetry, women of rank became divines, and young girls publicly exhorted Christian princes to take up arms for the recovery of the holy sepulchre. Hypatia, daughter of Theon of Alexandria, succeeded her father in the government of the Platonic school, and filled with reputation a seat, where many celebrated philosophers had taught. The people regarded her as an oracle, and magistrates consulted her in all important cases. No reproach was ever uttered against the perfect purity of her manners. She was unembarrassed in large assemblies of men, because their admiration was tempered with the most scrupulous respect. In the 13th century, a young lady of Bologna pronounced a Latin oration at the age of twenty-three. At twenty-six, she took the degree of doctor of laws, and began publicly to expound Justinian. At thirty, she was elevated to a professor's chair, and taught the law to a crowd of scholars from all nations. Italy produced many learned and gifted women, among whom, perhaps none was more celebrated than Victoria Colonna, Marchioness of Pescara. In Spain, Isabella of Rosera converted Jews by her eloquent preaching;" and in England the names of many women, from Lady Jane Gray down to Harriet Martineau, are familiar to every reader of history. Of the last mentioned authoress, Lord Brougham said that her writings on political economy were doing more good than those of any man in England. There is a contemporary of Harriet Martineau, who has recently rendered valuable services to her country. She presented a memorial to Parliament, stating the dangerous parts of the coast, where light-houses were needed, and at her suggestion, several were erected. She keeps a life-boat and sailors in her pay, and has been the means of saving many lives. Although she has been deprived of the use of her limbs since early childhood, yet even when the storm is unusually severe, she goes herself on the beach in her carriage, that she may be sure her men perform their duty. She understands several languages, and is now engaged in writing a work on the Northern languages of Europe. "In Germany, the influence of women on literature is considerable, though less obvious than in some other countries. Literary families frequently meet at each others houses, and learned and intelligent women are often the brightest ornaments of these social circles." France has produced many distinguished women, whose names are familiar to every lover of literature. And I believe it is conceded universally, that Madame de Stael was intellectually the greatest woman that ever lived. The United States have produced several female writers, some of whom have talents of the highest order. But women, even in this free republic, do not enjoy *all* the intellectual advantages of men, although there is a perceptible improvement within the last ten or twenty years; and I trust there is a desire awakened in my sisters for solid acquirements, which will elevate them to their "appropriate sphere," and enable them to "adorn the doctrine of God our Saviour in all things."

Thine in the bonds of womanhood,

SARAH M. GRIMKÉ.

LETTER XI.

Dress of Women.

Brookline, 9th Mo., 1837.

My Dear Sister,—When I view woman as an immortal being, travelling through this world to that city whose builder and maker is God,—when I contemplate her in all the sublimity of her spiritual existence, bearing the image and superscription of Jehovah, emanating from Him and partaking of his nature, and destined, if she fulfils her duty, to dwell with him through the endless ages of eternity,—I mourn that she has lived so far below her privileges and her obligations, as a rational and accountable creature; and I ardently long to behold her occupying that sphere in which I believe her Creator designed her to move.

Woman, in all ages and countries, has been the scoff and the jest of her lordly master. If she attempted, like him, to improve her mind, she was ridiculed as pedantic, and driven from the temple of science and literature by coarse attacks and vulgar sarcasms. If she yielded to the pressure of circumstances, and sought relief from the monotony of existence by resorting to the theatre and the ball-room, by ornamenting her person with flowers and with jewels, while her mind was empty and her heart desolate; she was still the mark at which wit and satire and cruelty levelled their arrows.

"Woman," says Adam Clarke, "has been invidiously defined, *an animal of dress.* How long will they permit themselves to be thus degraded?" I have been an attentive observer of my sex, and I am constrained to believe that the passion for dress, which so generally characterizes them, is one cause why there so is little of that solid improvement and weight of character which might be acquired under almost any circumstances, if the mind were not occupied by the love of admiration, and the desire to gratify personal vanity. I have already adduced some instances to prove the inordinate love of dress, which is exhibited by women in a state of heathenism; I shall, therefore, confine myself now to what are called Christian countres; only remarking that previous to the introduction of Christianity into the Roman empire, the extravagance of apparel had arisen to an unprecedented height. "Jewels, expensive embroidery, and delicious perfumes, were used in great profusion by those who could afford them." The holy religion of Jesus Christ came in at this period, and stript luxury and wealth of all their false attractions. "Women of the noblest and wealthiest families, surrounded by the seductive allurements of worldly pleasure, renounced them all. Undismayed by severe edicts against the new religion, they appeared before the magistrates, and by pronouncing the simple words, 'I am a Christian,' calmly resigned themselves to imprisonment, ignominy and death." Could such women have had their minds occupied by the foolish vanity of ornamental apparel? No! Christianity struck at the root of all sin, and consequently we find the early Christians could not fight, or swear, or wear costly clothing. Cave, in his work entitled "Primitive Christianity," has some interesting remarks on this subject, showing that simplicity of dress was not then esteemed an unimportant part of Christianity.

Very soon, however, when the fire of persecution was no longer blazing, pagan customs became interwoven with Christianity. The professors of the religion of a self-denying Lord, whose kingdom was not of this world, began to use the sword, to return railing for railing, to take oaths, to mingle heathen forms and ceremonies with Christian worship, to engraft on the beautiful simplicity of piety, the feasts and observances which were usual at heathen festivals in honor of the gods, and to adorn their persons with rich and ornamental apparel. And now if we look at Christendom, there is scarcely a vestige of that religion, which the Redeemer of men came to promulgate. The Christian world is much in the situation of the Jewish nation, when the babe of Bethlehem was born, full of outside observances, which they substitute for mercy and love, for self-denial and good works, rigid in the performance of religious duties, but ready, if the Lord Jesus came amongst them and judged them by their fruits, as he did the Pharisees formerly, to crucify him as a slanderer. Indeed, I believe the remark of a late author is perfectly correct:

Strange as it may seem, yet I do not hesitate to declare my belief that it is easier to make Pagan nations Christians, than to reform Christian communities and fashion them anew, after the pure and simple standard of the gospel. Cast your eye over Christian countries, and see what a multitude of causes combine to resist and impair the influence of Christian institutions. Behold the conformity of Christians to the world, in its prodigal pleasures and frivolous amusements, in its corrupt opinions and sentiments, of false honor. Behold the wide spread ignorance and degrading superstition; the power of prejudice and the authority of custom; the unchristian character of our systems of education; and the dread of the frowns and ridicule of the world, and we discover at once a host of more formidable enemies to the progress of *true religion* in Christian, than in heathen lands.

But I must proceed to examine what is the state of professing Christendom, as regards the subject of this letter. A few words will suffice. The habits and employments of fashionable circles are nearly the same throughout Christian communities. The fashion of dress, which varies more rapidly than the changing seasons, is still, as it has been from time immemorial, an all-absorbing object of interest. The simple cobbler of Agawam, who wrote in Massachusetts as early as 1647, speaking of women, says,

> It is no marvel they wear drailes on the hinder part of their heads, having nothing, as it seems, in the fore part, but a few squirrels' brains to help them frisk from one fashion to another.

It must, however, be conceded, that although there are too many women who merit this severe reprehension, there is a numerous class whose improvement of mind and devotion to the cause of humanity justly entitle them to our respect and admiration. One of the most striking characteristics of modern times, is the tendency toward a universal dissemination of knowledge in all Protestant communities. But the character of woman has been elevated more by participating in the great moral enterprises of the day, than by anything else. It would astonish us if we could see at a glance all the labor, the patience, the industry, the fortitude which woman has exhibited, in carrying on the causes of Moral Reform, Anti-Slavery, &c. Still, even these noble and ennobling pursuits have not destroyed personal vanity. Many of those who are engaged in these great and glorious reformations, watch with eager interest, the ever varying freaks of the goddess of fashion, and are not exceeded by the butterflies of the ballroom in their love of curls, artificial flowers, embroidery and gay apparel. Many a woman will ply her needle with ceaseless industry, to obtain money to forward a favorite benevolent scheme, while at the same time she will expend on useless articles of dress, more than treble the sum which she procures by the employment of her needle, and which she might throw into the Lord's treasury, and leave herself leisure to cultivate her mind, and to mingle among the poor and the afflicted more than she can possibly do now.

I feel exceedingly solicitous to draw the attention of my sisters to this subject. I know that it is called trifling, and much is said about dressing fashionably, and elegantly, and becomingly, without thinking about it. This I do not believe can be done. If we indulge our fancy in the chameleon caprices of fashion, or in wearing ornamental and extravagant apparel, the mind must be in no small degree engaged in the gratification of personal vanity.

Lest any one may suppose from my being a Quaker, that I should like to see a uniform dress adopted, I will say, that I have no partiality for their peculiar costume, except so far as I find it simple and convenient; and I have not the remotest desire to see it worn, where one more commodious can be substituted. But I do believe one of the chief obstacles in the way of woman's elevation to the same platform of human rights, and moral dignity, and intellectual improvement, with her brother, on which God placed her, and where he designed her to act her part as an immortal creature, is her love of dress. "It has been observed," says Scott, "that foppery and extravagance as to dress *in men* are most emphatically condemned by the apostle's silence on the subject, for this intimated that surely *they* could be under no temptation to such a childish vanity." But even those men who are superior to such a childish vanity in themselves, are, nevertheless, ever ready to encourage it in women. They know that so long as we submit to be dressed like dolls, we never can rise to the stations of duty and usefulness from which they desire to exclude us; and they are willing to grant us paltry indulgences, which forward their own design of keeping us out of our appropriate sphere, while they deprive us of essential rights.

To me it appears beneath the dignity of woman to bedeck herself in gewgaws and trinkets, in ribbons and laces, to gratify the eye of man. I believe, furthermore, that we owe a solemn duty to the poor. Many a woman, in what is called humble life, spends nearly all her earnings in dress, because she wants to be as well attired as her employer. It is often argued that, as the birds and the flowers are gaily adorned by nature's hand, there can be no sin in woman's ornamenting her person. My reply is, God created me neither a bird nor a flower; and I aspire to something more than a resemblance to them. Besides, the gaudy colors in which birds and flowers are arrayed, create in them no feelings of vanity; but as human beings, we are susceptible of these passions, which are nurtured and strengthened by such adornments. "Well," I am often asked, "where is the limitation?" This it is not my business to decide. Every woman, as Judson remarks, can best settle this on her knees before God. He has commanded her not to be conformed to this world, but to be transformed by the renewing of her mind, that she may know what is the good and acceptable and perfect will of God. He made the dress of the Jewish women the subject of special denunciation by his prophet—Is. 3. 16–26; yet the chains and the bracelets, the rings and the ear-rings, and the changeable suits of apparel, are still worn by Christian women. He has commanded them, through his apostles, not to adorn themselves with broidered hair, or gold, or pearls, or costly array. Not to let their adorning be the "outward adorning of plaiting the hair, or of wearing of gold, or of putting on of apparel, but let it be the hidden man of the heart, in that which is not corruptible, even the ornament of a meek and quiet spirit, which is in the sight of God of great price;" yet we disregard these solemn admonitions. May we not form some correct estimate of dress, by asking ourselves how we should feel, if we saw ministers of the gospel rise to address an audience with ear-rings dangling from their ears, glittering rings on their fingers, and a wreath of artificial flowers on their brow, and the rest of their apparel in keeping? If it would be wrong for a minister, it is wrong for every professing Christian. God makes no distinction between the moral and religious duties of ministers and people. We are bound to be "a chosen generation, a royal priesthood, a peculiar people, a holy nation; that we should show forth the praises of him who hath called us out of darkness into his marvellous light."

Thine in the bonds of womanhood,

SARAH M. GRIMKÉ.

LETTER XII.

Legal Disabilities of Women.

Concord, 9th Mo., 6th, 1837.

My Dear Sister,—There are few things which present greater obstacles to the improvement and elevation of woman to her appropriate sphere of usefulness and duty, than the laws which have been enacted to destroy her independence, and crush her individuality; laws which, although they are framed for her government, she has had no voice in establishing, and which rob her of some of her *essential rights.* Woman has no political existence. With the single exception of presenting a petition to the legislative body, she is a cipher in the nation; or, if not actually so in representative governments, she is only counted, like the slaves of the South, to swell the number of law-makers who form decrees for her government, with little reference to her benefit, except so far as her good may promote their own. I am not sufficiently acquainted with the laws respecting women on the continent of Europe, to say anything about them. But Prof. Follen, in his essay on "The Cause of Freedom in our Country," says, "Woman, though fully possessed of that rational and moral nature which is the foundation of all rights, enjoys amongst us fewer legal rights than under the civil law of continental Europe." I shall confine myself to the laws of our country. These laws bear with peculiar rigor on married women. Blackstone, in the chapter entitled "Of husband and wife," says:—

> By marriage, the husband and wife are one person in law; that is, *the very being, or legal existence of the woman* is suspended during the marriage, or at least is incorporated and consolidated into that of the husband under whose wing, protection and cover she performs everything. For this reason, a man cannot grant anything to his wife, or enter into covenant with her; for the grant would be to suppose her separate existence, and to covenant with her would be to covenant with himself; and therefore it is also generally true, that all compacts made between husband and wife when single, are voided by the intermarriage. A woman indeed may be attorney for her husband, but that implies no separation from, but is rather a representation of, her love.

Here now, the very being of a woman, like that of a slave, is absorbed in her master. All contracts made with her, like those made with slaves by their owners, are a mere nullity. Our kind defenders have legislated away almost all our legal rights, and in the true spirit of such injustice and oppression, have kept us in ignorance of those very laws by which we are governed. They have persuaded us, that we have no right to investigate the laws, and that, if we did, we could not comprehend them; they alone are capable of understanding the mysteries of Blackstone, &c. But they are not backward to make us feel the practical operation of their power over our actions.

> The husband is bound to provide his wife with necessaries by law, as much as himself; and if she contracts debts for them, he is obliged to pay for them; but for anything besides necessaries, he is not chargeable.

Yet a man may spend the property he has acquired by marriage at the ale-house, the gambling table, or in any other way that he pleases. Many instances of this kind have come to my knowledge; and women, who have brought their husbands handsome fortunes, have been left, in consequence of the wasteful and dissolute habits of their husbands, in straitened circumstances, and compelled to toil for the support of their families.

> If the wife be indebted before marriage, the husband is bound afterwards to pay the debt; for he has adopted her and her circumstances together.

The wife's property is, I believe, equally liable for her husband's debts contracted before marriage.

> If the wife be injured in her person or property, she can bring no action for redress without her husband's concurrence, and his name as well as her own: neither can she be sued, without making her husband a defendant.

This law that "a wife can bring no action," &c., is similar to the law respecting slaves. "A slave cannot bring a suit against his master, or any other person, for an injury—his master, must bring it." So if any damages are recovered for an injury committed on a wife, the husband pockets it; in the case of the slave, the master does the same.

> In criminal prosecutions, the wife may be indicted and punished separately, unless there be evidence of coercion from the fact that the offence was committed in the presence, or by the command of her husband. A wife is excused from punishment for theft committed in the presence, or by the command of her husband.

It would be difficult to frame a law better calculated to destroy the responsibility of woman as a moral being, or a free agent. Her husband is supposed to possess unlimited control over her; and if she can offer the flimsy excuse that he bade her steal, she may break the eighth commandment with impunity, as far as human laws are concerned.

> Our law, in general, considers man and wife as one person; yet there are some instances in which she is separately considered, as inferior to him and acting by his compulsion. Therefore, all deeds

> executed, and acts done by her during her coverture (i. e. marriage,) are void, except it be a fine, or like matter of record, in which case she must be solely and secretly examined, to learn if her act be voluntary.

Such a law speaks volumes of the abuse of that power which men have vested in their own hands. Still the private examination of a wife, to know whether she accedes to the disposition of property made by her husband is, in most cases, a mere form; a wife dares not do what will be disagreeable to one who is, in his own estimation, her superior, and who makes her feel, in the privacy of domestic life, that she has thwarted him. With respect to the nullity of deeds or acts done by a wife, I will mention one circumstance. A respectable woman borrowed of a female friend a sum of money to relieve her son from some distressing pecuniary embarrassment. Her husband was from home, and she assured the lender, that as soon as he returned, he would gratefully discharge the debt. She gave her note, and the lender, entirely ignorant of the law that a man is not obliged to discharge such a debt, actually borrowed the money, and lent it to the distressed and weeping mother. The father returned home, refused to pay the debt, and the person who had loaned the money was obliged to pay both principal and interest to the friend who lent it to her. Women should certainly know the laws by which they are governed, and from which they frequently suffer; yet they are kept in ignorance, nearly as profound, of their legal rights, and of the legislative enactments which are to regulate their actions, as slaves.

> The husband, by the old law, might give his wife moderate correction, as he is to answer for her misbehavior. The law thought it reasonable to entrust him with this power of restraining her by domestic chastisement. The courts of law will still permit a husband to restrain a wife of her liberty, in case of any gross misbehavior.

What a mortifying proof this law affords, of the estimation in which woman is held! She is placed completely in the hands of a being subject like herself to the outbursts of passion, and therefore unworthy to be trusted with power. Perhaps I may be told respecting this law, that it is a dead letter, as I am sometimes told about the slave laws; but this is not true in either case. The slaveholder does kill his slave by moderate correction, as the law allows; and many a husband, among the poor, exercises the right given him by the law, of degrading woman by personal chastisement. And among the higher ranks, if actual imprisonment is not resorted to, women are not unfrequently restrained of the liberty of going to places of worship by irreligious husbands, and of doing many other things about which, as moral and responsible beings, *they* should be the *sole* judges. Such laws remind me of the reply of some little girls at a children's meeting held recently at Ipswich. The lecturer told them that God had created four orders of beings with which he had made us acquainted through the Bible. The first was angels, the second was man, the third beasts; and now, children, what is the fourth? After a pause, several girls replied, "WOMEN."

> A woman's personal property by marriage becomes absolutely her husband's, which, at his death, he may leave entirely away from her.

And farther, all the avails of her labor are absolutely in the power of her husband. All that she acquires by her industry is his; so that she cannot, with her own honest earnings, become the legal purchaser of any property. If she expends her money for articles of furniture, to contribute to the comfort of her family, they are liable to be seized for her husband's debts: and I know an instance of a woman, who by labor and economy had scraped together a little maintenance for herself and a do-little husband, who was left, at his death, by virtue of his last will and testament, to be supported by charity. I knew another woman, who by great industry had acquired a little money which she deposited in a bank for safe keeping. She had saved this pittance whilst able to work, in hopes that when age or sickness disqualified her for exertion, she might have something to render life comfortable, without being a burden to her friends. Her husband, a worthless, idle man, discovered this hid treasure, drew her little stock from the bank, and expended it all in extravagance and vicious indulgence. I know of another woman, who married without the least idea that she was surrendering her rights to all her personal property. Accordingly, she went to the bank as usual to draw her dividends, and the person who paid her the money, and to whom she was personally known as an owner of shares in that bank, remarking the change in her signature, withdrew the money, informing her that if she were married, she had no longer a right to draw her dividends without an order from her husband. It appeared that she intended having a little fund for private use, and had not even told her husband that she owned this stock, and she was not a little chagrined, when she found that it was not at her disposal. I think she was wrong to conceal the circumstance. The relation of husband and wife is too near and sacred to admit of secrecy about money matters, unless positive necessity demands it; and I can see no excuse for any woman entering into a marriage engagement with a design to keep her husband ignorant that she was possessed of property. If she was unwilling to give up her property to his disposal, she had infinitely better have remained single.

The laws above cited are not very unlike the slave laws of Louisiana.

> All that a slave possesses belongs to his master; he possesses nothing of his own, except what his master chooses he should possess.
>
> By the marriage, the husband is absolutely master of the profits of the wife's lands during the coverture, and if he has had a living child, and survives the wife, he retains the whole of those lands, if they are estates of inheritance, during his life; but the wife is entitled only to one third if she survives, out of the husband's estates of inheritance. But this she has, whether she has had a child or not. With regard to the property of women, there is taxation without representation; for they pay taxes without having the liberty of voting for representatives.

And this taxation, without representation, be it remembered, was the cause of our Revolutionary war, a grievance so heavy, that it was thought necessary to purchase exemption from it at an immense expense of blood and treasure, yet the daughters of New England, as well as of all the other States of this free Republic, are suffering a similar injustice—but for one, I had rather we should suffer any injustice or oppression, than that my sex should have any voice in the political affairs of the nation.

The laws I have quoted, are, I believe, the laws of Massachusetts, and, with few exceptions, of all the States in this Union. "In Louisiana and Missouri, and possibly, in some other southern States, a woman not only has half her husband's property by right at his death, but may always be considered as possessed of half his gains during his life; having at all times power to bequeath that amount." That the laws which have generally been adopted in the United States, for the government of women, have been framed almost entirely for the exclusive benefit of men, and with a design to oppress women, by depriving them of all control over their property, is too manifest to be denied. Some liberal and enlightened men, I know, regret the existence of these laws; and I quote with pleasure an extract from Harriet Martineau's Society in America, as a proof of the assertion. "A liberal minded lawyer of Boston, told me that his advice to testators always is to leave the largest possible amount to the widow, subject to the condition of her leaving it to the children; but that it is with shame that he reflects that any woman should owe that to his professional advice, which the law should have secured to her as a right." I have known a few instances where men have left their whole property to their wives, when they have died, leaving only minor children; but I have known more instances of "the friend and helper of many years, being portioned off like a salaried domestic," instead of having a comfortable independence secured to her, while the children were amply provided for.

As these abuses do exist, and women suffer intensely from them, our brethren are called upon in this enlightened age, by every sentiment of honor, religion and justice, to repeal these unjust and unequal laws, and restore to woman those rights which they have wrested from her. Such laws approximate too nearly to the laws enacted by slaveholders for the government of their slaves, and must tend to debase and depress the mind of that being, whom God created as a help meet for man, or "helper like unto himself," and designed to be his equal and his companion. Until such laws are annulled, woman never can occupy that exalted station for which she was intended by her Maker. And just in proportion as they are practically disregarded, which is the case to some extent, just so far is woman assuming that independence and nobility of character which she ought to exhibit.

The various laws which I have transcribed, leave women very little more liberty, or power, in some respects, than the slave. "A slave," says the civil code of Louisiana, "is one who is in the power of a master, to whom he belongs. He can possess nothing, nor acquire anything, but what must belong to his master." I do not wish by any means to intimate that the condition of free women can be compared to that of slaves in suffering, or in degradation; still, I believe the laws which deprive married women of their rights and privileges, have a tendency to lessen them in their own estimation as moral and responsible beings, and that their being made by civil law inferior to their husbands, has a debasing and mischievous effect upon them, teaching them practically the fatal lesson to look unto man for protection and indulgence.

Ecclesiastical bodies, I believe, without exception, follow the example of legislative assemblies, in excluding woman from any participation in forming the discipline by which she is governed. The men frame the laws, and, with few exceptions, claim to execute them on both sexes. In ecclesiastical, as well as civil courts, woman is tried and condemned, not by a jury of her peers, but by beings, who regard themselves as her superiors in the scale of creation. Although looked upon as an inferior, when considered as an intellectual being, woman is punished with the same severity as man, when she is guilty of moral offences. Her condition resembles, in some measure, that of the slave, who, while he is denied the advantages of his more enlightened master, is treated with even greater rigor of the law. Hoping that in the various reformations of the day, women may be relieved from some of their legal disabilities, I remain,

Thine in the bonds of womanhood,

SARAH M. GRIMKÉ.

LETTER XIII.

Relation of Husband and Wife.

Brookline, 9th Mo., 1837.

My Dear Sister,—Perhaps some persons may wonder that I should attempt to throw out my views on the important subject of marriage, and may conclude that I am altogether disqualified for the task, because I lack experience. However, I shall not undertake to settle the specific duties of husbands and wives, but only to exhibit opinions based on the word of God, and formed from a little knowledge of human nature, and close observation of the working of generally received notions respecting the dominion of man over woman.

When Jehovah ushered into existence man, created in his own image, he instituted marriage as a part of paradisaical happiness: it was a *divine ordination*, not a civil contract. God established it, and man, except by special permission, has no right to annul it. There can be no doubt that the creation of Eve perfected the happiness of Adam; hence, our all-wise and merciful Father made her as he made Adam, in his own image after his likeness, crowned her with glory and honor, and placed in her hand, as well as in his, the sceptre of dominion over the whole lower creation. Where there was perfect equality, and the same ability to receive and comprehend divine truth, and to obey divine injunctions, there could be no superiority. If God had placed Eve under the guardianship of Adam, after having endowed her, as richly as him, with moral perceptions, intellectual faculties, and spiritual apprehensions, he would at once have interposed a fallible being between her and her Maker. He could not, in simple consistency with himself, have done this; for the Bible teems with instructions not to put any confidence in man.

The passage on which the generally received opinion, that husbands are invested by divine command with authority over their wives, as I have remarked in a previous letter, is a prediction; and I am confirmed in this belief, because the same language is used to Cain respecting Abel. The text is obscure; but on a comparison of it with subsequent events, it appears to me that it was a prophecy of the dominion which Cain would usurp over his brother, and which issued in the murder of Abel. It could not allude to any thing but physical dominion, because Cain had already exhibited those evil passions which subsequently led him to become an assassin.

I have already shown, that man has exercised the most unlimited and brutal power over woman, in the peculiar character of husband,—a word in most countries synonymous with tyrant. I shall not, therefore, adduce any further proofs of the fulfilment of that prophecy, "He will rule over thee," from the history of heathen nations, but just glance at the condition of woman in the relation of wife in Christian countries.

"Previous to the introduction of the religion of Jesus Christ, the state of society was wretchedly diseased. The relation of the sexes to each other had become so gross in its manifested forms, that it was difficult to perceive the pure conservative principle in its inward essence." Christianity came in, at this juncture, with its hallowed influence, and has without doubt tended to lighten the yoke of bondage, to purify the manners, and give the spiritual in some degree an empire over the animal nature. Still, that state which was designed by God to increase the happiness of woman as well as man, often proves the means of lessening her comfort, and degrading her into the mere machine of another's convenience and pleasure. Woman, instead of being elevated by her union with man, which might be expected from an alliance with a superior being, is in reality lowered. She generally loses her individuality, her independent character, her moral being. She becomes absorbed into him, and henceforth is looked at, and acts through the medium of her husband.

In the wealthy classes of society, and those who are in comfortable circumstances, women are exempt from great corporeal exertion, and are protected by public opinion, and by the genial influence of Christianity, from much physical ill treatment. Still, there is a vast amount of secret suffering endured, from the forced submission of women to the opinions and whims of their husbands. Hence they are frequently driven to use deception, to compass their ends. They are early taught that to appear to yield, is the only way to govern. Miserable sophism!

I deprecate such sentiments, as being peculiarly hostile to the dignity of woman. If she submits, let her do it openly, honorably, not to gain her point, but as a matter of Christian duty. But let her beware how she permits her husband to be her conscience-keeper. On all moral and religious subjects, she is bound to think and to act for herself. Where confidence and love exist, a wife will naturally converse with her husband as with her dearest friend, on all that interests her heart, and there will be a perfectly free interchange of sentiment; but *she is no more bound to be governed by his judgment*, than he is by hers. They are standing on the same platform of human rights, are equally under the government of God, and accountable to him, and him alone.

I have sometimes been astonished and grieved at the servitude of women, and at the little idea many of them seem to have of their own moral existence and responsibilities. A woman who is asked to sign a petition for the abolition of slavery in the District of Columbia, or to join a society for the purpose of carrying forward the annihilation of American slavery, or any other great reformation, not unfrequently replies, "My husband does not approve of it." She merges her rights and her duties in her husband, and thus virtually chooses him for a savior and a king, and rejects Christ as her Ruler and Redeemer. I know some women are very glad of so convenient a pretext to shield themselves from the performance of duty; but there are others, who, under a mistaken view of their obligations as wives, submit conscientiously to this species of oppression, and go mourning on their way, for want of that holy fortitude, which would enable them to fulfil their duties as moral and responsible beings, without reference to poor fallen man. O that woman may arise in her dignity as an immortal creature, and speak, think and act as unto God, and not unto man!

There is, perhaps, less bondage of mind among the poorer classes, because their sphere of duty is more contracted, and they are deprived of the means of intellectual culture, and of the opportunity of exercising their judgment, on many moral subjects of deep interest and of vital importance. Authority is called into exercise by resistance, and hence there will be mental bondage only in proportion as the faculties of mind are evolved, and woman feels herself as a rational and intelligent being, on a footing with man. But women, among the lowest classes of society, so far as my observation has extended, suffer intensely from the brutality of their husbands. Duty as well as inclination has led me, for many years, into the abodes of poverty and sorrow, and I have been amazed at the treatment which women receive at the hands of those, who arrogate to themselves the epithet of *protectors*. Brute force, the law of violence, rules to a great extent in the poor man's domicil; and woman is little more than his drudge. They are less under the supervision of public opinion, less under the restraints of education, and unaided or unbiased by the refinements of polished society. Religion, wherever it exists, supplies the place of all these; but the real cause of woman's degradation and suffering in married life is to be found in the erroneous notion of her inferiority to man; and never will she be rightly regarded by herself, or others, until this opinion, so derogatory to the wisdom and mercy of God, is exploded, and woman arises in all the majesty of her womanhood, to claim those rights which are inseparable from her existence as an immortal, intelligent and responsible being.

Independent of the fact, that Jehovah could not, consistently with his character as the King, the Lawgiver, and the Judge of his people, give the reins of government over woman into the hands of man, I find that all his commands, all his moral laws, are addressed to women as well as to men. When he assembled Israel at the foot of Mount Sinai, to issue his commandments, we may reasonably suppose he gave all the precepts, which he considered necessary for the government of moral beings. Hence we find that God says,—"Honor thy father and thy mother," and he enforces this command by severe penalties upon those who transgress it: "He that smiteth his father, or his mother, shall surely be put to death"—"He that curseth his father, or his mother, shall surely be put to death"—Ex. 21: 15, 17. But in the decalogue, there is no direction given to women to obey their husbands: both are commanded to have no other God but Jehovah, and not to bow down, or serve any other. When the Lord Jesus delivered his sermon on the Mount, full of the practical precepts of religion, he did not issue any command to wives to obey their husbands. When he is speaking on the subject of divorce, Mark 16: 11, 12, he places men and women on the same gound. And the Apostle, 1st Cor. 7: 12, 13, speaking of the duties of the Corinthian wives and husbands, who had embraced Christianity, to their unconverted partners, points out the same path to both, although our translators have made a distinction. "Let him not put her away," 12—"Let her not leave him," 13—is precisely the same in the original. If man is constituted the governor of woman, he must be her God; and the sentiment expressed to me lately, by a married man, is perfectly correct: "In my opinion," said he, "the greatest excellence to which a married woman can attain, is to worship her husband." He was a professor of religion—his wife a lovely and intelligent woman. He only spoke out what thousands think and act. Women are indebted to Milton for giving to this false notion, "confirmation strong as proof of holy writ." His Eve is embellished with every personal grace, to gratify the eye of her admiring husband; but he seems to have furnished the mother of mankind with just intelligence enough to comprehend her supposed inferiority to Adam, and to yield unresisting submission to her lord and master. Milton puts into Eve's mouth the following address to Adam:

> My author and disposer, what thou bidst,
> Unargued I obey; so God ordains—
> God is thy law, thou mine: to know no more,
> Is woman's happiest knowledge and her praise.

This much admired sentimental nonsense is fraught with absurdity and wickedness. If it were true, the commandment of Jehovah should have run thus: Man shall have no other gods before ME, and woman shall have no other gods before MAN.

The principal support of the dogma of woman's inferiority, and consequent submission to her husband, is found in some passages of Paul's epistles. I shall proceed to examine those passages, premising 1st, that the antiquity of the opinions based on the false construction of those passages, has no weight with me: they are the opinions of interested judges, and I have no particular reverence for them, *merely* because they have been regarded with veneration from generation to generation. So far from this being the case, I examine any opinions of centuries standing, with as much freedom, and investigate them with as much care, as if they were of yesterday. I was educated to think for myself, and it is a privilege I shall always claim to exercise. 2d. Notwithstanding my full belief, that the apostle Paul's testimony, respecting himself, is true, "I was not a whit behind the chiefest of the apostles," yet I believe his mind was under the influence of Jewish prejudices respecting women, just as Peter's and the apostles were about the uncleanness of the Gentiles. "The Jews," says Clarke, "would not suffer a woman to read in the synagogue, although a servant, or even a child, had this permission." When I see Paul shaving his head for a vow, and offering sacrifices, and circumcising Timothy, to accommodate himself to the prepossessions of his countrymen, I do not conceive that I derogate in the least from his character as an inspired apostle, to suppose that he may have been imbued with the prevalent prejudices against women.

In 1st Cor. 11: 3, after praising the Corinthian converts, because they kept the "ordinances," or "traditions," as the margin reads, the apostle says, "I would have you know, that the head of every man is Christ, and the head of the woman is the man; and the head of Christ is God." Eph. 5: 23, is a parallel passage. "For the husband is the head of the wife, even as Christ is the head of the Church." The apostle closes his remarks on this subject, by observing, "This is a great mystery, but I speak concerning Christ and the Church." I shall pass over this with simply remarking, that God and Christ are one. "I and my Father are one," and there can be no inferiority where there is no divisibility. The commentaries on this and similar texts, afford a striking illustration of the ideas which men entertain of their own superiority, I shall subjoin Henry's remarks on 1st Cor. 11: 5, as a specimen: "To understand this text, it must be observed, that it was a signification either of shame, or subjection, for persons to be veiled, or covered in Eastern countries; contrary to the custom of ours, where the being bare-headed betokens subjection, and being covered superiority and dominion; and this will help us the better to understand the reason on which he grounds his reprehension, 'Every man praying, &c. dishonoreth his head,' i. e. Christ, the head of every man, by appearing in a habit unsuitable to the rank in which God had placed him. The woman, on the other hand, that prays, &c. dishonoreth her head, i. e. the man. She appears in the dress of her *superior*, and throws off the token of her subjection; she might with equal decency cut her hair short, or cut it off, the common dress of the man in that age. Another reason against this conduct was, that the man is the image and glory of God, the representative of that glorious dominion and headship which God has over the world. It is the man who is set at the head of this lower creation, and therein bears the resemblance of God. The woman, on the other hand, is the glory of the man: she is his representative. Not but she has dominion over the inferior creatures, and she is a partaker of human nature, and so far is God's representative too, but it is at second hand. She is the image of God, inasmuch as she is the image of the man. The man was first made, and made head of the creation here below, and therein the image of the divine dominion; and the woman was made out of the man, and shone with a *reflection of his glory*, being made superior to the other creatures here below, but in subjection to her husband, and deriving that *honor from him*, out of whom she was made. The woman was made for the man to be his help meet, and not the man for the woman. She was, naturally, therefore, made subject to him, because made for him, for HIS USE AND HELP AND COMFORT."

We see in the above quotation, what degrading views even good men entertain of women. Pity the Psalmist had not thrown a little light on this subject, when he was paraphrasing the account of man's creation. "Thou hast made him a little lower than the angels, and hast crowned him with glory and honor. Thou madest him to have dominion over the works of thy hands; thou hast put all things under his feet." Surely if woman had been placed below man, and was to shine only by a lustre borrowed from him, we should have some clear evidence of it in the sacred volume. Henry puts her exactly on a level with the beasts; they were made for the use, help and comfort of man; and according to this commentator, this was the whole end and design of the creation of woman. The idea that man, as man is superior to woman, involves an absurdity so gross, that I really wonder how any man of reflection can receive it as of divine origin; and I can only account for it, by that passion for supremacy, which characterizes man as a corrupt and fallen creature. If it be true that he is more excellent than she, as man, independent of his moral and intellectual powers, then every man is superior by virtue of his manship, to every woman. The man who sinks his moral capacities and spiritual powers in his sensual appetites, is still, as a man, simply by the conformation of his body, a more dignified being, than the woman whose intellectual powers are highly cultivated, and whose approximation to the character of Jesus Christ is exhibited in a blameless life and conversation.

But it is strenuously urged by those, who are anxious to maintain their usurped authority, that wives are, in various passages of the New Testament, commanded to obey their husbands. Let us examine these texts.

> Eph. 5, 22. "Wives, submit yourselves unto your own husbands as unto the Lord." "As the church is subject unto Christ, so let the wives be to their own husbands in every thing."
>
> Col. 3, 18. "Wives, submit yourselves unto your own husbands, as it is fit in the Lord."
>
> 1st Pet. 3, 2. "Likewise ye wives, be in subjection to your own husbands; that if any obey not the word, they may also without the word be won by the conversation of the wives."

Accompanying all these directions to wives, are commands to husbands.

> Eph. 5, 25. "Husbands, love your wives even as Christ loved the Church, and gave himself for it." "So ought men to love their wives as their own bodies. He that loveth his wife, loveth himself."
>
> Col. 3, 19. "Husbands, love your wives, and be not bitter against them."
>
> 1st Pet. 3, 7. "Likewise ye husbands, dwell with them according to knowledge, giving honor unto the wife as unto the weaker vessel, and as being heirs together of the grace of life."

I may just remark, in relation to the expression "weaker vessel," that the word in the original has no reference to intellect: it refers to physical weakness merely.

The apostles were writing to Christian converts, and laying down rules for their conduct towards their unconverted consorts. It no doubt frequently happened, that a husband or a wife would embrace Christianity, while their companions clung to heathenism, and husbands might be tempted to dislike and despise those, who pertinaciously adhered to their pagan superstitions. And wives who, when they were pagans, submitted as a matter of course to their heathen husbands, might be tempted knowing that they were superior as moral and religious characters, to assert that superiority, by paying less deference to them than heretofore. Let us examine the context of these passages, and see what are the grounds of the directions here given to husbands and wives. The whole epistle to the Ephesians breathes a spirit of love. The apostle beseeches the converts to walk worthy of the vocation wherewith they are called, with all lowliness and meekness, with long suffering, forbearing one another in love. The verse preceding 5, 22, is "SUBMITTING YOURSELVES ONE TO ANOTHER IN THE FEAR OF GOD." Colossians 3, from 11 to 17, contains similar injunctions. The 17th verse says, "Whatsoever ye do in word, or in deed, do all in the name of the Lord Jesus." Peter, after drawing a most touching picture of Christ's sufferings for us, and reminding the Christians, that he had left us an example that we should follow his steps, "who did no sin, neither was guile found in his mouth," exhorts wives to be in subjection, &c.

From an attentive consideration of these passages, and of those in which the same words "submit," "subjection," are used, I cannot but believe that the apostles designed to recommend to wives, as they did to subjects and to servants, to carry out the holy principle laid down by Jesus Christ, "Resist not evil." And this without in the least acknowledging the right of the governors, masters, or husbands, to exercise the authority they claimed. The recognition of the existence of evils does not involve approbation of them. God tells the Israelites, he gave them a king in his wrath, but nevertheless as they chose to have a king, he laid down directions for the conduct of that king, and had him anointed to reign over them. According to the generally received meaning of the passages I have quoted, they directly contravene the laws of God, as given in various parts of the

Bible. Now I must understand the sacred Scriptures as harmonizing with themselves, or I cannot receive them as the word of God. The commentators on these passages exalt man to the station of a Deity in relation to woman. Clarke says, "As the Lord Christ is the head, or governor of the church, and the head of the man, so is the man the head, or governor of the woman. This is God's ordinance, and should not be transgressed. 'As unto the Lord.' The word church seems necessarily to be understood here: that is, act under the authority of your husbands, as the church acts under the authority of Christ. As the church submits to the Lord, so let wives submit to their husbands." Henry goes even further—"For the husband is the head of the wife. The metaphor is taken from the head in the natural body, which being the seat of reason, of wisdom and of knowledge, and the fountain of sense and motion, is more excellent than the rest of the body." Now if God ordained man the governor of woman, he must be able to save her, and to answer in her stead for all those sins which she commits by his direction. Awful responsibility. Do husbands feel able and willing to bear it? And what becomes of the solemn affirmation of Jehovah? "Hear this, all ye people, give ear all ye inhabitants of the world, both low and high, rich and poor." "None can by any means redeem his brother, or give to God a ransom for him, for the redemption of the soul is precious, and man cannot accomplish it."—*French Bible.*

Thine in the bonds of womanhood,

SARAH M. GRIMKÉ.

LETTER XIV.

Ministry of Women.

Brookline, 9th Mo. 1837.

My Dear Sister,—According to the principle which I have laid down, that man and woman were created equal, and endowed by their beneficent Creator with the same intellectual powers and the same moral responsibilities, and that consequently whatever is *morally* right for a man to do, is *morally* right for a woman to do, it follows as a necessary corollary, that if it is the duty of man to preach the unsearchable riches of Christ, it is the duty also of woman.

I am aware, that I have the prejudices of education and custom to combat, both in my own and the other sex, as well as "the traditions of men," which are taught for the commandments of God. I feel that I have no sectarian views to advance; for although among the Quakers, Methodists, and Christians, women are permitted to preach the glad tidings of peace and salvation, yet I know of no religious body, who entertain the Scripture doctrine of the perfect equality of man and woman, which is the fundamental principle of my argument in favor of the ministry of women. I wish simply to throw my views before thee. If they are based on the immutable foundation of truth, they cannot be overthrown by unkind insinuations, bitter sarcasms, unchristian imputations, or contemptuous ridicule. These are weapons which are unworthy of a good cause. If I am mistaken, as truth only can prevail, my supposed errors will soon vanish before her beams; but I am persuaded that woman is not filling the high and holy station which God allotted to her, and that in consequence of her having been driven from her "appropriate sphere," both herself and her brethren have suffered an infinity of evils.

Before I proceed to prove, that woman is bound to preach the gospel, I will examine the ministry under the Old Testament dispensation. Those who were called to this office were known under various names. Enoch, who prophesied, is designated as walking with God. Noah is called a preacher of righteousness. They were denominated men of God, seers, prophets, but they all had the same great work to perform, viz. to turn sinners from the error of their ways. This ministry existed previous to the institution of the Jewish priesthood, and continued after its abolition. *It has nothing to do with the priesthood.* It was rarely, as far as the Bible informs us, exercised by those of the tribe of Levi, and was common to all the people, women as well as men. It differed essentially from the priesthood, because there was no compensation received for calling the people to repentance. Such a thing as paying a prophet for preaching the truth of God is not even mentioned. They were called of Jehovah to go forth in his name, one from his plough, another from gathering of sycamore fruit, &c. &c. Let us for a moment imagine Jeremiah, when God says to him, "Gird up thy loins, and arise and speak unto the people all that I command thee," replying to Jehovah, "I will preach repentance to the people, if they will give me gold, but if they will not pay me for the truth, then let them perish in their sins." Now, this is virtually the language of the ministers of the present day; and I believe the secret of the exclusion of women from the ministerial office is, that that office has been converted into one of emolument, of honor, and of power. Any attentive observer cannot fail to perceive, that as far as possible, all such offices are reserved by men for themselves.

The common error that Christian ministers are the successors of the priests, is founded in mistake. In the particular directions given to Moses to consecrate Aaron and his sons to the office of the priesthood, their duties are clearly defined: see Ex. 28th, 29th and 30th chap. There is no commission to Aaron to preach to the people; his business was to offer sacrifice. Now why were sacrifices instituted?They were types of that one great sacrifice, which in the fulness of time was offered up through the eternal Spirit without spot to God. Christ assumed the office of priest; he "offered himself," and by so doing, abolished forever the order of the priesthood, as well as the sacrifices which the priests were ordained to offer.*

But it may be inquired, whether the priests were not to teach the people. As far as I can discover from the Bible, they were simply commanded to read the law to the people. There was no other copy that we know of, until the time of the kings, who were to write out a copy for their own use. As it was deposited in the ark, the priests were required, "When all Israel is come to appear before the Lord thy God in the place which he shall

*I cannot enter fully into this part of my subject. It is, however, one of great importance, and I recommend those who wish to examine it, to read "The Book of the Priesthood," by an English Dissenter, and Beverly's "View of the Present State of the Visible Church of Christ." They are both masterly productions.

choose, thou shalt read this law before all Israel in their hearing. Gather the people together, men, women, and children, that they may hear," Deut. 31: 9–33. See also Lev. 10: 11, Deut. 33: 10, 2d Chr. 17: 7–9, and numerous other passages. When God is enumerating the means he has used to call his people to repentance, he never, as far as I can discover, speaks of sending his priests to warn them; but in various passages we find language similar to this: "Since the day that your fathers came forth out of the land of Egypt unto this day, I have even sent unto you all my servants, the PROPHETS, daily rising up early and sending them. Yet they hearkened not unto me, nor inclined their ear, but hardened their neck; they did worse than their fathers." Jer. 7: 25, 26. See also, 25: 4. 2 Chr. 36: 15. and parallel passages. God says, Is. 9: 15, 16. "The prophet that teacheth lies, he is the tail; for the leaders of this people cause them to err." The distinction between priests and prophets is evident from their being mentioned as two classes. "The prophets prophesy falsely, and the priests bear rule by their means," Jer. 5: 31. See also, Ch. 2: 8. 8:1—10. and many others.

That women were called to the prophetic office, I believe is universally admitted. Miriam, Deborah and Huldah were prophetesses. The judgments of the Lord are denounced by Ezekiel on false prophetesses, as well as false prophets. And if Christian ministers are, as I apprehend, successors of the prophets, and not of the priests, then of course, women are now called to that office as well as men, because God has no where withdrawn from them the privilege of doing what is the great business of preachers, viz. to point the penitent sinner to the Redeemer. "Behold the Lamb of God, which taketh away the sins of the world."

It is often triumphantly inquired, why, if men and women are on an equality, are not women as conspicuous in the Bible as men? I do not intend to assign a reason, but I think one may readily be found in the fact, that from the days of Eve to the present time, the aim of man has been to crush her. He has accomplished this work in various ways; sometimes by brute force, sometimes by making her subservient to his worst passions, sometimes by treating her as a doll, and while he excluded from her mind the light of knowledge, decked her person with gewgaws and frippery which he scorned for himself, thus endeavoring to render her like unto a painted sepulchre.

It is truly marvellous that any woman can rise above the pressure of circumstances which combine to crush her. Nothing can strengthen her to do this in the character of a preacher of righteousness, but a call from Jehovah himself. And when the voice of God penetrates the deep recesses of her heart, and commands her to go and cry in the ears of the people, she is ready to exclaim, "Ah, Lord God, behold I cannot speak, for I am a woman." I have known women in different religious societies, who have felt like the prophet. "His word was in my heart as a burning fire shut up in my bones, and I was weary with forbearing." But they have not dared to open their lips, and have endured all the intensity of suffering, produced by disobedience to God, rather than encounter heartless ridicule and injurious suspicions. I rejoice that we have been the oppressed, rather than the oppressors. God thus prepared his people for deliverance from outward bondage; and I hope our sorrows have prepared us to fulfil our high and holy duties, whether public or private, with humility and meekness; and that suffering has imparted fortitude to endure trials, which assuredly await us in the attempt to sunder those chains with which man has bound us, galling to the spirit, though unseen by the eye.

Surely there is nothing either astonishing or novel in the gifts of the Spirit being bestowed on woman: nothing astonishing, because there is no respect of persons with God; the soul of the woman in his sight is as the soul of the man, and both are alike capable of the influence of the Holy Spirit. Nothing novel, because, as has been already shown, in the sacred records there are found examples of women, as well as of men, exercising the gift of prophecy.

We attach to the word prophecy, the exclusive meaning of foretelling future events, but this is certainly a mistake; for the apostle Paul defines it to be "speaking to edification, exhortation and comfort." And there appears no possible reason, why women should not do this as well as men. At the time that the Bible was translated into English, the meaning of the word prophecy, was delivering a message from God, whether it was to predict future events, or to warn the people of the consequences of sin. Governor Winthrop, of Massachusetts, mentions in a letter, that the minister being absent, he went to, —— to prophecy to the people.

Before I proceed to prove that women, under the Christian dispensation, were anointed of the Holy Ghost to preach, or prophecy, I will mention Anna, the (last) prophetess under the Jewish dispensation. "She departed not from the temple, but served God with fasting and prayers night and day." And coming into the temple, while Simeon was yet speaking to Mary, with the infant Savior in his arms, "spake of Christ to all them that looked for redemption in Jerusalem." Blackwall, a learned English critic, in his work entitled, "Sacred Classics," says, in reference to this passage, Luke 2: 37— "According to the *original* reading, the sense will be, that the devout Anna, who attended in the temple, both night and day, spoke of the Messiah to all the inhabitants of that city, who constantly worshipped there, and who prepared themselves for the worthy reception of that divine person, whom they expected at this time. And 'tis certain, that other devout Jews, not inhabitants of Jerusalem, frequently repaired to the temple-worship, and might, at this remarkable time, and several others, hear this admirable woman discourse upon the blessed advent of the Redeemer. A various reading has Israel instead of Jerusalem, which expresses that religious Jews, from distant places, came thither to divine offices, and would with high pleasure hear the discourses of this great prophetess, so famed for her extraordinary piety and valuable talents, upon the most important and desirable subject."

I shall now examine the testimony of the Bible on this point, after the ascension of our Lord, beginning with the glorious effusion of the Holy Spirit on the day of Pentecost. I presume it will not be denied, that women, as well as men, were at that time filled with the Holy Ghost, because it is expressly stated, that women were among those who continued in prayer and supplication, waiting for the fulfilment of the promise, that they should be enduced with power from on high. "When the day of Pentecost was fully come, they were ALL with one accord in one place. And there appeared unto them cloven tongues like as of fire, and it sat upon each of them; and they were all filled with the Holy Ghost, and began to speak with other tongues as the

Spirit gave them utterance." Peter says, in reference to this miracle, "This is that which was spoken by the prophet Joel. And it shall come to pass in the last days, said God, I will pour out my Spirit upon all flesh; and your sons and your daughters shall prophesy—and on my servants and on my hand-maidens, I will pour out in those days of my Spirit, and they shall prophesy." There is not the least intimation that this was a spasmodic influence which was soon to cease. The men and women are classed together; and if the power to preach the gospel was a supernatural and short-lived impulse in women, then it was equally so in men. But we are told, those were the days of miracles. I grant it; but the men, equally with the women, were the subjects of this marvellous fulfilment of prophecy, and of course, if women have lost the gift of prophesying, so have men. We are also gravely told, that if a woman pretends to inspiration, and thereupon grounds the right to plead the cause of a crucified Redeemer in public, she will be believed when she shows credentials from heaven, i. e. when she works a miracle. I reply, if this be necessary to prove her right to preach the gospel, then I demand of my brethren to show me their credentials; else I cannot receive their ministry, by their own showing. John Newton has justly said, that no power but that which created a world, can make a minister of the gospel; and man may task his ingenuity to the utmost, to prove that this power is not exercised on women as well as men. He cannot do it until he has first disclaimed that simple, but all comprehensive truth, "in Christ Jesus there is neither male nor female."

Women then, according to the Bible, were, under the New Testament dispensation, as well as the Old, the recipients of the gift of prophecy. That this is no sectarian view may be proved by the following extracts. The first I shall offer is from Stratton's "Book of the Priesthood."

> While they were assembled in the upper room to wait for the blessing, in number about one hundred and twenty, they received the miraculous gifts of the Holy Spirit's grace; they became the channels through which its more ordinary, but not less saving streams flowed to three thousand persons in one day. The whole company of the assembled disciples, male and female, young and

old, were all filled with the Holy Ghost, and began to speak with other tongues as the Spirit gave them utterance. They all contributed in producing that impression upon the assembled multitude, which Peter was instrumental in advancing to its decisive results.

Scott, in his commentary on this passage, says—

At the same time, there appeared the form of tongues divided at the tip and resembling fire; one of which rested on each of the whole company. They sat on every one present, as the original determines. At the time of these extraordinary appearances, the whole company were abundantly replenished with the gifts and graces of the Holy Spirit, so that they began to speak with other tongues.

Henry in his notes confirms this:

It seems evident to me that not the twelve apostles only, but all the one hundred and twenty disciples were filled with the Holy Ghost alike at this time,—all the seventy disciples, who were apostolical men and employed in the same work, and all the rest too that were to preach the gospel, for it is said expressly, Eph. 4: 8–12: "When Christ ascended up on high, (which refers to this) he gave gifts unto men." The all here must refer to the all that were together.

I need hardly remark that man is a generic term, including both sexes.

Let us now examine whether women actually exercised the office of minister, under the gospel dispensation. Philip had four daughters, who prophesied or preached. Paul calls Priscilla, as well as Aquila, his helpers; or, as in the Greek, his fellow laborers* in Christ Jesus. Divers other passages might be adduced to prove that women continued to be preachers, and that *many* of them filled this dignified station.

We learn also from ecclesiastical history, that female ministers suffered martyrdom in the early ages of the Christian church. In ancient councils, mention is made of deaconesses; and in an

*Rom. 16: 3, compare Gr. text of v. 21, 2. Cor. 8: 23; Phil. 2: 25; 1 Thes. 3: 2.

edition of the New Testament, printed in 1574, a woman is spoken of as minister of a church. The same word, which, in our common translation, is now rendered a servant of the church, in speaking of Phebe, Rom. 16: 1, is rendered minister, Eph. 6: 21, when applied to Tychicus. A minister, with whom I had lately the pleasure of conversing, remarked, "My rule is to expound scripture by scripture, and I cannot deny the ministry of women, because the apostle says, 'help those women who labored with me IN THE GOSPEL.' He certainly meant something more than pouring out tea for him."

In the 11th Ch. of 1 Cor., Paul gives directions to women and men how they should appear when they prophesy, or pray in public assemblies. It is evident that the design of the apostle, in this and the three succeeding chapters, is to rectify certain abuses which had crept into the Christian church. He therefore admonishes women to pray with their heads covered, because, according to the fashion of that day, it was considered immodest and immoral to do otherwise. He says, "that were all one as if she were shaven;" and shaving the head was a disgraceful punishment that was inflicted on women of bad character.

> "These things," says Scott, "the apostle stated as decent and proper, but if any of the Corinthian teachers inclined to excite contention about them, he would only add, v. 16, that he and his brethren knew of no such custom as prevailed among them, nor was there any such in the churches of God which had been planted by the other apostles."

John Locke, whilst engaged in writing his notes on the Epistles of St. Paul, was at a meeting where two women preached. After hearing them, he became convinced of their commission to publish the gospel, and thereupon altered his notes on the 11th Ch. 1 Cor. in favor of women's preaching. He says,—

> This about women seeming as difficult a passage as most in St. Paul's Epistles, I crave leave to premise some few considerations. It is plain that this covering the head in women is restrained to some peculiar actions which they performed in the assembly, expressed by the words praying, prophesying, which, whatever

> they signify, must have the same meaning applied to women in the 5th verse, that they have when applied to men in the 4th, &c. The next thing to be considered is, what is here to be understood by praying and prophesying. And that seems to me the performing of some public action in the assembly, by some one person which was for that time peculiar to that person, and whilst it lasted, the rest of the assembly silently assisted. As to prophesying, the apostle in express words tells us, Ch. 14: 3, 12, that it was speaking in the assembly. The same is evident as to praying, that the apostle means by it publicly with an audible voice, ch. 14: 19.

In a letter to these two women, Rebecca Collier and Rachel Bracken, which accompanied a little testimony of his regard, he says,

> I admire no converse like that of Christian freedom; and I fear no bondage like that of pride and prejudice. I now see that acquaintance by sight cannot reach the height of enjoyment, which acquaintance by knowledge arrives unto. Outward hearing may misguide us, but internal knowledge cannot err. Women, indeed, had the honor of first publishing the resurrection of the God of love—why not again the resurrection of the spirit of love? And let all the disciples of Christ rejoice therein, as doth your partner, John Locke.

See "The Friend," a periodical published in Philadelphia. Adam Clarke's comment on 1 Cor. 11: 5, is similar to Locke's:

> Whatever be the meaning of praying and prophesying in respect to the man, they have precisely the same meaning in respect to the woman. So that some women at least, as well as some men, might speak to others to edification and exhortation and comfort. And this kind of prophesying, or teaching, was predicted by Joel 2: 28, and referred to by Peter; and had there not been such gifts bestowed on women, the prophesy could not have had its fulfilment.

In the autobiography of Adam Clarke, there is an interesting account of his hearing Mary Sewall and another female minister preach, and he acknowledges that such was the power accompanying their ministry, that though he had been prejudiced against women's preaching, he could not but confess that these women were anointed for the office.

But there are certain passages in the Epistles of St. Paul, which seem to be of doubtful interpretation; at which we cannot much marvel, seeing that his brother Peter says, there are some things in them hard to be understood. Most commentators, having their minds preoccupied with the prejudices of education, afford little aid; they rather tend to darken the text by the multitude of words. One of these passages occurs in 1 Cor. 14. I have already remarked, that this chapter, with several of the preceding, was evidently designed to correct abuses which had crept into the assemblies of Christians in Corinth. Hence we find that the men were commanded to be silent, as well as the women, when they were guilty of any thing which deserved reprehension. The apostle says, "If there be no interpreter, let him keep silence in the church." The men were doubtless in the practice of speaking in unknown tongues, when there was no interpreter present; and Paul reproves them, because this kind of preaching conveyed no instruction to the people. Again he says, "If any thing be revealed to another that sitteth by, let the first hold his peace." We may infer from this, that two men sometimes attempted to speak at the same time, and the apostle rebukes them, and adds, "Ye may ALL prophesy one by one, for God is not the author of confusion, but of peace." He then proceeds to notice the disorderly conduct of the women, who were guilty of other improprieties. They were probably in the habit of asking questions, on any points of doctrine which they wished more thoroughly explained. This custom was common among the men in the Jewish synagogues, after the pattern of which, the meetings of the early Christians were in all probability conducted. And the Christian women, presuming on the liberty which they enjoyed under the new religion, interrupted the assembly, by asking questions. The apostle disapproved of this, because it disturbed the solemnity of the meeting: he therefore admonishes the women to keep silence in the churches. That the apostle did not allude to preaching is manifest, because he tells them, "If they will *learn* any thing, let them ask their husbands at home." Now a person endowed with a gift in the ministry, does not ask questions in the public exercise of that gift, for the purpose of gaining information: she is instructing others. Moreover, the apostle, in closing his remarks on this subject, says, "Wherefore, brethren, (a generic term, applying equally to men and women,) covet to prophesy, and forbid not to speak with tongues. Let all things be done decently and in order."

Clarke, on the passage, 'Let women keep silence in the churches,' says:

> This was a Jewish ordinance. Women were not permitted to teach in the assemblies, or even to ask questions. The rabbins taught that a woman should know nothing but the use of her distaff; and the saying of Rabbi Eliezer is worthy of remark and execration: "Let the words of the law be burned, rather than that they should be delivered by women."

Are there not many of our Christian brethren, whose hostility to the ministry of women is as bitter as was that of Rabbi Eliezer, and who would rather let souls perish, than that the truths of the gospel should be delivered by women?

> "This," says Clarke, "was their condition till the time of the gospel, when, according to the prediction of Joel, the Spirit of God was to be poured out on the women as well as the men, that they might prophesy, that is, teach. And that they did prophesy, or teach, is evident from what the apostle says, ch. 11: 5, where he lays down rules to regulate this part of their conduct while ministering in the church. But does not what the apostle says here, let your women keep silence in the churches, contradict that statement, and show that the words in ch. 11, should be understood in another sense? for here it is expressly said, that they should keep silence in the churches, for it was not permitted to a woman to speak. Both places seem perfectly consistent. It is evident from the context, that the apostle refers here to asking questions, and what we call dictating in the assemblies."

The other passage on which the opinion, that women are not called to the ministry, is founded, is 1 Tim. 2d ch. The apostle speaks of the duty of prayer and supplication, mentions his own ordination as a preacher, and then adds, "I will, therefore, that men pray everywhere, lifting up holy hands, without wrath and doubting. In like manner also, that women adorn themselves in modest apparel," &c. I shall here premise, that as the punctuation and division into chapters and verses is no part of the original arrangement, they cannot determine the sense of a passage. Indeed, every attentive reader of the Bible must observe, that the injudicious separation of sentences often destroys their meaning and their beauty. Joseph John Gurney, whose skill as a biblical critic is well known in England, commenting on this passage, says,

> It is worded in a manner somewhat obscure; but appears to be best construed according to the opinion of various commentators (See Pool's Synopsis) as conveying an injunction, that women as well as men should pray everywhere, lifting up holy hands without wrath and doubting. 1 Tim. 2: 8, 9. "I will therefore that men pray everywhere, &c.; likewise also the women in a modest dress." (Compare 1 Cor. 11: 5.) "I would have them adorn themselves with shamefacedness and sobriety."

I have no doubt this is the true meaning of the text, and that the translators would never have thought of altering it had they not been under the influence of educational prejudice. The apostle proceeds to exhort the women, who thus publicly made intercession to God, "not to adorn themselves with braided hair, or gold, or pearls, or costly array, but (which becometh women professing godliness) with good works." The word in this verse translated "professing," would be more properly rendered preaching godliness, or enjoining piety to the gods, or conducting public worship. After describing the duty of female ministers about their apparel, the apostle proceeds to correct some improprieties which probably prevailed in the Ephesian church, similar to those which he had reproved among the Corinthian converts. He says, "Let the women LEARN in silence with all subjection; but I suffer not a woman to teach, nor to usurp authority over the man, but to be in silence," or quietness. Here again it is evident that the women, of whom he was speaking, were admonished to learn in silence, which could not refer to their public ministrations to others. The verb to teach, verse 12, is one of very general import, and may in this place more properly be rendered dictate. It is highly probable that women who had long been in bondage, when set free by Christianity from the restraints imposed upon them by Jewish traditions and heathen customs, run into an extreme in their public assemblies, and interrupted the religious services by frequent interrogations, which they could have had answered as satisfactorily at home.

On a candid examination and comparison of the passages which I have endeavored to explain, viz., 1 Cor. chaps. 11 and 14, and 1 Tim. 2, 8—12. I think we must be compelled to adopt one of two conclusions; either that the apostle grossly contradicts himself on a subject of great practical importance, and that the fulfilment of the prophecy of Joel was a shameful infringement of decency and order; or that the directions given to women, not to speak, or to teach in the congregations, had reference to some local and peculiar customs, which were then common in religious assemblies, and which the apostle thought inconsistent with the purpose for which they were met together. No one, I suppose, will hesitate which of these two conclusions to adopt. The subject is one of vital importance. That it may claim the calm and prayerful attention of Christians, is the desire of

Thine in the bonds of womanhood,

SARAH M. GRIMKÉ.

LETTER XV.

Man Equally Guilty with Woman in the Fall.

Uxbridge, 10th Mo. 20th, 1837.

My Dear Sister,—It is said that "modern Jewish women light a lamp every Friday evening, half an hour before sunset, which is the beginning of their Sabbath, in remembrance of their original mother, who first extinguished the lamp of righteousness,—to remind them of their obligation to rekindle it." I am one of those who always admit, to its fullest extent, the popular charge, that woman brought sin into the world. I accept it as a powerful reason, why woman is bound to labor with double diligence, for the regeneration of that world she has been instrumental in ruining.

But, although I do not repel the imputation, I shall notice some passages in the sacred Scriptures, where this transaction is mentioned, which prove, I think, the identity and equality of man and woman, and that there is no difference in their guilt in the view of that God who searcheth the heart and trieth the reins of the children of men. In Is. 43: 27, we find the following passage—"Thy first father hath sinned, and thy teachers have transgressed against me"—which is synonymous with Rom. 5: 12. "Wherefore, as by ONE MAN sin entered into the world, and death by sin, &c." Here man and woman are included under one term, and no distinction is made in their criminality. The circumstances of the fall are again referred to in 2 Cor. 11: 3—"But I fear lest, by any means, as the serpent *beguiled* Eve through his subtility, so your mind should be beguiled from the simplicity that is in Christ." Again, 1st Tim. 2: 14—"Adam *was not deceived;* but the woman being *deceived*, was in the transgression." Now, whether the fact, that Eve was beguiled and deceived, is a proof that her crime was of deeper dye than Adam's, who was not deceived, but was fully aware of the consequences of sharing in her transgression, I shall leave the candid reader to determine.

My present object is to show, that, as woman is charged with all the sin that exists in the world, it is her solemn duty to labor for its extinction; and that this she can never do effectually and extensively, until her mind is disenthralled of those shackles which have been riveted upon her by a "*corrupt public opinion, and a perverted interpretation of the holy Scriptures.*" Woman must feel that she is the equal, and is designed to be the fellow laborer of her brother, or she will be studying to find out the *imaginary* line which separates the sexes, and divides the duties of men and women into two distinct classes, a separation not even hinted at in the Bible, where we are expressly told, "there is neither male nor female, for ye are all one in Christ Jesus."

My views on this subject are so much better embodied in the language of a living author than I can express them, that I quote the passage entire: "Woman's rights and man's rights are *both* contained in the *same* charter, and held by the *same* tenure. *All rights* spring out of the *moral* nature: they are both the root and the offspring of *responsibilities*. The physical constitution is the mere *instrument* of the *moral* nature; sex is a mere *incident* of this constitution, a provision necessary to this *form* of existence; its *only* design, not to give, nor to take away, nor in any respect to modify or even *touch* rights or responsibilities in any sense, except so far as the peculiar offices of each sex may afford less or more *opportunity* and ability for the exercise of rights, and the discharge of responsibilities; but merely to continue and enlarge the human department of God's government. Consequently, I know nothing of *man's* rights, or *woman's* rights; *human* rights are all that I recognise. The doctrine, that the *sex of the body* presides over and administers upon the rights and responsibilities of the moral, immortal nature, is to my mind a doctrine kindred to blasphemy, *when seen in its intrinsic nature*. It breaks up utterly the *relations* of the two natures, and reverses their functions; exalting the animal nature into a monarch, and humbling the moral into a slave; making the former a proprietor, and the latter its property."

To perform our duties, we must comprehend our rights and responsibilities; and it is because we do not understand, that we now fall so far short in the discharge of our obligations. Unaccustomed to think for ourselves, and to search the sacred volume, to see how far we are living up to the design of Jehovah in our creation, we have rested satisfied with the sphere marked out for us by man, never detecting the fallacy of that reasoning which forbids woman to exercise some of her noblest faculties, and stamps with the reproach of indelicacy those actions by which women were formerly dignified and exalted in the church.

I should not mention this subject again, if it were not to point out to my sisters what seems to me an irresistible conclusion from the literal interpretation of St. Paul, without reference to the context, and the peculiar circumstances and abuses which drew forth the expressions, "I suffer not a woman to teach"—"Let your women keep silence in the church," i. e. congregation. It is manifest, that if the apostle meant what his words imply, when taken in the strictest sense, then women have no right to *teach* Sabbath or day schools, or to open their lips to sing in the assemblies of the people; yet young and delicate women are engaged in all these offices; they are expressly trained to exhibit themselves, and raise their voices to a high pitch in the choirs of our places of worship. I do not intend to sit in judgment on my sisters for doing these things; I only want them to see, that they are as really infringing a *supposed* divine command, by instructing their pupils in the Sabbath or day schools, and by singing in the congregation, as if they were engaged in preaching the unsearchable riches of Christ to a lost and perishing world. Why, then, are we permitted to break this injunction in some points, and so sedulously warned not to overstep the bounds set for us by our *brethren* in another? Simply, as I believe, because in the one case we subserve *their* views and *their* interests, and act *in subordination to them;* whilst in the other, we come in contact with their interests, and claim to be on an equality with them in the highest and most important trust ever committed to man, namely, the ministry of the word. It is manifest, that if women were permitted to be ministers of the gospel, as they unquestionably were in the primitive ages of the Christian church, it would interfere materially with the present organized system of spiritual power and ecclesiastical authority, which is now vested solely in the hands of men. It would either show that all the paraphernalia of theological seminaries, &c. &c. to prepare men to become evangelists, is wholly unnecessary, or it would create a necessity for similar institutions in order to prepare women for the same office; and this would be an encroachment on that learning, which our hind brethren have so ungenerously monopolized. I do not ask any one to believe my statements, or adopt my conclusions, because they are mine; but I do earnestly entreat my sisters to lay aside their prejudices, and examine these subjects *for themselves*, regardless of the "traditions of men," because they are intimately connected with their duty and their usefulness in the present important crisis.

All who know any thing of the present system of benevolent and religious operations, know that women are performing an important part in them, in *subserviency to men*, who guide our labors, and are often the recipients of those benefits of education we toil to confer, and which we rejoice they can enjoy, although it is their mandate which deprives us of the same advantages. Now, whether our brethren have defrauded us intentionally, or unintentionally, the wrong we suffer is equally the same. For years, they have been spurring us up to the performance of our duties. The immense usefulness and the vast influence of woman have been eulogized and called into exercise, and many a blessing has been lavished upon us, and many a prayer put up for us, because we have labored by day and by night to clothe and feed and educate young men, whilst our own bodies sometimes suffer for want of comfortable garments, and our minds are left in almost utter destitution of that improvement which we are toiling to bestow upon the brethren.

> Full many a gem of purest ray serene,
> The dark unfathomed caves of ocean bear;
> Full many a flower is born to blush unseen
> And waste its sweetness on the desert air.

If the sewing societies, the avails of whose industry are now expended in supporting and educating young men for the ministry, were to withdraw their contributions to these objects, and give them where they are *more needed*, to the advancement of their *own sex* in useful learning, the next generation might furnish sufficient proof, that in intelligence and ability to master the whole circle of sciences, woman is not inferior to man; and instead of a sensible woman being regarded as she now is, is a lusses naturæ, they would be quite as common as sensible men. I confess, considering the high claim men in this country make to great politeness and deference to women, it does seem a little extraordinary that we should be urged to work for the brethren. I should suppose it would be more in character with "the generous promptings of chivalry, and the poetry of romantic gallantry," for which Catherine E. Beecher gives them credit, for them to form societies to educate their sisters, seeing our inferior capacities require more cultivation to bring them into use, and qualify us to be helps meet for them. However, though I think this would be but a just return for all our past kindnesses in this way, I should be willing to balance our accounts, and begin a new course. Henceforth, let the benefit be reciprocated, or else let each sex provide for the education of their own poor, whose talents ought to be rescued from the oblivion of ignorance. Sure I am, the young men who are now benefitted by the handy work of their sisters, will not be less honorable if they occupy half their time in earning enough to pay for their own education, instead of depending on the industry of women, who not unfrequently deprive themselves of the means of purchasing valuable books which might enlarge their stock of useful knowledge, and perhaps prove a blessing to the family by furnishing them with instructive reading. If the minds of women were enlightened and improved, the domestic circle would be more frequently refreshed by intelligent conversation, a means of edification now deplorably neglected, for want of that cultivation which these intellectual advantages would confer.

Duties of Women.

One of the duties which devolve upon women in the present interesting crisis, is to prepare themselves for more extensive usefulness, by making use of those religious and literary privileges and advantages that are within their reach, if they will only stretch out their hands and possess them. By doing this, they will become better acquainted with their rights as moral beings, and with their responsibilities growing out of those rights: they will regard themselves, as they really are, FREE AGENTS, immortal beings, amenable to no tribunal but that of Jehovah, and bound not to submit to any restriction imposed for selfish purposes, or to gratify that love of power which has reigned in the heart of man from Adam down to the present time. In contemplating the great moral reformations of the day, and the part which they are bound to take in them, instead of puzzling themselves with the harassing, because unnecessary inquiry, how far they may go without overstepping the bounds of propriety, which separate male and female duties, they will only inquire, "Lord, what wilt thou have us to do?" They will be enabled to see the simple truth, that God has made no distinction between men and women as moral beings; that the distinction now so much insisted upon between male and female virtues is as absurd as it is unscriptural, and has been the fruitful source of much mischief—granting to man a license for the exhibition of brute force and conflict on the battle field; forst ernness, selfishness, and the exercise of irresponsible power in the circle of home—and to woman a permit to rest on an arm of flesh, and to regard modesty and delicacy, and all the kindred virtues, as peculiarly appropriate to her. Now to me it is perfectly clear, that WHATSOEVER IT IS MORALLY RIGHT FOR A MAN TO DO, IT IS MORALLY RIGHT FOR A WOMAN TO DO; and that confusion must exist in the moral world, until women takes her stand on the same platform with man, and feels that she is clothed by her Maker with the *same rights*, and, of course, that upon her devolve the *same duties*.

It is not my intention, nor indeed do I think it is in my power, to point out the precise duties of women. To him who still teacheth by his Holy Spirit as never man taught, I refer my beloved sisters. There is a vast field of usefulness before them. The signs of the times give portentous evidence, that a day of deep trial is approaching; and I urge them, by every consideration of a Savior's dying love, by the millions of heathen in our midst, by the sufferings of woman in almost every portion of the world, by the fearful ravages which slavery, intemperance, licentiousness and other iniquities are making of the happiness of our fellow creatures, to come to the rescue of a ruined world, and to be found co-workers with Jesus Christ.

Ho! to the rescue, ho!
  Up every one that feels—
'Tis a sad and fearful cry of woe
  From a guilty world that steals.
Hark! hark! how the horror rolls,
  Whence can this anguish be?
'Tis the groan of a trammel'd people's souls,
  Now bursting to be free.

And here, with all due deference for the office of the ministry, which I believe was established by Jehovah himself, and designed by Him to be the means of spreading light and salvation through a crucified Savior to the ends of the earth, I would entreat my sisters not to *compel* the ministers of the present day to give their names to great moral reformations. The practice of making ministers life members, or officers of societies, when their hearts have not been touched with a live coal from the altar, and animated with love for the work we are engaged in, is highly injurious to them, as well as to the cause. They often satisfy their consciences in this way, without doing anything to promote the anti-slavery, or temperance, or other reformations; and we please ourselves with the idea, that we have done something to forward the cause of Christ, when, in effect, we have been sewing pillows like the false prophetesses of old under the arm-holes of our clerical brethren. Let us treat the ministers with all tenderness and respect, but let us be careful how we cherish in their hearts the idea that they are of more importance to a cause than other men. I rejoice when they take hold heartily. I love and honor some ministers with whom I have been associated in the anti-slavery ranks, but I do deeply deplore, for the sake of the cause, the prevalent notion, that the clergy must be had, either by persuasion or by bribery. They will not need persuasion or bribery, if their hearts are with us; if they are not, we are better without them. It is idle to suppose that the kingdom of heaven cannot come on earth, without their co-operation. It is the Lord's work, and it must go forward with or without their aid. As well might the converted Jews have despaired of the spread of Christianity, without the co-operation of Scribes and Pharisees.

Let us keep in mind, that no abolitionism is of any value, which is not accompanied with deep, heartfelt repentance; and that, whenever a minister sincerely repents of having, either by his apathy or his efforts, countenanced the fearful sin of slavery, he will need no inducement to come into our ranks; so far from it, he will abhor himself in dust and ashes, for his past blindness and indifference to the cause of God's poor and oppressed: and he will regard it as a privilege to be enabled to do something in the cause of human rights. I know the ministry exercise vast power; but I rejoice in the belief, that the spell is broken which encircled them, and rendered it all but blasphemy to expose their errors and their sins. We are beginning to understand that they are but men, and that their station should not shield them from merited reproof.

I have blushed for my sex when I have heard of their entreating ministers to attend their associations, and open them with prayer. The idea is inconceivable to me, that Christian women can be engaged in doing God's work, and yet cannot ask his blessing on their efforts, except through the lips of a man. I have known a whole town scoured to obtain a minister to open a female meeting, and their refusal to do so spoken of as quite a misfortune. Now, I am not glad that the ministers do wrong; but I am glad that my sisters have been sometimes compelled to act for themselves: it is exactly what they need to strengthen them, and prepare them to act independently. And to say the truth, there is something really ludicrous in seeing a minister enter the meeting, open it with prayer, and then take his departure. However, I only throw out these hints for the consideration of women. I believe there are solemn responsibilities resting upon us, and that in this day of light and knowledge, we cannot plead ignorance of duty. The great moral reformations now on the wheel are only practical Christianity; and if the ministry is not prepared to labor with us in these righteous causes, let us press forward, and they will follow on to know the Lord.

Conclusion.

I have now, my dear sister, completed my series of letters. I am aware, they contain some new views; but I believe they are based on the immutable truths of the Bible. All I ask for them is, the candid and prayerful consideration of Christians. If they strike at some of our bosom sins, our deep-rooted prejudices, our long cherished opinions, let us not condemn them on that account, but investigate them fearlessly and prayerfully, and not shrink from the examination; because, if they are true, they place heavy responsibilities upon women. In throwing them before the public, I have been actuated solely by the belief, that if they are acted upon, they will exalt the character and enlarge the usefulness of my own sex, and contribute greatly to the happiness and virtue of the other. That there is a root of bitterness continually springing up in families and troubling the repose of both men and women, must be manifest to even a superficial observer; and I believe it is the mistaken notion of the inequality of the sexes. As there is an assumption of superiority on the one part, which is not sanctioned by Jehovah, there is an incessant struggle on the other to rise to that degree of dignity, which God designed women to possess in common with men, and to maintain those rights and exercise those privileges which every woman's common sense, apart from the prejudices of education, tells her are inalienable; they are a part of her moral nature, and can only cease when her immortal mind is extinguished.

One word more. I feel that I am calling upon my sex to sacrifice what has been, what is still dear to their hearts, the adulation, the flattery, the attentions of trifling men. I am asking them to repel these insidious enemies whenever they approach them; to manifest by their conduct, that, although they value highly the society of pious and intelligent men, they have no taste for idle conversation, and for that silly preference which is manifested for their personal accommodation, often at the expense of great inconvenience to their male companions. As an illustration of what I mean, I will state a fact.

I was traveling lately in a stage coach. A gentleman, who was also a passenger, was made sick by riding with his back to the horses. I offered to exchange seats, assuring him it did not affect me at all unpleasantly; but he was too polite to permit a lady to run the risk of being discommoded. I am sure he meant to be very civil, but I really thought it was a foolish piece of civility. This kind of attention encourages selfishness in woman, and is only accorded as a sort of quietus, in exchange for those *rights* of which we are deprived. Men and women are equally bound to cultivate a spirit of accommodation; but I exceedingly deprecate her being treated like a spoiled child, and sacrifices made to her selfishness and vanity. In lieu of these flattering but injurious attentions, yielded to her as an inferior, as a mark of benevolence and courtesy, I want my sex to claim nothing from their brethren but what their brethren may justly claim from them, in their intercourse as Christians. I am persuaded woman can do much in this way to elevate her own character. And that we may become duly sensible of the dignity of our nature, only a little lower than the angels, and bring forth fruit to the glory and honor of Emanuel's name, is the fervent prayer of

Thine in the bonds of womanhood,

SARAH M. GRIMKÉ.

ANGELINA E. GRIMKÉ

SLAVERY AND THE BOSTON RIOT

Philadelphia, 8th month, 30th, 1835.

Respected Friend:

It seems as if I was compelled at this time to address thee, notwithstanding all my reasonings against intruding on thy valuable time, and the uselessness of so insignificant a person as myself offering thee the sentiments of sympathy at this alarming crisis.

I can hardly express to thee the deep and solemn interest with which I have viewed the violent proceedings of the last few weeks. Although I expected opposition, yet I was not prepared for it so soon—it took me by surprise, and I greatly feared Abolitionists would be driven back in the first onset, and thrown into confusion. So fearful was I, that though I clung with unflinching firmness to our *principles*, yet I was afraid of even opening one of thy papers, lest I should see some indications of compromise, some surrender, some palliation. Under these feelings, I was urged to read thy Appeal to the citizens of Boston. Judge, then, what were my feelings, on finding that my fears were utterly groundless, and that thou stoodest firm in the midst of the storm, determined to suffer and to die, rather than yield one inch. My heart was filled with thanksgiving and praise to the Preserver of men; I thanked God, and took courage, earnestly desiring that thousands may adopt thy language, and be *prepared* to meet the Martyr's doom, rather than give up the principles you (i. e. Abolitionists) have adopted. The ground upon which you stand is holy ground: never—never surrender it. If you surrender it, the hope of the slave is extinguished, and the chains of his servitude will be strengthened a hundred fold. But let no man take your crown, and success is as certain as the rising of to-morrow's sun. But remember you must be willing to suffer the loss of all things—willing to be the scorn and reproach of *professor* and profane. You must obey our great Master's injunction: "Fear *not* them that kill the body, and after that, have nothing more that they can do." You must, like Apostles, "count *not* your lives dear unto yourselves, so that you may finish your course with joy."

Religious persecution always begins with *mobs:* it is always unprecedented in the age or country in which it *commences*, and therefore there are *no laws*, by which Reformers can be punished; consequently, a lawless band of unprincipled men determine to take the matter into their hands, and act out in *mobs*, what they know are the *principles* of a large majority of those who are too high in *Church* and State to *condescend* to mingle with them, though they *secretly* approve and rejoice over their violent measures. The first martyr who ever died, was stoned by a *lawless mob;* and if we look at the rise of various sects—Methodists, Friends, &c.—we shall find that *mobs began* the persecution against them, and that it was not until *after* the people had thus spoken out their wishes, that laws were framed to fine, imprison, or destroy them. Let us, then, be prepared for the enactment of laws even in our *Free* States, against Abolitionists. And how ardently has the prayer been breathed, that God would prepare us for *all* he is preparing for us; that he would strengthen us in the hour of conflict, and cover our heads (if consistent with his holy will) in the day of battle! But O! how earnestly have I desired, *not* that we may escape suffering, but that we may be willing to endure unto the end. If we call upon the slave-holder to suffer the loss of what he calls property, then let us show him we make this demand from a deep sense of duty, by being ourselves willing to suffer the loss of character, property—yea, and life itself, in what we believe to be the cause of bleeding humanity.

My mind has been especially turned towards those, who are standing in the fore front of the battle; and the prayer has gone up for *their* preservation—not the preservation of their lives, but the preservation of their minds in humility and patience, faith, hope, and *charity*—that charity which is the bond of perfectness. If persecution is the means which God has ordained for the accomplishment of this great end, EMANCIPATION; then, in dependence *upon Him* for strength to bear it, I feel as if I could say, LET IT COME; for it is my deep, solemn, deliberate conviction, that *this is a cause worth dying for.* I say so, from what I have seen, and heard, and known, in a land of slavery, where rests the darkness of Egypt, and where is found the sin of Sodom. Yes! LET IT COME—let *us* suffer, rather than insurrections should arise.

At one time, I thought this system would be overthrown in blood, with the confused noise of the warrior; but a hope gleams across my mind, that *our* blood will be split, instead of the slaveholders'; *our* lives will be taken, and theirs spared—I say a *hope*, for all things I desire to be spared the anguish of seeing our beloved country desolated with the horrors of a servile war. If persecution can abolish slavery, it will also purify the Church; and who that stands between the porch and altar, weeping over the sins of the people, will not be willing to suffer, if such immense good will be accomplished. Let us endeavor, then, to put on the *whole* armor of God, and, having done all, to stand ready for whatever is before us.

I have just heard of Dresser's being flogged: it is no surprise at all; but the language of our Lord has been sweetly revived—"Blessed are ye when men shall revile you, and persecute you, and say all manner of evil against you *falsely,* for my sake. Rejoice, and be exceeding glad, for great is your reward in heaven." O! for a willingness and strength to suffer! But we shall have false brethren now, just as the Apostles had, and this will be one of our greatest griefs.

A. E. GRIMKÉ.

APPEAL TO THE CHRISTIAN WOMEN OF THE SOUTH

APPEAL, &C.

> "Then Mordecai commanded to answer Esther, Think not within thyself that thou shalt escape in the king's house more than all the Jews. For if thou altogether holdest thy peace at this time, then shall there enlargement and deliverance arise to the Jews from another place: but thou and thy father's house shall be destroyed: and who knoweth whether thou art come to the kingdom for such a time as this. And Esther bade them return Mordecai this answer: And so will I go in unto the king, which is not according to law, and if *I perish, I perish*."
>
> —ESTHER, iv. 13–16.

RESPECTED FRIENDS,

It is because I feel a deep and tender interest in your present and eternal welfare, that I am willing thus publicly to address you. Some of you have loved me as a relative, and some have felt bound to me in Christian sympathy and Gospel fellowship; and even when compelled by a strong sense of duty to break those outward bonds of union which bound us together as members of the same community, and members of the same religious denomination, you were generous enough to give me credit for sincerity as a Christian, though you believed I had been most strangely deceived. I thanked you then for your kindness, and I ask you *now,* for the sake of former confidence and former friendship, to read the following pages in the spirit of calm investigation and fervent prayer. It is because you have known me that I write thus unto you.

But there are other Christian women scattered over the Southern States, and these, a very large number of whom have never seen me, and never heard my name, and who feel *no* interest whatever in *me*. But I feel an interest in *you*, as branches of the same vine, from whose root I daily draw the principle of spiritual vitality. Yes! Sisters in Christ, I feel an interest in *you*, and often has the secret prayer arisen in your behalf,—Lord, "open thou their eyes, that they may see wondrous things out of thy law." It is, then, because I *do feel* and *do pray* for you, that I thus address you upon a subject about which, of all others perhaps, you would rather not hear anything; but, "would to God you could bear with me a little in my folly, and indeed bear with me, for I am jealous over you with godly jealousy." Be not afraid, then, to read my Appeal; it is *not* written in the heat of passion or prejudice, but in that solemn calmness which is the result of conviction and duty. It is true, I am going to tell you unwelcome truths, but I mean to speak those *truths in love*; and remember, Solomon says, "faithful are the *wounds* of a friend." I do not believe the time has yet come when *Christian women* "will not endure sound doctrine," even on the subject of slavery, if it is spoken to them in tenderness and love: therefore I now address *you*.

To all of you, then, known or unknown, relatives or strangers (for you are all *one* in Christ). I would speak. I have felt for you at this time, when unwelcome light is pouring in upon the world on the subject of slavery,—light which even Christians would exclude, if they could, from our country, or at any rate from the southern portion of it, saying, as its rays strike the rock-bound coasts of New England, and scatter their warmth and radiance over her hills and valleys, and from thence travel onward over the Palisades of the Hudson, and down the soft-flowing waters of the Delaware, and gild the waves of the Potomac,—"Hitherto shalt thou come, and no farther." I know that even professors of His name, who has been emphatically called the "Light of the world," would, if they could, build a wall of adamant around the Southern States, whose top might reach unto heaven, in order to shut out the light which is bounding from mountain to mountain, and from the hills to the plains and valleys beneath, through the vast extent of our Northern States. But believe me when I tell you, their attempts will be as utterly fruitless as were the efforts of the builders of Babel; and why? Because moral, like natural light, is so extremely subtle in its nature, as to overleap all human barriers, and laugh at the puny efforts of man to control it. All the excuses and palliations of this system must inevitably be swept away, just as other "refuges of lies" have been, by the irresistible torrent of a rectified public opinion. "The *supporters* of the slave system," says Jonathan Dymond, in his admirable work on the Principles of Morality, "will *hereafter* be regarded with the *same* public feeling as he who was an advocate for the slave trade *now is*." It will be, and that very soon, clearly perceived and fully acknowledged by all the virtuous and the candid, that in *principle* it is as sinful to hold a human being in bondage who has been born in Carolina, as one who has been born in Africa. All that sophistry of argument which has been employed to prove, that, although it is sinful to send to Africa to procure men and women as slaves, who have never been in slavery, that still it is *not* sinful to keep those in bondage who have come down by inheritance,—will be utterly overthrown. We must come back to the good old doctrine of our forefathers, who declared to the world this self-evident truth, "that *all* men are created *equal*, and that they have certain *inalienable* rights, among which are life, *liberty*, and the pursuit of happiness." It is even a greater absurdity to suppose a man can be legally born a slave under *our free republican* government, than under the petty despotisms of barbarian Africa. If, then, we have no right to enslave an African, surely we can have none to enslave an American. If it is a self-evident truth that *all* men, everywhere and of every colour, are born equal, and have an *inalienable right to liberty*, then it is equally true that *no* man can be born a slave, and no man can ever *rightfully* be reduced to *involuntary* bondage, and held as a slave, however fair may be the claim of his master or mistress, through wills and title-deeds.

But, after all, it may be said, our fathers were certainly mistaken, for the Bible sanctions slavery, and that is the highest authority. Now the Bible is my ultimate appeal in all matters of faith and practice, and it is to *this test* I am anxious to bring the subject at issue between us. Let us then begin with Adam, and examine the charter of privileges which was given to him: "Have dominion over the fish of the sea, and over the fowl of the air, and over every living thing that moveth upon the earth." In the eighth Psalm we have a still fuller description of this charter, which, through Adam, was given to all mankind: "Thou madest him to have dominion over the works of thy hands; thou hast put all things under his feet. All sheep and oxen, yea, and the beasts of the field, the fowl of the air, the fish of the sea, and whatsoever passeth through the paths of the seas." And after the flood, when this charter of human rights was renewed, we find *no additional* power vested in man: "And the fear of you and the dread of you shall be upon every beast of the earth, and every fowl of the air, and upon all that moveth upon the earth, and upon all the fishes of the sea; into your hand are they delivered." In this charter, although the different kinds of *irrational* beings are so particularly enumerated, and supreme dominion over *all of them* is granted, yet *man* is *never* vested with this dominion *over his fellow man*; he was never told that any of the human species were put *under his feet*; it was only *all things*,—and man, who was created in the image of his Maker, *never* can properly be termed a *thing*, though the laws of slave states do call him "a chattel personal." Man, then, I assert, *never* was put *under the feet of man* by that first charter of human rights which was given by God to the Fathers of the Antediluvian and Postdiluvian worlds: therefore the doctrine of equality is based on the Bible.

But it may be argued, that in the very chapter of Genesis from which I have last quoted, will be found the curse pronounced upon Canaan, by which his posterity was consigned to servitude under his brethern Shem and Japheth. I know this prophecy was uttered, and was most fearfully and wonderfully fulfilled, through the immediate descendants of Canaan, *i. e.* the Canaanites; and I do not know but it has been through all the children of Ham; but I do know that prophecy does *not* tell us what *ought to be*, but what actually does take place, ages after it has been delivered; and that if we justify America for enslaving the children of Africa, we must also justify Egypt for reducing the children of Israel to bondage, for the latter was foretold as explicitly as the former. I am well aware that prophecy has often been urged as an excuse for slavery; but be not deceived; the fulfilment of prophecy will *not cover one sin* in the awful day of account. Hear what our Saviour says on this subject: "It must needs be that offences come, but *woe unto that man through whom they come.*" Witness some fulfilment of this declaration in the tremendous destruction of Jerusalem, occasioned by that most nefarious of all crimes,—the crucifixion of the Son of God. Did the fact of that event having been foretold exculpate the Jews from sin in perpetrating it? No; for hear what the Apostle Peter says to them on this subject: "Him being delivered by the determinate counsel and foreknowledge of God, *ye* have taken, and by *wicked* hands have crucified and slain." Other striking instances might be adduced, but these will suffice.

But it has been urged that the patriarchs held slaves, and therefore, slavery is right. Do you really believe that patriarchal servitude was like American slavery? Can you believe it? If so, read the history of these primitive Fathers of the Church, and be undeceived. Look at Abraham, so great a man, going to the herd himself, and fetching a calf from thence, and serving it up with his own hands, for the entertainment of his guests. Look at Sarah, that princess, as her name signifies, baking cakes upon the hearth. If the servants they had were like Southern slaves, would they have performed such comparatively menial offices for themselves? Hear, too, the plaintive lamentation of Abraham when he feared he should have no son to bear his name down to posterity: "Behold thou hast given me no seed," &c., "one born in my house *is mine* heir." From this it appears that one of his *servants* was to inherit his immense estate. Is this like Southern slavery? I leave it to your own good sense and candour to decide. Besides, such was the footing upon which Abraham was with *his* servants, that he trusted them with arms. Are slaveholders willing to put swords and pistols into the hands of their slaves? He was as a father among his servants; what are planters and masters generally among theirs? When the institution of circumcision was established, Abraham was commanded thus:—"He that is eight days old shall be circumcised among you, *every* man-child in your generations; he that is born in the house, or bought with money of any stranger which is not of thy seed." And to render this command with regard to his *servants* still more impressive, it is repeated in the very next verse; and herein we may perceive the great care which was taken by God to guard the *rights of servants* even under this "dark dispensation." What, too, was the testimony given to the faithfulness of this eminent patriarch: "For I know him that he will command his children and his *household* after him, and they shall keep the way of the Lord to do justice and judgment." Now, my dear friends, many of you believe that circumcision has been superseded by baptism in the Church. *Are you* careful to have *all* that are born in your house, or bought with money of any stranger, baptised? Are *you* as faithful as Abraham to command *your household to keep the way of the Lord?* I leave it to your own consciences to decide. Was patriarchal servitude, then, like American slavery?

But I shall be told, God sanctioned slavery, yea, commanded slavery, under the Jewish Dispensation. Let us examine this subject calmly and prayerfully. I admit that a species of *servitude* was permitted to the Jews; but in studying the subject I have been struck with wonder and admiration at perceiving how carefully the servant was guarded from violence, injustice, and wrong. I will first inform you how these servants became servants, for I think this a very important part of our subject. From consulting Horne, Calmet, and the Bible, I find there were six different ways by which the Hebrews became servants legally.

1. If reduced to extreme poverty, a Hebrew might sell himself, *i. e.* his services, for six years, in which case *he* received the purchase money *himself*. Lev. xxv. 39.
2. A father might sell his children as servants, *i. e.* his *daughters*; in which circumstance it was understood the daughter was to be the wife or daughter-in-law of the man who bought her, and the *father* received the price. In other words, Jewish women were sold as *white women* were in the first settlement of Virginia,—as *wives, not* as slaves. Ex. xxi. 7.
3. Insolvent debtors might be delivered to their creditors as servants. 2 Kings iv. 1.
4. Thieves, not able to make restitution for their thefts, were sold for the benefit of the injured person. Ex. xxii. 3.
5. They might be born in servitude. Ex. xxi. 4.

6. If a Hebrew had sold himself to a rich Gentile, he might be redeemed by one of his brethren at any time the money was offered; and he who redeemed him, was *not* to take advantage of the favour thus conferred, and rule over him with rigour. Lev. xxv. 47–55.

Before going into an examination of the laws by which these servants were protected, I would just ask whether American slaves have become slaves in any of the ways in which the Hebrews became servants. Did they sell themselves into slavery and receive the purchase money into their own hands? No! Did they become insolvent, and by their own imprudence subject themselves to be sold as slaves? No! Did they steal the property of another, and were they sold to make restitution for their crimes? No! Did their present masters, as an act of kindness, redeem them from some heathen tyrant, to whom *they had sold themselves* in the dark hour of adversity? No! Were they born in slavery? No! No! not according to *Jewish Law;* for the servants who were born in servitude among them, were born of parents who had *sold themselves* for six years; Ex. xxi. 4. Were the female slaves of the South sold by their fathers? How shall I answer this question? Thousands and tens of thousands never were, *their* fathers *never* have received the poor compensation of silver or gold for the tears and toils, the suffering and anguish, and hopeless bondage of *their* daughters. They labour day by day, and year by year, side by side, in the same field, if haply their daughters are permitted to remain on the same plantation with them, instead of being, as they often are, separated from their parents and sold into distant states, never again to meet on earth. But do the *fathers of the South ever sell their daughters*? My heart beats, and my hand trembles, as I write the awful affirmative, Yes! The fathers of this Christian land often sell their daughters, *not* as Jewish parents did, to be the wives and daughters-in-law of the man who buys them, but to be the abject slaves of petty tyrants and irresponsible masters. Is it not so, my friends? I leave it to your own candour to corroborate my assertion. Southern slaves, then, have *not* become slaves in any of the six different ways in which Hebrews become servants, and I hesitate not to say that American masters *cannot*, according to *Jewish law*, substantiate their claim to the men, women, or children, they now hold in bondage.

But there was one way in which a Jew might illegally be reduced to servitude; it was this, he might be *stolen* and afterward sold as a slave, as was Joseph. To guard most effectually against this dreadful crime of manstealing, God enacted this severe law,—"He that stealeth a man and selleth him, or if he be found in his hand, he shall surely be put to death."* As I have tried American Slavery by *legal* Hebrew servitude, and found (to your surprise, perhaps), that Jewish law cannot justify the slaveholder's claim, let us now try it by *illegal* Hebrew bondage. Have the Southern slaves then been stolen? If they did not sell themselves into bondage; if they were not sold as insolvent debtors or as thieves; if they were not redeemed from a heathen master to whom *they had sold themselves;* if they were not born in servitude according to Hebrew Law; and if the females were not sold by their fathers as wives and daughters-in-law to those who purchased them; then what shall we say of them? what can we say of them? but that according *to Hebrew Law they have been stolen.*

But I shall be told that the Jews had other servants who were absolute slaves. Let us look a little into this also. They had other servants who were procured in two different ways.

1. Captives taken in war, were reduced to bondage instead of being killed; but we are not told that their children were enslaved. Deut. xx. 14.
2. Bondmen and bondmaids might be bought from the heathen round about them; these were left by fathers to their children after them, but it does not appear that the *children* of these servants ever were reduced to servitude. Lev. xxv. 44.

I will now try the right of the southern planter by the claims of Hebrew masters over their *heathen* slaves. Were the southern slaves taken captive in war? No! Were they bought from the

*And again, "If a man be found stealing any of his brethren of the children of Israel, and maketh merchandise of him, or selleth him, then *that thief shall die*, and thou shalt put away evil from among you." Deut. xxiv. 7.

heathen? No! for surely no one will *now* vindicate the slave-trade so far as to assert that slaves were bought from the heathen who were obtained by that system of piracy. The only excuse for holding southern slaves, is, that they were born in slavery; but we have seen that they were *not* born in servitude as Jewish servants were, and that the children of heathen slaves were not legally subjected to bondage, even under the Mosaic Law. How then have the slaves of the South been obtained?

I will next proceed to an examination of those laws which were enacted in order to protect the Hebrew and the Heathen servant; for I wish you to understand that *both* are protected by Him, of whom it is said "his mercies are over *all* his works." I will first speak of those which secured the rights of Hebrew servants. This code was headed thus:—

1. Thou shalt *not* rule over him with *rigour*, but shalt fear thy God.
2. If thou buy a Hebrew servant, six years shall he serve, and in the seventh year he shall go out free for nothing. Ex. xx. 2.*
3. If he come in by himself, he shall go out by himself; if he were married, then his wife shall go out with him.
4. If his master have given him a wife, and she have borne him sons and daughters, the wife and her children shall be his master's, and he shall go out by himself.
5. If the servant shall plainly say, I love my master, my wife, and my children, I will not go out free, then his master shall bring him unto the Judges, and he shall bring him to the door, or unto the door post, and his master shall bore his ear through with an awl, and he shall serve him *for ever.* Ex. xxi. 3–6.
6. If a man smite the eye of his servant, or the eye of his maid, that it perish, he shall let him go *free* for his eye's sake. And if he smite out his man servant's tooth, or

*And when thou sendest him out free from thee, thou shalt not let him go away empty: Thou shalt furnish him *liberally* out of thy flock, and out of thy floor, and out of thy wine-press: of that wherewith the Lord thy God hath blessed thee, shalt thou give unto him. Deut. xv. 13, 14.

his maid servant's tooth, he shall let him go free for his tooth's sake. Ex. xxi. 26, 27.

7. On the Sabbath, rest was secured to servants by the fourth commandment. Ex. xx. 10.
8. Servants were permitted to unite with their masters three times in every year in celebrating the Passover, the feast of Pentecost, and the feast of Tabernacles; every male throughout the land was to appear before the Lord at Jerusalem with a gift; here the bond and the free stood on common ground. Deut. xvi.
9. If a man smite his servant or his maid with a rod, and he die under his hand, he shall surely be punished. Notwithstanding, if he continue a day or two, he shall not be punished, for he is his money. Ex. xxi. 20, 21.

From these laws we learn that Hebrew men servants were bound to serve their masters *only six* years, unless their attachment to their employers, their wives and children, should induce them to wish to remain in servitude: in which case, in order to prevent the possibility of deception on the part of the master, the servant was first taken before the magistrate, where he openly declared his intention of continuing in his masters service (probably a public register was kept of such), he was then conducted to the door of the house (in warm climates doors are thrown open), and *there* his ear was *publicly* bored: and by submitting to this operation he testified his willingness to serve him *for ever, i. e.* during his life, for Jewish Rabbins, who must have understood Jewish *slavery* (as it is called), "affirm that servants were set free at the death of their masters, and did *not* descend to their heirs: or that he was to serve him until the year of Jubilee, when *all* servants were set at liberty. To protect servants from violence, it was ordained that if a master struck out the tooth or destroyed the eye of a servant, that servant immediately became *free*, for such an act of violence evidently showed he was unfit to possess the power of a master, and therefore that power was taken from him. All servants enjoyed the rest of the Sabbath and partook of the privileges and festivities of the three great Jewish feasts; and if a servant died under the infliction of chastisement, his master was surely to be punished. As a tooth for a tooth, and life for life, was the Jewish law, of course he was punished with death. I know that great stress has been laid upon the following verse, "Notwithstanding if he continue a day or two, he shall not be punished, for he is his money."

Slaveholders, and the apologists of slavery, have eagerly seized upon this little passage of Scripture, and held it up as the masters' Magna Charta, by which they were licensed by God himself to commit the greatest outrages upon the defenceless victims of their oppression. But, my friends, was it designed to be so? If our Heavenly Father would protect by law the eye and the tooth of a Hebrew servant, can we for a moment believe that he would abandon that same servant to the brutal rage of a master who would destroy even life itself. Do we not rather see in this, the *only* law which protected masters, and was it not right that in case of the death of a servant, one or two days after chastisement was inflicted, to which other circumstances might have contributed, that the master should be protected, when, in all probability, he never intended to produce so fatal a result? But the phrase "he is his money," has been adduced to show that Hebrew servants were regarded as mere *things*, "chattels personal;" if so, why were so many laws made to *secure their rights as men,* and to ensure their rising into equality and freedom? If they were mere *things,* why were they regarded as responsible beings, and one law made for them as well as for their masters? But I pass on now to the consideration of how the *female* Jewish servants were protected by *law.*

1. If she please not her master, who hath betrothed her to himself, then shall he let her be redeemed: to sell her unto another nation he shall have no power, seeing he hath dealt deceitfully with her.
2. If he have betrothed her unto his son, he shall deal with her after the manner of daughters.
3. If he take him another wife, her food, her raiment, and her duty of marriage, shall he not diminish.
4. If he do not these three unto her, then shall she go out *free* without money.

On these laws I will give you Calmet's remarks; "A father could not sell his daughter as a slave, according to the Rabbins, until she was at the age of puberty, and unless he were reduced to the utmost indigence. Besides, when a master bought an Israelitish girl, it was *always* with the presumption that he would take her to wife. Hence Moses adds, 'If she please not her master, and he does not think fit to marry her, he shall set her at liberty,' or according to the Hebrew, 'he shall let her be redeemed.' 'To sell her to another nation he shall have no power, seeing he hath dealt deceitfully with her;' as to the engagement implied, at least of taking her to wife. 'If he have betrothed her unto his son, he shall deal with her after the manner of daughters, *i. e.* he shall take care that his son uses her as his wife, that he does not despise or maltreat her. If he make his son marry another wife, he shall give her her dowry, her clothes and compensation for her virginity; if he does none of these three, she shall *go out free* without money.'" Thus were the *rights of female servants carefully secured by law* under the Jewish Dispensation; and now I would ask, are the rights of female slaves at the South thus secured? Are *they* sold only as wives and daughters-in-law, and when not treated as such, are they allowed to *go out free?* No! They have *all* not only been illegally obtained as servants according to Hebrew law, but they are also illegally *held* in bondage. Masters at the South and West have all forfeited their claims (*if they ever had any*), to their female slaves.

We come now to examine the case of those servants who were "of the heathen round about;" Were *they* left entirely unprotected by law? Horne, in speaking of the law, "Thou shalt not rule over him with rigour, but shalt fear thy God," remarks, "this law, Lev. xxv. 43, it is true, speaks expressly of slaves who were of Hebrew descent; but as *alien born* slaves were ingrafted into the Hebrew Church by circumcision, *there is no doubt* but that it applied to *all* slaves;" if so, then we may reasonably suppose that the other protective laws extended to them also; and that the only difference between Hebrew and Heathen servants lay in this, that the former served but six years unless they chose to remain longer, and were always freed at the death of their masters; whereas the latter served until the year of Jubilee, though that might include a period of forty-nine years,—and were left from father to son.

There are, however, two other laws which I have not yet noticed. The one effectually prevented *all involuntary* servitude, and the other completely abolished Jewish servitude every fifty years. They were equally operative upon the Heathen and the Hebrew.

1. "Thou shall *not* deliver unto his master the servant that is escaped from his master unto thee. He shall dwell with thee, even among you, in that place which he shall choose, in one of thy gates where it liketh him best: thou shall *not* oppress him." Deut. xxxiii. 15, 16.
2. "And ye shall hallow the fiftieth year, and proclaim *Liberty* throughout *all* the land, unto *all* the inhabitants thereof: it shall be a Jubilee unto you." Deut. xxv. 10.

Here, then, we see that by this first law, the *door of Freedom was opened wide to every servant who* had any cause whatever for complaint; if he was unhappy with his master, all he had to do was to leave him, and *no man* had a right to deliver him back to him again: and not only so, but the absconded servant was to *choose* where he should live, and no Jew was permitted to oppress him. He left his master just as our northern servants leave us; we have no power to compel them to remain with us, and no man has any right to oppress them; they go and dwell in that place where it chooseth them, and live just where they like. Is it so at the South? Is the poor runaway slave protected *by law* from the violence of that master whose oppression and cruelty has driven him from his plantation or his house? No! no! Even the free States of the North are compelled to deliver unto his master the servant that is escaped from his master unto them. By *human* law, under the *Christian Dispensation,* in the *nineteenth century, we* are commanded to do, what *God* more than *three thousand* years ago, under the *Mosaic Dispensation, positively commanded* the Jews *not* to do. In the wide domain even of our free states, there is not *one* city of refuge for the poor runaway fugitive; not one spot upon which he can stand and say, I am a free man—I am protected in my rights as a *man,* by the strong arm of the law; no! *not one.* How long the North will thus shake hands with the South in sin, I know not. How long she will stand by like the persecutor Saul *consenting* unto the death of Stephen, and keeping the raiment of them that slew him, I know not; but one thing I do know, the *guilt of the North* is increasing in a tremendous ratio as light is pouring in upon her on the subject and the sin of slavery. As the sun of righteousness climbs higher and higher in the moral heavens, she will stand still more and more abashed as the query is thundered down into her ear, "*Who* hath required *this* at thy hand!" It will be found *no* excuse then that the Constitution of our country required that *persons bound to service*, escaping from their masters, should be delivered up; no more excuse than was the reason which Adam assigned for eating the forbidden fruit. *He* was *condemned and punished because* he hearkened to the voice of *his wife*, rather than to the command of his Maker; and *we* will assuredly be condemned and punished for obeying *Man* rather than *God*, if we do not speedily repent, and bring forth fruits meet for repentance. Yea, are we not receiving chastisement even *now*?

But by the second of these laws a still more astonishing fact is disclosed. If the first effectually prevented *all involuntary servitude*, the last absolutely forbade even *voluntary servitude being perpetual*. On the great day of atonement, every fiftieth year, the Jubilee trumpet was sounded throughout the land of Judea, and *Liberty* was proclaimed to *all* the inhabitants thereof. I will not say that the servants' *chains* fell off, and their *manacles* were burst, for there is no evidence that Jewish servants *ever* felt the weight of iron chains, and collars, and handcuffs; but I do say, that even the man who had voluntarily sold himself, and the *heathen* who had been sold to a Hebrew master, were set free, the one as well as the other. This law was evidently designed to prevent the oppression of the poor, and the possibility of such a thing as *perpetual servitude* existing among them.

Where, then, I would ask, is the warrant, the justification, or the palliation of American Slavery from Hebrew servitude? How many of the southern slaves would now be in bondage according to the laws of Moses? Not one. You may observe that I have carefully avoided using the term *slavery* when speaking of Jewish servitude; and simply for this reason, that *no such thing* existed among that people; the word translated servant does *not* mean *slave*, it is the same that is applied to Abraham, to Moses, to Elisha, and the prophets generally. *Slavery*, then, *never* existed under the Jewish Dispensation at all, and I cannot but regard it as an aspersion on the character of Him who is "glorious in holiness," for any one to assert that "*God sanctioned, yea,* COMMANDED *slavery* under the old dispensation." I would fain lift my feeble voice to vindicate Jehovah's character from so foul a slander. If slaveholders are determined to hold slaves as long as they can, let them not dare to say that the God of mercy and of truth *ever* sanctioned such a system of cruelty and wrong. It is blasphemy against Him.

We have seen that the code of laws framed by Moses with regard to servants, was designed to *protect them as men and women:* to secure to them their *rights* as *human beings:* to guard them from oppression, and defend them from violence of every kind. Let us now turn to the Slave laws of the South and West, and examine them too. I will give you the substance only, because I fear I should trespass too much on your time, were I to quote them at length.

1. *Slavery* is hereditary and perpetual, to the last moment of the slave's earthly existence, and to all his descendants to the latest posterity.
2. The labour of the slave is compulsory and uncompensated; while the kind of labour, the amount of toil, the time allowed for rest, are dictated solely by the master. No bargain is made, no wages given. A pure despotism governs the human brute; and even his covering and provender, both as to quantity and quality, depend entirely on the master's discretion.*
3. The slave being considered a personal chattel, may be sold, or pledged, or leased, at the will of his master. He may be exchanged for marketable commodities, or taken in execution for the debts or taxes either of a living or

*There are laws in some of the slave states, limiting the labour which the master may require of the slave to fourteen hours daily. In some of the states there are laws requiring the masters to furnish a certain amount of food and clothing, as for instance, *one quart* of corn per day, or *one peck* per week, or *one bushel* per month, and "*one* linen shirt and pantaloons for the summer, and a linen shirt and woollen great-coat and pantaloons for the winter," &c. But "still," to use the language of Judge Stroud, "the slave is entirely under the control of his master,—is unprovided with a protector,—and, especially as he cannot be a witness or make complaint in any known mode against his master, the *apparent* object of these laws may *always* be defeated."—Ed.

dead master. Sold at auction, either individually, or in lots to suit the purchaser, he may remain with his family, or be separated from them for ever.

4. Slaves can make no contracts, and have no *legal* right to any property, real or personal. Their own honest earnings, and the legacies of friends, belong in point of law to their masters.
5. Neither a slave nor a free coloured person can be a witness against any *white,* or free person, in a court of justice, however atrocious may have been the crimes they have seen him commit, if such testimony would be for the benefit of a *slave;* but they may give testimony *against a fellow slave,* or free coloured man, even in cases affecting life, if the *master* is to reap the advantage of it.
6. The slave may be punished at his master's discretion,—without trial,—without any means of legal redress; whether his offence be real or imaginary; and the master can transfer the same despotic power to any person or persons he may choose to appoint.
7. The slave is not allowed to resist any free man under *any* circumstances: *his* only safety consists in the fact that his *owner* may bring suit and recover the price of his body, in case his life is taken, or his limbs rendered unfit for labour.
8. Slaves cannot redeem themselves, or obtain a change of masters, though cruel treatment may have rendered such a change necessary for their personal safety.
9. The slave is entirely unprotected in his domestic relations.
10. The laws greatly obstruct the manumission of slaves, even where the master is willing to enfranchise them.
11. The operation of the laws tends to deprive slaves of religious instruction and consolation.
12. The whole power of the laws is exerted to keep slaves in a state of the lowest ignorance.
13. There is in this country a monstrous inequality of law and right. What is a trifling fault in the *white* man, is considered highly criminal in the *slave;* the same offences which cost a white man a few dollars only, are punished in the negro with death.

14. The laws operate most oppressively upon free people of colour.*

Shall I ask you now, my friends, to draw the *parallel* between Jewish *servitude* and American *slavery?* No! For there is *no likeness* in the two systems; I ask you rather to mark the contrast. The laws of Moses *protected servants* in their *rights* as *men and women,* guarded them from oppression, and defended them from wrong. The Code Noir of the South *robs the slave of all his rights* as a *man*, reduces him to a chattel personal, and defends the *master* in the exercise of the most unnatural and unwarrantable power over his slave. They each bear the impress of the hand which formed them. The attributes of justice and mercy are shadowed out in the Hebrew code; those of injustice and cruelty in the Code Noir of America. Truly it was wise in the slaveholders of the South to declare their slaves to be "chattels personal;" for before they could be robbed of wages, wives, children, and friends, it was absolutely necessary to deny they were human beings. It is wise in them to keep them in abject ignorance, for the strong man armed must be bound before we can spoil his house,—the powerful intellect of man must be bound down with the iron chains of nescience before we can rob him of his rights as a man; we must reduce him to a *thing* before we can claim the right to set our feet upon his neck, because it was only *all things* which were originally *put under the feet of man* by the Almighty and Beneficent Father of all, who has declared himself to be *no respecter* of persons, whether red, white, or black.

But some have even said that Jesus Christ did not condemn slavery. To this I reply, that our holy Redeemer lived and preached among the Jews only. The laws which Moses enacted fifteen hundred years previous to his appearance among them, had never been annulled, and these laws protected every servant in Palestine. If, then, he did not condemn Jewish servitude, this does not prove that he would not have condemned such a monstrous system as that of American *slavery,* if that had existed among them. But did not Jesus condemn slavery? Let us

*See Mrs Child's Appeal, Chap. II.

examine some of his precepts. "*Whatsoever* ye would that men should do to you, do *ye even so to them.*" Let every slaveholder apply these queries to his own heart:—Am *I* willing to be a slave? Am *I* willing to see *my* wife the slave of another? Am *I* willing to see my mother a slave, or my father, my sister, or my brother? If *not*, then in holding others as slaves, I am doing what I would *not* wish to be done to me, or any relative I have; and thus have I broken this golden rule which was given *me* to walk by.

But some slaveholders have said, "we were never in bondage to any man," and therefore the yoke of bondage would be insufferable to us, but slaves are accustomed to it, their backs are fitted to the burden. Well, I am willing to admit that you who have lived in freedom would find slavery even more oppressive than the poor slave does, but then you may try this question in another form.—"Am I willing to reduce *my little child* to slavery?" You know that *if it is brought up a slave* it will never know any contrast, between freedom and bondage; its back will become fitted to the burden just as the negro child's does—*not by nature*—but by daily, violent pressure, in the same way that the head of the Indian child becomes flattened by the boards in which it is bound. It has been justly remarked that "*God never made a slave*:" he made man upright; his back was *not* made to carry burdens, nor his neck to wear a yoke; and the *man* must be crushed within him, before *his* back can be *fitted* to the burden of perpetual slavery; and that his back is *not* fitted to it, is manifest by the insurrections that so often disturb the peace and security of slaveholding countries. Who ever heard of a rebellion of the beasts of the field; and why not? simply because *they* were all placed *under the feet of man*, into whose hand they were delivered; it was originally designed that they should serve him, therefore their necks have been formed for the yoke, and their backs for the burden; but *not so with man*, intellectual, immortal man! I appeal to you, my friends, as mothers; Are you willing to enslave *your* children? You start back with horror and indignation at such a question. But why, if slavery is *no wrong* to those upon whom it is imposed? why, if, as has often been said, slaves are happier than their masters—free from the cares and perplexities of providing for themselves and their families! why not place *your children* in the way of being supported without your having the trouble to provide for them, or they for themselves? Do you not perceive that as soon as this golden rule of action is applied to *yourselves*, that you involuntarily shrink from the test; as soon as *your* actions are weighed in *this* balance of the sanctuary, that *you are found wanting?* Try yourselves by another of the Divine precepts,—"Thou shalt love thy neighbour as thyself." Can we love a man *as* we love *ourselves,* if we do, and continue to do, unto him, what we would not wish any one to do to us? Look, too, at Christ's example; what does he say of himself? "I came *not* to be ministered unto, but to minister." Can you for a moment imagine the meek, and lowly, and compassionate Saviour, *a slaveholder*? do you not shudder at this thought as much as at that of his being *a warrior*? But why, if slavery is not sinful?

Again, it has been said, the Apostle Paul did not condemn Slavery, for he sent Onesimus back to Philemon. I do not think it can be said he sent him back, for no coercion was made use of. Onesimus was not thrown into prison, and then sent back in chains to his master, as your runaway slaves often are. This could not possibly have been the case, because you know Paul, as a Jew, was *bound to protect* the runaway: *he had no right* to send any fugitive back to his master. The state of the case then seems to have been this. Onesimus had been an unprofitable servant to Philemon, and left him; he afterward became converted under the Apostle's preaching, and seeing that he had been to blame in his conduct, and desiring by future fidelity to atone for past error, he wished to return, and the Apostle gave him the letter we now have as a recommendation to Philemon, informing him of the conversion of Onesimus, and entreating him, as "Paul the aged," "to receive him, *not* now as a *servant*, but *above* a servant, a brother beloved, especially to me, but how much more unto thee, both in the flesh and in the Lord. If thou count *me* therefore as a partner, *receive him as myself.*" This, then, surely, cannot be forced into a justification of the practice of returning runaway slaves back to their masters, to be punished with cruel beatings and scourgings as they often are. Besides the word δουλος. here translated servant, is the same that is made use of in Matt. xviii. 27. Now it appears that this servant owed his lord ten thousand talents; he possessed property to a vast amount. Onesimus could not then have been a *slave*, for slaves do not own their wives, or children; no, not even their own bodies, much less property. But again, the servitude which the apostle was accustomed to, must have been very different from American slavery; for he says, "the heir (or son), as long as he is a child, differeth *nothing from a servant*, though he be lord of all, but is under *tutors* and governors until the time appointed of the father." From this it appears, that the means of *instruction* were provided for *servants* as well as children; and indeed we know it must have been so among the Jews, because their servants were not permitted to remain in perpetual bondage, and therefore it was absolutely necessary they should be prepared to occupy higher stations in society than those of servants. Is it so at the South, my friends? Is the daily bread of instruction provided for *your slaves?* are their minds enlightened, and they gradually prepared to rise from the grade of menials into that of *free*, independent members of the state? Let your own statute book, and your own daily experience, answer these questions.

If this apostle sanctioned *slavery*, why did he exhort masters thus, in his epistle to the Ephesians, "and ye, masters, do the same things unto them (*i. e.* perform your duties to your servants as unto Christ, not unto me), *forbearing threatening;* knowing that your master also is in heaven, neither is *there respect of persons with him.*" And in Colossians, "Masters give unto your servants that which is *just and equal,* knowing that ye also have a master in heaven." Let slaveholders only *obey* these injunctions of Paul, and I am satisfied slavery would soon be abolished. If he thought it sinful even to *threaten* servants, surely he must have thought it sinful to flog and to beat them with sticks and paddles; indeed, when delineating the character of a bishop, he expressly names this as one feature of it, "*no striker.*" Let masters give unto their servants that which is *just* and *equal*, and all that vast system of unrequited labour would crumble into ruin. Yes, and if they once felt they had no right to the *labour* of their servants without pay, surely they could not think they had a right to the wives, the children, and the bodies of slaves. Again, how can it be said Paul sanctioned slavery, when, as though to put this matter beyond all doubt, in that black catalogue of sins enumerated in his first epistle to Timothy, he mentions "*menstealers*," which word may be translated "*slavedealers*." But you may say, we all despise slavedealers as much as any one can; they are never admitted into genteel or respectable society. And why not? Is it not because even you shrink back from the idea of associating with those who make their fortunes by trading in the bodies and souls of men, women, and children? whose daily work it is to break human hearts, by tearing wives from their husbands, and children from their parents? But why hold slavedealers as despicable, if their trade is lawful and virtuous? and why despise them more than the *gentlemen of fortune and standing* who employ them as *their* agents? Why more than the *professors of religion* who barter their fellow-professors to them for gold and silver? We do not despise the land agent, or the physician, or the merchant: and why? Simply, because their professions are virtuous and honourable; and if the trade of men-jobbers was honourable, you would not despise them either. There is no difference in *principle*, in *Christian ethics*, between the despised slavedealer, and the *Christian* who buys slaves from, or sells slaves to him. Indeed, if slaves were not wanted by the respectable, the wealthy, and the religious in a community, there would be no slaves in that community, and of course no *slavedealers*. It is then the *Christians*, and the *honourable men* and *women* of the South, who are the *main pillars* of this grand temple built to Mammon and to Moloch. It is the *most enlightened* in every country who are *most* to blame when any public sin is supported by public opinion: hence Isaiah says, "*When* the Lord hath performed his whole work upon mount *Zion* and on *Jerusalem*, (then) I will punish the fruit of the stout heart of the king of Assyria, and the glory of his high looks." And was it not so? Open the historical records of that age: was not Israel carried into captivity B. C. 606? Judah B. C. 588? and the stout heart of the heathen monarchy not punished until B. C. 536, fifty-two years *after* Judah's, and seventy years *after* Israel's captivity, when it was overthrown by Cyrus, king of Persia? Hence, too, the apostle Peter says, "judgment must *begin at the house of God*." Surely this would not be the case, if the *professors of religion* were not *most worthy* of blame.

But it may be asked, why are *they* most culpable? I will tell you, my friends. It is because sin is imputed to us just in proportion to the spiritual light we receive. Thus the prophet Amos says, in the name of Jehovah, "*You only* have I known of all the families of the earth; *therefore* I will punish *you* for all your iniquities." Hear, too, the doctrine of our Lord on this important subject: "The servant who *knew* his Lord's will, and *prepared not* himself, neither did according to his will, shall be beaten with *many* stripes:" And why? "For unto whomsoever *much* is given, *of him* shall *much* be required; and to whom men have committed *much*, of *him* they will ask the *more*." Oh! then, that the *Christians* of the south would ponder these things in their hearts, and awake to the vast responsibilities which rest *upon them* at this important crisis.

I have thus, I think, clearly proved to you seven propositions, viz.: First, that slavery is contrary to the declaration of our independence. Second, that it is contrary to the first charter of human rights given to Adam, and renewed to Noah. Third, that the fact of slavery having been the subject of prophecy, furnishes *no* excuse whatever to slavedealers. Fourth, that no such system existed under the patriarchal dispensation. Fifth, that *slavery never* existed under the Jewish dispensation; but so far otherwise, that every servant was placed under the *protection of law*, and care taken, not only to prevent all *involuntary* servitude, but all *voluntary perpetual* bondage. Sixth, that slavery in America reduces a *man* to a *thing*, a "chattel personal," *robs him* of *all* his rights as a *human being*, fetters both his mind and body, and protects the *master* in the most unnatural and unreasonable power, whilst it *throws him out* of the protection of law. Seventh, that slavery is contrary to the example and precepts of our holy and merciful Redeemer, and of his apostles.

But, perhaps you will be ready to query, why appeal to *women* on this subject? *We* do not make the laws which perpetuate slavery. *No* legislative power is vested in *us*; *we* can do nothing to overthrow the system, even if we wished to do so. To this I reply, I know you do not make the laws, but I also know that *you are the wives and mothers, the sisters and daughters, of those who do;* and if you really suppose *you* can do nothing to overthrow slavery, you are greatly mistaken. You can do much in every way; four things I will name. 1st, You can read on this subject. 2d, You can pray over this subject. 3d, You can speak on this subject. 4th, You can *act* on this subject. I have placed reading before praying, not because I regard it more important, but because, in order to pray aright, we must understand what we are praying for; it is only then we can "pray with the understanding and the spirit also."

1. Read, then, on the subject of slavery. Search the Scriptures daily, whether the things I have told you are true. Other books and papers might be a great help to you in this investigation, but they are not necessary, and it is hardly probable that your Committees of Vigilance will allow you to have any other. The *Bible*, then, is the book I want you to read in the spirit of inquiry, and the spirit of prayer. Even the enemies of Abolitionists acknowledge that their doctrines are drawn from it. In the great mob in Boston, last autumn, when the books and papers of the Anti-Slavery Society were thrown out of the windows of their office, one individual laid hold of the Bible, and was about tossing it out to the ground, when another reminded him that it was the Bible he had in his hand. "*O! 'tis all one,*" he replied, and out went the sacred volume along with the rest. We thank him for the acknowledgment. Yes, "*it is all one,*" for our books and papers are mostly commentaries on the Bible, and the Declaration. Read the *Bible* then: it contains the words of Jesus, and they are spirit and life. Judge for yourselves, whether *he sanctioned* such a system of oppression and crime.

2. Pray over this subject. When you have entered into your closets, and shut to the doors, then pray to your father who seeth in secret, that he would open your eyes to see whether slavery is *sinful,* and if it is, that he would enable you to bear a faithful, open, and unshrinking testimony against it, and to do whatsoever your hands find to do, leaving the consequences entirely to Him, who still says to us, whenever we try to reason away duty from the fear of consequences, "*What is that to thee, follow thou me.*" Pray also for that poor slave, that he may be kept patient and submissive under his hard lot, until God is pleased to open the door of freedom to him, without violence or bloodshed. Pray, too, for the master, that his heart may be soft-

ened, and he made willing to acknowledge, as Joseph's brethren did, "Verily we are guilty concerning our brother," before he will be compelled to add, in consequence of Divine judgment, "therefore is all this evil come upon us." Pray also for all your brethren and sisters who are labouring in the righteous cause of Emancipation in the Northern States, England, and the world. There is great encouragement for prayer in these words of our Lord,—"Whatsoever ye shall ask the Father *in my name,* he *will give* it to you." Pray then without ceasing, in the closet and the social circle.

3. Speak on this subject. It is through the tongue, the pen, and the press, that truth is principally propagated. Speak, then, to your relatives, your friends, your acquaintances, on the subject of slavery; be not afraid if you are conscientiously convinced it is *sinful,* to say so openly, but calmly, and to let your sentiments be known. If you are served by the slaves of others, try to ameliorate their condition as much as possible; never aggravate their faults, and thus add fuel to the fire of anger already kindled in a master and mistress's bosom; remember their extreme ignorance, and consider them as your Heavenly Father does, the *less* culpable on this account, even when they do wrong things. Discountenance *all* cruelty to them, all starvation, all corporal chastisement; these may brutalize and *break* their spirits, but will never bend them to willing, cheerful obedience. If possible, see that they are comfortably and *seasonably* fed, whether in the house or the field; it is unreasonable and cruel to expect slaves to wait for their breakfast until eleven o'clock, when they rise at five or six. Do all you can to induce their owners to clothe them well, and to allow them many little indulgences which would contribute to their comfort. Above all, try to persuade your husband, father, brothers, and sons, that *slavery is a crime against God and man,* and that it is a great sin to keep *human beings* in such abject ignorance; to deny them the privilege of learning to read and write. The Catholics are universally condemned for denying the Bible to the common people, but *slaveholders must not* blame them, for *they* are doing the *very same thing,* and for the very same reason, neither of these systems can bear the light which bursts from the pages of that Holy Book. And lastly, endeavour to inculcate submission on the part of the

slaves, but whilst doing this be faithful in pleading the cause of the oppressed.

> Will *you* behold unheeding,
> Life's holiest feelings crushed;
> When *woman's* heart is bleeding,
> Shall *woman's* voice be hushed?

4. Act on this subject. Some of you *own* slaves yourselves. If you believe slavery is *sinful*, set them at liberty, "undo the heavy burdens, and let the oppressed go free." If they wish to remain with you, pay them wages; if not, let them leave you. Should they remain, teach them, and have them taught the common branches of an English education; they have minds, and those minds *ought to be improved*. So precious a talent as intellect, never was given to be wrapped in a napkin, and buried in the earth. It is the *duty* of all, as far as they can, to improve their own mental faculties, because we are commanded to love God with *all our minds*, as well as with all our hearts, and we commit a great sin, if we *forbid or prevent* that cultivation of the mind in others, which would enable them to perform this duty. Teach your servants then to read, &c., and encourage them to believe it is their *duty* to learn, if it were only that they might read the Bible.

But some of you will say, we can neither free our slaves nor teach them to read, for the laws of our state forbid it. Be not surprised when I say such wicked laws *ought to be no barrier* in the way of your duty, and I appeal to the Bible to prove this position. What was the conduct of Shiphrah and Puah, when the king of Egypt issued his cruel mandate, with regard to the Hebrew children? "*They* feared *God*, and did *not* as the king of Egypt commanded them, but saved the men children alive." Did these *women* do right in disobeying that monarch? "*Therefore* (says the sacred text), *God dealt well* with them, and made them houses," Ex. i. What was the conduct of Shadrach, Meshach, and Abednego, when Nebuchadnezzar set up a golden image in the plain of Dura, and commanded all people, nations, and languages, to fall down and worship it? "Be it known unto thee (said these faithful *Jews*), O king, that *we will not* serve thy gods, nor worship the image which thou hast set up." Did these men *do right in disobeying the law* of their sovereign? Let their miraculous deliverance from the burning fiery furnace, answer; Dan. iii. What was the conduct of Daniel, when Darius made a firm decree that no one should ask a petition of any man or God for thirty days? Did the prophet cease to pray? No! "When Daniel *knew that the writing was signed,* he went into his house, and his windows being *open* toward Jerusalem, he kneeled upon his knees three times a day, and prayed and gave thanks before his God, as he did aforetime." Did Daniel do right thus to *break* the law of his king? Let his wonderful deliverance out of the mouths of the lions answer; Dan. vii. Look, too, at the Apostles Peter and John. When the rulers of the Jews, "*commanded them not* to speak at all, nor teach in the name of Jesus," what did they say? "Whether it be right in the sight of God, to hearken unto you more than unto God, judge ye." And what did they do? "They spake the word of God with boldness, and with great power gave the Apostles witness of the *resurrection* of the Lord Jesus;" although *this* was the very doctrine, for the preaching of which, they had just been cast into prison, and further threatened. Did these men do right? I leave *you* to answer, who now enjoy the benefits of their labours and sufferings, in that Gospel they dared to preach when positively commanded *not to teach any more* in the name of Jesus. Acts iv.

But some of you may say, if we do free our slaves they will be taken up and sold, therefore there will be no use in doing it. Peter and John might just as well have said we will not preach the Gospel, for if we do, we shall be taken up and put in prison, therefore there will be no use in our preaching. *Consequences,* my friends, belong no more to *you,* than they did to these apostles. Duty is ours, and events are God's. If you think slavery is sinful, all *you* have to do is to set your slaves at liberty; do all you can to protect them; and in humble faith and fervent prayer, commend them to your common Father. He can take care of them; but if for wise purposes he sees fit to allow them to be sold, this will afford you an opportunity of testifying openly, wherever you go, against the crime of *manstealing.* Such an act will be *clear robbery,* and if exposed, might, under the Divine direction, do the cause of Emancipation more good, than any thing that could happen:—for, "He makes even the wrath of man to praise him, and the remainder of wrath he will restrain."

I know that this doctrine of obeying *God,* rather than man, will be considered as dangerous, and heretical by many, but I am not afraid openly to avow it, because it is the doctrine of the Bible; but I would not be understood to advocate resistance to any law, however oppressive, if, in obeying it, I was not obliged to commit *sin.* If, for instance, there was a law, which imposed imprisonment or a fine upon me if I manumitted a slave, I would on no account resist that law, I would set the slave free, and then go to prison, or pay the fine. If a law commands me to *sin, I will break it;* if it calls me to *suffer,* I will let it take its course *unresistingly.* The doctrine of *blind* obedience and *unqualified* submission to *any human* power, whether civil or ecclesiastical, is the doctrine of despotism, and ought to have no place among Republicans and Christians.

But you will perhaps say, such a course of conduct would inevitably expose us to great suffering. Yes! my christian friends, I believe it would, but this will *not* excuse you or any one else for the neglect of *duty.* If Prophets and Apostles, Martyrs and Reformers, had not been willing to suffer for the truth's sake, where would the world have been now? If they had said, we cannot speak the truth, we cannot do what we believe is right, because the *laws of our country or public opinion are against us,* where would our holy religion have been now? The Prophets were stoned, imprisoned, and killed by the Jews. And why? Because they exposed and openly rebuked public sins; they opposed public opinion; had they held their peace, they all might have lived in ease, and died in favour with a wicked generation. Why were the Apostles persecuted from city to city, stoned, incarcerated, beaten, and crucified? Because they dared to *speak the truth;* to tell the Jews, boldly and fearlessly, that *they* were the *murderers* of the Lord of Glory, and that, however great a stumbling block the Cross might be to them, there was no other name given under heaven by which men could be saved, but the name of Jesus. Because they declared, even at Athens, the seat of learning and refinement, the self-evident truth, "that they be no gods that are made with men's hands," and exposed to the

Grecians the foolishness of worldly wisdom, and the impossibility of salvation but through Christ, whom they despised on account of the ignominious death he died. Because at Rome, the proud mistress of the world, they thundered out the terrors of the law upon that idolatrous, war-making, and slaveholding community. Why were the martyrs stretched upon the rack, gibbeted, and burnt, the scorn and diversion of a Nero, whilst their tarred and burning bodies sent up a light which illuminated the Roman capital? Why were the Waldenses hunted like wild beasts upon the mountains of Piedmont, and slain with the sword of the Duke of Savoy, and the proud monarch of France? Why were the Presbyterians chased like the partridge over the highlands of Scotland,—the Methodists pumped upon, and stoned, and pelted with rotten eggs,—the Quakers incarcerated in filthy prisons, beaten, whipped at the cart's tail, banished, and hanged? Because they dared to *speak* the *truth;* to *break* the unrighteous *laws* of their country; and chose rather to suffer affliction with the people of God, "not accepting deliverance," even under the gallows. Why were Luther and Calvin persecuted and excommunicated, and Cranmer, Ridley, and Latimer burnt? Because they fearlessly proclaimed the truth, though that truth was contrary to public opinion, and the authority of Ecclesiastical councils and conventions. Now, all this vast amount of human suffering might have been saved. All these Prophets and Apostles, Martyrs and Reformers, might have lived and died in peace with all men; but following the example of their great pattern, "they despised the shame, endured the cross, and are now set down on the right hand of the throne of God," having received the glorious welcome of "well *done* good and faithful servants, enter ye into the joy of your Lord."

But you may say we are *women*, how can *our* hearts endure persecution? And why not? Have not *women* stood up in all the dignity and strength of moral courage to be the leaders of the people, and to bear a faithful testimony for the truth whenever the providence of God has called them to do so? Are there no *women* in that noble army of martyrs who are now singing the song of Moses and the Lamb? Who led out the women of Israel from the house of bondage, striking the timbrel, and singing the song of deliverance on the banks of that sea, whose waters stood up like walls of crystal, to open a passage for their escape? It was a *woman*; Miriam, the prophetess, the sister of Moses and Aaron. Who went up with Barak to Kadesh to fight against Jabin, King of Canaan, into whose hand Israel had been sold, because of their iniquities? It was a *a woman!* Deborah the wife of Lapidoth, the judge, as well as the prophetess of that backsliding people; Judges iv. 9. Into whose hands was Sisera, the captain of Jabin's host delivered? Into the hand of a *woman.* Jael the wife of Heber! Judges vi. 21. Who dared to *speak the truth* concerning those judgments which were coming upon Judea, when Josiah, alarmed at finding that his people "had not kept the word of the Lord, to do after all that was written in the book of the Law," sent to inquire of the Lord concerning these things? It was a *woman.* Huldah the prophetess, the wife of Shallum; 2 Chron. xxxiv. 22. Who was chosen to deliver the whole Jewish nation, from that murderous decree of Persia's King, which wicked Haman had obtained by calumny and fraud? It was a *woman*; Esther the Queen. Yes, weak and trembling *woman* was the instrument appointed by God, to reverse the bloody mandate of the eastern monarch, and save the *whole visible church* from destruction. What human voice first proclaimed to Mary that she should be the mother of our Lord? It was a *woman!* Elizabeth, the wife of Zacharias; Luke i. 42, 43. Who united with the good old Simeon in giving thanks publicly in the temple, when the child, Jesus, was presented there by his parents, "and spake of him to all them that looked for redemption in Jerusalem?" It was a *woman!* Anna the prophetess. Who first proclaimed Christ as the true Messiah in the streets of Samaria, once the capital of the ten tribes? It was a *woman!*

Who ministered to the Son of God whilst on earth, a despised and persecuted Reformer, in the humble garb of a carpenter? They were *women!* Who followed the rejected King of Israel, as his fainting footsteps trod the road to Calvary? "A great company of people and of *women*;" and it is remarkable that to *them alone,* he turned and addressed the pathetic language, "Daughters of Jerusalem, weep not for me, but weep for yourselves and your children." Ah! who sent unto the Roman Governor when he was set down on the judgment seat, saying unto him, "Have thou nothing to do with that just man, for I have suffered many things this day in a dream because of him?" It was a *woman!* the wife of Pilate. Although "*he knew* that for envy the Jews had delivered Christ," yet *he* consented to surrender the Son of God into the hands of a brutal soldiery, after having himself scourged his naked body. Had the *wife* of Pilate sat upon that judgment seat, what would have been the result of the trial of this "just person?"

And who last hung round the cross of Jesus, on the mountain of Golgotha? Who first visited the sepulchre early in the morning on the first day of the week, carrying sweet spices to embalm his precious body, not knowing that it was incorruptible, and could not be holden by the bands of death? These were *women!* To whom did he *first* appear after his resurrection? It was to a *woman!* Mary Magdalene; Mark xvi. 9. Who gathered with the apostles to wait at Jerusalem, in prayer and supplication, for "the promise of the Father;" the spiritual blessing of the Great High Priest of his Church, who had entered, *not* into the splendid temple of Solomon, there to offer the blood of bulls and of goats, and the smoking censer upon the golden altar, but into Heaven itself, there to present his intercessions, after having "given himself for us, an offering and a sacrifice to God for a sweet-smelling savour?" *Women* were among that holy company; Acts i. 14. And did *women* wait in vain? Did those who had ministered to his necessities, followed in his train, and wept at his crucifixion, wait in vain? No! No! Did the cloven tongues of fire descend upon the heads of *women* as well as men? Yes, my friends, "it sat upon *each of them;*" Acts ii. 3. *Women*, as well as men, were to be living stones in the temple of grace, and therefore *their* heads were consecrated by the descent of the Holy Ghost, as well as those of men. Were *women* recognized as fellow-labourers in the gospel field? They were! Paul says, in his epistle to the Philippians, "help those *women* who laboured with me in the gospel;" Phil. iv. 3.

But this is not all. Roman *women* were burnt at the stake; *their* delicate limbs were torn joint from joint by the ferocious beasts of the Amphitheatre, and tossed by the wild bull in his fury, for the diversion of that idolatrous, warlike, and slaveholding people. Yes, *women* suffered under the ten persecutions of heathen Rome, with the most unshrinking constancy and fortitude; not all the entreaties of friends, nor the claims of new born infancy, nor the cruel threats of enemies, could make *them* sprinkle one grain of incense upon the altars of Roman idols. Come now with me to the beautiful valleys of Piedmont. Whose blood stains the green sward, and decks the wild flowers with colours not their own, and smokes on the sword of persecuting France? It is *woman's*, as well as man's! Yes, *women* were accounted as sheep from the slaughter, and were cut down as the tender saplings of the wood.

But time would fail me to tell of all those hundreds and thousands of *women* who perished in the low countries of Holland, when Alva's sword of vengeance was unsheathed against the Protestants, when the Catholic Inquisitions of Europe became the merciless executioners of vindictive wrath upon those who dared to worship God, instead of bowing down in holy adoration before "my Lord God, the *Pope*," and when England, too, burnt her Ann Ascoes at the stake of martyrdom. Suffice it to say, that the Church, after having been driven from Judea to Rome, and from Rome to Piedmont, and from Piedmont to England, and from England to Holland, at last stretched her fainting wings over the dark bosom of the Atlantic; and found, on the shores of a great wilderness, a refuge from tyranny and oppression, as she thought; but *even here* (the warm blush of shame mantles my cheek as I write it), *even here, woman* was beaten and banished, imprisoned, and hung upon the gallows, a trophy to the Cross.

And what, I would ask in conclusion, have *women* done for the great and glorious cause of Emancipation? Who wrote that pamphlet which moved the heart of Wilberforce to pray over the wrongs, and his tongue to plead the cause of the oppressed African? It was a *woman*, Elizabeth Heyrick. Who laboured assiduously to keep the sufferings of the slave continually before the British public? They were *women*. And how did they do it? By their needles, paint-brushes, and pens; by speaking the truth, and petitioning Parliament for the abolition of slavery. And what was the effect of their labours? Read it in the Emancipation bill of Great Britain. Read it in the present state of her West India Colonies. Read it in the impulse which has been given to the cause of freedom in the United States of America. Have

English women, then, done so much for the negro, and shall American women do nothing? Oh no! Already are there sixty female Anti-Slavery Societies in operation. These are doing just what the English women did: telling the story of the coloured man's wrongs; praying for his deliverance; and presenting his kneeling image constantly before the public eye on bags and needle-books, card-racks, pen-wipers, pin-cushions, &c. Even the children of the north have inscribed on their handy-work, "May the points of our needles prick the slaveholder's conscience." Some of the reports of these Societies exhibit not only considerable talent, but a deep sense of religious duty, and a determination to persevere through evil as well as good report, until every scourge, and every shackle, is buried under the feet of the manumitted slave.

The Ladies' Anti-Slavery Society of Boston was called last autumn to a severe trial of their faith and constancy. They were mobbed by "the gentlemen of property and standing," in that city, at their anniversary meeting; and their lives were jeoparded by an infuriated crowd; but their conduct on that occasion did credit to our sex, and affords a full assurance that they will *never* abandon the cause of the slave. The pamphlet, "Right and Wrong in Boston," issued by them, in which a particular account is given of that "mob of broad cloth in broad day," does equal credit to the head and the heart of her who wrote it. I wish my Southern sisters could read it; they would then understand that the women of the North have engaged in this work from a sense of *religious duty*, and that nothing will ever induce them to take their hands from it until it is fully accomplished. They feel no hostility to you, no bitterness or wrath; they rather sympathize in your trials and difficulties; but they well know, that the first thing to be done to help you, is to pour in the light of truth on your minds, to urge you to reflect on, and pray over the subject. This is all *they* can do for you, *you* must work out your own deliverance with fear and trembling; and with the direction and blessing of God, *you can do it.* Northern women may labour to produce a correct public opinion at the North, but if Southern women sit down in listless indifference and criminal idleness, public opinion cannot be rectified and purified at the South. It is manifest to every reflecting mind, that slavery must be abolished; the era in which we live, and the light which is overspreading the whole world on this subject, clearly show that the time cannot be distant when it will be done. Now, there are only two ways in which it can be effected, by *moral* power, or *physical* force, and it is for *you* to choose which of these you prefer. Slavery always has, and always will, produce insurrections wherever it exists, because it is a violation of the natural order of things, and no human power can much longer perpetuate it. The opposers of abolitionists fully believe this; one of them remarked to me not long since, "there is no doubt there will be a most terrible overturning at the South in a few years, such cruelty and wrong must be visited with Divine vengeance soon." Abolitionists believe, too, that this must inevitably be the case if you do not repent, and they are not willing to leave you to perish without entreating you to save yourselves from destruction; well may they say with the apostle, "am I then your enemy because I tell you the truth," and warn you to flee from impending judgments.

But why, my dear friends, have I thus been endeavouring to lead you through the history of more than three thousand years, and to point you to that great cloud of witnesses who have gone before, "from works to rewards?" Have I been seeking to magnify the sufferings, and exalt the character of woman, that she "might have praise of men?" No! no! my object has been to arouse *you*, as the wives and mothers, the daughters and sisters of the South, to a sense of your duty as *women*, and as Christian women, on that great subject, which has already shaken our country, from the St Lawrence and the lakes to the Gulf of Mexico, and from the Mississippi to the shores of the Atlantic; *and will continue mightily to shake it*, until the polluted temple of slavery fall and crumble into ruin. I would say unto each one of you, "what meanest thou, O sleeper! arise and call upon thy God, if so be that God will think upon us that we perish not." Perceive you not that dark cloud of vengeance which hangs over our boasting Republic? Saw you not the lightnings of Heaven's wrath in the flame which leaped from the Indian's torch to the roof of yonder dwelling, and lighted with its horrid glare the darkness of midnight? Heard you not the thunders of Divine anger, as the distant roar of the cannon came rolling onward from the Texian country, where Protestant American Rebels are fighting with Mexican Republicans—for what? For the re-establishment of *slavery;* yes! of American slavery in the bosom of a Catholic Republic, where that system of robbery, violence, and wrong, had been legally abolished for seven years. Yes! citizens of the United States, after plundering Mexico of her land, are now engaged in deadly conflict for the privilege of fastening chains, and collars, and manacles—upon whom? upon the subjects of some foreign prince? No! upon native born American Republican citizens, although the fathers of these very men declared to the whole world, while struggling to free themselves from the three-penny taxes of an English king, that they believed it to be a *self-evident* truth that *all men* were created equal, and had an *unalienable right to liberty.*

Well may the poet exclaim in bitter sarcasm,

> The fustian flag that proudly waves,
> In solemn mockery *o'er a land of slaves.*

Can you not, my friends, understand the signs of the times; do you not see the sword of retributive justice hanging over the South, or are you still slumbering at your posts?—Are there no Shiphrahs, no Puahs among you, who will dare in Christian firmness and Christian meekness, to refuse to obey the *wicked laws* which require *woman to enslave, to degrade, and to brutalize woman?* Are there no Miriams who would rejoice to lead out the captive daughters of the Southern States to liberty and light? Are there no Huldahs there who will dare to *speak the truth* concerning the sins of the people, and those judgments, which it requires no prophet's eye to see, must follow, if repentance is not speedily sought? Is there no Esther among you who will plead for the poor devoted slave? Read the history of this Persian queen, it is full of instruction; she at first refused to plead for the Jews; but hear the words of Mordecai, "Think not within thyself that *thou* shalt escape in the king's house more than all the Jews, for *if thou altogether holdest thy peace at this time,* then shall there enlargement and deliverance arise to the Jews from another place: but *thou and thy father's house shall be destroyed.*" Listen, too, to her magnanimous reply to this powerful appeal; "*I will* go in unto the king, which is *not* according to law, and if I perish, I perish." Yes! if there were but *one* Esther at the South, she *might* save her country from ruin; but let the Christian women there arise, as the Christian women of Great Britain did, in the majesty of moral power, and that salvation is certain. Let them embody themselves in societies, and send petitions up to their different legislatures, entreating their husbands, fathers, brothers, and sons, to abolish the institution of slavery; no longer to subject *woman* to the scourge and the chain, to mental darkness and moral degradation; no longer to tear husbands from their wives, and children from their parents; no longer to make men, women, and children, work *without wages;* no longer to make their lives bitter in hard bondage; no longer to reduce *American citizens* to the abject condition of *slaves*, of "chattels personal;" no longer to barter the *image of God* in human shambles for corruptible things such as silver and gold.

The *women of the South can overthrow* this horrible system of oppression and cruelty, licentiousness and wrong. Such appeals to your legislatures would be irresistible, for there is something in the heart of man which *will bend under moral suasion.* There is a swift witness for truth in his bosom, which *will respond to truth* when it is uttered with calmness and dignity. If you could obtain but six signatures to such a petition in only one state, I would say, send up that petition, and be not in the least discouraged by the scoffs and jeers of the heartless, or the resolution of the house to lay it on the table. It will be a great thing if the subject can be introduced into your legislatures in any way, even by *women,* and *they* will be the most likely to introduce it there in the best possible manner, as a matter of *morals* and *religion,* not of expediency or politics. You may petition, too, the different ecclesiastical bodies of the slave states. Slavery must be attacked with the whole power of truth and the sword of the spirit. You must take it up on *Christian* ground, and fight against it with Christian weapons, whilst your feet are shod with the preparation of the gospel of peace. And *you are now* loudly called upon by the cries of the widow and the orphan, to arise and gird yourselves for this great moral conflict, with the whole armour of righteousness upon the right hand and on the left.

There is every encouragement for you to labour and pray, my friends, because the abolition of slavery as well as its existence has been the theme of prophecy. "Ethiopia (says the Psalmist) shall stretch forth her hands unto God." And is she not now doing so? Are not the Christian negroes of the south lifting their hands in prayer for deliverance, just as the Israelites did when their redemption was drawing nigh? Are they not sighing and crying by reason of the hard bondage? And think you that He, of whom it was said, "and God heard their groaning, and their cry came up unto him by reason of the hard bondage," think you that his ear is heavy that he cannot *now* hear the cries of his suffering children? Or that He who raised up a Moses, an Aaron, and a Miriam, to bring them up out of the land of Egypt from the house of bondage, cannot now, with a high hand, and a stretched out arm, save the poor negroes out of the hands of their masters? Surely you believe that his arm is *not* shortened that he cannot save. And would not such a work of mercy redound to his glory? But another string of the harp of prophecy vibrates to the song of deliverance: "But they shall sit every man under his vine, and under his fig-tree, and *none shall make them afraid;* for the mouth of the Lord of Hosts hath spoken it." The *slave* never can do this as long as he is a *slave;* whilst he is a "chattel personal," he can own *no* property; but the time *is to come* when *every* man is to sit under *his own* vine and *his own* fig-tree, and no domineering driver, or irresponsible master, or irascible mistress, shall make him afraid of the chain or the whip. Hear, too, the sweet tones of another string: "Many shall run to and fro, and *knowledge* shall be increased." Slavery is an insurmountable barrier to the increase of knowledge in every community where it exists; *slavery, then, must be abolished before* this prediction can be fulfilled. The last chord I shall touch will be this, "They shall *not* hurt nor destroy in all my holy mountain."

Slavery, then, must be overthrown before the prophecies can be accomplished; but how are they to be fulfilled? Will the wheels of the millennial car be rolled onward by miraculous power? No! God designs to confer this holy privilege upon *man;* it is through *his* instrumentality that the great and glorious work of reforming the world is to be done. And see you not how the mighty engine of *moral power* is dragging in its rear the Bible and peace societies, anti-slavery and temperance, sabbath schools, moral reform, and missions? or to adopt another figure, do not these seven philanthropic associations compose the beautiful tints in that bow of promise which spans the arch of our moral heaven? Who does not believe, that if these societies were broken up, their constitutions burnt, and the vast machinery with which they are labouring to regenerate mankind was stopped, that the black clouds of vengeance would soon burst over our world, and every city would witness the fate of the devoted cities of the plain? Each one of these societies is walking abroad through the earth scattering the seeds of truth over the wide field of our world, not with the hundred hands of a Briareus, but with a hundred thousand.

Another encouragement for you to labour, my friends, is, that you will have the prayers and co-operation of English and Northern philanthropists. You will never bend your knees in supplication at the throne of grace for the overthrow of slavery, without meeting there the spirits of other Christians, who will mingle their voices with yours, as the morning or evening sacrifice ascends to God. Yes, the spirit of prayer and of supplication has been poured out upon many, many hearts; there are wrestling Jacobs who will not let go of the prophetic promises of deliverance for the captive, and the opening of prison doors to them that are bound. There are Pauls who are saying, in reference to this subject, "Lord, what wilt thou have me to do?" There are Marys sitting in the house now, who are ready to arise and go forth in this work as soon as the message is brought, "the master is come and calleth for thee?" And there are Marthas, too, who have already gone out to meet Jesus, as he bends his footsteps to their brother's grave, and weeps, *not* over the lifeless body of Lazarus bound hand and foot in grave-clothes, but over the politically and intellectually lifeless slave, bound hand and foot in the iron chains of oppression and ignorance. Some may be ready to say, as Martha did, who seemed to expect nothing but sympathy from Jesus, "Lord, by this time he stinketh, for he hath been dead four days." She thought it useless to remove the stone and expose the loathsome body of her brother; she could not believe that so great a miracle could be wrought, as to raise *that putrified body* into life; but "Jesus said, take *ye* away the stone; and when *they* had taken away the stone where the dead was laid, and uncovered the body of Lazarus, then it was that "Jesus lifted up his eyes and said, Father, I thank thee that thou hast heard me," &c. "And when he had thus spoken, he cried with a loud voice, Lazarus, come forth." Yes, some may be ready to say of the coloured race, how can *they* ever be raised politically and intellectually, they have been dead four hundred years? But *we* have *nothing* to do with *how* this is to be done; *our business* is to take away the stone which has covered up the dead body of our brother, to expose the putrid carcass, to show *how* that body has been bound with the grave-clothes of heathen ignorance, and his face with the napkin of prejudice, and having done all it was our duty to do, to stand by the negro's grave, in humble faith and holy hope, waiting to hear the life-giving command of "Lazarus, come forth." This is just what Anti-Slavery Societies are doing; they are taking away the stone from the mouth of the tomb of slavery, where lies the putrid carcass of our brother. They want the pure light of heaven to shine into that dark and gloomy cave; they want all men to see *how* that dead body has been bound, *how* that face has been wrapped in the *napkin of prejudice;* and shall they wait beside that grave in vain? Is not Jesus still the resurrection and the life? Did He come to proclaim liberty to the captive, and the opening of prison doors to them that are bound in vain? Did He promise to give beauty for ashes, the oil of joy for mourning, and the garment of praise for the spirit of heaviness unto them that mourn in Zion, and will He refuse to beautify the mind, anoint the head, and throw around the captive negro the mantle of praise for that spirit of heaviness, which has so long bound him down to the ground? Or shall we not rather say with the prophet, "the zeal of the Lord of Hosts *will* perform this?" Yes, his promises are sure, and amen in Christ Jesus, that he will assemble her that halteth, and gather her that is driven out, and her that is afflicted.

But I will now say a few words on the subject of Abolitionism. Doubtless you have all heard Anti-Slavery Societies denounced as insurrectionary and mischievous, fanatical and dangerous. It has been said they publish the most abominable untruths, and that they are endeavouring to excite rebellions at the South.

Have you believed these reports, my friends? have *you* also been deceived by these false assertions? Listen to me, then, whilst I endeavour to wipe from the fair character of Abolitionism such unfounded accusations. You know that *I* am a Southerner; you know that my dearest relatives are now in a slave state. Can you for a moment believe I would prove so recreant to the feelings of a daughter and a sister, as to join a society which was seeking to overthrow slavery by falsehood, bloodshed, and murder? I appeal to you who have known and loved me in days that are passed, can *you* believe it? No! my friends. As a Carolinian, I was peculiarly jealous of any movements on this subject; and before I would join an Anti-Slavery Society, I took the precaution of becoming acquainted with some of the leading Abolitionists, of reading their publications and attending their meetings, at which I heard addresses both from coloured and white men; and it was not until I was fully convinced that their principles were *entirely pacific,* and their efforts *only moral,* that I gave my name as a member to the Female Anti-Slavery Society of Philadelphia. Since that time, I have regularly taken the Liberator, and read many Anti-Slavery pamphlets and papers and books, and can assure you I *never* have seen a single insurrectionary paragraph, and never read any account of cruelty which I could not believe. Southerners may deny the truth of these accounts, but why do they not *prove* them to be false. Their violent expressions of horror at such accounts being believed, *may* deceive some, but they cannot deceive *me,* for I lived too long in the midst of slavery, not to know what slavery is. When *I* speak of this system, "I speak that I do know," and I am not at all afraid to assert, that Anti-Slavery publications have *not* overdrawn the monstrous features of slavery at all. And many a Southerner *knows* this as well as I do. A lady in North Carolina remarked to a friend of mine about eighteen months since, "Northerners know nothing at all about slavery; they think it is perpetual bondage only; but of the *depth of degradation* that word involves, they have no conception; if they had, *they would never cease* their efforts until so *horrible* a system was overthrown." She did not know how faithfully some Northern men and Northern women had studied this subject; how diligently they had searched out the cause of "him who had none to help him," and how fearlessly they had told the story of the negro's wrongs. Yes, Northerners know *every* thing about slavery now. This monster of iniquity has been unveiled to the world, her frightful features unmasked, and soon, very soon will she be regarded with no more complacency by the American Republic, than is the idol of Juggernaut, rolling its bloody wheels over the crushed bodies of its prostrate victims.

But you will probably ask, if Anti-Slavery societies are not insurrectionary, why do Northerners tell us they are? Why, I would ask you in return, did Northern senators and Northern representatives give their votes, at the last sitting of congress, for the admission of Arkansas Territory as a State? Take those men, one by one, and ask them in their parlours, do you *approve of slavery?* ask them on *Northern* ground, where they will speak the truth, and I doubt not *every man* of them will tell you, *no!* Why then, I ask, did *they* give their votes to enlarge the mouth of that grave which has already destroyed its tens of thousands? All our enemies tell *us* they are as much anti-slavery as we are. Yes, my friends, thousands who are helping you to bind the fetters of slavery on the negro, despise you in their hearts for doing it; they rejoice that such an institution has not been entailed upon them. Why then, I would ask, do *they* lend you their help? *I* will tell you, "they love *the praise of men more* than the praise of God." The Abolition cause has not yet become so popular as to induce them to believe, that by advocating it in congress, they shall sit more securely in their seats there, and like the *chief rulers* in the days of our Saviour, though *many* believed on him, yet they did *not* confess him, lest they should *be put out of the synagogue;* John xii. 42, 43. Or, perhaps like Pilate, thinking they could prevail nothing, and fearing a tumult, they determined to release Barabbas and surrender the just man, the poor innocent slave to be stripped of his rights and scourged. In vain will such men try to wash their hands, and say, with the Roman governor, "I am innocent of the blood of this just person." Northern American statesmen are no more innocent of the crime of slavery, than Pilate was of the murder of Jesus, or Saul of that of Stephen. These are high charges, but I appeal to *their hearts;* I appeal to public opinion ten years from now. Slavery then is a national sin.

But you will say, a great many other Northerners tell us so, who can have no political motives. The interests of the North, you must know, my friends, are very closely combined with those of the South. The Northern merchants and manufacturers are making *their* fortunes out of the *produce of slave labour;* the grocer is selling your rice and sugar; how then can these men bear a testimony against slavery without condemning themselves? But there is another reason, the North is most dreadfully afraid of Amalgamation. She is alarmed at the very idea of a thing so monstrous, as she thinks. And lest this consequence *might* flow from emancipation, she is determined to resist all efforts at emancipation without expatriation. It is not because *she approves of slavery*, or believes it to be "the corner stone of our republic," for she is as much *anti-slavery* as we are; but amalgamation is too horrible to think of. Now I would ask *you*, is it right, is it generous, to refuse the coloured people in this country the advantages of education, and the privilege, or rather the *right*, to follow honest trades and callings merely because they are coloured. The same prejudice exists here against our coloured brethren that existed against the Gentiles in Judea. Great numbers cannot bear the idea of equality, and fearing lest, if they had the same advantages we enjoy, they would become as intelligent, as moral, as religious, and as respectable and wealthy, they are determined to keep them as low as they possibly can. Is this doing as they would be done by? Is this loving their neighbour *as themselves?* Oh! that *such* opposers of Abolitionism would put their souls in the stead of the free coloured man's and obey the apostolic injunction, "remember them that are in bonds *as bound with them*." I will leave you to judge whether the fear of amalgamation ought to induce men to oppose anti-slavery efforts, when *they* believe *slavery* to be *sinful*. Prejudice against colour is the most powerful enemy we have to fight with at the North.

You need not be surprised, then, at all, at what is said *against* Abolitionists by the North, for they are wielding a two-edged sword, which, even here, cuts through the *cords of caste*, on the one side, and the *bonds of interest* on the other. They are only sharing the fate of other reformers, abused and reviled whilst they are in the minority; but they are neither angry nor discouraged by the invective which has been heaped upon them by slaveholders at the South, and their apologists at the North. They know that when George Fox and William Edmundson were labouring in behalf of the negroes in the West Indies, in 1671, that the very *same* slanders were propagated against them, which are *now* circulated against Abolitionists. Although it was well known that Fox was the founder of a religious sect which repudiated *all* war, and *all* violence, yet *even he* was accused of "endeavouring to excite the slaves to insurrection, and of teaching the negroes to cut their master's throats." And these two men who had their feet shod with the preparation of the Gospel of Peace, were actually compelled to draw up a formal declaration, that *they were not* trying to raise a rebellion in Barbadoes. It is also worthy of remark, that these Reformers did not at this time see the necessity of emancipation under seven years, and their principal efforts were exerted to persuade the planters of the necessity of instructing their slaves; but the slaveholder saw then, just what the slaveholder sees now, that an *enlightened* population *never* can be a *slave* population, and therefore they passed a law, that negroes should not even attend the meetings of Friends. Abolitionists know that the life of Clarkson was sought by slavetraders, and that even Wilberforce was denounced on the floor of Parliament as a fanatic and a hypocrite, by the present king of England, the very man who, in 1834, set his seal to that instrument which burst the fetters of eight hundred thousand slaves in his West India colonies. They know that the first Quaker who bore a *faithful* testimony against the sin of slavery, was cut off from religious fellowship with that society. That Quaker was a *woman*. On her deathbed she sent for the committee who dealt with her,—she told them the near approach of death had not altered her sentiments on the subject of slavery, and, waving her hand toward a very fertile and beautiful portion of country which lay stretched before her window, she said with great solemnity, "Friends, the time will come when there will not be friends enough in all this district to hold one meeting for worship, and this garden will be turned into a wilderness."

The aged friend, who, with tears in his eyes, related this interesting narrative to me, remarked, that at that time there were seven meetings of friends in that part of Virginia, but that when he was there ten years ago, not a single meeting was held, and the country was literally a desolation. Soon after her decease, John Woolman began his labours in our society, and instead of disowning a member for testifying *against* slavery, they have for fifty-two years positively forbidden their members to hold slaves.

Abolitionists understand the slaveholding spirit too well to be surprised at anything that has yet happened at the South or the North; they know that the greater the sin is, which is exposed, the more violent will be the efforts to blacken the character, and impugn the motives of those who are engaged in bringing to light the hidden things of darkness. They understand the work of Reform too well to be driven back by the furious waves of opposition, which are only foaming out their own shame. They have stood "the world's dread laugh," when only twelve men formed the first Anti-Slavery Society in Boston, in 1831. They have faced and refuted the calumnies of their enemies, and proved themselves to be emphatically *peace men*, by *never resisting* the violence of mobs, even when driven by them from the temple of God, and dragged by an infuriated crowd through the streets of the emporium of New England, or subjected by *slaveholders* to the pain of corporal punishment. "None of these things move them;" and, by the grace of God, they are determined to persevere in this work of faith, and labour of love: they mean to pray, and preach, and write, and print, until slavery is completely overthrown,—until Babylon is taken up and cast into the sea, to "be found no more at all." They mean to petition Congress year after year, until the seat of our government is cleansed from the sinful traffic in "slaves and the souls of men." Although that august assembly may be like the unjust judge who "feared not God, neither regarded man," yet it *must* yield, just as he did, from the power of importunity. Like the unjust judge, Congress *must* redress the wrongs of the widow, lest by the continual coming up of petitions it be wearied. This will be striking the dagger into the very heart of the monster, who will soon after sink to the earth and expire.

Abolitionists have been accused of abusing their Southern brethren. Did the prophet Isaiah *abuse* the Jews when he addressed to them the cutting reproofs contained in the first chapter of his prophecies, and ended by telling them they would be *ashamed* of the oaks they had desired, and *confounded* for the garden they had chosen? Did John the Baptist *abuse* the Jews when he called them "*a generation of vipers*," and warned them "to bring forth fruits meet for repentance?" Did Peter abuse the Jews when he told them they were the *murderers* of the Lord of Glory? Did Paul abuse the Roman Governor when he reasoned before him of righteousness, temperance, and judgment, so as to send conviction home to his guilty heart, and cause him to tremble in view of the crimes he was living in? Surely not. No man will *now* accuse the prophets and apostles of *abuse*, but what have Abolitionists done more than they? No doubt the Jews thought the prophets and apostles in their day just as harsh and uncharitable as slaveholders now think Abolitionists; if they did not, why did they beat, and stone, and kill them?

Great fault has been found with the prints which have been employed to expose slavery at the North, but, my friends, how could this be done so effectually in any other way? Until the pictures of the slave's sufferings were drawn and held up to public gaze, no Northerner had any idea of the cruelty of the system; it never entered their minds that such abominations could exist in Christian, Republican America; they never suspected that many of the *gentlemen* and *ladies* who came from the South to spend the summer months in travelling among them, were petty tyrants at home. And those who had lived at the South, and came to reside at the North, were too *ashamed of slavery* even to speak of it; the language of their hearts was, "tell it *not* in Gath, publish it *not* in the streets of Askelon;" they saw no use in uncovering the loathsome body to popular sight, and, in hopeless despair, wept in secret places over the sins of oppression. To such hidden mourners the formation of Anti-Slavery Societies was as life from the dead: the first beams of hope which gleamed through the dark clouds of despondency and grief. Prints were made use of to effect the abolition of the Inquisition in Spain; and Clarkson employed them when he was labouring to break up the Slave trade; and English Abolitionists used them just as we are now doing. They are powerful appeals, and have invariably done the work they were designed to do, and we cannot consent to abandon the use of them until the *realities* no longer exist.

With regard to those white men, who, it was said, sought to raise an insurrection in Mississippi a year ago, and who were stated to be Abolitionists, none of them were proved to be members of Anti-Slavery Societies, and it must remain a matter of great doubt whether, even they, were guilty of the crimes alleged against them; because, when any community is thrown into such a panic as to inflict Lynch law upon accused persons, they cannot be supposed to be capable of judging with calmness and impartiality. *We know* that the papers of which the Charleston mail was robbed, were *not* insurrectionary, and that they were *not* sent to the coloured people as was reported. *We know* that Amos Dresser was *no insurrectionist*, though he was accused of being so, and on this false accusation, was publicly whipped in Nashville (Tennessee) in the midst of a crowd of infuriated *slaveholders*. Was that young man disgraced by this infliction of corporal punishment? No more than was the great apostle of the Gentiles who five times received forty stripes, save one. Like him, he might have said, "henceforth I bear in my body the marks of the Lord Jesus," for it was for the *truth's sake he suffered*, as much as did the Apostle Paul. Are Nelson, and Garrett, and Williams, and other Abolitionists, who have recently been banished from Missouri, insurrectionists? *We know* they are *not*, whatever slaveholders may choose to call them. The spirit which now asperses the character of the Abolitionists, is the *very same* which dressed up the Christians of Spain in the skins of wild beasts and pictures of devils, when they were led to execution as heretics. Before we condemn individuals, it is necessary, even in a wicked community, to accuse them of some crime; hence, when Jezebel wished to compass the death of Naboth, men of Belial were suborned to bear *false* witness against him: and so it was with Stephen, and so it ever has been, and ever will be, as long as there is any virtue to suffer on the rack, or the gallows. *False* witnesses must appear against Abolitionists before they can be condemned.

I will now say a few words on George Thompson's mission to this country. This philanthropist was accused of being a foreign emissary. Were La Fayette, and Steuben, and De Kalb, foreign emissaries when they came over to America to fight against the tories, who preferred submitting to what was termed, "the yoke of servitude," rather than bursting the fetters which bound them to the mother county? *They* came with *carnal weapons* to engage in *bloody* conflict against American citizens, and yet, where do their names stand on the page of History. Among the honourable, or the low? Thompson came here to war against the giant sin of slavery, *not* with the sword and the pistol, but with the smooth stones of oratory taken from the pure waters of the river of Truth. His splendid talents and commanding eloquence rendered him a powerful coadjutor in the Anti-Slavery cause, and in order to neutralize the effects of these upon his auditors, and rob the poor slave of the benefits of his labours, his character was defamed, his life was sought, and he at last driven from our Republic, as a fugitive. But was *Thompson* disgraced by all this mean and contemptible and wicked chicanery and malice? No more than was Paul, when in consequence of a vision he had seen at Troas, he went over to Macedonia to help the Christians there, and was beaten and imprisoned, because he cast out a spirit of divination from a young damsel, which had brought much gain to her masters. Paul was as much a *foreign emissary* in the Roman colony of Philippi, as George Thompson was in America, and it was because he was a *Jew*, and taught customs it was not lawful for them to receive or observe, being Romans, that the Apostle was thus treated.

What have the foes of freedom in this land gained by the expulsion of George Thompson from these shores? Look at him now pouring the thundering strains of his eloquence upon crowded audiences in Great Britain, and see in this a triumphant vindication of his character. The slaveholder, and his obsequious apologist, have gained nothing by all their violence and falsehood. No! the stone which struck Goliath of Gath, had already been thrown from the sling. The giant of slavery who had so proudly defied the armies of the living God, had received his death-blow before he left our shores. But what is George Thompson doing there? Is he not now labouring as effectually to abolish American slavery as though he trod our own soil, and lectured to New York or Boston assemblies? What is he doing, but constructing a stupendous dam, which will turn the overwhelming tide of public opinion over the wheels of that machinery which Abolitionists are working here. He is now lecturing to *Britons* on *American Slavery*, to the *subjects* of a *King*, on the abject condition of the *slaves* of a *Republic*. He is telling them of that mighty confederacy of petty tyrants, which extends over thirteen States of our Union. He is telling them of the munificent rewards offered by slaveholders, for the heads of the most distinguished advocates for freedom in this country. He is moving the British Churches to send out to the churches of America the most solemn appeals, reproving, rebuking, and exhorting them with all long-suffering and patience, to abandon the sin of slavery immediately. Where then, I ask, will the name of George Thompson stand on the page of History? Among the honourable or the base?

What can I say more, my friends, to induce *you* to set your hands, and heads, and hearts to this great work of justice and mercy. Perhaps you have feared the consequences of immediate Emancipation, and been frightened by all those dreadful prophecies of rebellion, bloodshed, and murder, which have been uttered. "Let no man deceive you;" they are the predictions of that same "lying spirit' which spoke through the four thousand prophets of old, to Ahab king of Israel, urging him on to destruction. *Slavery* may produce these horrible scenes if it is continued five years longer, but Emancipation *never will*.

I can prove the *safety* of immediate Emancipation by history. In St Domingo, in 1793, six hundred thousand slaves were set free in a white population of forty-two thousand. That island "marched as by enchantment towards its ancient splendour, cultivation prospered, every day produced perceptible proofs of its progress, and the negroes all continued quietly to work on the different plantations, until in 1802, France determined to reduce these liberated slaves again to bondage. It was at *this time* that all those dreadful scenes of cruelty occurred, which we so often *unjustly* hear spoken of, as the effects of Abolition. They were occasioned *not* by Emancipation, but by the base attempt to fasten the chains of slavery on the limbs of liberated slaves.

In Guadaloupe, eighty-five thousand slaves were freed in a white population of thirteen thousand. The same prosperous effects followed manumission here, that had attended it in Hayti, every thing was quiet until Bonaparte sent out a fleet to reduce these negroes again to slavery, and in 1802, this institution was re-established in that island. In 1834, when Great Britain determined to liberate the slaves in her West India colonies, and proposed the apprenticeship system, the planters of Bermuda and Antigua, after having joined the other planters in their representations of the bloody consequences of Emancipation, in order, if possible, to hold back the hand which was offering the boon of freedom to the poor negro; as soon as they found such falsehoods were utterly disregarded, and Abolition must take place, came forward voluntarily, and asked for the compensation which was due to them, saying, *they preferred immediate emancipation*, and were not afraid of any insurrection. And how is it with these islands now? They are decidedly more prosperous than any of those in which the apprenticeship system was adopted, and England is now trying to abolish that system, so fully convinced is she that immediate Emancipation is the *safest* and the best plan.

And why not try it in the Southern States, if it *never* has occasioned rebellion; if *not* a *drop* of *blood* has ever been shed in consequence of it, though it has been so often tried, why should we suppose it would produce such disastrous consequences now? "Be not deceived then, God is not mocked," by such false excuses for not doing justly and loving mercy. There is nothing to fear from immediate Emancipation, but *every thing* from the continuance of slavery.

Sisters in Christ, I have done. As a Southerner, I have felt it was my duty to address you. I have endeavoured to set before you the exceeding sinfulness of slavery, and to point you to the example of those noble women who have been raised up in the church to effect great revolutions, and to suffer for the truth's sake. I have appealed to your sympathies as women, to your sense of duty as *Christian women*. I have attempted to vindicate the Abolitionists, to prove the entire safety of immediate Emancipation, and to plead the cause of the poor and oppressed. I have done—I have sowed the seeds of truth, but I well know, that even if an Apollos were to follow in my steps to water them, "*God only* can give the increase." To Him, then, who is able to prosper the work of his servant's hand, I commend this appeal in fervent prayer, that as he "hath *chosen the weak things of the world* to confound the things which are mighty," so He may cause His blessing to descend and carry conviction to the hearts of many Lydias through these speaking pages. Farewell—count me not your "enemy because I have told you the truth," but believe me in unfeigned affection,

Your sympathizing Friend,

ANGELINA E. GRIMKÉ.

AN APPEAL TO THE WOMEN OF THE NOMINALLY FREE STATES

Issued by an Anti-Slavery Convention of American Women,

Held by adjournments from the 9th to the 12th of May, 1837.

We are thy sisters;—God has truly said,
That of one blood the nations He has made.
Oh! Christian woman, in a Christian land,
Canst thou unblushing read this great command?
Suffer the wrongs which wring our inmost heart,
To draw one throb of pity on thy part!
Our skins may differ, but from thee we claim,
A sister's privilege, and a sister's name.

—*Sarah Forten.*

The trembling earth, the low murmuring thunders, already admonish us of our danger; and if females can exert any saving influence in this emergency, *it is time for them to awake.*

—*Catharine E. Beecher.*

BELOVED SISTERS,

The wrongs of outraged millions, and the foreshadows of coming judgments, constrain us, under a solemn sense of responsibility, to press upon your consideration the subject of American Slavery. The women of the North have high and holy duties to perform in the work of emancipation—duties to themselves, to the suffering slave, to the slaveholder, to the church, to their country, and to the world at large, and, above all to their God. Duties, which if not performed now, may never be performed at all.

Multitudes will doubtless deem such an address ill-timed and ill-directed. Many regard the excitement produced by the agitation of this subject as an evidence of the impolicy of free discussion, and a sufficient excuse for their own inactivity. Others, so undervalue the rights and responsibilities of woman, as to scoff and gainsay whenever she goes forth to duties beyond the parlor and the nursery. The cry of such is, that the agitation of this subject has rolled back the cause of emancipation 50, or 100, or it may be 200 years, and that this is a *political* subject with which women have nothing to do. To the first, we would reply, that the people of the South are the *best judges* of the effects of Anti-Slavery discussions upon their favorite "domestic institution;" and the universal alarm which has spread through the Slave States, is conclusive evidence of *their* conviction that *Slavery cannot survive discussion. They know* full well, that this terrific Upas must fall when the axe of free discussion is laid at its root. "From how many statesmen at the South has not the confession been extorted—extorted by the remorse and fear which they could neither dissipate nor conceal—that the infamy with which they are already branded by all the philanthropists of Christendom, *was fast becoming insupportable!* The plunder of our goods we do not dread, they exclaim; but what is more to be deprecated, *the loss of character.* What can our goods be worth, *while we are constrained to bear the scorn and execration of the civilized world, as a nest of pirates?*" A similar sentiment was uttered by John C. Calhoun, in speaking of his Southern opponents, in the session of Congress, 1835, in the Senate. "Do they expect the Abolitionists will resort to arms, and commence a crusade to liberate our slaves by force? Is this what they mean when they speak of the attempt to abolish Slavery? If so, let me tell our friends of the South who differ from us, that the war which the Abolitionists wage against us, is of a very different character, AND FAR MORE EFFECTIVE; it is waged *not* against our *lives,* but our *character.*" Gen. Duff Green, the Editor of the United States Telegraph, and the great champion of "Southern rights," has expressed the same views: "We believe we have *most* to fear from the organized action upon the *consciences* and fear of the *Slaveholders themselves,* from the insinuation of their (Abolitionists) dangerous heresies into our schools, our pulpits, and our domestic circles. It is only by alarming the consciences of the weak and feeble, and diffusing among our own people a *morbid sensibility* on the question of Slavery, that the Abolitionists can accomplish their object."

Here then is the unequivocal testimony of Southerners as to what *they expect* to be the influence of free discussion. Has this expectation been realized? Has the *conscience* of the slaveholder been reached? In answer to these enquiries, we quote from a work recently published by James Smylie, a Presbyterian minister of the Amite Presbytery. "From his intercourse with religious societies of *all* denominations in Mississippi and Louisiana, he was aware that the Abolition maxim, viz: that *Slavery is in itself sinful, had gained on and entwined itself among the religious and conscientious scruples of many* in the community, so far as to render them *unhappy.* The eye of the mind, resting on Slavery itself as a *corrupt fountain,* from which, of necessity, *nothing but corrupt* streams could flow, was *incessantly* employed in search of some plan by which, with safety, the fountain could, in some future time, be *entirely* dried up." An illustration of this important acknowledgement, will be found in the following fact, extracted from the Herald of Freedom: "A young gentleman who has been residing in S. Carolina, says our movements, (Abolitionists) are producing the best effects upon the South, *rousing the consciences of Slaveholders,* while the slaves seem to be impressed as a body with the idea, that help is coming—that an interest is felt for them, and plans devising for their relief somewhere—which keeps them quiet. He says it is not uncommon for ministers and good people to make confession like this. One, riding with him broke forth, "O, I fear that the groans and wails from our slaves enter into the ear of the Lord of Sabbaoth. I am distressed on this subject: my *conscience* will let me have no peace. I go to bed, but not to sleep. I walk my room in agony, and resolve that I will never hold slaves another day; but in the morning, my heart like Pharaoh's, is hardened."

And there are others who have liberated their slaves to the number of 5 or 600. Others again, who are weeping in secret places, over the abominations of Slavery, and praying for the success of our efforts. These things we have learned from Southern lips, and Southern pens. Let them stimulate us to unremitted effort to "deliver him that is spoiled out of the hand of the oppressor, lest the fury of the Lord go out like fire, and burn that none can quench it, because of the evil of our doings," as a nation.

To the second objection, that Slavery is a political question, we would say: every citizen should feel an intense interest in the political concerns of the country, because the honor, happiness, and well being of every class, are bound up in its politics, government and laws. Are we aliens because we are women? Are we bereft of citizenship because we are the *mothers, wives,* and *daughters* of a mighty people? Have *women* no country—no interest staked in public weal—no liabilities in common peril—no partnership in a nation's guilt and shame?—Has *woman* no home nor household altars, nor endearing ties of kindred, nor sway with man, nor power at a mercy seat, nor voice to cheer, nor hand to raise the drooping, and to bind the broken?

But before we can appreciate the bearing of this subject, and our duties with regard to it, we must first know what Slavery is; and then trace out its manifold and monstrous relations. We can thus discover whether women have any duties to discharge in its abolition. We will then attempt to show WHY Northern women should labor for its overthrow, and lastly HOW they can aid in this work of faith, and labor of love.

What then is Slavery? It is that *crime* which casts man down from that exaltation where God has placed him, "a little lower than the angels," and sinks him to a level with the beasts of the field. This intelligent and immortal being is confounded with the brutes that perish; he whose spirit was formed to rise in aspirations of gratitude and praise whilst here, and to spend an eternity with God in heaven, is herded with the beasts, whose spirits go downward with their bodies of clay, to the dust of which they were made. Slavery is that crime by which man is robbed of his inalienable right to liberty, and the pursuit of happiness, the diadem of glory, and honor, with which he was crowned, and that sceptre of dominion which was placed in his hand when he was ushered upon the theatre of creation, and was divinely commissioned to "have dominion over the fish of the sea, and over the fowls of the air, and over the cattle, and over all the earth, and every creeping thing that creepeth upon the earth." Slavery throws confusion into the arrangements of Infinite Wisdom, breaks up the divine harmony, and tears up the very foundations of human society. It produces a state of things at war with nature, and hence those unnatural expedients to preserve this system from destruction—hence the severity of those laws which disgrace the statute books of our Southern States. A compend of these was published in 1827, by Judge Stroud of Philadelphia, and to this work we would refer our sisters for a full and correct exposition of American Slavery. Let us first hear what a Slave *is* according to the laws of South Carolina. "Slaves shall be deemed, taken, and reputed and adjudged in law to be *chattels personal* in the hands of their masters, owners, and possessors, and their executors, administrators and assigns, to all intents, constructions and purposes whatsoever." As "*chattels personal*," they are held in 12 of the Southern States, but in Louisiana they are held as *real estate*. Her law runs thus: "Slaves shall always be reputed and considered as *real estate*, shall be as such, subject to be mortgaged, according to the rules prescribed by law, and they shall be seized and sold as *real estate*." She further says "A Slave is one who is in the power of the master to whom he belongs. The master may sell him, dispose of his person, his industry, and his labor; he can do nothing, possess nothing, nor acquire any thing but what must belong to his master." In the one case he is held as bank stock, or the shares in a rail-road company, in the other as houses or lands. In both he is equally liable to be seized at any time, and sold for the debts of a living or deceased master.

These definitions of a slave, then, plainly declare, "that the slave is not to be ranked among *sentient* beings, but among *things*, is an article of property, a chattel personal." The code therefore which has been framed to keep this rational being on a level with the brutes, this sentient creature on an equality with inanimate objects, must necessarily be terribly severe, a permanent index to the *hearts* of those who framed it, and those who, although invested with the power, refuse to abrogate it. The following carrolleries are amply sustained by the language of the slave codes themselves:

I. MAN, created in the image of God, is reduced to a *thing*.

II. MAN is robbed of his "inalienable right to liberty," and is held in perpetual captivity.

III. MAN can own *no* property, and is daily plundered of the fruits of his toil. Says God, "The laborer is worthy of his hire:" says the slaveholder, "*I* will yoke him with the brutes, and he shall *toil* for ME."

IV. MAN "can make *no* contract." God has established the marriage relation; and Christ has said, "What therefore God hath joined together, let *not* man put asunder." The slaveholder denies the right, and forbids to marry. *Not a single slave in the United States is legally married*. The nominal marriages which they contract may be broken at any time by the master, and are continually and most cruelly sundered every day. Look, then, at the awful state of concubinage to which two millions and a quarter of our citizens are reduced, by the Statute Laws of our land.

V. MAN is denied the benefits of education, and compelled to disobey the divine command to "search the Scriptures:" they are a sealed book to him—sealed by the express provisions of the legal code of the South.

VI. MAN is required to yield unqualified submission to his fellowman—ay, and WOMAN, too, is bound to submit, and become the unconsenting victim of unspeakable indignities. Resistance may be punished with death.

VII. MAN is thrown entirely out of the protection of law: *the murder* of the slave is *legalized* in four different ways; and the same laws which reduce him to the condition of a brute, and deny him legal protection, punish him with unparallelled severity. In Virginia, there are seventy-one offences for which the slave may suffer death, and thirty-six in South Carolina. In all these cases, we must remember he is denied the right of a presentation by a grand jury, and a trial by a petit jury—and this, too, in direct violation of the Constitution of the United States.

VIII. MAN is deprived of all hope of redemption from this horrible condition, either for himself, his wife, or his children. Slavery is to be (according to the slave laws) "hereditary and perpetual."

Here, then, is a faint description of American Slavery. This is the republican despotism under which the slaves of our country are groaning out a life of ignorance, degradation, and anguish. Let every American citizen ponder this question, which bears with momentous power on the destinies of our country, whether we regard it in a political, a moral, or a religious point of view.

SLAVERY, A POLITICAL SUBJECT.

I. Let us first look at it as a *political* subject. Such incongruous elements as freedom and slavery, republicanism and despotism, cannot long exist together: the unnatural and unhallowed union between these things must sooner or later be broken. Not only are one-sixth part of the inhabitants of this republic held in abject slavery, but the Free and the Slave States are unequally yoked together—they do not enjoy equal privileges. In the former, persons only are represented in our National Congress; in the latter, *property* as well as persons send their representatives there. The slaveholding and non-slaveholding States have antagonist interests, which are continually conflicting, and producing jealousies and heart-burnings between the contending parties. Our

Congressional debates have presented one unvaried scene of unreasonable demands and haughty threats on the one hand—of tame compromise, and unmanly, and in many cases most *unprincipled* submission on the other. Slavery not only robs the slave of all his rights as a man in thirteen of the States of this Confederacy, but it vaults over the barrier of Mason's and Dixon's line, swims the Ohio and the Potomac, and bribes Northern citizens to kidnap and enslave freemen of the North—drags them into hopeless bondage, and sells them under the hammer of the auctioneer. Not only so—it outlaws every Northerner who openly avows the sentiments of the Declaration of our Independence, and destroys the free communication of our sentiments through the medium of the mail, so that the daughters of America cannot now send the productions of their pen to the parent who resides in a slaveholding state. It threatens even our Representatives in Congress with assassination, if they dare to open their lips in defence of the rights of the oppressed and the dumb—tramples in the dust the right of petition, when exercised by free men and free women—brands them with the opprobrious epithets of "white slaves" and "devils," and rides triumphant over the bowed heads of the senators and representatives of our Free States. Slavery nurses within the bosom of our country her deadliest foes, and threatens to bring down the "exterminating thunders" of Divine vengeance upon our guilty heads. "The dark spirit of slavery" rules in our national councils, and menaces the severance of the bonds which bind together these United States, and to shake from our star-spangled banner, as with a mighty wind, those glittering emblems of our country's pre-eminence among the nations of the earth, and to burn our Declaration as a "splendid absurdity," a "rhetorical flourish;" to offer the glorious character of our constitutional liberties and alliance upon the same altar—to the horns of which the bleeding slave is now bound by the chain of his servitude, and the colored freeman by "the cord of caste."

This is a very imperfect outline of the political bearings of this great question; and it is gravely urged, that as it is a *political subject, women* have no concernment with it: this doctrine of the North is a sycophantic response to the declaration of a Southern representative, that women have *no right* to send up petitions to Congress. We know, dear sisters, that the open and the secret enemies of freedom in our country have dreaded our influence, and therefore have reprobated our interference; and in order to blind us to our responsibilities, have thrown dust into our eyes, well knowing that if the organ of vision is only clear, the whole body, the moving and acting faculties will become full of light, and will soon be thrown into powerful action. Some, who pretend to be very jealous for the honor of our sex, and are very anxious that *we* should scrupulously maintain the dignity and delicacy of female propriety, continually urge this objection to female effort. We grant that it is a political, as well as a moral subject: does this exonerate women from their duties as subjects of the government, as members of the great human family? Have women never wisely and laudably exercised political responsibilities?

When the Lord led out his chosen people like a flock into the wilderness, from the house of bondage, was it not a WOMAN whom He sent before them with Moses and Aaron? Did she not lead her manumitted sisters in that sublime peon of thanksgiving and praise which ascended from their grateful hearts as they answered the chorus of their brethren with the inspired words, "Sing ye to the Lord, for he hath triumphed gloriously: the horse and his rider hath he thrown into the sea." And was not the deliverance of Israel from Egyptian bondage a *political concern?* Did it not shake the throne of the Pharaohs, desolate the land of Egypt, and strike terror into the stubborn hearts of subtle politicians. Miriam then interfered with the *political concerns* of Egypt; and we doubt not, had the monarch been permitted to lay his hand upon the sister of Moses, she would have suffered as a leader in this daring attempt to lead out her sisters from the house of bondage. Would not her fate have been similar to that of the heroine of the fifteenth century?

When Barak received the divine command to go down to Mount Tabor, and the promise that with ten thousand men he should overcome the hosts of Sisera with their iron chariots, to whom did he appeal in those memorable words—"If *thou* wilt go with me, then I will go; but if *thou* wilt not go with me, then I will not go"? It was to Deborah: and this *woman* intermeddled so far with the *political concerns* of Israel, as to go up with him to the battle; and when, as she predicted, Sesira was sold into the hands of a woman, she united with Barak in a song of triumphant praise, that the ancient Kishon had swept down in the current of its waters the lifeless bodies of the Canaanitish warriors.

But many seem to think, that although women may have been called to the performance of extraordinary duties in the days of miracle and of inspiration, that under no other circumstances could such conduct have been warranted. Let us turn, then, to the history of Rome. When Coriolanus, who had been banished by the Roman Senate, returned with a host of barbarians, to wreak his vengeance upon the proud mistress of the world, and after the embassies of senators, and priests, and augurs, had failed to move his unrelenting heart, who were sent out to try the magic power of their tears and prayers? Were they not the *wife* and *mother* of the Roman warrior, and were they not followed by a train of matrons, who approached the Volician camp to plead their country's cause? And what was the success of this embassage of mercy and of love? The hero's icy heart was melted by the tears and pleadings of these feebler ones: he bowed his stubborn will to theirs, turned back his disappointed freebooters from the gates of Rome, and sent these *women* home with the glad tidings of peace upon their trembling lips.

But perhaps the sage objector may say, "True; but these women were delegated by the Roman Senate—*they* were vested with authority by 'the powers that be'—*they* did not rush uncalled into the field of action." Was this, then, *their* commission for intermeddling with the *political concerns* of their country? Where, then, was the commission of those Sabine women, who threw themselves between the hostile armies, when they were just about plunging their javelins into the hearts of their own fathers, brothers, and sons? Were *they* deputed by the Roman Senate? No! they held higher credentials. The angel of mercy commissioned them each to do and to dare all that might become a woman, in such a fearful hour of agony and boding. They rushed between the embattled hosts. At the sight of their tears and prayers, the iron grasp relaxed—the weapons fell—and they who met in hate to kill, embraced in love, and thenceforth mingled into one. These *women* poured the assuasive oil over the troubled waters of strife. *Woman* became the healer of breaches—the restorer of paths to dwell in.

But are these the doings of olden time alone? are there no instances of woman's "interference" in modern history? About the middle of the fifteenth century, when the kingdom of France had fallen, and the infant monarch of England had placed her crown upon his youthful head, lo! a woman arose as the deliverer of her country. *She* led on the broken-spirited troops of France to the siege of Orleans, 1428—compelled the English to surrender—conducted Charles the Seventh to the city of Rheims—witnessed the coronation of the astonished prince—and then retired from the plaudits of a grateful nation, who hailed the deliverance she had wrought as almost miraculous. And who was this Joan of Arc? An uneducated country girl, who stepped so far beyond the sphere of her humble duties, as the servant of a tavern-keeper, as to intermeddle with the *political concerns* of one of the greatest kingdoms of Europe. What wonderful presumption! No marvel, then, that she suffered the penalty of her strange temerity, being burned alive as a witch, by the English, in the town of Rouen.

But let us turn over the pages of our own history. When the British army had taken possession of our beautiful city of brotherly love, who arose at midnight, to listen to the plots which were laid in an upper chamber, by General Howe in his council of war? It was a *woman:* and when she stole the secret from their unconscious lips, she kept it locked within her own bosom, until under an ingenious pretext she repaired to Frankford, gained an interview with Washington, and disclosed to him the important intelligence which saved the lives of her countrymen. Did Lydia Darrah confer a benefit upon the American army—did she perform the duties of an American citizen? Or, was this act an impertinent intermeddling with the *political concerns* of her country, with which, as a *woman*, she had nothing to do? Let the daughters of this republic answer the question.*

It is related of Buonaparte, that he one day rebuked a French lady for busying herself with politics. "Sire," replied she, "in a

*We would here remark, that these instances of interference on the part of women of different ages and countries, in the political concerns of states and kingdoms, are NOT cited as *approbatory* of the *measures* they employed, but as illustrations of the principle that *women are citizens*, and that they have important duties to perform for their country.

country where *women* are put to death, it is very natural that *women* should wish to know the reason why." And, dear sisters, in a country where women are degraded and brutalized, and where their exposed persons bleed under the lash—where they are sold in the shambles of "negro brokers"—robbed of their hard earnings—torn from their husbands, and forcibly plundered of their virtue and their offspring; surely, in *such* a country, it is very natural that *women* should wish to know "the reason *why*"—especially when these outrages of blood and nameless horror are practised in violation of the principles of our national Bill of Rights and the Preamble of our Constitution. We do not, then, and cannot concede the position, that because this is a *political subject* women ought to fold their hands in idleness, and close their eyes and ears to the "horrible things" that are practised in our land. The denial of our duty to act, is a bold denial of our right to act; and if we have no right to act, then may *we* well be termed "the white slaves of the North"—for, like our brethren in bonds, we must seal our lips in silence and despair.

SLAVERY A MORAL SUBJECT.

II. This, however, is not merely a political subject, it is highly moral, and as such claims the attention of every *moral* being. Slavery exerts a most deadly influence over the morals of our country, not only over that portion of it, where it actually exists as "a domestic institution," but like the miasma of some pestilential pool, it spreads its desolating influence far beyond its own boundaries. Who does not know that licentiousness is a crying sin at the North as well as at the South, and who does not admit that the manners of the South in this respect have had a wide and destructive influence on northern character. Can crime be fashionable and common in one part of the Union and unrebuked by the other, without corrupting the very heart's-blood of the nation, and lowering the standard of morality every where? Can northern men go down to the well watered plains of the South to make their fortunes, without bowing themselves in the house of Rimmon and drinking of the waters of that river of pollution which rolls over the plain of Sodam and Gomorrah? Do they return uncontaminated to their homes, or does not many and many a northerner dig the grave of his virtue in the Admahs and Zeboims of our southern states. And can our theological and academic institutions be opened to the sons of the planter, without endangering the purity of the morals of our own sons, by associations with men who regard the robbery of the poor as no crime, and oppression as no wrong? Impossible!

Then again, the interest of the North and the South are closely interwoven, and this circumstance has contributed to blind the eyes of the North to the sin of the slaveholder, and to steel his heart against the sufferings of the helpless slave. She has learned to look with cold indifference, if not with approbation, upon that organized system of robbery which is dignified with the mild epithet of "peculiar institution of the South," and to hear unmoved, those wailings of agony and despair which come up from the sultry fields of Louisiana and Mississippi, Alabama, and Georgia. Yes, so demoralizing has been the influence of southern commerce and southern custom of dollars and of cents, that millions in the free states stand up on the side of the oppressor, and pour out all the sympathies of their souls into the bosoms of those who buy and sell and degrade and brutalize their fellow-creatures. What further need have we of evidence that the North has been most deeply corrupted, than the fact that *her* hands are busy in daubing this idol temple with untempered mortar, and *her* lips in crying peace! peace! to the South, when God has declared, "there is no peace to the wicked." Look, too, at her citizens, even her *ministers* becoming slaveholders and marrying slaveholders, instead of rebuking this presumptuous insurrection against the rights of God and man, and refusing to be partaker in their evil deeds. But this is not all, our people have erected a false standard by which to judge of men's character. Because in the slaveholding states colored men are plundered and kept in abject ignorance, are treated with disdain and scorn, so here too, in profound deference to the South, we refuse to eat or ride, or walk, or associate, or open our institutions of learning, or even our zoological institutions to people of color, unless they visit them in the capacity of *servants,* of menials in humble attendance upon the Anglo-American,* Who ever heard of a more wicked absurdity in a Republican country?

Have northern women then, nothing to do with slavery, when its demoralizing influence is polluting their domestic circles and blasting the fair character of *their* sons and brothers. Nothing to do with slavery when *their* domestics are often dragged by the merciless kidnapper from the hearth of their nurseries and the arms of their little ones. Nothing to do with slavery when northern women are chained and driven like criminals, and incarcerated in the great prison-house of the South. Nothing to do with slavery—but we forbear, and pass on to consider it in a religious point of view.

SLAVERY A RELIGIOUS SUBJECT.

III. It is as a religious question that we regard it as most important. O! it is when we look at the effort made by slaveholders to destroy the *mind* of the slave that we fear and tremble. "It is," says the North Carolina Manumission Society, in 1826, "the maxim of slavemasters in common with *other tyrants,* the more ignorance the more safety." Hear, too, the language of Berry, in the Virginia House of Delegates, in 1832.—"We have, as far as possible, closed every avenue by which light might enter their minds. If we could *extinguish the capacity* to see the light, our work would be completed; they would be on a level with the beasts of the field, and we should be safe. I am *not* certain that we would not do it, if we could find out the necessary process—and that under the plea of necessity." And these testimonies are corroborated by James A. Thome, a minister of the Gospel of Kentucky. "The plantations of the South are graveyards of the *mind,* the inexpressive countenances of the slaves are monuments of souls expired, and their spiritless eyes their epitaphs."

*The restriction to which we allude is contained in the following extract from the pamphlet, published by the Institute. "The *proprietors wish it to be understood, that* PEOPLE OF COLOR *are not permitted to enter,* EXCEPT WHEN IN ATTENDANCE UPON CHILDREN AND FAMILIES."

And Robert J. Breckenridge, of Baltimore, affirms, that one feature of American slavery is, "to deprive them of the means and opportunities of moral and *intellectual* culture."

Not only are the means of *mental* improvement withheld from the slave, but the opportunities of receiving *moral* culture also. Not only is the privilege of learning to read and write, &c. denied, but no provision is made by law for his religious instruction, and hardly any by the church or the master. Indeed the slaveholder possesses *legally* supreme dominion over the *soul* of his slave. This was admitted in 1831, by C. C. Jones, now a Professor in the Theological Seminary of Columbia, South Carolina, in a sermon preached by him before two associations of planters in Georgia. These are his own words,—"In the exercise of that *supreme power* over them, *vested in us by the laws of our country, we can* forbid any man's coming on our plantations for the purpose of religiously instructing them—*we can* forbid all meetings for religious purposes on our plantations—*we can* refuse to instruct them ourselves—*we can* forbid them the privileges of God's sanctuary on the Sabbath—*we can literally bar the door of entrance into heaven against them; nor is there any power in our government that can compel us to swerve a hair from such treatment of them.* The moral destinies of these people are submitted to our disposal." Here then is the despotic power with which *every* slaveholder in our land is vested. We would now ask, do they exercise it? We appeal to the South for an answer. We condemn her *not* by northern testimony, but *out of her own mouth.* What is the condition of her slaves? In the same sermon from which the above extract is taken, we find the following:—"The description which the apostle Paul, in his epistle to the Romans gives of the Heathen world, will apply with *very little* abatement, to our negroes. . . . . Chastity is an exceeding rare virtue. Poligamy is common, and there is little sacredness attached to the marriage contract. It is entered into for the most part without established forms and is dissolved at the will of the parties.* Nor is there any sacredness attached to the Sabbath. It is a day of idleness and sleep, of sinful amusement, of visiting, and of labor. Numbers of them do not go to church, and

*Just as frequently at the will of tyrannical masters.

cannot tell who Jesus Christ is, nor have they ever heard so much as the Ten Commandments read and explained. Of the professors of religion among them, there are many of questionable piety, who occasion the different churches great trouble in discipline, for they are extremely ignorant, and frequently are guilty of the grossest vices. Generally speaking, they appear to us to be without hope and without God in the world. A NATION OF HEATHEN IN OUR VERY MIDST. And if we believe the testimony of our own eyes and ears, and the testimony of those who know these people most intimately, we must conclude, that they need the Gospel, and need it AS MUCH AS ANY PEOPLE IN THE WORLD. We have been shocked at the death of 40,000 men annually, by intemperance. But it is probable that as many die annually among the negroes in slaveholding states, whose death is *equally as hopeless* as that of the drunkard, and yet we have not thought of this, neither have we felt it. The majority do not hear the Gospel for weeks and months together. But whenever the negroes hear the preaching of the Gospel, they hear it to a very great disadvantage. The sermons are almost wholly delivered to their masters, and are not only for the greater part inapplicable to them, but *entirely above their comprehension*, both as to language and thought. The Gospel is preached to them in *an unknown tongue*. Many of them are guilty of notorious sins and know *not* that they are sins at all.

We might quote more abundantly from official southern testimony, but these have so often been printed and reprinted that we have purposely avoided introducing them into this address. We feel then that the supreme power of the master over his slaves has been put forth, *not* "to compel them to come" into the Gospel kingdom, but to keep them in the lowest possible state of ignorance, degradation, and crime. Have northern women then nothing to do with this "NATION OF HEATHEN IN OUR VERY MIDST." Shall we pour our treasures into the funds of the Foreign Missionary Society to send the glad tidings of redeeming love to "the isles of the Gentiles," to Russia and Greece, to China and Burmah, and the coast of Africa, and yet sit down in indifference to the perishing souls of *our own countrymen?* Shall we busy ourselves to send the Bible to nations afar off, and yet neglect to do all that our hands and lips and pens and purses can do, to induce the South to abolish a system which forbids almost entirely the labors of missionaries among one-half of her population, and altogether seals up the pages of divine inspiration to them. Nothing to do with slavery! O! our sisters, some of us feel ready to exclaim—if we forget the complicated wrongs of our brethren and sisters in chains, let our right hands forget their cunning! If we remember not, "them that are in bonds as bound with them," and plead not the cause of the dumb, let our tongues cleave to the roofs of our mouths, if we prefer not to suffer reproach and afflictions for these outraged ones, to all the joys of worldly power and human praise. Nothing to do with slavery?—Then we would ask, what have *we* to do with the frantic screams of that Hindoo widow who ascends the funeral pile of her husband, and offers up her own body a living sacrifice to the demon of superstition. What have *we* to do with that Indian mother who plunges her innocent babe into the Ganges, or with that father, who, when it lifts its little hands for help, strikes it down with the paddle of his boat. What have *we* to do with the Sumatrian who carries his decrepid parent into the pathless woods, and leaves him to perish with hunger and thirst. Ah! dear sisters, *we know* that as human beings and as Christians, *we* are "debtors, both to the Greeks and to the Barbarians" of other lands; and are *we* not *much more so* to the bond and the Heathen of our own?

We have hitherto addressed you more as moral and responsible beings, than in the distinctive character of women; we have appealed to you on the broad ground of *human rights* and human responsibilities, rather than on that of your peculiar duties as women. We have pursued this course of argument designedly, because, in order to prove that you have any duties to perform, it is necessary first to establish the principle of moral being, for all our rights and all our duties grow out of this principle. *All moral beings have essentially the same rights and the same duties,* whether they be male or female. This is a truth the world has yet to learn, though she has had the experience of fifty-eight centuries by which to acquire the knowledge of this fundamental axiom. Ignorance of this has involved her in great inconsistencies, great errors, and great crimes and hurled confusion over that beautiful and harmonious structure of human society which infinite wisdom had established. We will now endeavour to enumerate some reasons why we believe northern women, as *women,* are solemnly called upon to labor in the great and glorious work of emancipation.

I.—Slave Trade Sanctioned by a Woman.

We know that our country is very anxious to throw all the blame of the origin of slavery here upon England, although it is a well established fact, that the first slaves ever introduced into the colonies, were *voluntarily* purchased by the colonists from a *Dutch* vessel in 1620.—Upon the head of England, however, *we* pour the execrations of our wrath for having brought upon us the curse of slavery. Let us now turn over the pages of her history to find out WHO filled her throne at the time that Captain Hawkins was authorized to carry on the horrible traffic of the slave trade. It was a WOMAN! This first British pirate on the coast of Africa, assisted by some rich persons in London, fitted out three ships, and sailed to Africa, where he plundered the towns and carried off three hundred of the defenceless inhabitants to Hispaniola. This noble exploit of Christian chivalry was followed by the express authority of Elizabeth, to perpetrate a series of such depredations upon the shores of this devoted continent.* If then, a WOMAN was the first British Sovereign who legalized the African slave trade, through whose instrumentality so many thousands of the victims of oppression have been brought to our land, then *women* are bound to do all they can to exterminate the evil which *woman* exerted her power and authority to bring upon our country and the world.

II.—Women the Victims of Slavery.

Out of the millions of slaves who have been stolen from Africa, a very great number must have been women, who were torn from the arms of their fathers and husbands, brothers and children,

*Perhaps it is but justice to the Queen to say, that at the very time she granted this commission to Hawkins, "she expressed her concern lest any of the Africans should be carried off without their free consent, declaring that such a thing would be detestable, and call down the vengeance of heaven upon the undertakers."

and subjected to all the horrors of the middle passage and the still greater sufferings of slavery in a foreign land. Multitudes of these were cast upon our inhospitable shores, some of them now toil out a life of bondage "one hour of which is fraught with more misery than ages of that" which our fathers rose in rebellion to oppose. But the great mass of female slaves in the southern states are the descendants of these hapless strangers: 1,000,000 of them now wear the iron yoke of slavery in this land of boasted liberty and law. They are our countrywomen—*they are our sisters,* and to us, as women, they have a right to look for sympathy with their sorrows, and effort and prayer for their rescue. Upon those of us especially, who have named the name of Christ, they have peculiar claims, and claims which *we must answer or we shall incur a heavy load of guilt.*

Women, too, are constituted by nature the peculiar guardians of children, and children are the victims of this horrible system. Helpless infancy is robbed of the tender care of the mother, and the protection of the father. There are in this Christian land, thousands of little children who have been made orphans by the "domestic institution" of the South; and whilst woman's hand is stretched out to gather in the orphans and the half orphans whom *death* has made in our country, and to shelter them from the storms of adversity, O! let us not forget the orphans whom *crime* has made in our midst, but let us plead the cause of *these* innocents. Let us expose the heinous wickedness of the internal slave-trade. It is an organized system for the disruption of family ties, a manufactory of widows and orphans.

III.—Women Are Slaveholders.

Multitudes of the Southern women, hold men, women and children as *property. They* are pampered in luxury, and nursed in the school of tyranny; *they* sway the iron rod of power, and *they* rob the laborer of his hire. Immortal beings tremble at *their* nod, and bow in abject submission at *their* word, and under the cowskin, too often wielded by *their* own delicate hands. Women at the South hold *their own sisters* and brothers in bondage. Start not at this dreadful assertion—we speak that which some of us do know—we testify that which some of us have seen. Such facts ought to be known, that the women of the North may understand *their* duties, and be incited to perform *them.*

Southern families often present the most disgusting scenes of dissension, in which the Mistress acts a part derogatory to her own character as a woman. Jefferson has so exactly described the bitter fruits of Slavery in the domestic circle that we cannot forbear re-quoting it: "The whole commerce between master and slave, is a *perpetual exercise* of the most boisterous passions, the most unremitting despotism on the one hand, and degrading submission on the other. The parent *storms,* the child looks on, catches the lineaments of wrath, puts on the same airs in a circle of smaller slaves, gives loose to the worst of passions; and thus *nursed educated, and daily exercised* in *tyranny,* cannot but be stamped by it with odious peculiarities." We wish this picture applied only to the "commerce between *master* and slave;" but we know that there are *female tyrants* too, who are prompt to lay their complaints of misconduct before their husbands, brothers, and sons, and to urge them to commit acts of violence against their helpless slaves. Others still more cruel, place the lash in the hands of some trusty domestic, and stand by whilst he lays the heavy strokes upon the unresisting victim, deaf to the cries for mercy which rend the air, or rather the more enraged at such appeals, which are only answered by the Southern lady with the prompt command of "give her more for that." This work of chastisement is often performed by a brother, or other relative of the poor sufferer, which circumstance stings like an adder the very heart of the slave, while her body writhes under the lash. Other mistresses who cannot bear that their delicate ears should be pained by the screams of the poor sufferers, write an order to the master of the Charleston Work House, or the New Orleans Calaboose, where they are most cruelly stretched, in order to render the stroke of the whip, or the blow of the paddle, more certain to produce cuts and wounds, which cause the blood to flow at every stroke. And let it be remembered that these poor creatures are often *women* who are most indecently divested of their clothing, and exposed to the gaze of the executioner of a *woman's* command.

What then, our beloved sisters, must be the effects of such a system upon the domestic character of the white females? Can a corrupt tree bring forth good fruit? Can such despotism mould the character of the Southern woman to gentleness and love, or may we not fairly conclude that all that suavity, for which slaveholding ladies are so conspicuous, is in many instances the paint and the varnish of hypocrisy, the fashionable polish of a heartless superficiality.

But it is not the character alone of the mistress that is deeply injured by the possession and exercise of such despotic power, nor is it the degradation and suffering to which the slave is continually subject, but another important consideration is, that in consequence of the dreadful state of morals at the South, the wife and the daughter sometimes find their homes a scene of the most mortifying, heart-rending preference of the degraded domestic, or the colored daughter of the head of the family. There are alas, too many families, of which, the contentions of Abraham's household is a fair example. But we forbear to lift the veil of private life any higher; let these few hints suffice to give you some idea of what is daily passing *behind* that curtain which has been so carefully drawn before the scenes of domestic life in Christian America.

And now, dear sisters, let us not forget that *Northern* women are participators in the crime of Slavery—too many of *us* have surrendered our hearts and hands to the wealthy planters of the South, and gone down with them to live on the unrequited toil of the Slave. Too many of *us* have ourselves become slaveholders, our hearts have been hardened under the searing influence of the system, and we too, have learned to be tyrants in the school of despots. Too few of us have replied to the matrimonial proposals of the slaveholder:

> Go back, haughty Southron, thy treasures of gold,
> Are dimmed by the blood of the hearts thou hast sold;
> Thy home may be lovely, but round it I hear,
> The crack of the whip, and the footsteps of fear.
>
> Full low at thy bidding thy negroes may kneel,
> With the iron of bondage on spirit and heel;
> Yet know that the Northerner sooner would be,
> *In fetters with them, than in freedom with thee.*

But let it be so no longer. Let us henceforward resolve, that the women of the free states *never* again will barter their principles for the blood bought luxuries of the South—*never* again will regard with complacency, much less with the tender sentiments of love, any man "who buildeth his house by unrighteousness, and his chambers by wrong, that useth his neighbor's service *without* wages, and giveth him *not* for his work."

And there are others amongst us, who, though not slaveholders ourselves, yet have those who are nearest and dearest to us involved in this sin. Ah! yes, some of us have fathers and mothers, sisters and brothers, who are living in the slave states, and are daily served by the unremunerated servant; and for the enlightenment of these, *we* are most solemnly bound to labor and to pray without ceasing. Vast responsibilities are rolled upon us by the fact that we believe we have received the truth on this subject, whilst they are in ignorance and error. Some Northern women too, are the wives of slaveholders, and of those who hold mortgages on the slaves of the South.

IV.—Women Use the Products of Slave Labor.

Multitudes of Northern women are daily making use of the products of slave labor. They are clothing themselves and their families in the cotton, and eating the rice and the sugar, which they well know has cost the slave his unrequited toil, his blood and his tears; and if the maxim in law be founded in justice and truth, that "the receiver *is as bad* as the thief," how much *greater* the condemnation of those who, not merely receive the stolen products of the slave's labor, but *voluntarily* purchase them, and *continually appropriate them to their own use.*

We frequently meet with individuals who, though very particular in not using sugar which has been raised by the slave, yet feel no compunction in purchasing slave grown cotton, and assign as a reason, that there is not that waste of life in the culture of cotton, which attends that of sugar. *But is there less waste of blood?* We copy the following description of the *whip* which is *made by Northern men,* and used by Southern overseers on *cotton plantations.* "The staff is about 20 or 22 inches in length, with a large and heavy head, which is often loaded with a quarter or half a pound of lead, wrapped in cat gut, and securely fastened on, so that nothing but the greatest violence can separate it from the staff. The lash is 10 feet long, made of small strips of buckskin, tanned so as to be dry and hard, and plaited carefully and closely together, of the thickness, in the largest part, of a man's little finger, but quite small at each extremity. At the furthest end of this thong, is attached a cracker, nine inches in length, made of strong sewing silk, twisted and knotted, until it feels as firm as the hardest twine.

This whip in an unpractised hand, is a very awkward and inefficient weapon; but the *best* qualification of the overseer of a *cotton* plantation, is the ability of using this whip with adroitness, and when wielded by an experienced arm, it is one of the *keenest instruments of torture* ever invented by the ingenuity of man. The cat-o-nine-tails, used in the British military service, is but a clumsy instrument beside this whip, which has superseded the cow hide, the hickory, and every other species of lash on the *cotton* plantations. The cowhide and the hickory, bruise and mangle the flesh of the sufferer; but *this whip cuts,* when expertly applied, *almost as keen as a knife,* and never bruises the flesh, nor injures the bones." What then do our sisters say to using *cotton* which is raised under the keen and cutting lash of this whip, by the mancipated mothers, wives, and daughters of the South? Can these sufferers really believe we are remembering them that are in bonds *as bound with them,* whilst we freely use what costs them so much agony?

And has the Lord uttered no rebuke to us in these fearful times? Is there *no* lesson for *us* to learn in recent events? Who are the men that now weep and mourn over their broken fortunes—their ruined hopes? Are they not the merchants and manufacturers, who have traded largely in the unrequited labor of the slave? Men who have joined hand in hand with the wicked, and entered into covenant to rivet the chains of the captive?

We are often told that free articles cannot be obtained, but why not? Our answer is, because there is so little demand for them. Only let the moral sense of the free states become so pure and so elevated as to induce them to refuse to purchase slave grown products, and the manufacturers, and merchants, and grocers, will soon devise some plan by which to supply their factories and stores with free labor cotton and goods. But we may be asked what are we to do until the market is supplied? We unhesitatingly reply, suffer the inconvenience of deprivation, and then will *you,* dear sisters, become the favored instruments in the Lord's hand, of producing that change in public feeling which will lead to such action, as will bring the desired supply into our market. We find that those who really wish to obtain such articles, are almost universally able to do so, if they will pay a little higher price, and be satified to wear what may not be of quite so good a quality, but it is frequently the case that even this trifling self denial is not necessary.

We would remind you of the course pursued by our Revolutionary fathers and mothers, when Great Britain levied upon her colonies what they regarded as unjust taxes. Read the words of the Historian, and ponder well the noble self-denial of the men and *women* of this country, when they considered their own liberties endangered by the encroachments of England's bad policy. Look then, at the influence which their measures produced in making it the interest of the merchants and manufacturers in Great Britain to second the petitions of her colonies for a redress of grievances, and judge for yourselves whether the Southern planters would not gladly second the efforts of the abolitionists, by petitioning their National and State Legislatures, for the abolition of Slavery, if they found they could no longer sell their slave grown products.

"In most departments, by common consent, business was carried on as though no Stamp Act had existed. This was accompanied by spirited resolutions to *risk all consequences,* rather than submit to use the paper required by law. While these matters were in agitation, the Colonists entered into associations against importing British manufactures, till the Stamp Act should be repealed. By suspending their future purchases on the repeal of the Stamp Act, the Colonists made it the *interest* of merchants and manufacturers to solicit for that repeal. They had usually taken so great a proportion of British manufactures, that the sudden stoppage of all their orders, amounting annually to two or three millions sterling, threw some thousands in the mother country out of employment, and induced them, from a regard to their own interests, to advocate the measures wished for by America. The petitions by the Colonists were seconded by petitions from the merchants and manufacturers of Great Britain. What the former prayed for, as a matter of right, and connected with their liberties, the latter also solicited from motives of immediate interest.

"In order to remedy the deficiency of British goods, the Colonists betook themselves to a variety of necessary domestic manufactures. In a little time, large quantities of common cloths were brought to market; and these, though *dearer,* and of a *worse quality,* were cheerfully preferred to similar articles imported from Britain. That wool might not be wanting, they entered into resolutions to abstain from eating lamb. Foreign elegancies were laid aside. The *women* were as exemplary as the men, in various instances of self-denial. With great readiness, they refused every article of decoration for their persons, and luxury for their tables. These restrictions, which the Colonists had voluntarily imposed on themselves, were so well observed, that multitudes of artificers in England were reduced to great distress, and some of their most flourishing manufactories were in a great measure at a stand."—*Ramsay's History, U. S.,* pp. 345–6.

Would not a similar effect be produced in *this* country at *this* time, if the *women* of the Free States would practice the same self-denial which distinguished our mothers. Let them refuse "every article of decoration for their persons and luxury for their tables," and of convenience and comfort, the use of which imposes upon the down-trodden slave *not* a paltry tax of pennies upon paper and tea, but the heavy tribute of tears, and groans, and blood, and perpetual bondage.

Our fathers and mothers were quick to discern the working of the principle of oppression when it was applied to themselves: their necks were galled by the friction of a very easy yoke, and they were prompt to devise means and ways by which to rid themselves of it. But to us, dear sisters, is committed a *far nobler work.* *We* are called upon, *not* to break the yoke which is fastened on *our own* necks, but to aid in the generous, disinterested effort to break asunder that which bows the heads of the poor in the very dust of degradation and wo. *We* are called upon by the cries of a people "scattered and peeled, meted out and trodden down," to obey the divine injunction, "Deliver the poor and needy, rid them out of the hand of the wicked." Our fathers asserted their right to freedom at the point of the bayonet and the mouth of the cannon, but we repudiate all war and violence—"Our weapons are *not* carnal, but spiritual:" we wield no other sword than "the sword of the Spirit;" we encounter the fees of freedom with "the word of God," whilst our feet are shod with the preparation of the Gospel of peace, our breasts covered with the shield of faith, our heads with the helmet of salvation. We need no other armory, for this is a moral conflict, and we know that "Truth is mighty, and will prevail."

V.—Northern Women Apologize for the Sin of Slavery.

Many have no correct views of the height and depth, the length and breadth, and innumerable horrors of this enormous system of crime. They too easily allow themselves to be persuaded of the mildness of American Slavery, by those who go to the South, *not* to search out the hidden works of darkness, *not* to visit the sighing captive in the house of his bondage; but to make their fortunes, and to sit in the drawing-rooms of the rich and the great. Such see no more of the internal machinery of slavery, than the man who goes to the theatre and sits in the pit or the boxes sees of what passes behind the curtain. Some of us have been *behind* the scenes of the South, and we feel it to be an imperative duty to assure you, that slavery is a whited sepulchre, which however fair and beautiful it may outwardly appear, is nevertheless "full of dead men's bones and all uncleanness." We entreat you, therefore, no longer to apologize for slavery, for we feel assured, that in so doing you are helping to deceive the North as to the real state of things in the Slave States, and to paralyze her moral energies—to rivet the chains of the colored man, and to blind the eyes and steel the heart of the master to his highest interests and monstrous obligations.

VI.—Northern Women Have Deep Rooted Prejudices Against Our Colored Brethren and Sisters.

They gravely talk of their intellectual inferiority and their physical organization, as sufficient reasons why they never should be permitted to rise to an equality with the whites in this country, forgetting that they have not yet proved the position assumed, with regard to mental inferiority. This we utterly deny, and appeal to history and facts to show that the colored is equal in capacity to the white man.

Intellect of the Colored Man.

The Honorable Alexander H. Everett, in a speech delivered in Boston about ten years ago, says, "Trace this very civilization of which we are so proud to its origin, and see where you will find it. We received it from our European ancestors—they had it from the Greeks and Romans, and the Jews. But where did the Greeks, and the Romans, and the Jews get it? They derived it from Ethiopia and Egypt—in one word, from Africa. Moses, we are told, was instructed in all the learning of the Egyptians. The founders of the principal Grecian cities, such as Athens, Thebes, and Delphi, came from Egypt, and for centuries afterwards their descendants returned to that country, as the source and centre of civilization. There it was that the generous and stirring spirits of the time—Herodotus, Homer, Plato, Pythagoras, and the rest—made their noble voyages of intellectual and moral discovery, as ours now make them in England, France, Germany, and Italy. . . . Well, sir, who were the Egyptians? They were Africans. And of what race? It is sometimes pretended, that though Africans, and of Ethiopian extraction, they were not black. But what says the father of history, who had travelled among them, and knew their appearance as well as we know that of our neighbors in Canada? Herodotus tells us they were black, with curled hair. . . . It seems, therefore, that for this very civilization of which we are so proud, and which is the only ground of our present claim of superiority, we are indebted to the ancestors of these very blacks, whom we are pleased to consider as naturally incapable of civilization. And it is worth while, Mr. President, to remark, that the prejudice which is commonly entertained in this country, and which does not exist to any thing like the same extent in Europe, against the color of the blacks, seems to have grown out of the unnatural position which they occupy among us. At the period to which I have just alluded, when the *blacks took precedence of the whites* in civilization, science, and political power, no such prejudice appears to have existed."

In this extract from Alexander H. Everett, the most unexceptionable evidence seems to be afforded, as to the intellectual capacity of the colored man. And in speaking of the doctrine of his mental imbecility, he says, "I reject with contempt and indignation this miserable heresy." Dr. J. Mason Good also spurns the idea of his inferiority, and thinks "that of all the arguments which have ever been offered to support the doctrine of different species, *this is the feeblest and most superficial*." "It may," says he, "suit the narrow purposes of a slave merchant—of a trafficker in human nerves and muscles; it may suit *their* purpose to introduce such a distinction into their creed, and to let it constitute the whole of their creed; but it is a distinction too trifling and evanescent to claim the notice of a physiologist for a moment."

Blumenbach, of Germany, had a private library composed entirely of works written by colored men; but it has been the policy of Americans to exclude such books from our public and private collections of taste and talent—at least, so far as we have been able to ascertain.

In a sermon preached about thirty years since by Dr. Griffin, late President of Williams College, in which he endeavors to refute the false and malicious assertions relative to the inferiority of the colored man, he says, "Passing by many ancient Ethiopians, to whom I have only seen a reference, and some instances of energy and prowess in the field, I have arranged the names of more than fifty negroes and mulattoes which are worthy to be preserved from oblivion. Among these, I could show you a handsome portrait painter*—a distinguished physician†—skilful

*Cugoano, once a slave. †James Durham, also at one time a slave.

navigators[*]—and useful ministers of religion.[†] I could show you those who could repeat from memory the Koran,[‡] and those who without rules and figures could perform the most difficult calculations with the rapidity of thought.[§] I could show you those who were skilled in Latin, Greek, and Hebrew; and an instance or two, I might add, of Arabic and Chaldaic. I could show you teachers of the Latin language, a teacher of mathematics,[¶] and a publisher of almanacs.[**] I could show you poets—authors of letters,[††] histories, memoirs[‡‡]—essays,[§§] petitions to legislative bodies,[¶¶] and Latin verses and dissertations.[***] I could show you a man "of great wisdom and profound knowledge, several who were truly learned, and one who gave private lectures on philosophy at a university[†††]. I could show you members of the universities of Cambridge, Leyden, and Wittemburg. I could show you one who took the degree of doctor of philosophy, and was raised to the chair of a professor in one of the first universities of Europe; another who was corresponding member of the French Academy;[‡‡‡] and a third who was an associate of the National Institute of France. I could show you one who for many ages has been surnamed in Arabia the Wise, and whose authority Mahomet himself frequently appealed to in the Koran, in support of his own opinion. I could show you men of wealth and active benevolence: here a sable Howard, spending his life in visiting prisons, to relieve and reclaim the wretched tenants, and consecrating all his property to charitable uses;[§§§] there another founding a hospital for poor negroes and mulattoes, and devoting his life and fortune to their comfort for more than forty years.[¶¶¶] In another place, a third, making distant and expensive voyages, to promote the improvement of his brethren and the colonization of Africa."[¶¶¶¶]

We hope, dear sisters, that we shall be excused for dwelling so long on the intellectual capacity of the colored man: we have

*Paul Cuffee and G. Vassa. †Capetein and others. ‡Stedman mentions one. §Thomas Fuller and others. ¶Francis Williams. **Bannaker, a slave. ††Sancho. ‡‡Vassa. §§Othello. ¶¶Sancho. ***Capitein and Williams. †††Anthony William Amo. ‡‡‡L. Islet Geoffroy. §§§Joseph Rachel. ¶¶¶Jazmin Thomazeau. ¶¶¶¶Paul Cuffee.

done so, because we believe it is of vital importance to his interest, that the ungenerous and unfounded aspersions of his enemies should be completely refuted, in order that all pretexts for treating him as an inferior should be entirely destroyed. We must remember, that if in this country he has not risen to an equality with the whites, it is solely because he has not had the same advantages. In schools for colored children, we have witnessed the same ability and anxiety to learn; and our experience is not only corroborated by the testimony of many living teachers, but by that of Anthony Benezet, who had the honor of being the first individual in America who opened a school for colored children. He says, "I can with truth declare, that among my negro scholars I have found *as great a variety of talent* as among the like number of whites;" and then proceeds to assign the reason *why we* regard them as our inferiors: "and I am bold to assert, that the notion of their inferiority is a *vulgar prejudice*, founded on the *pride* of those who keep them at so great *a distance as to be unable to form a right judgment of them*."

We are, however, often told that those colored men who have excelled in intellect, are not black, and that their superiority arises from a mixture with the white race. The testimony of the Abbe Gregoire, who wrote a book on the Intellect of Negroes, is directly contrary to this opinion; he says, "the number of negro writers is *greater* than that of mulattoes." And Wadstrom, who travelled extensively in Africa, thought the blacks *superior* to the whites, for says he, "the intellect of Africans is *so far from being of an inferior order*, that one finds it difficult to account for their acuteness which so far transcends their means of improvement."*

But what further evidence of the intellectual capacities of colored men do we need, than the attainments of those who are now living in our free states, and occupying the station of ministers of the gospel. Let any one who counts them inferior, only go and hear a Cornish, a Raymond, a Wright, and a Williams,

*This testimony is very valuable, because he had previously kept a school for whites.

of New York; a Charleton, of Virginia, a Meacham, of St. Louis, a Graham of Nashville, a Small, of Boston, or a Gardner and a Douglass of Philadelphia, and we feel assured he will be ashamed of ever having entertained an opinion so unjust to them, and so derogatory to his own heart and head. We cannot appeal to the abilities of our colored brethren here as lawyers, physicians, and statesmen, but why? It is *not* because *they could not fill* such stations among us, had they the same advantages which white men enjoy, but simply because American prejudice has closed the doors of our literary institutions against them, and pertinaciously refused to grant them the privilege of drinking freely from that river of knowledge which flows so abundantly throughout our borders. But we can point you to the West India Islands, first to Hayti, whose government was organized by colored men, among whom Toussaint L'Ouverture shines pre-eminent as a statesman, as well as a warrior, and which has been for more than 30 years entirely under their control. We will next point you to the Island of St. Thomas, a Danish island, where Slavery still exists, and yet the aid-de-camp of the Governor General of all the Danish West Indies, is a colored man, who it is supposed is the wealthiest man in the island, being worth a million, which vast sum he made by merchandize. In the Island of St. Cristophers, the proportion of colored members in the Assembly is increasing every year; it is supposed that at least one eighth of the present Assembly are colored men. Several of the special magistrates are colored men. The editor of the "St. Christopher Weekly Intelligencer and Advertiser," is a colored man, who has been a bold advocate of liberal principles. He is described as a thorn in the side of the planters, and a great blessing to the island. In the Island of Dominica, 4 or 5 of the members of the Assembly are colored men. In Antigua there is now a colored Methodist minister, who is represented by a planter who is well acquainted with the clergymen of the island, as the most clear and logical reasoner, and finished writer among them. In Jamaica, out of five representatives from the town of Kingston, 4 of them are colored; and a colored lawyer lately died in this island, who was acknowledged to be an ornament to his profession. Many other instances of talent and worth and wealth might be adduced, but it seems impossible after all which has been said, any doubt can remain on your minds as to the equality of the colored with the white man. To the above instances we would add that of James McCune Smith, who after being cast out of the seminaries of learning in this Republican Despotism, was received into the University of Glasgow, where he has recently graduated and taken the highest honor, though he competed with hundreds of *white* men.

Now beloved sisters, what do you say to these proofs of the intellectual abilities of our colored brethren? Can you *rejoice* to find that you were mistaken in your opinion of their inferiority? Are you ready to extend to them the hand of a sister, to welcome them upon that platform of equal rights, social, civil, and religious, on which they are as much entitled to stand erect as any white man in our land?

II.—Physical Organization.

But we will now endeavor to answer the second objection urged against the colored man's equality, which is his physical organization. He has a black, or it may be a yellow skin. From these peculiarities, it is argued that he belongs to a *different race*. This we confess we cannot understand, if the Bible account of man's creation is authentic; for we are there told that Eve was the "mother of all living." There can therefore be but *one race* of human beings, as they have all sprung from one common parentage. This holy book speaks of different nations, people, kindreds, and tongues, but tells us nothing of different *races*; so far from it that it expressly declares "God hath made of one blood all the nations, to dwell on all the face of the earth." But there are others who gravely tell us that Noah was the second father of mankind, and that he had three sons, one of whom was white, one red, and one black, and that from them have descended the varieties of the human family. This is an assertion without proof, and it does appear to us to be a very absurd one, as learned physiologists all agree in the opinion, that difference of color is produced by climate, food, &c. Buffon says that "man though white in Europe, black in Africa, yellow in

Asia, and red in America, is still *the same animal,* tinged only with the *color* of the *climate.*" It appears self-evident then, that Noah's sons were of but one complexion, when they separated after the flood, to people the three then known continents, and that the color of their descendants has been produced by the difference of climate into which they emigrated. "No matter what the original complexion of the emigrants to any country may have been, it is always found to accommodate itself to the hue peculiar to that country or climate. Hence the Jews, who were doubtless originally all of the *same* complexion, and who never intermarry with the nations among whom they sojourn, are found to be *white* in Germany and Poland, *swarthy* in Spain and Portugal, *olive* in the Barbary states, and Egypt, and *black* in Hindoostan. And hence a colony of Ethiopians, who settled at Colchis, on the Black Sea, 2,000 years ago, have now become white, and the Portuguese who settled 200 years since on the coast of Africa, black."

"But still we shall be asked, if color be the effect of climate, why the negroes born in the United States are not white. We answer, that it should be remembered, ours "is *not* the *native climate* of the *white* man." The copper color is that which is incident to this climate, therefore it would be very unnatural for the black man to turn white on our shores.

The learned professor of Gottengen remarks, that in Guinea, not only men, but dogs, birds, and particularly the gallinaceous tribe are black; whilst near the frozen seas, bears and other animals are white. Here it may be asked why are not men who live under the same parallels of latitude in Africa and America of the same color. We reply that climate does not depend entirely upon latitude, but very materially upon the face of a country also. In Africa a vast extent of sandy desert stretches across that continent, which renders the reflection of the sun's rays far more intense than it can be in America, where the surface is broken by mountains and hills covered with verdure, and diversified and cooled by lakes and rivers. The products of these two countries are also different, and therefore the food of the inhabitants is dissimilar. Hence even in Africa, the inhabitants of the mountain and the plain, differ greatly in their complexions. This will be fully understood when we remember that the sun's rays have no heat until they have come in contact with the earth's surface, from the diversified reflecting power of which, our atmosphere derives its comparative degrees of heat.

The simple reason which the Bible assigns for the color of black in the human species is truly philosophical. "Look not upon me," said the bride in Canticles, "because I am *black*, for the sun hath looked upon me." Her blackness was occasioned by the intense heat of a tropical sun, and so is the African's.

If then the black skin is *not* the mark of a distinct *race*, but merely the peculiarity incident to climate and food, what shall we say about it—how shall we regard it? As an insuperable barrier between our colored brethren and sisters and ourselves—as a sufficient reason for their being deprived of valuable privileges and social enjoyments among us—or a trivial distinction, as unworthy of our notice, as the difference of color in the hair and the eyes of our fairer companions and friends. Is it not wonderful and humiliating to us as Republicans and Christians, that we should ever have made the sinful distinctions and silly assertions which we have, because some of our fellow creatures wear a skin not colored like our own? Let the time past then suffice, and let us now resolve to do all we can in vindicating the character of our colored brethren from the unjust aspersions which the world and the church have united in heaping upon them. Women ought to feel a peculiar sympathy in the colored man's wrongs, for like him, *she* has been accused of mental inferiority, and denied the privileges of a liberal education.

VII.—Northern Women Are Lending Their Aid to the Colonization Society.

If the advocates of this scheme would only call it by its true name, the EXPATRIATION Society we would be spared the trouble of entering into an explanation of its character and objects. But the very fact of its having been clothed with the mantle of benevolence, is a powerful reason why we should attempt to exhibit it, just in that light which its own friends and advocates have thrown upon it, in their public speeches and its official documents.

Before enumerating our reasons for condemning the principles of this society, we will give some little account of its origin. As early as the year 1777, Jefferson formed a plan for colonizing the free colored population of the United States, on some of the western vacant lands, but it proved a failure. In 1787, Dr. Thornton, of Washington, formed another scheme to effect the same purpose on the western coast of Africa, and published an address to the colored people residing in Massachusetts and Rhode Island, inviting them to accompany him. A sufficient number agreed to go, and were prepared for the expedition, but this project likewise failed for want of funds. About the year 1800 or 1801, soon after the insurrection of Gabriel, at Richmond, Virginia, the impulse of fear prompted another effort to throw from our shores the free people of color, and any slaves who might be suspected of insurrectionary intentions. The legislature of Virginia, in secret session, instructed Mr. Monroe, then Governor of the State, to apply to the President of the United States, and urge him to institute negociations with some of the powers of Europe possessed of colonies on the coast of Africa, to grant an asylum, to which our emancipated negroes might be sent. Mr. Jefferson opened a negociation with the Sierra Leone Company, for that purpose, but without success. He subsequently applied to the Government of Portugal, but failed. The project was then abandoned, as hopeless. In the Legislature of Virginia of 1816, the subject was again brought forward, and the following resolution was adopted by a large majority: "Resolved, that the Executive be requested to correspond with the President of the United States, for the purpose of obtaining a territory on the coast of Africa, or at some other place, not within any of the states or territorial governments of the United States, to serve as an asylum for such persons of color as are now free, and may desire the same, and for those who may hereafter be emancipated within the commonwealth, and that the senators and representatives of this State in the Congress of the United States, be requested to exert their best efforts to aid the President of the United States in the attainment of the above object."

This resolution was passed in the Virginia House of Delegates, some time before the formation in the city of Washington of the American Colonization Society. The origin of this society is thus spoken of in a memorial presented by the managers of the Colonization Society to Congress in 1817: "The design of this institution, the committee are apprised, *originated* in the disclosure of the secret resolutions of prior legislatures of that State; to which may also be ascribed, it is understood, the renewal of their obvious purpose in the resolution subjoined to this report—a resolution which was first adopted by the House of Delegates of Virginia, on the 14th December, 1816, with an unanimity which denoted the deep interest that it inspired, and which openly manifested to the world a steady adherence to the humane policy which had secretly animated the same councils at a much earlier period. This brief but correct history of the origin of the American Colonization Society, evinces that it sprang from a deep solicitude for *Southern* interest, and *among those* most competent to discern and promote them," *i.e.*, among *slaveholders*. The African Repository informs us, that at its formation, *every* one who spoke was a slaveholder. In an address of the Rockbridge (Virginia) Colonization Society, published in Vol. IV. p. 274, we find this assertion: "About twelve years ago, some of the wisest men in the nation, *mostly slaveholders*, formed in the city of Washington the present American Colonization Society." Its first president, Bushrod Washington, was a slaveholder all his life, and *during his continuance in office* sold fifty-four human beings, who were driven off in chains to Louisiana.

From that time to the present, it has been principally managed by slaveholders. We make this assertion on the authority of the African Repository, the official organ of the Colonization Society; which, in speaking of the members of the Society, repeatedly asserts that they are "mostly slaveholders"—"chiefly slaveholders"—"by far the larger part citizens of slaveholding states;" and that "from the first it obtained its *most decided* and efficient support from the slaveholding states." Charles Carroll, its second president, who signed the Declaration that all men are created free and equal, died owning near one thousand slaves. Its third president, James Madison, also died a slaveholder; and its fourth president, Henry Clay, is now a slaveholder. This society, then, originated in the Ancient Dominion, in the midst of slavery; and its members and publications have again and again urged the fact of their being slaveholders as an incontrovertible evidence of their peculiar fitness to manage its concerns, and their claims to Southern confidence and Southern aid. Thus, in the African Repository, Vol. VII. p. 100, we find the following: "Being *mostly slaveholders ourselves*, having a *common interest with you* on this subject, an equal opportunity of understanding it, and the *same motives* to prudent action, what better guarantee can be afforded for the just discrimination and the safe operation of our measures." The league, then, which has been formed between the colonizationist and the slaveholder seems to us to be as close as that which existed between Jehoram and Jehoshaphat, when the latter said unto the former, "I am as thou art, my people as thy people, my horses as thy horses." Read now our objections, and judge for yourselves whether this assertion be not true. We condemn it—

I. Because it surrenders the great principle, that man cannot justly hold man as property, and regards the wresting of the slaves from their masters as great an outrage as the invasion of their right of property in houses, cattle, and land. To substantiate this charge, we quote from the African Repository, Vol. I. p. 283: "We hold their *slaves*, as we *hold their other property*, SACRED." In Vol. II. p. 13, we find these words: "Does this society wish to meddle with our slaves as our *rightful property?* I answer, *no*—I think not." And in a speech delivered by Henry Clay, he said, "It was proper again and again to repeat, that it was far from the intention of the society to *affect in any manner* the tenure by which a *certain species of property is held*." He was himself a slaveholder; *and he considered that kind of property as inviolable as any other in the country.*

II. Because it not only is *not* hostile to slavery, but in its reports and in its official organ, and by its auxiliary societies and principal supporters, exonerates slaveholders from guilt, and represents their *criminality* as their *misfortune*. In the VIIth vol. of the African Repository, are these declarations: "It (the society) *condemns no man because he is a slaveholder*"—p. 200. "They (the abolitionists) confound the *misfortunes* of one generation with the *crimes* of another, and would sacrifice both individual and public good to *an unsubstantial theory of the rights of man*"—p. 202. From the Second Annual Report of the New-York State Colonization Society, we extract the following exculpation of slaveholders: "The existence of slavery among us, though *not at all* to be objected to our Southern brethren as a *fault*, is yet a blot on our national character," &c.

III. Because it openly, actively, uncompromisingly denounced the immediate abolition of slavery as injustice to the masters, a calamity to the slaves, dangerous to society, and contrary to the requirements of Christianity. We prove this assertion by an extract from the First Annual Report of the New-Jersey Colonization Society: "The inhabitants of the South cannot and *ought not* suddenly to emancipate their slaves, to remain among them free. Such a measure would be *no blessing* to the slaves, but the very madness of self-destruction to the whites." In Vol. III. of African Repository, p. 97, are these words: "The scope of the society is large enough, but it is in no wise mingled and confounded with the broad sweeping views of a *few fanatics* in America, who would urge us on to the total abolition of slavery."

IV. Because it formally lays down the doctrine, that it is *not* incumbent on all oppressors to do justly and love mercy *now*, and that it is proper to cease from robbery and sin by a slow process. In Vol. V. of the African Repository, is this sentiment, p. 329: "Were the very spirit of angelic charity to pervade and fill the hearts of all the slaveholders in our land, it would *by no means* require that all the slaves should be instantaneously liberated."

V. Because it confesses that its measures are calculated to secure the slave system from destruction—to remove the apprehensions of slaveholders—to increase the value of slave property—and thus to perpetuate the thraldom of native Americans. John Randolph, in a speech delivered at the first meeting of the Colonization Society, remarked, "So far from being connected with the abolition of slavery, the measures proposed *would prove one of the greatest securities to enable the master to keep in possession his own property.*" In the 3d Volume of the African Repository, we find the following: "To remove these people (free colored persons) from among us, will *increase the usefulness* and improve the moral character of those who remain in servitude, and with whose labors the country is unable to dispense." And in Vol. II. p. 344: "THE EXECUTION OF ITS SCHEME WOULD AUGMENT, INSTEAD OF DIMINISHING, THE VALUE OF THE PROPERTY LEFT BEHIND."

VII. Because it positively denies that it has any reference to the work of emancipation. In a speech of James S. Green, published with the First Annual Report of the New-Jersey Colonization Society, is this explicit avowal: "Our society, and the friends of colonization, wish to be distinctly understood upon this point. From the beginning, they have DISAVOWED, and they do yet *disavow*, that their object is *the emancipation of the slaves.*" In the 3d. Vol. of African Repository, p. 197, this official organ of the society declares, "*It is no abolition society*: it addresses as yet *arguments to no master*, and disavows with horror the idea of offering temptations to any slave. *It denies the design of attempting emancipation, either partial or gradual.*" And again: "The Colonization Society, as such, have renounced *wholly* the name and the characteristics of abolitionists. On this point, they have been unjustly and injuriously slandered. *Into their account, the subject of Emancipation does not enter at all.*"—p. 306.

VIII. Because it holds that slaveholders are such from *necessity*,—that the oppressive laws which are enacted against the free colored and slave population, are justified by sound policy, and that it is wrong to increase the number of the free blacks by emancipation. We quote now from the North American Review of July, 1832: "Thousands are connected with the system of slavery from *necessity*, and not from choice. . . . The vast majority of those who would emancipate, we have no hesitation in saying, are deterred from it by a PATRIOTISM AND A PHILANTHROPY, which look beyond the bound of their particular district, and beyond the ostensible quality of the mere abstract act." And in the Ninth Annual Report of the Colonization

Society we find the following declaration with regard to the oppressive laws against the people of color: "Such, unhappily, is the case: but there is a *necessity* for it; and so long as they remain among us, will that necessity continue."

IX. Because it denies the power of the Gospel to overcome prejudice, and maintains that no moral or educational means can ever raise the colored population from their degradation to respectability and usefulness *in this country*. By inculcating this monstrous doctrine, it measurably paralyzes in the breasts of those who embrace it all efforts to improve the character and condition of this depressed and injured class. The following may be found in the African Repository, Vol. IV. p. 118, 119: "In every part of the United States, there is a broad and *impassable* line of demarcation between every one who has *one drop* of African blood in his veins, and every other class in the community. The habits, the feelings, all the prejudices of society—prejudices which neither *refinement*, nor *argument*, nor education, NOR RELIGION ITSELF, can subdue—mark the people of color, whether bond or free, as the subjects of a degradation, *inevitable and incurable*. The African belongs by birth to the very lowest station in society; and from that station HE CAN NEVER RISE, be his talents, his enterprise, his virtues what they may. . . . They constitute a class by themselves—a class out of which *no individual can be elevated*, and below which none can be depressed."

X. Because, while it professes to remove those emigrants only who go "with *their own consent*" to Africa, it is the instrument of a cruel persecution against the free people of color, by its abuse of their character, representing them as seditious, dangerous, and useless. It contends, moreover, that emancipation should not take place without the simultaneous expatriation of the liberated—thus leaving to the slave the choice of *banishment* or *perpetual servitude*. In the African Repository, Vol. II. p. 188, the following sentiment is found: "No scheme of abolition will meet any support that leaves the emancipated blacks among us." In Vol. III. p. 26, "*We would say, liberate them only on condition of their going to Africa*." In Vol. IV. p. 226. "*I am not complaining of the owners of slaves:* it would be as humane to throw them from the decks in the middle passage, as to set them free in our country." And on p. 300, "*A scheme of emancipation without colonization* (*i.e.* expatriation) they know, and see, and feel to be productive of *nothing but evil;* evil to all whom it affects—to the white population, to the slaves, *to the manumitted themselves.*"

XI. Because it is held in abhorrence by the free people of color, wherever they possess the liberty of speech and the means of intelligence, as a scheme full of evil to themselves and to their enslaved brethren. This may be amply proved, by quoting resolutions passed at hundreds of meetings held by them to protest against the scheme of expatriation many years BEFORE any Anti-Slavery Society was ever formed in this country. We will transcribe but one, which we regard as a noble specimen of that true elevation of moral feeling to which many of our colored brethren have attained, notwithstanding the withering, crushing influence of prejudice in this land: "Resolved, That we never will separate ourselves voluntarily from the slave population in this country: they are our brethren by the ties of consanguinity, of suffering, and of wrong; and we feel that there is more virtue in suffering privations with them, than fancied advantages for a season."

XII. Our last objection is founded on the fact, that this society, although it professes to be the greatest friend of the colored people, is exerting no influence to produce a correct public sentiment with regard to their rights in this the land of their birth. Far otherwise—their love is a love to get rid of them—a love to keep them low in the dust under the feet of oppression, and the scowl of contempt, and the ban of a separate and inferior caste, as long as they remain in *their own native* America. Of the principles of Colonization, then, we fully and freely express our entire disapprobation. We believe them to be utterly unchristian—calculated alike to foster the feelings of pride and prejudice in the aristocracy of the North, and the unjust, unreasonable oppression of our colored brethren and sisters—and to blind the eyes, sear the conscience, and steel the heart of the slaveholder at the South.

The effect which this scheme is to produce upon Africa is quite another thing: were that influence ever so favorable, our opinion of its *principles* and its tendency to strengthen the unholy feeling of prejudice in the United States, must remain the same. An immense amount of evil has been done here: our colored brethren have entreated and protested in vain—they have lifted up their voices in vain, and besought Colonizationists to spare them the abuse which they have heaped upon their defenceless heads—to roll back from off their prostrate bodies and minds the ponderous wheels of that American Juggernaut, Prejudice, which their hands have dragged over them by incessantly preaching up the doctrine that "*they never can rise*" in this country, and that *even Religion itself* cannot subdue in the hearts of Americans that hatred of the colored man which now fills their bosoms.

We consider it our duty then, solemnly to protest against the influence of colonization principles on the free and the bond in our land, and to urge our sisters to examine them for themselves, and to judge for themselves whether they are not evil, unsound, and unsustainable on the broad basis of human rights and Christian love. To those who justify this scheme on the ground of its evangelizing Africa, we would point to this emphatic, tremendous declaration of the apostle Paul, when vindicating the purity of Christian principles from the false accusations of his enemies, some of whom affirmed that the apostles said "*let us do evil that good may come, whose condemnation is just.*"

We would then turn to the effects which colonization has already produced on Africa. Its deleterious influence on that devoted country had become so manifest to the English philanthropists that Dr. Philip was recalled from South Africa, that he might lay before the British public the working of this system *on the natives*. From a speech delivered by him in Exeter Hall, we copy the following:

"The system has been put into operation and supported by the nations of Europe, to the manifest *injury of the natives of America, Africa, and other parts of the world.*" After noticing some of these, the Doctor proceeded—"In the beginning of the last century, the European colony in Africa was confined to within a few miles of Cape Town. From that period it has advanced, till it now includes many more square miles than are to be found in England, Scotland, and Ireland. (If a traveller, who had visited that country twenty-five years ago, were to take his stand on the banks of the Koiskama river, and ask what had become of the natives whom he saw there on his former visit; if he took his stand on the banks of the Sunday river, and looked forward to a country seventy miles in breadth before him, he might ask the same question; if he were to take his stand again on the Fish river, and there extend his views to Caffraria, he might ask the same question; and were he to take his stand upon the snow mountains called Craaff Reinet, (he would have before him a country containing 40,000 square miles,)—and ask where was the immense concourse that he saw there twenty-five years ago, no man could tell him where they were.")

In Zion's Watchman, we find the succeeding remarks on this extract, and as they contain our own views and give some interesting facts relative to Liberia, which are not generally known, we have inserted them without any alteration.

"A fine illustration this, of the benefits of colonization to the *natives* of any country? It shows that colonization is only another name for extermination. As long as human wickedness is what it is, such will ever be the result. Such it ever has been. 'You can't civilize the Hottentots,' was the doctrine of South Africa. 'An Indian will be an Indian—you can't civilize him,' was the doctrine in the United States; and accordingly the natives have melted away and been destroyed in both cases, just in proportion as the tide of colonization has moved onward. Such, too, thus far, has been, as a matter-of-fact, the result at Liberia. To this moment, there has been no amalgamation of the natives and colonists. On the contrary, the same line of distinction, and the same separate interests and mutual jealousies exist there as have existed in other cases. The colonists are called by the natives, ''Mericans,' their customs, ''Merica man's fash.' Governor Pinney himself, (see letter some three years since,) declared that 'the natives are, as to wealth and intellectual cultivation, related to the colonists as the negro in America is to the white man—and this fact, added to their mode of dress, leads to the same distinction as exists in America between colors,' so that 'a colonist of any dye, (and many southern are of a darker hue than the Vey, or Dey, or Croo, or Bassoo,) would, if at all respectable, think himself *degraded* by marrying a native; the missionaries of the American Board, Wilson, and Wynkoop, (Missionary Herald, June, 1834,) select the site for the 'mission settlement,' half a mile from the colonial settlement; 'and then,' say they 'we took all the pains we could to impress the mind of the king and his people with the fact, that the mission is to be entirely distinct from the colony, and will be identified with the interests of the natives,' as if it were vain to secure their confidence, so strong their jealousies, and so separate their interests from those of the colonists, except by taking *sides* with them; and finally, in August, 1835, (Note African Repository, May, 1836,) we find the citizens of Monrovia enacting as a law, 'that all Kroomen residing at Krootown, on that side of the Mesurado river, shall pay annually to the town of Monrovia the sum of one dollar and fifty cents, and do *any* kind of fatigue duty required by the president of the town council; and further, that all Kroomen coming there to reside 'shall report themselves within five days to the president of the town council, and receive a certificate, granting them *permission* to reside (not in Monrovia but even) in Krootown—for which they shall pay the sum of one dollar and fifty cents; and all neglecting to comply with this resolution shall, on conviction, pay the sum of two dollars, and leave the settlement; and in case of failure to pay the fine, shall be compelled to do public labor until the fine is satisfied;' and not these only, but 'that all *other* natives, not in the employment of the colonists of the town, *shall* when called upon by proper authority, do fatigue duty of ANY NATURE, that may be assigned them'—thus, instead of amalgamating them with the colony, they are branding them as a suspected and servile class, and giving their president the semi-power of a slaveholder.

"Now, be it remembered, (see Phillips' South Africa,) that all this is the very kind of encroachment which marked the early history of colonization in South Africa. A more perfect counterpart could not be found. But with such a beginning, and proceeding as it did from bad to worse, why was it that colonization there did not long ago, result in the utter extermination of the natives? Simply and only because that colony was under the control of a *home government*, and was to some extent, restricted in its powers of mischief. With no restriction whatever, then, of this kind, what will—nay, what must be, the end of such a beginning in Liberia? Evil, and evil only, and evil continually; and if the gospel makes progress among the natives, it will be only by the instrumentality of those who keep 'entirely distinct from the colony, and identified with the interest of the natives,' and who do what they do, not by the help, but in spite of the influence of the colony. Such has been the case in South Africa—and such, as the facts already show, must be the case in Liberia."

If, then, colonization has already proved such a curse to Africa, and if Liberia is treading in the footsteps of the colonies which preceded her; if the missionary is indeed compelled to plant the standard of the cross *beyond* the limits of Cape Palmas, and to *disavow all connection with it;* how can we possibly flatter ourselves any longer with the delusive hope that the land of Ham will be evangelized by colonization, particularly when we remember, that according to the declaration of colonizationists, these very colonists are "a nuisance from which it were a blessing to be free," "*the subjects of a degradation inevitable and incurable.*"

But here we shall be met with the assertion, that these colonies will put an end to the slave trade. What have they done towards the attainment of this object? We here copy from the most favorable account which we have seen of the state of the colonies, contained in an official communication to the Secretary of the Navy from Captain Joseph J. Nicholson, of the Navy, dated January 8th, 1837. "The slave trade within the last three years has seriously injured the colony. Not only has it diverted the industry of the natives, but it has effectually cut off the communication with the interior. WITHIN A YEAR FOUR SLAVE FACTORIES HAVE BEEN ESTABLISHED ALMOST WITHIN SIGHT OF THE COLONY."—[Bassa Cove.]

"And what assurance have we that the colony itself when grown up and independent will not follow the example of Christian Maryland, and the Christian capital of our own Christian land, and set up a trade in the bodies and souls of its own citizens or in the "menials" that it may buy of the heathen? In doing so, it would only imitate the example of the Honorable Bushrod Washington, the first President of the Colonization

Society, who sold a large number of slaves into the hopeless bondage of the South." We doubt not that such will actually be the case in Liberia, unless a correct public sentiment is created by anti-slavery efforts and anti-slavery principles, which will throw a healthful influence over the colony before it becomes strong enough to govern itself. Colonization principles could not certainly pacify public opinion there any more than it has done it here; and if slavery is a *necessary* evil in America, why may it not be a *necessary* evil in Africa? If the society condemns no man for being a slaveholder here, how could it possibly condemn any of the colonists for holding slaves there? The holy principles of truth change not with climate, nor with color, nor with circumstance, but are like their great Author the *same yesterday, to-day, and for ever*; the same on the hill tops and green valleys of America, and the sickly shores and sandy deserts of Africa. O! then our sisters, for the sake of the slave, whose condition as *property* is rendered *more secure* by colonization, according to the showing of the society itself; for the sake of the free people of color, whose hopes of usefulness and respectability in *their own native land*, are completely blasted by the vituperation and slanders which are heaped upon them by its advocates; for the sake of the manumitted slave, to whom is offered the sad alternative of *exile or bondage*, and for the sake of our white brethren and sisters in whose hearts the weed of prejudice grows with frightful luxuriance, nursed by the transplanting hand of colonization—O! for the sake of the bond and the free, the colored and the white, we beseech you to pause and reflect, and pray over this subject, before you any longer throw your influence into the scale of unholy prejudice and cruel expatriation, rather than into that of human rights and Christian philanthropy. We pray you give no countenance to a society which seeks to banish our free colored citizens from *their own* country.—Do not admit for a moment that they have "no right to live in the white man's homestead," as colonizationists have denominated the United States. But on the contrary, let us openly and constantly plead their cause, assert their rights as Americans and do all that we can to produce that correct public sentiment, which will throw open our literary institutions to them, and that spirit of true repentance which will induce us as a nation, to nurse and cherish in the bosom of fraternal love these trembling injured outcasts of society. Let us protest against that cruelty which would cast our brethren on the barbarous and sickly shores of Africa, and that strange philanthropy which while it builds a college in Liberia, refuses to grant to the colored man in this country the privileges of a liberal education. Let us then endeavor to hasten the time, when "for their shame they shall have double, and for confusion they shall rejoice in their portion."

VIII.—The Colored Women of the North Are Oppressed.

The eighth reason we would urge for the interference of northern women with the system of slavery is, that in consequence of the odium which the degradation of slavery has attached to *color* even in the free states, our *colored sisters* are dreadfully oppressed here. Our seminaries of learning are closed to them,* they are almost entirely banished from our lecture rooms, and even in the house of God they are separated from their white brethren and sisters as though we were afraid to come in contact with a colored skin. Listen now to the sad experience of one of these oppressed and injured ones. We quote from a letter recently received from a colored young woman of a neighbouring city. "For the last three years of my life, I can truly say, my soul has hungered and thirsted after knowledge, and I have looked to the right hand and to the left, but there was none to give me food. Prejudice has strictly guarded every avenue to science, and cruelly repulsed all my efforts to gain admittance to her presence." Hear, too, her description of her

*To the honor of Oberlin Institution, we would say that it is a noble exception to the ban of proscription which denies to our sisters the privilege of obtaining a liberal education in our high schools. It stands erect in our land like a pillar of marble bearing on its capital these words, "Of all monopolies, a monopoly of knowledge is the worst. Let it be as active as the ocean, as free as the wind—as universal as the sunbeams." It is a city set upon an hill in the midst of this "hypocritical nation." A light revealing that prejudice which hangs like a dark cloud over the literary institutions of the "Freest Government in the world."

feelings in attending a place of worship in this city.—"I have been to meeting to-day, and can say of a truth, it was good to be there, for the Master of assemblies was present and the broad wing of his love rested on us as a canopy. Notwithstanding I am so often blessed in going to meeting, I find it a grievous cross. My heart sinks within me at times when I look around me and do not see one familiar face, and feel that *I am despised for my complexion*, and perhaps considered as an intruder."

Here then, are some of the bitter fruits of that inveterate prejudice, which the vast proportion of Northern women are cherishing, towards their colored sisters, and let us remember that every one of us who denies the sinfulness of this prejudice, under the false pretext of its being "an ordination of Providence," "no more to be changed than the laws of nature," and fixed beyond the control of any *human power*, yea! a feeling which *religion itself cannot subdue;" every one of us* who make these colonization excuses for hugging to our bosoms the viper which strikes such deadly stings into the very hearts of our oppressed sisters, is awfully guilty in the sight of Him who is no respecter of persons. If it be a sin to despise the man clothed in vile raiment, and to say to such an one "stand thou there, or sit here under my foot-stool," how much greater must be the crime of despising our sister, because *God has clothed her* in a darker skin than our own. How solemn the reflection, that "Whoso oppresseth the poor *reproacheth his Maker*." Yes, our sisters, little as we may be willing to admit it, yet it is assuredly true, that whenever we treat a colored brother or sister in a way different from that in which we would treat them, were they white, we do virtually *reproach our Maker* for having dyed their skins of a sable hue.

IX.—True Cause of the Increase of Prejudice.

It is said that this prejudice has increased to a dreadful extent since Anti-Slavery Societies were formed in our country, and we are often told that upon *us* must rest all the blame. Now we contend that the victims of this prejudice are the very best judges of this matter, and we appeal to the sister from whose letters we have already quoted, to know what are the views of the colored people with regard to it. In another letter she says, "They know the American Colonization Society to be their *most potent enemy* at home, they feel its iron grasp upon their necks, pressing them to the very dust, and behold with horror and dismay *that prejudice grows more fierce and bitter wherever its influence is felt.*" And again in a letter of a still more recent date: "I solemnly believe that the American Colonization Society is the most cruel and potent enemy of the free people of color, that it seeks to rivet faster the fetters of the slave, by driving the free people from their native land, that it originated in hatred to us, and that *it has increased prejudice a thousand fold*, by asserting that we are "too debased to be reached by heavenly light. It is sustained by constant and artful appeals to the prejudices of our white brethren and sisters, against our complexions, and we view all their proceedings with abhorrence, and receive their protestations of kindness, as the most bitter mockery." And again in speaking of an Anti-Slavery lecturer whom she had heard, she writes thus: "He proved so clearly *what we feel so deeply*, that the *Colonization Society originated in hatred to the free people of color.*"* Shall we refuse then, the testimony of this sufferer, shall we turn a deaf ear to her experience, when she lifts her voice in the accents of agony and warning, as to the true cause of the increase of this soul withering prejudice. In the bitterness of her heart she exclaims, "O! the guilt! the heavy load of guilt that rests on the heads of Colonizationists, may God in his mercy open their eyes before it be too late. *We pity, while we fear them.*"

But look at the *principles* of our two Societies, and judge for yourselves which of them would legitimately produce the monster prejudice. On the banner of one is written "*the people of color must*, in this country, REMAIN FOR AGES, PROBABLY FOREVER, A SEPARATE AND INFERIOR CASTE, weighed down by causes powerful, universal, *inevitable*, which neither *legislation nor christianity can remove.*" On that of the other is inscribed

*In good keeping with this assertion, we would state, that when the only official agent they ever sent to England, was about to sail, a friend observed to him that he had heard of his intended visit to England. "Yes," said he, "*but I am not going out of any love to the niggers.*" Would abolitionists have sent out such an agent?

in characters of light. Human rights—prejudice vincible. "Whatsoever ye would that men should do to you, do ye even so to them." If ye have respect to colors, ye commit sin. Let the swift witness for truth in your own bosoms decide the question.

But our colored sisters are oppressed in other ways. As they walk the streets of our cities, they are continually liable to be insulted with the vulgar epithet of "nigger," no matter how respectable or wealthy, they cannot visit the Zoological Institute of New York, except in the capacity of nurses or servants—no matter how worthy, they cannot gain admittance into, or receive assistance from any of the charities of this city. In Philadelphia, they are cast out of our Widow's Assylum, and their children are refused admittance to the House of Refuge, the Orphan's House and the Infant School connected with the Alms House, though into these are gathered the very offscouring of our population. These are only specimens of that soul crushing influence from which the colored women of the North are daily suffering. Then again, some of them have been robbed of their husbands and children by the heartless kidnapper, and others have themselves been dragged into Slavery. If they attempt to travel, they are exposed to great indignities and great inconveniences. Instances have been known of their actually dying in consequence of the exposure to which they were subjected on board of our steam-boats. No money could purchase the use of a berth for a delicate female, because she had a colored skin. Prejudice, then degrades and fetters the minds, persecutes and murders the bodies, of our free colored sisters. Shall *we* be silent at such a time as this—shall we say prejudice is an innate feeling, implanted by God in our hearts—shall we blaspheme his holy name by saying in other words that He has taught us, yea *caused* us to hate our brother? Or shall we not rather arise in the moral strength of our womanhood and our Christianity, and cast out this foul demon from our hearts, our houses, and our churchs, in the name of the Lord of light and of love?

X.—The South Is Appealing to the North.

The last reason we shall urge, is the fact that the South is appealing to us for help in the overthrow of Slavery. From the

"Appeal to Christian women of the South" we learn that a lady in North Carolina, made the following remark about two years ago: "Northerners know nothing at all about Slavery; they think it is perpetual bondage only, but of the depth of degradation that word involves they have no conception, if they had, *they would never cease their efforts until so horrible a system was over-thrown.*" Here then, is a strong appeal to *Northerners* to put forth *their* unceasing energies to overthrow the system of Southern oppression. Those women in the slave states who are mourning over the abominations of the land, feel that a spirit of reform on this subject, can no more be expected to originate among slaveholders, than a temperance reform, or a moral reformation, among those most deeply involved in the sins of drunkenness, and licentiousness. *Their appeal is to the North.* Another lady from the South, a slaveholder, who visited Philadelphia last fall, remarked to an abolitionist, that, until Northern women did their duty on this great subject, it could not be expected that Southern women would do theirs. She appeared surprised at the apathy of the free states when she became acquainted with the extent to which *they* were involved in the crime of slavery—she had never thought on these things before, and encouraged her friends, who had enlisted in the Anti-Slavery cause, saying, if you accomplish your object, you will do a great work, and be a blessing to our country. These appeals are from *Southern women*—shall we disregard them?

We will now relate a circumstance that occurred to Theodore D. Weld, when he was lecturing in Pittsburgh, Pa. in 1835. At the close of one of his evening lectures, a man sought him through the crowd, and extending his hand to him through his friends, by whom he was surrounded, solicited him to step aside with him for a moment. After they had retired by themselves to some corner of the house, says the man, "I am a slaveholder from Maryland—*and you are right—the doctrine you advocate is the truth.*" "Why then," said the lecturer, "do you not emancipate your slaves?" "Because," replied the Marylander, "*I have not religion enough*"—he was a professed Christian—"I have not sufficient moral courage to do so under the existing state of public sentiment—I dare not subject myself to the torrent of opposition which, from the present state of public sentiment, would be poured upon me; but do you abolitionists go on, and you will effect a change in public sentiment, which will render it possible and easy for us to emancipate our slaves. I know," continued he, "a great many slaveholders in my state, who stand on precisely the same ground that I do in relation to this matter. *Only produce a correct public sentiment at the North, and the work is done; for all that keeps the South in countenance while continuing this system, is the apology and argument afforded so generally by the North; only produce a right feeling in the North generally, and the South cannot stand before it; let the North be thoroughly converted, and the work is at once accomplished at the South.*" Another fact which may be adduced to prove that the South is looking to the North for help, is the following: At an Anti-Slavery concert of prayer for the oppressed, held in New York city, in 1836, a gentleman arose in the course of the meeting, declaring himself a Virginian and a slaveholder. He said he came to that city filled with the deepest prejudice against the abolitionists, by the reports given of their character in papers published at the North. But he determined to investigate their character and designs for himself. He even boarded in the family of an abolitionist, and attended the monthly concert of prayer for the slaves and the slaveholders. And now as the result of his investigations and observations, he was convinced that *not only the spirit but the principles and measures of the abolitionists* ARE RIGHTEOUS. He was now ready to emancipate his own slaves, and had commenced advocating the doctrine of immediate emancipation—"and here," said he, pointing to two men sitting near him, "are the first fruits of my labors—these two fellow Virginians and slaveholders, are converts with myself to abolitionism. And I know a thousand Virginians who need only to be made acquainted with the true spirit and principles of abolitionists in order to their becoming converts as we are. *Let the abolitionists go on in the dissemination of their doctrines, and let the Northern papers cease to misrepresent them at the South—let the true light of abolitionism be fully shed upon the Southern mind, and the work of immediate and general emancipation will be speedily accomplished.*"—*Morn. Star.*

But a still more powerful appeal has been made to us. Two of our Southern sisters who were once slaveholders, have come up from the land of worse than Egyptian bondage, and besought us, as women, as Americans, as Christians, to awake from the slumber of apathy, and to rise in all the power of female influence, to the high and holy duty of rebuking the sin of oppression at the South, and the sin of prejudice at the North. Their testimony against the abominations of Slavery is fully laid before the public—that testimony must be admitted, by every candid mind, to be unexceptionable, for what but a deep and solemn sense of duty to the suffering slave could induce them to throw themselves out so prominently as witnesses against a system, of which their nearest and dearest relatives are now the advocates and practical supporters. They have declared to us that no one who has not been an *integral* part of this system, can form any idea of the wreck of temper and of morals which Slavery produces. They have told us that it is not for the slave alone that they plead, but for the master and the mistress also—for the oppressor cannot wield the iron rod of his power, without having his conscience seared, his heart hardened, his moral susceptibilities blunted, and his spiritual eye darkened. They have been nursed in the arms, pillowed on the bosom, and cradled on the lap of Slavery. They have lived from infancy up to womanhood behind that painted curtain which hangs before the scenes of private life. They tell us, and surely *they* ought to know whereof they affirm, that the folds of this tapestry are too artfully and studiously disposed by the hands of petty tyrants, to admit of the heedless glances of Northern visitors, discovering the wretchedness, and crime, and cruelty which exists behind it.—Take one single instance as an illustration. A gentleman of this city was in New Orleans 4 years ago, at the time that the atrocious cruelties of Madame La Loirie were discovered, and her house torn down by the mob. He said that only a few days previous to this circumstance, he had dined with that—what shall we call her—not *woman*—that were too noble a title—that *slaveholder*—and that he had not the least suspicion of those deeds of darkness and of death which were transacting even then in the garret and the cellar. The sunshine of Southern hospitality illuminated her parlor, with all the light of fashionable etiquette and hollow-hearted politeness, and the sounding brass and the tinkling symbol drowned the groan of the captive sufferer, and the stifled wail of the lacerated and dying Slave, and the clank of his fetters, and the moanings which told how the iron had entered into his soul. He was the guest of the *mistress*, he sat in *her* parlor, he sat down to *her* board, and what did he know? How could he know of those hidden works of darkness which she understood as well how to *conceal* as how to perpetrate?

These sisters tell us that the testimony of a Northern woman, who, when she went to the South two years since, made it her business to inquire into the real condition of things, is correct. In a letter to a friend in Philadelphia, she says, "On coming South, we found that although we had heard so much of Slavery, the *half*, the *worst half* too had never been told us; not that we have *seen* any thing of cruelty ourselves, though truly we have felt its deadening influence, and the accounts we hear from every tongue, *that nobly dares to speak the truth*, are deplorable indeed." They are now in our free states to which they were driven by the cries of the sufferers they had no power to relieve—they remonstrated, and rebuked, and entreated in vain—there was no spirit of reform there—no wish to deliver those who were drawn unto death—no ear open to receive the truth—no heart to feel for the multiplied wrongs of the outraged victim of oppression. They fled to our Northern states, and their hearts beat high with the expectation of mingling with spirits who could weep over the down trodden slave—but did they find such spirits—did they meet with those who sympathised in his sorrows, and labored for his redemption? No! To their grief and amazement they found that the North was wrapt in profound darkness and apathy—the gushing fountain of feeling was almost frozen, and they had well nigh despaired of the bondman ever being released, except by the strong arm of vengeance in the midst of the war-cry, the roar of the cannon, and the exterminating judgments of an angry God. A lowering cloud had gathered over the land of their birth, full of the judgments of God, and in awful suspense they watched it, deepening and expanding, as the oppressor, year after year, treasured up for himself wrath against the day of wrath, and the righteous retribution of heaven.—They had well nigh sunk down in utter hopelessness, as their aching eyes rested on the dark cloud that thickened with gloomy portents, and careered with thunderings, but a star had already arisen in the east, though they knew it not. They had heard some rumor of a fiery comet which had glared on the sky, and thrown far and wide its wild and fierce sweepings, threatening murder and war. Their hearts trembled with fear—they turned away from the spectacle—they refused to listen for a while—but duty, solemn duty, forced upon their minds the necessity of seeing for themselves—they seized the telescope of truth—they scanned the frightful meteor—and what was their joy at finding that it was the star of hope, the harbinger of certain and speedy deliverance to those over whom they had so often wept in secret places. And now, beloved sisters, they have given themselves wholly to the cause of immediate, unconditional, universal emancipation—they ask our help—they invite us all to join battle with the foes of freedom in this great moral contest—they beckon us onward—shall we respond? or shall we stop our ears to the cry of the poor, sent up to our Northern states through their lips and their pens?

HOW NORTHERN WOMEN CAN HELP THE CAUSE OF EMANCIPATION.

We come next to the second grand division of our subject: we are now to show you *how* Northern women can help the cause of abolition. That we be not further tedious unto you, we will endeavor to be concise. We would answer, they can organize themselves into Anti-Slavery Societies, and thus add to the number of those beaming stars which are already pouring their cheering rays upon the dreary pathway of the slave. Let the women of the Free States multiply these, until a perfect galaxy of light and glory stretches over our Northern hemisphere. By joining an Anti-Slavery Society, we assume a responsibility—we pledge ourselves to the cause—we openly avow that we are on the side of the down-trodden and the dumb—we declare that Slavery is a crime against God and against man—and we swell the tide of that public opinion which in a few years is to sweep from our land this vast system of oppression, and robbery, and licentiousness, and heathenism. But be not satisfied with merely setting your names to a constitution—this is a very little thing: read on the subject—none of us have yet learned half the abominations of slavery. We wish that every Northern woman could read "Stroud's Sketch of the Slave Laws;" they are as a code worthy of the remark made by Summers of Virginia, when speaking of the laws of that state alone. "How will the provisions of our slave code be viewed in after time? I fear some learned antiquary may use them as a portion of his evidence to prove the *barbarism* of the present enlightened and Christian era; I fear lest *he* may not *understand* the necessity which with us *justifies our attempt to annihilate the mind* of a portion of our race." How monstrous must be those statutes which seek the annihilation of the immortal mind of man! how tremendous the crime!

Anti-Slavery publications abound; and *no intelligent woman ought to be ignorant of this great subject—no Christian woman can escape the obligation now resting upon her, to examine it for herself.* If Anti-Slavery principles and efforts are right, *she is bound* to embrace and to aid them; if they are wrong, as the vestal virgins of her country's honor and safety, and the church's purity and faith, she is bound to oppose them, to crush them if she can. Read, then, beloved sisters; and as many of you as are able, subscribe for one or more Anti-Slavery papers or periodicals, and exert your influence to induce your friends to do the same; and when memory has been stored with interesting facts, lock them not up in her store-house, but tell them from house to house, and strive to awaken interest, and sympathy, and action in others, who, like Galleo of old, "care for none of these things." The seeds of knowledge must be sown broad-cast over our land—light must be increased a thousand-fold—and woman ought to be in this field: it is *her duty, her privilege* to labor in it, "as woman never yet has labored."

By spreading correct information on the subject of slavery, you will prepare the way for the circulation of numerous petitions, both to the ecclesiastical and civil authorities of the nation. Presbyterians ought to petition their Presbyteries and Synods, and the General Assembly. Baptists ought to petition their Annual and the Triennial Conventions. Protestant Episcopalians their Conventions, and Methodists their Annual and General Conferences: beseeching and entreating that they would banish slavery from the communion table and the pulpit, and rebuke iron-hearted prejudice from our places of worship. Such memorials must ultimately produce the desired effect.

Every woman, of every denomination, whatever may be her color or her creed, *ought to sign* a petition to Congress for the abolition of slavery and the slave trade in the district of Columbia—slavery in Florida—and the inter-state slave traffic. Seven thousand of our brethren and sisters are now languishing in the chains of servitude in the capital of this republican despotism: their hands are stretched out to *us* for help—they have heard what the women of England did for the slaves of the West Indies—800,000 women signed the petition which broke the fetters of 800,000 slaves; and when there are as many signatures to the memorials sent up by the women of the United States to Congress, as there are slaves in our country, oh! then will the prison-doors of the South be opened by the earthquake of public opinion.

We believe you may also help this cause by refraining from the use of slave-grown products. Wives and mothers, sisters and daughters, can exert a very extensive influence in providing for the wants of a family; and those women whose fortunes have been accumulated by their husbands and fathers out of the manufacture and merchandize of such produce, ought to consider themselves deeply indebted to the slave, and be peculiarly anxious to bear a testimony against such participation in the gains of oppression, as well as to aid by liberal donations in spreading Anti-Slavery principles.

Much may be done, too, by sympathizing with our oppressed colored sisters, who are suffering in our very midst. Extend to them the right hand of fellowship on the broad principles of humanity and Christianity—treat them as *equals*—visit them as *equals*—invite them to co-operate with you in Anti-Slavery, and Temperance, and Moral Reform Societies—in Maternal Associations, and Prayer Meetings, and Reading Companies. If you regard them as your inferiors, then remember the apostolic injunction to "condescend to men of low estate:" here is a precious opportunity; and if it is improved, dear sisters, we feel assured you will find your own souls watered and refreshed, whilst you are watering others. Opportunities frequently occur in travelling, and in other public situations, when your countenance, your influence, and your hand, might shield a sister from contempt and insult, and procure for her comfortable accommodations. Then, again, you can do a great deal towards the elevation of our free colored population, by visiting their day schools, and teaching in their Sabbath and evening schools, and shedding over them the smile of your approbation, and aiding them with pecuniary contributions. Go to their places of worship; or, if you attend others, sit not down in the highest seats, among the white aristocracy, but go down to the despised colored woman's pew, and sit side by side with her. Multitudes of instances will continually occur in which you will have the opportunity of *identifying yourselves with this injured class* of our fellow-beings: embrace these opportunities at all times and in all places, in the true nobility of our great Exemplar, who was ever found among the *poor and the despised*, elevating and blessing them with his counsels and presence. In this way, and this alone, will you be enabled to subdue that deep-rooted prejudice which is doing the work of oppression in the Free States to a most dreadful extent.

When this demon has been cast out of your own hearts, when *you* can recognize the colored woman as a WOMAN—*then* will you be prepared to send out an appeal to our Southern sisters, entreating them to "go and do likewise." The South has been addressed by a Southern woman—she is doubtless expecting, perhaps waiting, for an appeal from her Northern sisters. *When* will Northern women be ready to make such an appeal? Can they be ready *before* they have fulfilled their duties to the colored people around their own doors? A Southern woman, a slaveholder, who visited the North last summer, remarked she was astonished to find that prejudice against color was so strong and malignant—yes, she was indignant. How, then, would an address on behalf of the slave from *Northern* women appeal to the hearts of such a Southerner? Could she believe its sincerity? or would she not rather turn and say, Go, break the cord of caste in the Free States, and then come and persuade us to break the yoke of bondage here. Go back to the North, and lift the colored woman from her low estate there, and then come and talk to us about the slavery of the colored woman here. Go, pluck the beam out of your own eye first, and then will you see clearly how to pull the mote from ours. Go, "physician, heal thyself." Go, and *when you* have performed *your* duties, then, aided by that correct public sentiment which you shall have created at the North—*then we will* do our duties at the South.

We solemnly believe that the North can labor effectually with the South *only so far* as she overcomes her deadly hatred to the free colored man. Prejudice, dear sisters, is that Achan in the camp of abolitionists which *must be brought out, and stoned before all the people,* before we ever can successfully storm the citadel of slavery, or even its out-works. Look, then, at the tremendous responsibility resting on us at the North. If we do not abandon this cherished sin, *we must* inevitably become individually guilty of keeping our brethren and sisters at the South in bondage, just as the Israelites would have been individually guilty of producing the continued defeat of the army at Ai, if they had refused to surrender Achan to the exterminating sentence of the law.

And since we have set before our white sisters of the North their duties to our sisters of color, so now we would tenderly solicit their indulgence whilst we throw out some suggestions to them. *You*, beloved sisters, have important duties to perform at this crisis—duties no less dignified, and far more delicate and difficult. You daily feel the sorrowful effects of the prejudices which is exercised towards those peculiarities of form with which our Heavenly Father has stamped you. It is your allotment to bear the cruel scorn and aversion in a thousand different ways. Your hearts often bleed at the heedless expression and studied avoidance—your spirits are often cast down under the glance of contempt and the smile of heartless courtesy, and you feel afraid to come into our presence, unless assured that we can greet you as human beings, as women, as sisters, and often, perhaps, when duty calls you into associations with us, you shrink back and refuse to come, lest haply some among us may be too delicate to sit beside you, too fastidious to bear the contact. We know such things must be mortifying, and hard, very hard, to endure especially from your *professed friends*, but we entreat you to "bear with us a little in *our folly*," for we have so long indulged this prejudice, that some of us find it exceedingly difficult to divest our minds of it. We fully believe that it is *not* a plant of our Father's planting, we are striving to root it up; have patience then with us *whilst* the struggle continues and when it is over, we shall be able to labor more effectually than ever for you. You must be willing to mingle with us whilst we have the prejudice, because it is only by associating with you that we shall ever be able to overcome it. You must not avoid our society whilst we are in this *transition state.* "And indeed bear with us" for our *own sakes;* as women, as Christians, we are ashamed of our folly and sin, and we entreat *your aid* to help us to overcome and abandon it.—We know that we have not the same mind in us, which was in Christ Jesus, and you can confer no greater favor upon *us* than in thus for a season, "bearing all things, believing all things, hoping all things, enduring all things." Put on, therefore, towards us, your weak and erring sisters, that charity which is the bond of perfectness, that charity which never faileth. We crave your sympathy and prayers: we deeply feel our need of them.

But there is one thing which above all others we beseech you to do for this glorious cause. *Pray for it.* Pray without ceasing, for unless all your efforts are baptized with prayer, they can never return into your own bosoms with the blessing of heaven—they can never effectually help forward this work. We have no confidence in *effort without prayer*, and no confidence *in prayer without effort.* We believe them as inseparably connected as are faith and works. And if any woman tell us that she prays but cannot labor for the slave, we must reply to her in the language of James, in reference to faith and works—show me prayers *without* effort, and we will show thee our prayers *by our* efforts. Yes! sisters—we want you to be persuaded of this, because we are assured, that an utter fallacy passes among us for sound doctrine. There is nothing more common than to hear such expressions as these from the lips of men and women who are *doing nothing* to set the bondman free—we are as much Anti-Slavery as you, we abhor slavery as much as any one possibly can. Away with such hypocritical pretensions to sympathy!—It is just that kind of sympathy which says to the naked and hungry, "Depart in peace, be you warmed and filled, notwithstanding ye give them not those things which are needful to the body." Well may *we* exclaim with the Apostle "what doth it profit?" *We* believe in no such Anti-Slavery principles, for full well do *we know* that our principles possess a *life and power which must prompt to action, a spirit which will live in our life, and breathe in our words.*

Ah! but we are told—the measures, the measures, we cannot unite with. What is the matter with the measures? Why there is such a daring of public opinion—such a determination to carry on this work in spite of opposition when you see that the public are not prepared for it—when you know that they have so often produced mobs.

And how, we would ask, is the public to be prepared for the reception of these great doctrines? By throwing a bushel over the candle of truth, because the organs of spiritual vision are pained by its radiance, in consequence of the moral darkness in which they have so long been involved—or, by still continuing to *hold forth* the word of life until the eye gradually becomes accustomed to the light, and at last receives it without pain. What did our Lord mean by calling his disciples *the light of the world*, and by commanding them *to let their light so shine before men*, that they might *see* their good works. Did he mean they must cease to preach the truth as soon as wicked and deceitful men opposed the truth, and blasphemed it? Let us learn his meaning from his actions, for *He* embodied all his principles in his glorious *life. He* did not speak or profess one thing while *He* acted another. Let us then trace the history of Jesus—let us see whether he propagated doctrines obnoxious to public opinion, adverse to the views of the dignitaries of Church and of State, and whether, when he was traduced and opposed, he bowed to popular tumult and clamour, or stood erect, uprearing the light of truth in the tempest of passion which howled around him.

EXAMPLE OF JESUS AND HIS APOSTLES.

In early childhood his life was sought by Herod, and during all his sojourn in the flesh, "he was a man of sorrows and acquainted with grief," beset by cruel enemies, who went about to kill him. Some times the Jews were so incensed, that they took up stones to cast at him because "they perceived that he spake his parables *against* them." At one time "they thrust him out of the city (of Nazareth) and led him to the brow of the hill that they might cast him down head-long, but he passing through the midst of them went his way." At last a great mob, armed with swords and with staves, came out to take him, and after being betrayed by one of his own disciples, and mocked and scourged by his enemies, he was put to death, although "He did *no* sin, neither was guile found in his mouth." Judea was in a ferment, and the hearts of the people were moved as the trees of the wood by the sweeping blast. But did all this opposition silence the tongue of *Him*, who "spake as never man spake?" No! he went about from city to city, and from village to village, here in the synagogue and there by the sea shore, and then again in Peter's ship as it floated on Genezareth, every where preaching *those very truths, which excited to wrath* the unbelieving Jews.

But from the example of him who was "God manifest in the flesh," let us turn to those who were "men of like passions with ourselves." Was Stephen deterred from proclaiming the truth, because "the Jews stirred up the people, and elders, and the scribes, and came upon him, and brought him to the council, and set up *false* witnesses against him?" No! he seized upon this very opportunity to trace their history from the call of Abraham, and to prove by recorded facts, that they had "always resisted the Holy Ghost," as their fathers did, so also had they done, in being the betrayers and murderers of that Just One, whose coming their own prophets had foretold. And what were the consequences? Did the Spirit and the power by which he spake convince them? No! they were cut to the heart, and gnashed upon him with their teeth, and even whilst he was full of the Holy Ghost, "they cried out with a loud voice, and stopped their ears, and ran upon him with one accord, and cast him out of the city, and stoned him." He died by the hands of a lawless mob. And what effect did this violent opposition produce on the Apostles? Did they withhold the truth because the people were unwilling to hear it? or did they fearlessly and perseveringly "dare public opinion," by their obnoxious *doctrines?* Let the conduct of Peter and John answer this query.

And how did the great Apostle of the Gentiles bear himself? Was he deterred from his work by what he had witnessed at the stoning of Stephen? And when converted to that faith which he once destroyed, was he satisfied with merely ceasing to do evil, or did he also go about preaching that gospel, which was to the Jews a stumbling block, and to the Greeks foolishness? After the scales fell from his eyes, "straightway he preached Christ in the synagogue, that he is the Son of God," and when, by the power of his arguments, he confounded the Jews that dwelt at Damascus, and they took counsel to slay him, he was let down by night in a basket from the wall, and fled to Arabia. We afterwards find him in Jerusalem, where he preached until "the Grecians went about to slay him," when he was sent to Arabia. At Antioch he preached the humiliating doctrine, that through the very man Christ Jesus, who had been condemned and executed as a malefactor, the Jews must obtain forgiveness of sins, and be justified from all things from which they could not be justified by the law of Moses. This roused their malice and envy, so that they contradicted and blasphemed, and spake against those things which were spoken by Paul; and even succeeded in stirring up the people, and the *devout and honorable women*, and raised persecution against Paul and Barnabas, and expelled them out of their coasts.

At Iconium they preached with such power that a great multitude, both of the Jews and also of the Greeks, believed, yet still the unbelieving Jews stirred up the people, and made their minds evil affected towards the brethren, and when an assault was made, both by the people and their *rulers*, to use them despitefully and to stone them, they fled into Lystra. Here too, Paul was beset by a mob, and stoned, and drawn out of the city and left as dead. Did all these persecutions prevent him from promulgating the truths of the gospel? No? In labors he was more abundant than any of the Apostles, and his zeal was equalled only by the virulence with which he was opposed every where. We next find him at Thessalonica, where the Jews set all the city in an uproar, and assaulted the house of Jason, and sought to bring the Apostles out to the people, but they fled to Berea, where it is stated "they received the word with all readiness of mind and *searched the Scriptures daily to know whether these things were so:*" the consequence of which was, that *honorable women here believed the very truths* which the devout and honorable women of Antioch rejected, through ignorance and prejudice, having suffered themselves to become dupes of those malignant Jews, who stirred up the people against the Apostles.

OPPOSITION TO TRUTH SHOULD NOT SILENCE ITS ADVOCATES.

It is *no new thing* for the truth to be opposed by violence, and its promulgators mobbed from city to city.—And if Paul felt it his duty to persevere in preaching it, notwithstanding the uproars, confusion and insurrections, which were raised to crush it, we can see no reason why abolitionists should cease their efforts on behalf of the suffering slave, because mobs are raised against them in New York, Boston, Utica, and Cincinnatti. If (as some have asserted) *abolitionists* raised these mobs, then with equal truth it may be said, that Paul and Barnabas raised those of Antioch, Lystra, Ephesus, and Jerusalem. In view of these facts, what is the duty of the friend of the Slave? We answer unhesitatingly, to *go on* fearlessly, uncompromisingly, and pacifically, to preach the truth and nothing but the truth, in the whole length and breadth of our land. Those who raise these mobs, are responsible for that spirit of anarchy and violence which they are producing, and *not* those who are the innocent victims of such outrages.

In the lives of Jesus and his Apostles, do we find our warrant for breasting the furious waves of public opinion, for keeping our ranks in righteousness unbroken, and for steadily holding up the unflickering flame of truth, in the midst of a crooked and perverse generation. And we must believe that if there were any real principle, any living sympathy in the hearts of those who are "as much Anti-Slavery as we are," and yet condemn our measures, that instead of doing *nothing*, they would devise measures of their own, and if their measures were the right measures, doubtless they would prevail, and we should be driven from the field. If we do wrong, it is *no excuse for their doing nothing*, at such an awful crisis as the present.

MINISTERIAL ADVOCATES OF SLAVERY.

The abolitionists have stood by that altar which avarice and lust of power have consecrated to the demon of Slavery, and they have solemnly protested that the priests who offered human sacrifices upon her shrine, would themselves be doomed by the indignant voice of coming generations. The Jeroboams of the South and the North, have put forth their hands from that altar, saying, "lay hold on them," but their hands, like that of the presumptious monarch of Israel, have withered in the impious attempt to close the lips of those who have been raised up in this "hypocritical nation," to "show the people their transgressions, and the house of Jacob their sins." Yes! those ministers of the gospel, who defend Slavery from the Bible, are the priests of this bloody Moloch, and as the light of day makes manifest the pollutions which cover objects around us, so will the light of truth reveal the corruption of those *professed* ministers of Christ, who have blasphemed the name of our God, by affixing the counterfeit seal of his approbation to the abominations of this system of moral, mental night and ruin. For the bold utterance of the truth, and delivering the message to the people which was entrusted to them, they have been traduced and persecuted even unto strange cities.

IT IS THE PROVINCE OF WOMAN TO LABOR IN THIS CAUSE.

If our brethren, then, have suffered and dared so much in the cause of bleeding humanity, shall *we* not stand side by side with them in the bloodless contest? Is it true, that the women of France often follow their husbands and their brothers to the sanguinary contest, putting on the soldier's armour, and facing the fierceness of war's grim visage of death? And shall American women refuse to follow their husbands, fathers, and brothers, into the wide field of moral enterprise and holy aggressive conflict with the master sin of the American republic, and the American church? Oh no! we know the hearts of our sisters too well—we see them already girding on the whole armour of

God—already gathering in the plain and on the mountain, in the crowded cities of our seaboard, and the little villas and hamlets of the country—we see them cheering with their smiles, and strengthening with their prayers, and aiding with their efforts, that noble band of patriots, philanthropists, and Christians, who have come up to the help of the Lord against the mighty. We see them meekly bowing to the obloquy, and uncovering their heads to the curses, which are heaped by Southern slaveholders upon all who remember those who are in bonds. Woman is now rising in her womanhood, to throw from her, with one hand, the paltry privileges with which *man* has invested her, of conquering by fashionable charms and winning by personal attractions, whilst, with the other, she grasps the right of woman, to unite in holy copartnership with man, in the renovation of a fallen world. She tramples these glittering baubles in the dust, and takes from the hand of her *Creator*, the Magna Charta of her high prerogatives as a *moral*, an *intellectual*, an accountable being—a *woman*, who, though placed in subjection to the monarch of the world, is still the crown and "the glory of the man."

When Jehovah was about to erect in the wilderness of Sinai a tabernacle in which he was to walk amidst his chosen people, was it builded by the contributions and the labors of man only? Did not *woman* lend her aid to the holy work? What saith the Scripture? "The children of Israel brought a willing offering unto the Lord, every man and every *woman*, whose heart made them willing to bring for all manner of work, which the Lord had commanded to be made by the hand of Moses." And if Bezaleel and Aholiab were "filled with wisdom of heart to work all manner of work, so also the *women* that were wise-hearted, and did spin with their hands, and brought that which they had spun, both of purple and of blue, and of scarlet, and of fine linen."

Woman, as well as man, put forth her energy and ingenuity, in preparing materials for the building of the tabernacle. She labored unitedly with him, and shared with him the toils and the honors of bringing *willing offerings* to the tabernacle of the congregation of the Lord. And when our fathers pitched the tabernacle of freedom in this Western wilderness, did not *woman* cheer him onward in the privations and sufferings he was called to endure? They well knew that the government they erected could not be permanent: it was like the tabernacle of Sinai, set up in the midst of thunderings and lightnings, and a thick cloud, and the voice of the trumpet, waxing louder and louder.

But we live, beloved sisters, in a very different era. The Lord has raised up men whom he has endowed with "wisdom, and understanding, and knowledge," to lay deep and broad the foundations of the *temple of liberty.* This is a great moral work in which they are engaged. No war-trumpet summons to the field of battle, but wisdom crieth without: "she uttereth her voice in the streets"—"whosoever is of a willing heart, let him bring an offering." Shall *woman* refuse her response to the call? or, will she not rather surrender herself to the work, and throw the sympathies of her heart, and the gems of her intellect, into the treasury of this temple? Was she originally created to be a helpmeet to man—his sorrows to divide, his joys to share, and all his toils to lighten, by her willing aid? and shall she refuse to aid him with her prayers, her labors, and her counsels, too, *at such a time, in such a cause as this?*

LETTERS TO CATHERINE E. BEECHER IN REPLY TO AN ESSAY ON SLAVERY AND ABOLITIONISM, ADDRESSED TO A. E. GRIMKÉ. REVISED BY THE AUTHOR.

LETTER I.

Fundamental Principle of Abolitionists.

Brookline, Mass. 6 month, 12th, 1837.

My Dear Friend: Thy book has appeared just at a time, when, from the nature of my engagements, it will be impossible for me to give it that attention which so weighty a subject demands. Incessantly occupied in prosecuting a mission, the responsibilities of which task all my powers, I can reply to it only by desultory letters, thrown from my pen as I travel from place to place. I prefer this mode to that of taking as long a time to answer it, as thou didst to determine upon the best method by which to counteract the effect of my testimony at the north—which, as the preface of thy book informs me, was thy main design.

Thou thinkest I have not been "sufficiently informed in regard to the feelings and opinions of Christian females at the North" on the subject of slavery; for that in fact they hold the same *principles* with Abolitionists, although they condemn their measures. Wilt thou permit me to receive their principles from thy pen? Thus instructed, however misinformed I may heretofore have been, I can hardly fail of attaining to accurate knowledge. Let us examine them, to see how far they correspond with the principles held by Abolitionists.

The great fundamental principle of Abolitionists is, that man cannot rightfully hold his fellow man as property. Therefore, we affirm, that *every slaveholder is a man-stealer.* We do so, for the following reasons: to steal a man is to rob him of himself. It matters not whether this be done in Guinea, or Carolina; a man is a *man*, and *as* a man he has *inalienable* rights, among which is the right to personal *liberty.* Now if every man has an *inalienable* right to personal liberty, it follows, that he cannot rightfully be reduced to slavery. But I find in these United States, 2,250,000 men, women and children, robbed of that to which they have an *inalienable* right. How comes this to pass? Where millions are plundered, are there no *plunderers?* If, then, the slaves have been robbed of their liberty, *who* has robbed them? Not the man who stole their forefathers from Africa, but he who now holds them in bondage; no matter *how* they came into his possession, whether he inherited them, or bought them, or seized them at their birth on his own plantation. The only difference I can see between the original man-stealer, who caught the African in his native country, and the American slaveholder, is, that the former committed *one* act of robbery, while the other perpetrates the same crime *continually.* Slaveholding is the perpetrating of acts, all of the same kind, in a *series,* the first of which is technically called man-stealing. The *first* act robbed the man of himself; and the same state of mind that prompted *that act, keeps up the series,* having *taken* his all from him: it *keeps* his all from him, not only *refusing* to *restore*, but still robbing him of all he gets, and as fast as he gets it. Slaveholding, then, is *the constant or habitual perpetration of the act of man-stealing. To make* a slave is *man-stealing—the* ACT *itself*—to *hold* him such is man-stealing—the *habit*, the *permanent* state, made up of *individual* acts. In other words—to *begin* to hold a slave is man-stealing—to *keep on* holding him is merely a *repetition* of the first act—a doing the same identical thing *all the time.* A series of the same acts continued for a length of time is a *habit—a permanent state.* And the *first* of this series of the *same* acts that make up this *habit* or state is just like all the rest.

If every slave has a right to freedom, then surely the man who withholds that right from him to-day is a man-stealer, though he may not be the first person who has robbed him of it. Hence we find that Wesley says—"Men-*buyers* are *exactly on a level* with men-*stealers*." And again—"Much less is it possible that any child of man should ever be *born a slave*." Hear also Jonathan Edwards—"To hold a man in a state of slavery, is to be *every day guilty* of robbing him of his liberty, or of *man-stealing*." And Grotius says—"Those are men-stealers who abduct, *keep*, sell or buy *slaves* or freemen."

If thou meanest merely that *acts* of that *same nature*, but differently located in a series, are designated by different terms, thus pointing out their different *relative positions,* then thy argument concedes what we affirm,—the identity in the *nature* of the acts, and thus it dwindles to a mere philological criticism, or rather a mere play upon words.

These are Abolition sentiments on the subject of slaveholding; and although our principles are universally held by our opposers at the North, yet I am told on the 44th page of thy book, that "the word man-stealer has one peculiar signification, and is no more synonymous with slaveholder than it is with sheep-stealer." I must acknowledge, thou hast only confirmed my opinion of the difference which I had believed to exist between Abolitionists and their opponents. As well might Saul have declared, that he held similar views with Stephen, when he stood by and kept the raiment of those who slew him.

I know that a broad line of distinction is drawn between our principles and our measures, by those who are anxious to "avoid the appearance of evil"—very desirous of retaining the fair character of enemies to slavery. Now, our *measures* are simply the carrying out of our *principles;* and we find, that just in proportion as individuals embrace our principles, in spirit and in truth, they cease to cavil at our measures. Gerrit Smith is a striking illustration of this. Who cavilled more at Anti-Slavery *measures*, and who more ready now to acknowledge his former blindness? Real Abolitionists know full well, that the slave never has been, and never can be, a whit the better for mere abstractions, floating in the *head* of any man; and they also know, that *principles, fixed in the heart,* are things of another sort. The former have never done any good in the world, because they possess no vitality, and therefore cannot bring forth *the fruits* of holy, untiring effort; but the latter live in the lives of their possessors, and breathe in their words. And I am free to express my belief, that *all* who really and heartily approve our *principles*, will also approve our *measures;* and that, too, just as certainly as a good tree will bring forth good fruit.

But there is another peculiarity in the views of Abolitionists. We hold that the North is guilty of the crime of slaveholding—we assert that it is a *national* sin: on the contrary, in thy book, I find the following acknowledgement:—"*Most* persons in the non-slaveholding States, have considered the matter of southern slavery as one in which they were no more called to interfere, than in the abolition of the press-gang system in England, or the tithe-system in Ireland." Now I cannot see how the same principles can produce such entirely different opinions. "Can a good tree bring forth corrupt fruit?" This I deny, and cannot admit what thou art anxious to prove, viz. that "Public opinion may have been *wrong* on this point, and yet *right* on all those great *principles* of rectitude and justice relating to slavery." If Abolition principles are generally adopted at the North, how comes it to pass, that there is no abolition action here, except what is put forth by a few despised fanatics, as they are called? Is there any living faith without works? Can the sap circulate vigorously, and yet neither blossoms put forth nor fruit appear?

Again, I am told on the 7th page, that all Northern Christians believe it is a sin to hold a man in slavery for "*mere purposes of gain*"; as if this was the *whole* abolition principle on this subject. I can assure thee that Abolitionists do not stop here. Our principle is, that *no circumstances can ever justify* a man in holding his fellow man as *property;* it matters not what *motive* he may give for such a monstrous violation of the laws of God. The claim to him as *property* is an annihilation of his right to himself, which is the foundation upon which all his other rights are built. It is high-handed robbery of Jehovah; for He has declared, "All souls are *mine*." For myself, I believe there are hundreds of thousands at the South, who do *not* hold their slaves, by any means, as much "for purposes of gain," as they do from *the lust of power:* this is the passion that reigns triumphant there, and those who do not know this, have much yet to learn. Where, then, is the similarity in our views?

I forbear for the present, and subscribe myself,

Thine, but not in the bonds of gospel Abolitionism,

A. E. GRIMKÉ.

LETTER II.

Immediate Emancipation.

Brookline, Mass. 6th month, 17th, 1837.

DEAR FRIEND: Where didst thou get thy statement of what Abolitionists mean by immediate emancipation? I assure thee, it is a novelty. I never heard any abolitionist say that slaveholders "were physically unable to emancipate their slaves, and of course are not bound to do it," because in some States there are laws which forbid emancipation. This is truly what our opponents affirm; but *we* say that all the laws which sustain the system of slavery are unjust and oppressive—contrary to the fundamental principles of morality, and, therefore, null and void.

We hold, that all the slaveholding laws violate the fundamental principles of the Constitution of the United States. In the preamble of that instrument, the great objects for which it was framed are declared to be "to establish justice, to promote the *general* welfare, and to secure the blessings of *liberty* to us and to our posterity." The slave laws are flagrant violations of these fundamental principles. Slavery subverts justice, promotes the welfare of the *few* to the manifest injury of the many, and robs thousands of the *posterity* of our forefathers of the blessings of liberty. This cannot be denied, for Paxton, a Virginia slaveholder, says, "the *best* blood in Virginia flows in the veins of slaves!" Yes, even the blood of a Jefferson. And every southerner knows, that it is a common thing for the *posterity of our forefathers* to be sold on the vendue tables of the South. *The posterity of our fathers* are advertised in American papers as runaway slaves. Such advertisements often contain expressions like these: "has sometimes passed himself off as a *white* man,"—"has been mistaken for a *white* man,"—"*quite white*, has *straight* hair, and would not readily be taken for a slave," &c.

Now, thou wilt perceive, that, so far from thinking that a slaveholder is bound by the *immoral* and *unconstitutional* laws of the Southern States, *we* hold that he is solemnly bound as a man, as an American, to *break* them, and that *immediately* and openly; as much so, as Daniel was to pray, or Peter and John to preach—or every conscientious Quaker to refuse to pay a militia fine, or to train, or to fight. *We* promulgate no such time-serving doctrine as that set forth by thee. When *we* talk of immediate emancipation, we speak that we do mean, and the slaveholders understand us, if thou dost not.

Here, then, is another point in which we are entirely at variance, though the *principles* of abolitionism are "generally adopted by our opposers." What shall I *say* to these things, but that I am glad thou hast afforded me an opportunity of explaining to thee what *our principles* really are? for I apprehend that *thou* "hast not been sufficiently informed in regard to the feelings and opinions" of abolitionists.

It matters not to me what meaning "Dictionaries or standard writers" may give to immediate emancipation. My Dictionary is the Bible; my standard authors, prophets and apostles. When Jehovah commanded Pharaoh to "let the people go," he meant that they should be *immediately emancipated*. I read his meaning in the judgments which terribly rebuked Pharaoh's repeated and obstinate refusal to "let the people go." I read it in the *universal* emancipation of near 3,000,000 of Israelites in *one awful night*. When the prophet Isaiah commanded the Jews "to loose the bands of wickedness, to undo the heavy burdens, and to let the oppressed go free, and that ye break every yoke," he taught no gradual or partial emancipation, but *immediate, universal emancipation.* When Jeremiah said, "Execute judgment in the MORNING, and deliver him that is spoiled out of the hand of the oppressor," he commanded *immediate* deliverance. And so also with Paul, when he exhorted masters to render unto their servants that which is just and equal. Obedience to this command would *immediately* overturn the whole system of American Slavery; for liberty is justly *due* to every American citizen, according to the laws of God and the Constitution of our country; and a fair recompense for his labor is the right of every man. Slaveholders know this is just as well as we do. John C. Calhoun said in Congress, in 1833—"He who *earns* the money—who *digs it out of the earth* with the sweat of his brow, has a *just title* to it against the Universe. *No one* has a right to touch it *without his consent,* except his government, and *it only* to the extent of its *legitimate* wants: to take more is *robbery.*"

If our fundamental principle is right, that no man can rightfully hold his fellow man as *property*, then it follows, of course, that he is bound *immediately* to cease holding him as such, and that, too, in *violation of the immoral and unconstitutional laws* which have been framed for the express purpose of "turning aside the needy from judgment, and to take away the right from the poor of the people, that widows may be their prey, and that they may rob the fatherless." Every slaveholder is bound to cease to do evil *now,* to emancipate his slaves *now.*

Dost thou ask what I mean by emancipation? I will explain myself in a few words. 1. It is "to reject with indignation, the wild and guilty phantasy, that man can hold *property* in man." 2. To pay the laborer his hire, for he is worthy of it. 3. No longer to deny him the right of marriage, but to "let every man have his own wife, and let every woman have her own husband," as saith the apostle. 4. To let parents have their own children, for they are the gift of the Lord to *them*, and no one else has any right to them. 5. No longer to withhold the advantages of education and the privilege of reading the Bible. 6. To put the slave under the protection of equitable laws.

Now, why should not *all* this be done immediately? Which of these things is to be done next year, and which the year after? and so on. *Our* immediate emancipation means, doing justice and loving mercy *to-day*—and this is what we call upon every slaveholder to do.

I have seen too much of slavery to be a gradualist. I dare not, in view of such a system, tell the slaveholder, that "he is physically unable to emancipate his slaves." I say *he is able* to let the oppressed go free, and that such heaven-daring atrocities ought to *cease now,* henceforth and forever. Oh, my very soul is grieved to find a northern woman thus "sewing pillows under all arm-holes," framing and fitting soft excuses for the slaveholder's conscience, whilst with the same pen she is *professing* to regard slavery as a sin. "An open enemy is better than such a secret friend."

Hoping that thou mayest soon be emancipated from such inconsistency, I remain until then,

Thine *out* of the bonds of Christian Abolitionism,

A. E. GRIMKÉ.

LETTER III.

Main Principle of Action.

Lynn, 6th Month, 23d, 1837.

DEAR FRIEND:—I now pass on to the consideration of "the main principle of action in the Anti-Slavery Society." Thou art pleased to assert that it "rests wholly on a false deduction from past experience." In this, also, thou "hast not been sufficiently informed." Our main principle of action is embodied in God's holy command—"Wash you, make you clean, put away the evil of your doings from before mine eyes, cease to do evil, learn to do well; seek judgment, relieve the oppressed, judge the fatherless, plead for the widow." Under a solemn conviction that it is our duty as Americans to "cry aloud and spare not, to lift up our voices as a trumpet, and to show our people their transgressions, and the house of Jacob their sins," we are striving to rouse a slumbering nation to a sense of the retributions which must soon descend upon her guilty head, unless like Ninevah she repent, and "break off her sins by righteousness, and her transgressions by showing mercy to *the poor.*" *This* is our "main principle of action." Does it rest "wholly on a false deduction from past experience?" or on the experience of Israel's King, who exclaimed, "In keeping of them (thy commandments,) there is great reward."

Thou art altogether under a mistake, if thou supposest that our "main principle of action" is the successful effort of abolitionists in England, in reference to the abolition of the slave-trade; for I hesitate not to pronounce the attempts of Clarkson and Wilberforce, at that period of their history, to have been a *complete failure;* and never have the labors of any philanthropists so fully showed the inefficacy of halfway principles, as have those of these men of honorable fame. The doctrines now advocated by the American Anti-Slavery Society, were not advanced by the abolitionists of that day. *They* were *not* immediate abolitionists, but just such gradualists as thou art even now. If I supposed that our labors in the cause of the slave would produce *no better* results than those of these worthies, I should utterly despair. I need not remind thee, that they bent all their energies to the annihilation of the slave-trade, under the impression that *this* was the mother of slavery; and that after toiling for twenty years, and obtaining the passage of an act to that effect, the result was a mere *nominal* abolition; for the atrocities of the slave-trade are, if possible, *greater* now than ever. I will explain what I mean. A friend of mine one evening last winter, heard a conversation between two men, one of whom had, until recently, been a slave-trader. He had made several voyages to the coast of Africa, and said that once his vessel was chased by an English man of war, and that, in order to avoid a search and the penalty of death, he threw every slave overboard; and when his companion expressed surprise and horror at such a wholesale murder, "Why," said the trader, "it was the fault of the English; they had no business to make a law to hang a man on the yard arm, if they caught him with slaves in his ship." He intimated that it was not an uncommon thing for the captains of slavers thus to save their lives.* Where, then, I ask, is this glorious success of which we *hear* so much, but *see* so little?

Let us travel onward, from the year 1806, when England passed her abolition act. What were British philanthropists doing for the emancipation of the slave, for the next twenty years? Nothing at all; and it was the voice of Elizabeth Heyrick which first awakened them from their dream of *gradualism* to an understanding of the simple doctrine of immediate emancipation; but even though they saw the injustice and inefficiency of *their own* views, yet several years elapsed before they had the courage to promulgate hers. And now I can point thee to the success of these efforts in the emancipation bill of 1834. But even this success was paltry, in comparison with what it would have been, had all the conspicuous abolitionists of England been true to these just and holy principles. Some of them were false to those principles, and hence the compensation and apprenticeship system. A few months ago, it was my privilege to converse with Joseph Sturge, on his return from the West Indies, via New York, to Liverpool, whither he had gone to examine the working of England's plan of emancipation. I heard him speak of the bounty of £20,000,000 which she had put into the hands of the planters, of their mean and cruel abuse of the apprenticeship system, and of the hearty approbation he felt in the thorough-going principles of the Anti-Slavery Societies in this country, and his increased conviction that *ours* were the *only right* principles on this important subject. That even the

*And in "Laird's Expedition to Africa, &c." a work recently published in England, this assertion of the slave trader is fully sustained. Laird relates that "there is *proof* of the horrid fact, that several of the wretches engaged in this traffic, when hotly pursued, consigned *whole cargoes* to the deep." He then goes on to state several such instances, from which I select the following: "In 1833, the Black Joke and Fair Rosamond fell in with the Hercule and Regule, two slave vessels off the Bonny River. On perceiving the cruisers, they attempted to regain the port, and pitched overboard upwards of 500 human beings, chained together, before they were captured; from the abundance of sharks in the river, their track was literally a blood-stained one. The slaver not only does this, but *glories in it:* the first words uttered by the captain of the Maria Isabelle, seized by captain Rose, were, 'that if he had seen the man of war in chase an hour sooner, he would have thrown *every* slave in his vessel overboard, as *he was fully insured.*'"

apprenticeship system is viewed by British philanthropists as a complete failure, is evident from the fact that they are now re-organizing their Anti-Slavery Societies, and circulating petitions for the substitution of immediate emancipation in its stead.

Hence it appears, that so far from our resting "wholly upon *a false deduction from past experience*," we are resting on *no* experience at all; for no class of men in the world ever have maintained the principles which we now advocate. Our main principle of action is "obedience to God"—our hope of success is faith in Him, and that faith is as unwavering as He is true and powerful. "Blessed is the man who trusteth in the Lord, and whose hope the Lord is."

With regard to the connection between the North and the South, I shall say but little, having already sent thee my views on that subject in the letter to "Clarkson," originally published in the New Haven Religious Intelligencer. I there pointed out fifteen different ways in which the North was implicated in the guilt of slavery; and, therefore, I deny the charge that abolitionists are endeavoring "to convince their fellow citizens of the faults of *another* community." Not at all. We are spreading out the horrors of slavery before Northerners, in order to show them *their own sin* in sustaining such a system of complicated wrong and suffering. It is because we are politically, commercially, and socially connected with our southern brethren, that we urge our doctrines upon those of the free States. We have begun our work *here*, because pro-slavery men of the North are to the system of slavery just what temperate drinkers were to the vice of intemperance. Temperance reformers did not *begin* their labors among drunkards, but among temperate drinkers: so Anti-Slavery reformers did not *begin* their labors among slaveholders, but among those who were making their fortunes out of the unrequited toil of the slave, and receiving large mortgages on southern plantations and slaves, and trading occasionally in "slaves and the souls of men," and sending men to Congress to buy up southern land to be converted into slave States, such as Louisiana and Florida, which cost *this nation* $20,000,000—men who have admitted seven slave States into the Union—men who boast on the floor of Congress, that "there is no cause in which they would sooner buckle a knapsack on their backs and shoulder a musket, than that of putting down a servile insurrection at the South," as said the present Governor of Massachusetts, which odious sentiment was repeated by Governor Lincoln only last winter—men who, trained up on Freedom's soil, yet go down to the South and marry slaveholders, and become slaveholders, and then return to our northern cities with slaves in their train. This is the case with a native of this town, who is now here with his southern wife and southern *slave*. And as soon as we reform the recreant sons and daughters of the North,—as soon as we rectify public opinion at the North,—then I, for one, will promise to go down into the midst of slaveholders themselves, to promulgate our doctrines in the land of the slave. But how can we go now, when northern pulpits and meeting-houses are closed, and northern ministers are dumb, and northern Governors are declaring that "the discussion of the subject of slavery ought to be made an offence indictable at common law," and northern women are writing books to paralyze the efforts of southern women, who have come up from the South, to entreat their northern sisters to exert their influence in behalf of the slave, and in behalf of the slaveholder, who is as deeply corrupted, though not equally degraded, with the slave. No! No! the taunts of a New England woman will induce no abolitionist to cease his rebuke of *northern slaveholders* and apologists for slavery. Southerners see the wisdom of *this*, if *thou* canst not; and over against thy opinion, I will place that of a Louisiana planter, who, whilst on a visit to his relatives at Uxbridge, Mass. this summer, unhesitatingly admitted that the *North was the right place to begin Anti-Slavery efforts*. Had I not been convinced of this before, surely thy book would have been all-sufficient to satisfy me of it; for a more subtle defence of the slaveholder's right to property in his helpless victims, I never saw. It is just such a defence as the hidden enemies of Liberty will rejoice to see, because, like thyself, they earnestly desire to "avoid the *appearance of evil*;" they are as much opposed to slavery as we are, only they are as much opposed to Anti-Slavery as the slaveholders themselves. Is there any middle path in this reformation? Or may we not fairly conclude, that he or *she* that is not for the slave, in deed and in truth, is *against* him, no matter how specious their professions of pity for his condition?

In haste, I remain thy friend,

A. E. GRIMKÉ.

LETTER IV.

Connection Between the North and South.

Danvers, Mass., 7th mo., 1837.

DEAR FRIEND:—I thank thee for having furnished me with just such a simile as I needed to illustrate the connection which exists between the North and the South. Thou sayest, "Suppose two rival cities, one of which becomes convinced that certain practices in trade and business in the other are dishonest, and have an oppressive bearing on certain classes in that city. Suppose, also, that these are practices, which, by those who allow them, are considered as honorable and right. Those who are convinced of this immorality wish to alter the opinions and the practices of the citizens of their rival city, and to do this they commence the collection of facts, that exhibit the tendencies of these practices and the evils they have engendered. But, instead of going among the community in which the evil exists, and endeavoring to convince them, they proceed to form voluntary associations among their neighbors at home, and spend their time, money, and efforts to convince their fellow citizens that the inhabitants of their rival city are guilty of a great sin." Now I will take up the comparison here, and suppose a few other things about these two cities. Suppose that the people in one city were *known never* to pay the laborer his wages, but to be in the constant habit of keeping back the hire of those who reaped down their fields; and that, on examination, it was found that the people in the other city were continually going over to live with these gentlemen oppressors, and instead of rebuking them, were joining hands in wickedness with them, and were actually *more* oppressive to the poor than the native inhabitants. Suppose, too, it was found that many of the merchants in the city of Fairdealing, as it was called, were known to hold mortgages, not only upon the property which ought to belong to the unpaid laborers, but mortgages, too, on the *laborers themselves*, ay, and *their wives and children also*, a thing altogether contrary to the laws of their city, and the customs of their people, and the principles of fundamental morality. Suppose, too, it was found that the people in the city of Oppression were in the constant practice of sending over to the city of Fairdealing, and bribing their citizens to seize the poorest, most defenceless of their people for them, because they were so lazy they would not do their own work, and so mean they would not pay others for doing it, and chose thus to supply themselves with laborers, who, when they once got into the city, were placed under such severe laws, that it was almost impossible for them ever to return to their afflicted wives and children. Suppose, too, that whenever any of these oppressed, unpaid laborers happened to escape from the city of Oppression, and after lying out in the woods and fastnesses which lay between the two cities, for many weeks, "in weariness and painfulness, in watchings, in hunger and thirst, in cold and nakedness," that, as soon as they reached the city of Fairdealing, they were most unmercifully hunted out and sent back to their cruel oppressors, who it was well known generally treated such laborers with great cruelty, "*stern necessity*" demanding that they should be punished and "rebuked before all, that others might fear" the consequences of such elopement. In short, suppose that the city of Fairdealing was so completely connected with the city of Oppression, that the golden strands of their interests were twisted together so as to form a bond of Union stronger than death, and that by the intermarriages which were constantly taking place, there was also a silken cord of love tying up and binding together the tender feelings of their hearts with all the intricacies of the Gordian knot; and then, again, that the identity of the political interests of these cities were wound round and round them like bands of iron and brass, altogether forming an union so complicated and powerful, that it was impossible even to *speak* in the most solemn manner, in the city of Fairdealing, of the enormous crimes which were common in the city of Oppression, without having brickbats and rotten eggs hurled at the speaker's head. Suppose, too, that although it was perfectly manifest to every reflecting mind, that a most guilty copartnership existed between these two cities, yet that the "gentlemen of property and standing" of the city of Fairdealing were continually taunting the people who were trying to represent *their* iniquitous league with the city of Oppression in its true and sinful bearings, with the query of "Why don't you go to the city of Oppression, and tell the people there, not to rob the poor?" Might not these reformers very justly remark, we cannot go there *until* we have persuaded *our own* citizens to cease *their unholy cooperation with them*, for they will certainly turn upon us in bitter irony and say—"Physician, heal thyself;" go back to your own city, and tell your own citizens "to break off *their* sins by righteousness, and *their* transgressions by showing mercy to the poor," who fly from our city into the gates of theirs for protection, but receive it not. Would not common sense bear them out in refusing to go there, until they had *first* converted *their own* people from the error of their ways? I will leave thee and my other readers to make the application of this comparison; and if thou dost not acknowledge that abolitionists have been governed by the soundest common sense in the course they have pursued at the North with regard to slavery, then I am very much disappointed in thy professions of *candor.* With regard to the parallel thou hast drawn (p. 16,) between abolitionists, and the "men (who) are daily going into the streets, and calling all bystanders around them" and pointing out certain men, some as liars, some as dishonest, some as licentious, and then bringing proofs of their guilt and rebuking them before all; at the same time exhorting all around to point at them the finger of scorn; thou sayest, "they persevere in this course till the whole community is thrown into an uproar; and assaults and even bloodshed ensue." But why, I should like to know, if these people are themselves *guiltless* of the crimes alleged against the others? I cannot understand why they should be so angry, unless, like the Jews of old, they perceived that the parable had been spoken "*against them.*" To my own mind, the exasperation of the North at the discussion of slavery is an undeniable proof of *her guilt*, a certain evidence of the necessity of her plucking the beam out of her own eye, *before* she goes to the South to rebuke sin there. To thee, and to all who are continually crying out, "Why don't you go to the South?" I retort the question by asking, why don't YOU go to the South? *We* conscientiously believe that this work must be commenced *here* at the North; this is an all-sufficient answer for US; but YOU, who are "as much anti-slavery as we are," and differ *only* as to the modus operandi, believing that the South and *not* the North ought to be the field of Anti-Slavery labors—YOU, I say, have no excuse to offer, and are bound to go there now.

But there is another view to be taken of this subject. By all our printing and talking at the North, we *have actually reached the very heart of the disease at the South.* They acknowledge it themselves. Read the following confession in the Southern Literary Review. "There are *many good men even among us, who have begun to grow timid.* They think that what the virtuous and high-minded men of the North look upon as a crime and a plague-spot, *cannot* be perfectly innocent or quite harmless in a slaveholding community." James Smylie, of Mississippi, a minister of the gospel, *so called*, tells us on the very first page of his essay, written to uphold the doctrines of Governor McDuffie, "that the abolition maxim, viz. that slavery is *in itself sinful*, had gained on and entwined itself among the *religious* and *conscientious* scruples of *many* in the community, so far as to render them *unhappy.*" I could quote other southern testimony to the same effect, but will pass on to another fact just published in the New England Spectator; a proposition from a minister in Missouri "to have separate organizations for slavery and anti-slavery professors," and indeed "all over the *slaveholding States.*" Has our labor then been in vain in the Lord? Have we failed to rouse the slumbering consciences of the South?

Thou inquirest—"Have the northern States power to rectify evils at the South, as they have to remove their own moral deformities?" I answer unhesitatingly, certainly they have, for *moral* evils can be removed only by *moral* power; and the close connection which exists between these two portions of our country, affords the greatest possible facilities for exerting a *moral* influence on it. Only let the North exert as much moral influence over the South, as the South has exerted demoralizing influence over the North, and slavery would die amid the flame of Christian remonstrance, and faithful rebuke, and holy indignation. The South has told us so. In the report of the committee on federal relations in the Legislature of South Carolina last winter, we find the following acknowledgement: "Let it be admitted, that by reason of an efficient police and judicious internal legislation, we may render abortive the designs of the fanatic and incendiary within our limits, and that the torrent of pamphlets and tracts which the abolition presses of the North are pouring forth with an inexhaustible copiousness, is arrested the moment it reaches our frontier. Are we to wait until our enemies have built up, by the grossest misrepresentations and falsehoods, a *body of public opinion, which it would be impossible to resist*, without separating ourselves from the social system of the rest of the civilized world?" Here is the acknowledgement of a southern legislature, that it will be *impossible for the South to resist the influence* of that body of *public opinion*, which abolitionists are building up against them at the North. If further evidence is needed, that anti-slavery societies are producing a powerful influence at the South, look at the efforts made there to vilify and crush them. Why all this turmoil, and passion, and rage in the slaveholder, if we have indeed rolled back the cause of emancipation 200 years, as thy father has asserted? Why all this terror at the distant roar of free discussion, if they feel not the earth quaking beneath them? Does not the *South* understand what really will affect her interests and break down her domestic institution? Has *she* no subtle politicians, no far-sighted men in her borders, who can scan the practical bearings of these troublous times? Believe me, she has; and did they not know that we are springing a mine beneath the great bastile of slavery, and laying a train which will soon whelm it in ruin, she would not be quite so eager "to cut out our tongues, and hang us as high as Haman."

I will just add, that as to the committee saying that abolitionists are building up a body of public opinion at the North "by the grossest misrepresentations and falsehoods," I think it was due to *their* character for veracity, to have cited and refuted some of these calumnies. Until they do, we must believe them; and as a Southerner, I can bear the most decided testimony against slavery as the mother of *all* abominations. Farewell for the present.

I remain thy friend,

A. E. GRIMKÉ.

LETTER V.

Christian Character of Abolitionism.

Newburyport, 7th mo. 8th, 1837.

DEAR FRIEND: As an Abolitionist, I thank thee for the portrait thou hast drawn of the character of those with whom I am associated. They deserve all thou hast said in their favor; and I will now endeavor to vindicate those "men of pure morals, of great honesty of purpose, of real benevolence and piety," from some objections thou hast urged against their measures.

"Much evidence," thou sayest, "can be brought to prove that the character and measures of the Abolition Society are not either peaceful or christian in tendency, but that they are in their nature calculated to generate party spirit, denunciation, recrimination, and angry passion." Now I solemnly ask thee, whether the character and measures of our holy Redeemer did not produce exactly the same effects? Why did the Jews lead him to the brow of the hill, that they might cast him down headlong; why did they go about to kill him; why did they seek to lay hands on him, if the tendency of *his* measures was so very pacific? Listen, too, to his own declaration: "I came not to send peace on earth, but a sword;" the effects of which, he expressly said, would be to set the mother against her daughter, and the daughter-in-law against her mother-in-law. The rebukes which he uttered against sin were eminently calculated to produce "recriminations and angry passions," in all who were determined to *cleave* to their sins; and they did produce them even against "him who did no sin, neither was guile found in his mouth." He was called a winebibber, and a glutton, and Beelzebub, and was accused of casting out devils by the prince of the devils. Why, then, protest against our measures as *unchristian*, because they do not smooth the pillow of the poor sinner, and lull his conscience into fatal security? The truth is, the efforts of abolitionists have stirred up the *very same spirit* which the efforts of *all thorough-going* reformers have ever done; we consider it a certain proof that the truths we utter are sharper than any two edged sword, and that they are doing the work of conviction in the hearts of our enemies. If it be not so, I have greatly mistaken the character of Christianity. I consider it pre eminently aggressive; it waits not to be assaulted, but moves on in all the majesty of Truth to *attack* the strong holds of the kingdom of darkness, carries the war into the enemy's camp, and throws its fiery darts into the midst of its embattled hosts. Thou seemest to think, on the contrary, that Christianity is just such a weak, dependent, puerile creature as thou hast described woman to be. In my opinion, thou hast robbed both the one and the other of all their *true dignity* and glory. Thy descriptions may suit the prevailing christianity of this age, and the general character of woman; and if so, we have great cause for shame and confusion of face.

I feel sorry that thy unkind insinuations against the christian character of Wm. Lloyd Garrison, have rendered it necessary for me to speak of him individually, because what I shall feel bound to say of him may, to some like thyself, appear like flattery; but I must do what justice seems so clearly to call for at my hands. Thou sayest that "though he professes a belief in the christian religion, he is an avowed opponent of most of its institutions." I presume thou art here alluding to his views of the ordinances of baptism and the Lord's supper, and the Sabbath. Permit me to remind thee, that in *all* these opinions, he coincides entirely with the Society of Friends, whose views of the Sabbath never were so ably vindicated as by his pen: and the insinuations of hypocrisy which thou hast thrown out against him, may with just as much truth be cast upon *them*. The Quakers think that these are not *christian* institutions, but thou hast assumed it without any proof at all. Thou sayest farther, "The character and spirit of *this man* have for years been exhibited in the Liberator." I have taken that paper for two years, and therefore understand its character, and am compelled to acknowledge, that harsh and severe as is the language often used, I have never seen any expressions which *truth* did not warrant. The abominations of slavery *cannot* be otherwise described. I think Dr. Channing exactly portrayed the character of brother Garrison's writings when he said, "That deep feeling of evils, which is *necessary* to *effectual* conflict with them, which marks *God's most powerful messengers to mankind, cannot* breathe itself in soft and tender accents. The deeply moved soul *will* speak strongly, and *ought* to speak strongly, so as to move and shake nations." It is well for the slave, and well for this country, that such a man was sent to sound the tocsin of alarm before slavery had completed its work of moral death in this "hypocritical nation." Garrison begun that discussion of the subject of slavery, which J. Q. Adams declared in his oration, delivered in this town on the 4th inst. "to be the only safety-valve by which the high pressure boiler of slavery could be prevented from a most fatal explosion in this country;" and as a Southerner, I feel truly grateful for all his efforts to redeem not the slave only, but the *slaveholder*, from the polluting influences of such a system of crime.

In his character as a man and a Christian, I have the highest confidence. The assertion thou makest, "that there is to be found in that paper, or *any thing else, any* evidence of his possessing the peculiar traits of Wilberforce, (benignity, gentleness and kind heartedness, I suppose thou meanest,) not even his warmest admirers will maintain," is altogether new to me; and I for one feel ready to declare, that I have never met in any one a more lovely exhibition of these traits of character. I might relate several anecdotes in proof of this assertion, but let one suffice. A friend of mine, a member of the Society of Friends, told me that after he became interested in the Anti-Slavery cause through the Liberator, he still felt so much prejudice against its editor, that, although he wished to labor in behalf of the slaves, he still felt as if he could not identify himself with a society which recognized such a leader as he had heard Wm. L. Garrison was. He had never seen him, and after many struggles of feeling, determined to go to Boston on purpose to see "this man," and judge of his character for himself. He did so, and when he entered the office of the Liberator, soon fell into conversation with a person he did not know, and became very much interested in him. After some time, a third person came in and called off the attention of the stranger, whose benevolent countenance and benignant manners he had so much admired. He soon heard him addressed as Mr. Garrison, which astonished him very much; for he had expected to see some coarse, uncouth and rugged creature, instead of the perfect gentleman he now learned was Wm. L. Garrison. He told me that the effect upon his mind was so great, that he sat down and wept to think he had allowed himself to be so prejudiced against a person, who was so entirely different from what his enemies had represented him to be. He at once felt as if he could most cheerfully labor, heart and hand, with such a man, and has for the last three or four years been a faithful co-worker with him, in the holy cause of immediate emancipation. And his confidence in him as a man of pure, *christian* principle, has grown stronger and stronger, as time has advanced, and circumstances have developed his true character. I think it is impossible thou canst be personally acquainted with brother Garrison, or thou wouldst not write of him in the way thou hast. If thou really wishest to have thy erroneous opinions removed, embrace the first opportunity of being introduced to him; for I can assure thee, that with the fire of a Paul, he does possess some of the most lovely traits in the character of Wilberforce.

In much haste, I remain thy friend,

A. E. GRIMKÉ.

LETTER VI.

Colonization.

Amesbury, 7th mo. 20th, 1837.

DEAR FRIEND: The *aggressive* spirit of Anti-Slavery papers and pamphlets, of which thou dost complain, so far from being a repulsive one to me, is very attractive. I see in it that uncompromising integrity and fearless rebuke of sin, which will bear the enterprize of emancipation through to its consummation.

And I most heartily desire to see these publications scattered over our land as abundantly as the leaves of Autumn, believing as I do that the principles they promulgate will be as leaves for the healing of this nation.

I proceed to examine thy objections to "one of the first measures of Abolitionists:" their attack on a *benevolent* society.

That the Colonization Society is a *benevolent* institution, we deny: therefore our attack upon it was not a sacrilegious one; it was absolutely necessary, in order to disabuse the public mind of the false views they entertained of its character. And it is a perfect mystery to me how men and women can *conscientiously* persevere in upholding a society, which the very objects of its professed benevolence have repeatedly, solemnly, constantly and universally condemned. To say the least, this is a very suspicious kind of benevolence, and seems too nearly allied to that, which induces some southern professors to keep their brethren in bonds *for their benefit*. Yes, the free colored people are to be exiled, because public opinion is crushing them into the dust; instead of their friends protesting against that corrupt and unreasonable prejudice, and living it down by a practical acknowledgement of their *right* to *every* privilege, social, civil and religious, which is enjoyed by the white man. I have never yet been able to learn, how our hatred to our colored brother is to be destroyed by driving him away from us. I am told that when a colored republic is built up on the coast of Africa, then we shall respect that republic, and acknowledge that the character of the colored man can be elevated; we will become connected with it in a commercial point of view, and welcome it to the sympathies of our hearts. Miserable sophistry! deceitful apology for present indulgence in sin! What man or woman of common sense now doubts the intellectual capacity of the colored people? Who does not know, that with all our efforts as a nation to crush and "*annihilate the mind* of this portion of our race," we have never yet been able to do it? Henry Berry of Virginia, in his speech in the Legislature of that State, in 1832, expressly acknowledged, that although slaveholders had "as far as possible closed every avenue by which light might enter their minds," yet that they never had found out the process by which they "could extinguish the *capacity* to see the light." No! that capacity remains—it is indestructible—an integral part of their nature, as moral and immortal beings.

If it is true that white Americans only need a demonstration of the colored man's capacity for elevation, in order to make them willing to receive him on the same platform of human rights upon which they stand, why has not the intelligence of the Haytians convinced them? *Their* free republic has grown up under the very eye of the slaveholder, and as a nation we have for many years been carrying on a lucrative trade with her merchants; and yet we have never recognized her independence, never sent a minister there, though we have sent ambassadors to European countries whose commerce is far less important to us us than that of St. Domingo.*

These professions of a wish to plant the tree of Liberty on the shores of Africa, in order to convince our Republican Despotism of the high moral and intellectual worth of the colored man, are perfectly absurd. Hayti has done that long ago. A friend of mine (not an Abolitionist) whose business called him to that island for several months, told me that in the society of its citizens, he often felt his own inferiority. He was astonished at the elegance of their manners, and the intelligence of their conversation. Instead of going into an examination of Colonization principles, I refer thee to the Appeal to the Women of the nominally free States, issued by the Convention of American Women, in which we set forth our reasons for repudiating them.

Thou hast given a specimen of the manner in which Abolitionists deal with their Colonization opponents. Thy friend remarked, after an interview with an abolitionist, "I love truth and sound argument; but when a man comes at me with a sledge hammer, I cannot help dodging." I presume thy friend only felt the truth of the prophet's declaration, "Is not my word like as a fire, saith the Lord, and like a *hammer* that breaketh the rock in

*Although there are some who like to discant on the worthless character of the Haytians, and the miserable condition of the Island, yet it is an indisputable fact, that a population of nearly 1,000,000 are supported on its soil, and that in 1833, the value of its exports to the United States exceeded in value those of Prussia, Sweden, and Norway—Denmark and the Danish West Indies—Ireland and Scotland—Holland—Belgium—Dutch East Indies—British West Indies—Spain—Portugal—all Italy—Turkey and the Levant, or any one Republic in South America.

pieces?" I wonder not that he did *dodge,* when the sledge hammer of truth was wielded by an abolition army. Many a Colonizationist has been compelled to dodge, in order to escape the blows of this hammer of the Lord's word, for there is no other way to get clear. We must either *dodge* the arguments of abolitionists, or like J. G. Birney, Edward C. Delevan, and many others, be willing to be broken to pieces by them. I greatly like this specimen of private dealing, and hope it is not the only instance which has come under thy notice, of Colonizationists acknowledging the absolute necessity of *dodging* Anti-Slavery arguments, when they were unwilling that the *rock of prejudice* should be broken to pieces by them.

Thy next complaint is against the *manner* in which this benevolent EXPATRIATION Society was attacked. "The style in which the thing was done was at once offensive, inflammatory and exasperating,"—"the feelings of many sincere, upright, and conscientious men were harrowed by a sense of the injustice, the indecorum and the unchristian treatment they received." But why, if *they* were entirely innocent of the charges brought against Colonizationists? I have been in the habit, for several years past, of watching the workings of my own mind under true and false charges against myself; and my experience is, that the more clear I am of the charge, the less I care about it. If I really feel a sweet assurance that "my witness is in heaven—my record is on high," I then realize to its fullest extent that "it is a small thing to be judged of *man's* judgment," and I can bear *false* charges unmoved; but true ones always nettle me, if I am unwilling to confess that "I have sinned;" if I am, and yield to conviction, O then! how sweet the reward! Now I am very much afraid that these sincere, upright and conscientious Colonizationists are something like the *pious professors* of the South, who are very angry because abolitionists say that all slaveholders are men-stealers. Both find it 'hard to kick against the pricks' of conviction, and both are unwilling to repent. A northern man remarked to a Virginia slaveholder last winter, "that as the South denied the charges brought against her by abolitionists, he could not understand why she was so enraged; for," continued he, "if you were to accuse us at the North of being sheep-stealers, we should not care about the charge—we should ridicule it." "O!" said the Virginian with an oath, "what the abolitionists say about slaveholders is *too true*, and *that's the reason* we are vexed." Is not this the reason why our Colonization brethren and sisters are so angry? Is not what we say of them also *too true*? Let them examine these things with the bible and prayer, and settle this question between God and their own souls.

Every true friend of the oppressed American has great cause to rejoice, that the cloak of benevolence has been torn off from the monster Prejudice, which could love the colored man *after* he got to Africa, but seemed to delight to pour contumely upon him whilst he remained in the land of his birth. I confess it would be very hard for me to believe that any association of men and women loved me or my family, if, because we had become obnoxious to them, they were to meet together, and concentrate their energies and pour out their money for the purpose of transporting us back to France, whence our Hugenot fathers fled to this country to escape the storm of persecutions. Why not let us live in America, if you really *love* us? Surely you never want to "*get rid*" of people whom you *love*. *I* like to have such near me; and it is because I love the colored Americans, that I want them to stay in this country; and in order to make it a happy home to them, I am trying to talk down, and write down, and live down this horrible prejudice. Sending a few to Africa cannot destroy it. No—we must dig up the weed by the roots out of each of our hearts. *It is a sin*, and we must repent of it and forsake it—and then we shall no longer be so anxious to "*be clear of them,*" "*to get rid of them.*"

Hoping, though against hope, that thou mayest one day know how precious is the reward of those who can love our oppressed brethren and sisters in this day of their calamity, and who, despising the shame of being identified with these peeled and scattered ones, rejoice to stand side by side with them, in the glorious conflict between Slavery and Freedom, Prejudice and Love unfeigned, I remain thine in the bonds of universal love,

A. E. GRIMKÉ.

LETTER VII.

Prejudice.

Haverhill, Mass. 7th mo. 23, 1837.

DEAR FRIEND:—Thou sayest, "the *best* way to make a person like a thing which is disagreeable, is to try in some way to make it agreeable." So, then, instead of convincing a person by sound argument and pointed rebuke that sin is *sin*, we are to *disguise* the opposite virtue in such a way as to make him like that, in preference to the sin he had so dearly loved. We are to *cheat* a sinner out of his sin, rather than to compel him, under the stings of conviction, to give it up from deep-rooted principle.

If this is the course pursued by ministers, then I wonder not at the kind of converts which are brought into the church at the present day. Thy remarks on the subject of prejudice, show but too plainly how strongly thy own mind is imbued with it, and how little thy colonization principles have done to exterminate this feeling from thy own bosom. Thou sayest, "if a certain class of persons is the subject of unreasonable prejudice, the peaceful and christian way of removing it would be to endeavor to render the unfortunate persons who compose this class, so useful, so *humble, so unassuming*, &c. that prejudice would be supplanted by complacency in their goodness, and *pity* and sympathy for their disabilities." "If the friends of the blacks had quietly set themselves to work to increase their intelligence, their usefulness, &c. and then had appealed to the *pity* and benevolence of their fellow citizens, a very different result would have appeared." Or in other words, if one person is guilty of a sin against another person, I am to let the sinner go entirely unreproved, but to persuade the injured party to bear with humility and patience all the outrages that are inflicted upon him, and thus try to soothe the sinner "into complacency with their goodness" in "bearing all things, and enduring all things." Well, suppose I succeed:—is that sinner won from the evil of his ways by *principle?* No! Has he the principle of love implanted in his breast? No! Instead of being in love with the virtue exhibited by the individual, because *it is virtue*, he is delighted with the personal convenience he experiences from the exercise of that virtue. He feels kindly toward the individual, *because* he is an *instrument* of his enjoyment, a mere *means* to promote his wishes. There is *no* reformation there at all. And so the colored people are to be taught to be "very *humble*" and "*unassuming*," "*gentle*" and "*meek*," and then the "*pity* and generosity" of their fellow citizens are to be appealed to. Now, no one who knows anything of the influence of Abolitionists over the colored people, can deny that it has been *peaceful* and christian; had it not been so, they never would have seen those whom they had regarded as their best friends, mobbed and persecuted, without raising an arm in their defence. Look, too, at the rapid spread of thorough temperance principles among them, and their moral reform and other laudable and useful associations; look at the rising character of this people, the new life and energy which have been infused into them. Who have done it? Who have exerted by far the greatest influence on these oppressed Americans? I leave thee to answer. I will give thee one instance of this salutary influence. In a letter I received from one of my colored sisters, she incidentally makes this remark:—"Until very lately, I have lived and acted more for *myself* than for the good of others. I confess that I am *wholly indebted to the Abolition cause* for arousing me from apathy and indifference, and shedding light into a mind which has been too long wrapt in selfish darkness." The Abolition cause has exerted a powerful and healthful influence over this class of our population, and it has been done by quietly going into the midst of them, and identifying ourselves with them.

But Abolitionists are complained of, because they, at the same time, fearlessly exposed the *sin* of the unreasonable and unholy prejudice which existed against these injured ones. Thou sayest "that reproaches, rebukes and sneers were employed to convince the whites that their prejudices were sinful, and *without* any just cause." *Without any just cause!* Couldst thou think so, if thou really loved thy colored sisters as *as thyself?* The unmeasured abuse which the Colonization Society was heaping upon this despised people, was no *just cause* for pointed rebuke, I suppose! The manner in which they are thrust into one corner of our meeting-houses, as if the plague-spot was on their skins;

the rudeness and cruelty with which they are treated in our hotels, and steamboats, rail road cars and stages, is *no just cause* of reproach to a professed christian community, I presume. Well, all that I can say is, that I believe if Isaiah or James were now alive, they would pour their reproaches and rebukes upon the heads and *hearts* of those who are thus despising the Lord's poor, and saying to those whose spirits are clothed by God in the "vile raiment" of a *colored skin*, Stand thou there in yonder gallery, or sit thou here in "the negro-pew." "Sneers," too, are complained of. Have abolitionists ever made use of greater sarcasm and irony than did the prophet Elijah? When things are ridiculous as well as wicked, it is unreasonable to expect that every cast of mind will treat them with solemnity. And what is more ridiculous than American prejudice; to proscribe and persecute men and women, because their *complexions* are of a darker hue than our own? Why, it is an outrage upon common sense; and as my brother Thomas S. Grimké remarked only a few weeks before his death, "posterity will laugh at our prejudices." Where is the harm, then, if abolitionists should laugh now at the wicked absurdity?

Thou sayest, "this tended to irritate the whites, and to increase their prejudices against the blacks." The *truth always* irritates the proud, impenitent sinner. To charge abolitionists with this irritation, is something like the charge brought against the English government by the captain of the slaver I told thee of in my second letter, who threw all his human merchandize overboard, in order to escape detection, and then charged this horrible wholesale murder upon the government; because, said he, they had no business to make a law to hang a man if he was found engaged in the slave trade. So *we* must bear the guilt of man's angry passions, because the *truth* we preach, is like a two-edged sword, cutting through the bonds of interest on the one side, and the cords of caste on the other.

As to our increasing the prejudice against color, this is just like the North telling us that we have increased the miseries of the slave. Common sense cries out against the one as well as the other. With regard to prejudice, I believe the truth of the case to be this: the rights of the colored man *never* were advocated by any body of men in their length and breadth, before the rise of the Anti-Slavery Society in this country. The propagation of these ultra principles has produced in the northern States exactly the same effect, which the promulgation of the doctrine of immediate emancipation has done in the southern States. It has *developed* the latent principles of pride and prejudice, not *produced* them. Hear John Green, a Judge of the Circuit Court of Kentucky, in reference to abolition efforts having given birth to the opposition against emancipation now existing in the South: "I would rather say, it has been the means of *manifesting* that opposition, which *previously* existed, but *laid dormant* for want of an exciting cause." And just so has it been with regard to prejudice at the North—when there was no effort to obtain for the colored man his *rights* as a man, as an American citizen, there was no opposition exhibited, because it "laid dormant for want of an exciting cause."

I know it is alleged that some individuals, who treated colored people with the greatest kindness a few years ago, have, since abolition movements, had their feelings so embittered towards them, that they have withdrawn that kindness. Now I would ask, could such people have acted from *principle*? Certainly not; or nothing that others could do or say would have driven them from the high ground they *appeared* to occupy. No, my friend, they acted precisely upon the false principle which thou hast recommended; their *pity* was excited, their *sentiments* of *generosity* were called into exercise, because they regarded the colored man as an *unfortunate inferior*, rather than as an *outraged* and *insulted equal*. Therefore, as soon as abolitionists demanded for the oppressed American the *very same treatment*, upon the high ground of *human rights*, why, then it was instantly withdrawn, simply because *it never had been conceded on the right* ground; and those who had previously granted it became afraid, lest, during the æra of abolition excitement, persons would presume *they* were acting on the fundamental principle of abolitionism—the principle of *equal rights*, irrespective of color or condition, instead of on the mere principle of "*pity* and *generosity*."

It is truly surprising to find a professing christian excusing the unprincipled opposition exhibited in New Haven, to the erection of a College for young men of color. Are we indeed to succumb to a corrupt public sentiment at the North, and the abominations of slavery at the South, by refraining from asserting the *right* of Americans to plant a literary institution in New Haven, or New York, or *any where* on the American soil? Are we to select "some retired place," where there would be the least prejudice and opposition to meet, rather than openly and fearlessly to face the American monster, who, like the horse-leach, is continually crying give, give, and whose demands are only increased by compromise and surrender? No! there is a spirit abroad in this country, which will not consent to barter principle for an *unholy* peace; a spirit which seeks to be "pure from the blood of all men," by a bold and christian avowal of truth; a spirit which will not hide God's eternal principles of right and wrong, but will stand erect in the storm of human passion, prejudice and interest, "holding forth the light of truth in the midst of a crooked and perverse generation;" a spirit which will never slumber nor sleep, till man ceases to hold dominion over his fellow creatures, and the trump of universal liberty rings in every forest, and is re-echoed by every mountain and rock.

Art thou not aware, my friend, that this College was projected in the year 1831, previous to the formation of the first Anti-Slavery Society, which was organized in 1832? How, then, canst thou say that the circumstances relative to it occurred "at a time when the public mind was excited on the subject?" I feel quite amused at the *presumption* which thou appearest to think was exhibited by the projectors of this institution, in wishing it to be located in New Haven, where was another College "embracing a large proportion of southern students," &c. It was a great offence; to be sure, for colored men to build a College by the walls of the white man's "College, where half the shoe-blacks and waiters were *colored men*." But why so? The other half of the shoe-blacks and waiters were *white*, I presume; and if these *white* servants could be satisfied with *their* humble occupation *under the roof* of Yale College, why might not the colored waiters be contented also, though an institution for the education of colored Americans might *presume* to lift its head "beside the very walls of this College?" Is it possible that any professing christian can calmly look back at these disgraceful transactions, and tell me that such opposition was manifested "*for the best reasons?*" And what is still worse, censure the projectors of a literary institution, in free, republican, enlightened America, because they did not meekly yield to "*such reasonable objections,*" and refused "to soothe the feelings and apprehensions of those who had been excited" to opposition and clamor by the simple fact that some American born citizens wished to give their children a liberal education in a separate College, only because the white Americans despised their brethren of a darker complexion, and scorned to share with them the privileges of Yale College? It was very wrong, to be sure, for the friends of the oppressed American to consider such outrageous conduct "as a mark of the force of sinful prejudice!" Vastly uncharitable! Great complains are made that "the worst motives were ascribed to some of the most respectable, and venerated, and *pious* men who opposed the measure." Wonderful indeed, that men should be found so true to their principles, as to dare in this age of sycophancy to declare the truth to those who stand in high places, wearing the badges of office or honor, and fearlessly to rebuke the puerile and unchristian prejudice which existed against their colored brethren! "Pious men!" Why, I would ask, how are we to judge of men's piety—by professions or products? Do men gather thorns of grapes, or thistles of figs? Certainly not. If, then, in the lives of men we do not find the fruits of christian principle, we have no right, according to our Saviour's criterion, "by their fruits ye shall know them," to suppose that men are really pious who can be perseveringly guilty of despising others, and denying them equal rights, because they have colored skins. "A great deal was said and done that was calculated to throw the community into an angry ferment." Yes, and I suppose the friends of the colored man were just as guilty as was the great Apostle, who, by the angry, and excited, and *prejudiced* Jews, was accused of being "a pestilent fellow and a mover of sedition," because he declared himself called to preach the everlasting gospel to the Gentiles, whom they considered as "dogs," and utterly unworthy of being placed on the same platform of human rights and a glorious immortality.

Thy friend,

A. E. GRIMKÉ.

LETTER VIII.

Vindication of Abolitionists.

Groton, Mass. 6th month, 1837.

DEAR FRIEND:—In my last, I commented upon the opposition to the establishment of a College in New Haven, Conn., for the education of colored young men. The same remarks are applicable to the persecutions of the Canterbury School. I leave thee and our readers to apply them. I cannot help thinking how strange and unaccountable thy soft excuses for the *sins of prejudice* will appear to the next generation, if thy book ever reach their eye.

As to Cincinnati having been chosen as the city in which the Philanthropist should be published after the retreat of its editor from Kentucky, thou hast not been "sufficiently informed," for James G. Birney pursued exactly the course which *thou* hast marked out as the most prudent and least offensive. He edited his paper at New Richmond, in Ohio, for nearly three months before he went to Cincinnati, and did not go there until the excitement appeared to have subsided.

And so, thou thinkest that abolitionists are accountable for the outrages which have been committed against them; they are the tempters, and are held responsible by God, as well as the tempted. Wilt thou tell me, who was responsible for the mob which went with swords and staves to take an innocent man before the tribunals of Annas and Pilate, some 1800 years ago? And who was responsible for the uproar at Ephesus, the insurrection at Athens, and the tumults at Lystra and Iconium? Were I a mobocrat, I should want no better excuse than thou hast furnished for such outrages. Wonderful indeed, if, in free America, her citizens cannot *choose* where they will erect their literary institutions and presses, to advocate the self-evident truths of our Declaration of Independence! And still more wonderful, that a New England woman should, *after years of reflection*, deliberately write a book to condemn the advocates of liberty, and plead excuses for a relentless prejudice against her colored brethren and sisters, and for the persecutors of those, who, according to the opinion of a *Southern* member of Congress, are prosecuting "the *only plan* that can ever overthrow slavery at the South." I am glad, *for thy own sake*, that thou hast exculpated abolitionists from the charge of the "deliberate intention of fomenting illegal acts of violence." Would it not have been still better, if thou hadst spared the remarks which rendered such an explanation necessary?

I find that thou wilt not allow of the comparison often drawn between the effects of christianity on the hearts of those who obstinately rejected it, and those of abolitionism on the hearts of people of the present day. Thou sayest, "Christianity is a system of *persuasion*, tending by kind and gentle influences to make men *willing* to leave their sins." Dost thou suppose the Pharisees and Sadducees deemed it was very *kind* and *gentle* in its influences, when our holy Redeemer called them "a generation of vipers," or when he preached that sermon "full of harshness, uncharitableness, rebuke and denunciation," recorded in the xxiii. chapter of Matthew? But I shall be told that Christ knew the hearts of all men, and therefore it was right for him to use terms which mere human beings never ought to employ. Read, then, the prophecies of Isaiah, Ezekiel, and others, and also the Epistles of the New Testament. They employed the most offensive terms on many occasions, and the sharpest rebukes, knowing full well that there are some sinners who can be reached by nothing but death-thrusts at their consciences. An anecdote of JOHN RICHARDSON, who was remarkable for his urbanity of manners, occurs to me. He one day preached a sermon in a country town, in which he made use of some *hard* language; a friend reproved him after meeting, and inquired whether he did not know that hard wood was split by soft knocks. Yes, said Richardson, but I also know that there is some wood so rotten at the heart, that nothing but tremendously hard blows will ever split it open. Ah! John, replied the elder, I see thou understandest *how* to do thy master's work. Now, I believe this nation is *rotten at the heart*, and that nothing but the most tremendous blows with the sledge-hammer of abolition truth, could ever have broken the false rest which we had taken up for ourselves on the very brink of ruin.

"Abolitionism, on the contrary, is a system of *coercion* by public opinion." By this assertion, I presume thou "hast not been correctly informed" as to the reasons which have induced abolitionists to put forth all their energies to rectify public opinion. It is *not* because we wish to wield this public opinion like a rod of iron over the heads of slaveholders, to *coerce* them into an abandonment of the system of slavery; not at all. We are striving to purify public opinion, first, because as long as the North is so much involved in the guilt of slavery, by its political, commercial, religious, and social connexion with the South, *her own citizens* need to be converted. Second, because we know that when public opinion is rectified at the North, it will throw a flood of light from its million of reflecting surfaces upon the heart and soul of the South. The South sees full well at what we are aiming, and she is so unguarded as to acknowledge that "if she does not resist the danger in its inception, it will *soon* become *irresistible.*" She exclaims in terror, "the truth is, the *moral* power of the world is against us; it is idle to disguise it." The fact is, that the slaveholders of the South, and their northern apologists, have been overtaken by the storm of free discussion, and are something like those who go down to the sea and do business in the great waters: "they reel to and fro, and stagger like a drunken man, and are at their wit's end."

Our view of the doctrine of expediency, thou art pleased to pronounce "wrong and very pernicious in its tendency." Expediency is emphatically the doctrine by which the children of this world are wont to guide their steps, whilst the rejection of it as a rule of action exactly accords with the divine injunction, to "walk by faith, *not* by sight." Thy doctrine that "the wisdom and rectitude of a given course depend entirely on the *probabilities of success,*" is not the doctrine of the Bible. According to this principle, how absurd was the conduct of Moses! What probability of success was there that he could move the heart of Pharaoh? None at all; and thus did *he* reason when he said, "Who am *I*, that I should go unto Pharaoh?" And again, "Behold, they will not believe *me*, nor hearken unto my voice." The *success* of Moses's mission in persuading the king of Egypt to "let the people go," was not involved in the duty of obedience to the divine command. Neither was the success of Isaiah, Jeremiah, and others of the prophets who were singularly *unsuccessful* in their mission to the Jews. All who see the path of duty plain before them, are bound to walk in that path, end where it may. They then can realize the meaning of the Apostle, when he exhorts Christians to cast all their burden on the Lord, with the promise that He would sustain them. This is walking by *faith*, not by sight. In the work in which abolitionists are engaged, they are compelled to "walk by faith;" they feel called upon to preach the truth in season and out of season, to lift up their voices like a trumpet, to show the people their transgressions and the house of Jacob their sins. The *success* of this mission, *they* have no more to do with, than had Moses and Aaron, Jeremiah or Isaiah, with that of theirs. Whether the South will be saved by Anti-Slavery efforts, is not a question for us to settle—and in some of our hearts, the *hope of its salvation has utterly gone out*. All nations have been punished for oppression, and why should ours escape? Our light, and high professions, and the age in which we live, convict us not only of enormous oppression, but of the vilest hypocrisy. It may be that the rejection of the truth which we are now pouring in upon the South, may be the final filling up of their iniquities, just previous to the bursting of God's exterminating thunders over the Sodoms and Gomorrahs, the Admahs and Zeboims of America. The *result* of our labors is hidden from our eyes; whether the preaching of Anti-Slavery truth is to be a savor of life unto life, or of death unto death to this nation, we know not; and we have no more to do with it, than had the Apostle Paul, when he preached Christ to the people of his day.

If American Slavery goes down in blood, it will but verify the declarations of those who uphold it. A committee of the North Carolina Legislature acknowledged this to an English Friend ten years ago. Jefferson more than once uttered his gloomy forebodings; and the Legislators of Virginia, in 1832, declared that if the opportunity of escape, through the means of emancipation, were rejected, "though they might *save themselves*, they would rear their posterity to the business of the dagger and the torch." I have myself known several families to leave the South, solely from a fear of insurrection; and this twelve and fourteen years ago, long before any Anti-Slavery efforts were made in this country. And yet, I presume, *if* through the cold-hearted apathy and obstinate opposition of the North, the South should become strengthened in her desperate determination to hold on to her outraged victims, until they are goaded to despair, and if the Lord in his wrath pours out the vials of his vengeance upon the slave States, why then, Abolitionists will have to bear all the blame. Thou hast drawn a frightful picture of the final issue of Anti-Slavery efforts, as thou art pleased to call it; but none of these things move me, for with just as much truth mayest thou point to the land of Egypt blackened by God's avenging fires, and exclaim, "Behold the issue of Moses's mission." Nay, verily! See in that smoking, and blood-drenched house of bondage, the consequences of oppression, disobedience, and an obstinate rejection of truth, and light, and love. What had Moses to do with those judgment plagues, except to lift his rod? And if the South soon finds her winding sheet in garments rolled in blood, it will *not* be because of what the North has told her, but because, like impenitent Egypt, she hardened her heart against it, whilst the voices of some of her own children were crying in agony, "O! that thou hadst known, even thou, in this thy day, the things which belong to thy peace; but now they are hid from thine eyes."

Thy friend,

A. E. GRIMKÉ.

LETTER IX.

Effect on the South.

Brookline, Mass. 8th month, 17th, 1837.

DEAR FRIEND:—Thou sayest "There are cases also, where differences in age, and station, and character, forbid all interference to modify the conduct and character of others." Let us bring this to the only touchstone by which Christians should try their principles of action.

How was it when God designed to rid his people out of the hands of the Egyptian monarch? Was *his* station so exalted "as to forbid all interference to modify his character and conduct?" And *who* was sent to interfere with his conduct towards a stricken people? Was it some brother monarch of exalted station, whose elevated rank might serve to excuse such interference "to modify his conduct and character?" No. It was an obscure shepherd of Midian's desert; for let us remember, that Moses, in pleading the cause of the Israelites, identified himself with the *lowest* and *meanest* of the King's subjects. Ah! he was *one of that despised caste;* for, although brought up as the son of the princess, yet he had left Egypt as an outlaw. He had committed the crime of murder, and fled because the monarch "sought to slay him." This exiled outlaw is the instrument chosen by God to vindicate the cause of his oppressed people. Moses was in the sight of Pharaoh as much an object of scorn, as Garrison now is to the tyrants of America. Some seem to think, that great moral enterprises can be made honorable only by Doctors of Divinity, and Presidents of Colleges, engaging in them: when all powerful Truth cannot be dignified by *any* man, but *it* dignifies and ennobles all who embrace it. *It* lifts the beggar from the dunghill, and sets him among princes. Whilst it needs no great names to bear it onward to its glorious consummation, it is continually making great characters out of apparently mean and unpromising materials; and in the intensity of its piercing rays, revealing to the amazement of many, the insignificance and *moral* littleness of those who fill the highest stations in Church and State.

But take a few more examples from the bible, of those in high stations being reproved by men of inferior rank. Look at David rebuked by Nathan, Ahab and Jezebel by Elijah and Micaiah. What, too, was the conduct of Daniel and Shadrach, Meshack and Abednego, but a *practical* rebuke of Darius and Nebuchadnezzar? And *who* were these men, apart from these acts of daring interference? They were the Lord's prophets, I shall be told; but what cared those monarchs for *this fact?* How much credit did they give them for holding this holy office? None. And why? Because all but David were impenitent sinners, and rejected with scorn all "interference to modify their conduct or characters." Reformers are rarely estimated in the age in which they live, whether they be called prophets or apostles, or abolitionists, or what not. They stand on the rock of Truth, and calmly look down upon the careering thunder-clouds, the tempest, and the roaring waves, because they well know that where the atmosphere is surcharged with pestilential vapors, a conflict of the elements *must* take place, before it can be purified by that moral electricity, beautifully typified by the cloven tongues that sat upon *each* of the heads of the 120 disciples who were convened on the day of Pentecost. Such men and women expect to be "blamed and opposed, because their measures are deemed inexpedient, and calculated to increase rather than diminish the evil to be cured." They know full well, that *intellectual* greatness cannot give *moral* perception—therefore, *those who have no clear views of the irresistibleness of moral power, cannot see the efficacy of moral means.* They say with the apostle, "The natural man receiveth not the things of the Spirit of God; for they are foolishness unto him: neither can he know them, because they are spiritually discerned." We know full well, that northern men and women laugh at the inefficacy of Anti-Slavery measures; *but slaveholders never have ridiculed them:* not that their moral perceptions are any clearer than those of our northern opponents, but where men's *interests* and *lust of power* are immediately affected by moral effort, they instinctively feel that it is so, and tremble for the result.

But suppose even that our measures were calculated to *increase* the evils of slavery. *The measures adopted by Moses, and sanctioned by God, increased the burdens of the Israelites.* Were they, therefore, *inexpedient?* And yet, if *our* measures produce a similar effect, O then! they are very inexpedient indeed. The truth is, when we look at Moses and his measures, we look at them in connection with the emancipation of the Israelites. The *ultimate* and glorious success of the measures proves their wisdom and expediency. But when Anti-Slavery measures are looked at *now*, we see them long *before the end is accomplished.* We see, according to thy account, the burdens increased; but we do not yet see the triumphant march through the Red Sea, nor do we hear the song of joy and thanksgiving which ascended from Israel's redeemed host. But canst thou not give us twenty years to complete our work? Clarkson, thy much admired model, worked twenty years; and the benevolent Colonization Society has been in operation twenty years. Just give us as long a time, or half that time, and then thou wilt be a far better judge of the expediency or inexpediency of our measures. Then thou wilt be able to look at them in connection with their success or their failure, and instead of writing a book on thy opinions and my opinions, thou canst write a *history*.

I cannot agree with thee in the sentiment, that the station of a nursery maid makes it inexpedient for her to turn reprover of the master who employs her. This is the doctrine of *modern aristocracy*, not of primitive christianity; for ecclesiastical history informs us that, in the first ages of christianity, kings were converted through the faithful and solemn rebukes of their slaves and captives. I have myself been reproved by a *slave*, and I thanked her, and still thank her for it. Think how this doctrine robs the nursery maid of her responsibility, and shields the master from reproof; for it may be that she alone has seen him ill-treat his wife. Now it appears to me, so far from her station forbidding all interference to modify the character and conduct of her employer, that that station peculiarly qualifies her for the difficult and delicate task, because nursery maids often know secrets of oppression, which no other persons are fully acquainted with. For my part, I believe it is *now the duty of the slaves of the South to rebuke their masters* for their robbery, oppression and crime; and so far from believing that such "reproof would do no good, but only evil," I think it would be attended by the happiest results in the main, though I doubt not it would occasion some instances of severe personal suffering. No station or character can destroy individual responsibility, in the matter of reproving sin. I feel that a slave has a right to rebuke me, and so has the vilest sinner; and the sincere, humble christian will be thankful for rebuke, let it come from whom it may. Such, I am confident, never would think it inexpedient for their chamber maids to administer it, but would endeavor to profit by it.

Thou askest very gravely, why James G. Birney did not go quietly into the southern States, and collect facts? Indeed! Why should he go to the South to collect facts, when he had lived there forty *years*? Thou mayest with just as much propriety ask me, why I do not go to the South to collect facts. The answer to both questions is obvious:—We have lived at the South, as *integral* parts of the system of slavery, and therefore we know from practical observation and sad experience, quite enough about it already. I think it would be absurd for either of us to spend our time in such a way. And even if J. G. Birney had not lived at the South, why should he go there to collect facts, when the Anti-Slavery presses are continually throwing them out before the public? Look, too, at the Slave Laws! What more do we need to show us the bloody hands and iron heart of Slavery?

Thou sayest on the 89th page of thy book, "Every avenue of approach to the South is shut. No paper, pamphlet, or preacher, that touches on that topic, is admitted in their bounds." Thou art greatly mistaken; every avenue of approach to the South is *not* shut. The American Anti-Slavery Society sends between four and five hundred of its publications to the South by mail, *to subscribers*, or as exchange papers. One slaveholder in North Carolina, not long since, bought $60 worth of our pamphlets, &c. which he distributed in the slave States. Another slaveholder from Louisiana, made a large purchase of our publications last fall, which he designed to distribute among professors of religion who held slaves. To these I may add another from South Carolina, another from Richmond, Virginia, numbers from Kentucky, Tennessee, and Missouri, and others from New Orleans, besides persons connected with at least three Colleges and Theological Seminaries in slave States, have applied for our publications for their own use, and for distribution. Within a few weeks, the South Carolina Delegation in Congress have sent on an order to the publishing Agent of the American Anti-Slavery Society, for all the principal bound volumes, pamphlets, and periodicals of the Society. At the same time, they addressed a very courteous letter to J. G. Birney, the Corresponding Secretary, propounding nearly a score of queries, embracing the principles, designs, plans of operation, progress and results of the Society. I know in the large cities, such as Charleston and Richmond, that Anti-Slavery papers are not suffered to reach their destination through the mail; but *it is not so* in the smaller towns. But even in the cities, I doubt not they are read by the postmasters and others. The South may pretend that she will not read our papers, but it is all pretence; the fact is, she is very anxious to see what we are doing, so that when the mail-bags were robbed in Charleston in 1835, *I know* that the robbers were very careful to select a few copies of each of the publications *before* they made the bonfire, and that these were handed round in a private way through the city, so that they were *extensively read*. This fact I had from a friend of mine who was in Charleston at the time, and *read* the publications himself. My relations also wrote me word, that they had seen and read them.

In order to show that our discussions and publications have already produced a great effect upon many individuals in the slave States, I subjoin the following detail of facts and testimony now in my possession.

My sister, S. M. Grimké, has just received a letter from a Southerner residing in the far South, in which he says, "On the 4th of July, the friends of the oppressed met and contributed six or eight dollars, to obtain some copies of Gerrit Smith's letter, and some other pamphlets for our own benefit and that of the vicinity. The leaven, we think, is beginning to work, and we hope that it will ere long purify the whole mass of corruption."

An intelligent member of the Methodist Church, who resides in North Carolina, was recently in the city of New York, and told the editor of Zion's Watchman, that "our publications were read with great interest at the South—that there was great curiosity there to see them." A bookseller also in one of the most southern States, only a few months ago, ordered a package of our publications. And within a very short time, an influential slaveholder from the far South, who called at the Anti-Slavery Office in New York, said he had had misgivings on the subject ever since the formation of the American Society—that he saw some of our publications *at the South* three years ago, and is now convinced and has emancipated his slaves.

A correspondent of the Union Herald, a clergyman, and a graduate of one of the colleges of Kentucky, says, "I find in this State *many* who are decidedly opposed to slavery—but few indeed take the ground that it is right. I trust the cause of human rights is onward—*weekly, I receive two copies of the Emancipator,* which I send out as battering rams, to beat down the citadel of oppression." In a letter to James G. Birney, from a gentleman in a slave State, we find this declaration: "Your paper, the Philanthropist, is regularly distributed here, and as yet works no incendiary results; and indeed, so far as I can learn, general satisfaction is here expressed, both as to the temper and spirit of the paper, and no disapprobation as to the results." At an Anti-Slavery meeting last fall in Philadelphia, a gentleman from Delaware was present, who rose and encouraged Abolitionists to go on, and said that he could assure them the influence of their measures was felt there, and their principles were gaining ground secretly and silently. The subject, he informed them, was discussed there, and he believed Anti-Slavery lectures could be delivered there with safety, and would produce important results. Since that time, a lecturer has been into that State, and a State Society has been formed, the secretary of which was the first editor of the Emancipator, and is now pastor of the Baptist church in the capital of the State. The North Carolina Watchman, published at Salisbury, in an article on the subject of Abolition, has the following remarks of the editor: "It [the abolition party] is the growing party at the North: we are inclined to believe, that there is even *more of it at the South,* than prudence will permit to be openly avowed." It rejoices our hearts to find that there are some southerners who feel and acknowledge the infatuation of the politicians of the South, and the philanthropy of abolitionists. The Maryville Intelligencer of 1836, exclaims, "What sort of madness, produced by a jaundiced and distorted conception of the feelings and motives by which northern abolitionists are actuated, can induce the southern political press to urge a severance of the tie that binds our Union together? To offer rewards for those very individuals who stand as *mediators* between masters and slaves, urging the one to be obedient, and the other to do justice?"

A southern Minister of the Methodist Episcopal Church, at the session of the New York Annual Conference, in June of 1836, said: "Don't give up Abolitionism—don't bow down to slavery. You have thousands at the South who are secretly praying for you." In a subsequent conversation with the same individual, he stated, that the South is not that unit of which the pro-slavery party boast—there is a diversity of opinion among them in reference to slavery, and the REIGN OF TERROR alone suppresses the free expression of sentiment. That there are thousands who believe slaveholding to be sinful, who secretly wish the abolitionists success, and believe God will bless their efforts. That the ministers of the gospel and ecclesiastical bodies who indiscriminately denounce the abolitionists, without doing any thing themselves to remove slavery, have *not* the thanks of thousands at the South, but on the contrary are viewed as *taking sides with slaveholders,* and *recreant to the principles of their own profession.—Zion's Watchman, November,* 1836.

The Christian Mirror, published in Portland, Maine, has the following letter from a minister who has lately taken up his abode in Kentucky, to a friend in Maine:—"Several ministers have recently left the State, I believe, on account of slavery; and many of the members of churches, as I have understood, have sold their property, and removed to the free States. Many are becoming more and more convinced of the evil and *sin* of slavery, and would gladly rid themselves and the community of this scourge; and I feel confident that influences are already in operation, which, if properly directed and regulated by the principles of the gospel, may 'break every yoke and let the oppressed go free' in Kentucky."

In 1st month, 1835, when Theodore D. Weld was lecturing in Pittsburgh, Pennsylvania, at the close of one of his evening lectures, a man sought him through the crowd, and extending his hand to him through his friends, by whom he was surrounded, solicited him to step aside with him for a moment. After they had retired by themselves, the gentleman said to him with great earnestness, "I am a slaveholder from Maryland—*you are right—the doctrine you advocate is truth.*" Why, then, said the lecturer, do you not emancipate your slaves? "Because," said the Marylander, "I have not religion enough"—He was a professing christian—"I dare not subject myself to the torrent of opposition which, from the present state of public sentiment, would be poured upon me; but do you abolitionists go on, and you will effect a change in public sentiment, which will render it possible and easy for us to emancipate our slaves. I know," continued he, "a great many slaveholders in my State, who stand on precisely the same ground that I do in relation to this matter. *Only produce a correct public sentiment at the North, and the work is done; for all that keeps the South in countenance while continuing this system, is the apology and argument afforded so generally by the North; only produce a right feeling in the North generally, and the South cannot stand before it; let the North be thoroughly converted, and the work is at once accomplished at the South.*" Another fact which may be adduced to prove that the South is looking to the North for help, is the following: At an Anti-Slavery concert of prayer for the oppressed, held in New York city, in 1836, a gentleman arose in the course of the meeting, declaring himself a Virginian and a slaveholder. He said he came to that city filled with the deepest prejudice against the abolitionists, by the reports given of their character in papers published at the North. But he determined to investigate their character and designs for himself. He even boarded in the family of an abolitionist, and attended the monthly concert of prayer for the slaves and the slaveholders. And now, as the result of his investigations and observations, he was convinced that *not only the spirit but the principles and measures of the abolitionists* ARE RIGHTEOUS. He was now ready to emancipate his own slaves, and had commenced advocating the doctrine of immediate emancipation—"and here," said he, pointing to two men sitting near him, "are the first fruits of my labors—these two fellow Virginians and slaveholders, are converts with myself to abolitionism. And I know a thousand Virginians, who need only to be made acquainted with the true spirit and principles of abolitionists, in order to their becoming converts as we are. *Let the abolitionists go on in the dissemination of their doctrines, and let the Northern papers cease to misrepresent them at the South—let the true light of abolitionism be fully shed upon the Southern mind, and the work of immediate and general emancipation will be speedily accomplished.*"—*Morning Star, N. Y.*

A letter from a gentleman in Kentucky to Gerrit Smith, dated August, 1836, contains the following expressions:—

> I am fully persuaded, that the voice of the free States, lifted up in a proper manner against the evil, [Slavery] will awaken them [slaveholders] from their midnight slumbers, and produce a happy change. I rejoice, dear brother in Christ, to hear that you are with us, and

feel deeply to plead the cause of the oppressed, and undo the heavy burdens. May God bless you, and the cause which you pursue.

In the summer of 1835, William R. Buford, of Virginia, who had then recently emancipated his slaves, wrote a letter which was published in the Hampshire Gazette, North Hampton, Mass. from which I give thee some extracts.

Dear Sir:—As you are ardently engaged in the discussion of Slavery, I think it likely I may be of service to you, and through you to the cause which you are advocating. * * * I was born and brought up at the South in the midst of slavery, as you know. My father inherited slaves from his father, and I from him. So far from thinking slavery a sin, or that I had no right to own the slaves inherited from my father, I thought no one could venture to dispute that right, any more than he could my right to his land or his stock. I advocated Colonization, as I thought it on many accounts a good plan to get rid of such colored persons as wished to go to Africa; but my conscience as a slaveholder was not much troubled by it. Of course, I had no tendency to make me disclaim my right to my slaves. Abolition—immediate abolition, began afterwards to be discussed in various parts of the country. My right to the slaves I owned began to be disputed. I had to defend myself. In vain did I say I inherited my slaves from a pious father, who seemed to be governed in his dealings by a sense of duty to his slaves. In vain did I say that nearly all my property consisted in slaves, and to free them would make me a poor man. My duty to emancipate was still urged. At length my eyes were opened—partly by the arguments used by the abolitionists: but mainly, by long being compelled *by them* to examine the subject for myself. No longer could I close my eyes to the evils of slavery, nor could I any longer despise the abolitionists, "the only true friends of their country and kind." I now think, I know, I have no more right to own slaves, whether I inherited them or not, than I have to encourage the African slave trade. By declaring this sentiment, I expect and design to abet the cause of Abolition at the North, and through the North the emancipation of the slaves at the South. I know that in doing this, I condemn the South. No one can suppose, however, that I have any unkind feelings towards the South.

All my relatives live in the slaveholding States, and are almost all slaveholders.

I think the abolitionists have done, and are doing a great deal of good, by holding slavery up to the public gaze. Sentiment at the North on the subject of slavery must have the same effect on the South, that their opinions have on any other matter.

The writer of the foregoing is, as I am told, still a resident of Virginia, where he has long been known, and is highly respected.

In the 11th month, 1835, the United States Telegraph, published at Washington city, contains the following remarks by the Editor, Duff Green.

We are of those who believe the South has nothing to fear from a servile war. We do not believe that the abolitionists intend, nor could they if they would, excite the slaves to insurrection. The danger of this is remote. We believe that we have most to fear from the *organised action upon the consciences* and fears of the slaveholders themselves; *from the insinuations of their dangerous heresies into our schools, our pulpits, and our domestic circles. It is only by alarming the consciences of the weak and feeble, and diffusing among our own people a morbid sensibility on the question of slavery, that the abolitionists can accomplish their object.* PREPARATORY TO THIS, they are now laboring to saturate the non-slaveholding States with the belief that slavery is a "sin against God." We must meet the question in all its bearings. We must SATISFY THE CONSCIENCES, we must allay the fears of our own people. We must satisfy them that slavery is of itself right—that it is not a sin against God—that it is not an evil, moral or political. To do this, we must discuss the subject of slavery itself. We must examine its bearing upon the moral, political, and religious institutions of the country. In this way, and this way only, can we prepare our own people to *defend their own institutions*.

In another number of the same paper, the Editor says,

We hold that our sole reliance is on ourselves; that we have *most to fear from the gradual operation on public opinion among ourselves*; and that those are the most insidious and dangerous invaders of our rights and interests, who, coming to us in the guise of friendship, endeavor to *persuade* us that slavery is a sin, a curse, an evil. It is not true that the South sleeps on a volcano—that we are afraid to go to bed at night—that we are fearful of murder and pillage. *Our greatest cause of apprehension is from the operation of the morbid sensibility which appeals to the consciences of our own people*, and would make them the voluntary instruments of their own ruin.

In 1835, I think about the close of the year, a series of articles on Slavery appeared in the Lexington (Kentucky) Intelligencer. In one of the numbers, the writer says:—

> Much of the preceding matter was inserted (May, 1833) in the Louisville Herald. A *great change* has since taken place in public sentiment. Colonization, then a favorite measure, is now rejected for instant emancipation. Were this last feasible, I would gladly join its advocates, &c.

In a letter to the publisher of the Emancipator, dated "April 1, 1837," from a Southerner, I find the following language:—

> Though a —— born and bred, I now consider the Anti-Slavery cause as a just and holy one. Deep reflection, the reading of your excellent publications, and—years of travel in Europe, have made me, what I am now proud to call myself, an abolitionist.
>
> For the present, accept the assurances of my unswerving devotion to the cause of liberty and justice. Any letter from yourself will always give me sincere pleasure, and whenever I go to New York, I shall call upon you, *sans ceremonie*, as I would upon an old friend.

A short time since, J G. Birney received a donation of $20 for the Anti-Slavery Society, from an individual residing in a slave State, accompanied with a request that his name might not be mentioned.

About the time of the robbery of the U. S. Mail, and the burning of Abolition papers by the infatuated citizens of my own city, the Editor of the Charleston Courier made the following remarks in his paper, which plainly reveal the cowering of the spirit of slavery, under the searching scrutiny occasioned by the Anti-Slavery discussions in the free States.

> *Mart for Negroes.*—We understand that a proposition is before the city council, relative to the establishment of a mart for the sale of negroes in this city, in a place *more remote from observation*, and less offensive to the public eye, than the one now used for that purpose. We doubt not that the proposition before the council will be acceptable to the community, and that it may be so matured as to promote public decency, without prejudice to the interest of individuals.

Hear, too, the acknowledgement of the Southern Literary Review, published at Charleston, South Carolina, which was got up in 1837, to sustain the system of Slavery.

> There are *many* good men even among us, who have begun to grow *timid*. They think that what the virtuous and high-minded men of the North look upon as a crime and a plague-spot, cannot be perfectly innocent or quite harmless in a slaveholding community. * * * Some timid men among us, whose ears have been long assailed with outcries of tyranny and oppression, wafted over the ocean and land from North to South, begin to look *fearfully* around them.

A correspondent of the Pittsburgh Witness, detailing the particulars of an Anti-Slavery meeting in Washington co. Pennsylvania, says:—"After Dr. Lemoyne, the President of the Pennsylvania Anti-Slavery Society, had finished his address, in which the principles and measures of the Anti-Slavery Society were fully exhibited, the Rev. Charles Stewart, of Kentucky, a slaveholding clergyman of the Presbyterian church, who was casually present, rose and addressed the audience, and instead of opposing our principles as might have been expected, fully endorsed every thing that had been said, declaring his conviction that such a speech would have been well received by the truly religious part of the community in which he resided, and would have been opposed only by those who were actuated by party politics alone, or those who 'neither feared God nor regarded man."

I give thee now a letter from a gentleman in a South Western slaveholding State, to J. G. BIRNEY.

> *Very Dear Sir*:—I knew you in the days of your prosperity at the South, though you will not recognize me. Ever since you first took your stand in defence of *natural rights*, I have been looking upon you with intense interest. I *was* violently opposed to Abolitionists, and verily thought I was doing service to both church and State, in decrying them as *incendiaries* and *fanatics*. What blindness and infatuation! Yet I was *sincere*. Ah! my dear sir, God in mercy has taught me that something more than *sincerity*, in the common acceptation of the term, is necessary to preserve our understandings from idiocy, and our hearts from utter ruin. How could I have been such a *madman*, as coolly and composedly to place my foot upon the necks of immortal beings, and from that horrid point of elevation, hurl the deep curses of church and State at the heads of —— whom? Fanatics? No, sir!—*but of the only persons on the face of the earth, who had* HEART *enough to* FEEL, *and* SOUL *enough to* ACT, *in behalf of the* RIGHTS OF MAN! Yet I was just such a madman! Yes, sir, I was a *fanatic*, and an *incendiary* too—setting on fire the worst passions of our fallen nature. But I have repented. I have become a convert to political, and I trust, also, to *Christian Freedom*. The spectacle exhibited by yourself, and your compatriots and fellow-christians, has completely overcome me. Your reasonings convince my judgment, and your ACTIONS win my heart. God speed you in your work of love! The hopes of the world depend, under God, upon the success of your cause.
>
> Very respectfully and with undying affection,
>
> Your friend and brother, A SOUTHERNER.

Another of J. G. Birney's southern correspondents says, in 1836,

> That portion of the Church with which I am connected, seem to have no sympathy with the indignation against the abolitionists, which prevails so extensively North and South; but, on the other hand, consider the *South as infatuated* to the highest degree.

> There is more credit for philanthropy given those who manumit their slaves, without *expatriation,* than formerly.
>
> The thirst for information is increasing, while the "*non liquetism*" [voting on neither side] of brethren in church courts is becoming less and less satisfactory; and such of them as advocate the perpetuity of the system, are looked upon with surprise and regret.
>
> Those who view with horror the traffic in slaves by ministers of the gospel, express more freely their pain at its indulgence, *than I have ever known.* I am acquainted with several such cases. In no instances have they left the brother's standing where it was, before it took place. Of such cases—even those, too, where the usual allowances might be called for—I have heard professors of religion remark, "Mr. A. could not get an audience to hear him preach"—"Mr. B. has more assurance than I could have, to preach, after selling my slaves as he has done"—"He can never make me believe he has any religion"—"This is the first time you have done so, but repeat it, and I think I shall never hear you preach again."

These remarks were made by slaveholding professors of religion themselves, and under circumstances neither calculated nor intended to deceive.

The following letter was written by an intelligent gentleman in the interior of Alabama, to Arthur Tappan, of New York, who had sent him some Anti-Slavery publications. The date is March 21, 1834.

> Dear Sir—Your letter of Dec. last, I read with much interest. The numbers of the Anti-Slavery Reporter, also, which you were so kind as to send me, I carefully examined, and put them in circulation.
>
> Your operations have produced considerable excitement in some sections of this country, but humanity has lost nothing. The more the subject of slavery is agitated, the better. A distinguished gentleman remarked to me a day or two since, that "there was a great change going on in public sentiment." Few would acknowledge that it was to be ascribed to the influence of your Society. There can be no doubt, however, that this is directly and indirectly the principal cause.

During the same year, the Editor of the New York Evangelist received a letter from a christian friend in North Carolina, from which I give thee an extract.

To the Editor of the Evangelist—

The subject of slavery, recently brought up and discussed in your paper, is the one which elicits the following remarks.

In the first place I will state, that I entertain very different views *now*, to what I did six months ago. I was among those who thought (and honestly too) that there was no more moral guilt attached to the holding our fellow beings in bondage, regarding them as property, than to the holding of a mule or an ox. It was natural enough for me to think so, for I had been trained from my very infancy to view the subject in no other light. I shall never forget my feelings when the subject was first hit upon in the Evangelist. I became angry, and was disposed to attribute sinister motives to all who were concerned in the matter. With some others, I determined to stop the paper forthwith.

Though I made every effort to turn my mind away from the subject, my conscience in spite of me began to awake, and to be troubled. The word of God was resorted to, with the hope of finding something to bring peace and quietude, but all in vain. It was but adding fuel to the flame. I determined, let others do as they would, to meet the subject, to examine it in all its bearings, and to abide the result; and if it should be found that God regards slavery as an evil, and incompatible with the gospel, I would give it up. If not, I should be made wiser without incurring any harm by the investigation.

In the very nature of God's dealings with men, this subject must and will be agitated, until conviction shall be brought home to the heart and conscience of every man, and *slavery shall be banished from our land*. And woe be to him who wilfully closes his eyes, and stops his ears against the light of God's truth.

In 8th month of the same year, the same paper contained the following extract from another correspondent in North Carolina.

——— N. C. July 9, 1834.

Rev. and dear Sir—If I owe an apology for intruding on you, and introducing myself, I must find it in the fact, that I wish to bid you God speed in the good cause in which you are so heartily engaged. While so many at the North are opposing, I wish to cheer you by one voice from the South. If it is unpopular to plead the cause of the oppressed negro in New York, how dangerous to be known as his friend in the far South, where, as a correspondent in the Evangelist justly observes, a minister cannot enforce the law of love, without being suspected of favoring emancipation. I am glad the people with you are beginning to feel and to act. I pray God that you may go on with all the light and love of the gospel, and that the cry of "Let us alone," will not frighten you from your labor of love.

James A. Thome, a Presbyterian clergyman, a native, and still a resident of Kentucky, said in a speech at New York, at the Anniversary of the American Anti-Slavery Society in 1834:

Under all these disadvantages, you are doing much. The very little leaven which you have been enabled to introduce, is now working with tremendous power. One instance has lately occurred within my acquaintance, of an heir to slave property—a young man of growing influence, who was first awakened by reading a single number of the Anti-Slavery Reporter, sent to him by some unknown hand. He is now a whole-hearted abolitionist. I have facts to show that cases of this kind are by no means rare. A family of slaves in Arkansas Territory, another in Tennessee, and a third, consisting of 88, in Virginia, were successively emancipated through the influence of one abolition periodical. Then do not hesitate as to duty. Do not pause to consider the propriety of interference. It is as unquestionably the province of the North to labor in this cause, as it is the duty of the church to convert the world. The call is urgent—it is imperative. We want light. The ungodly are saying, "the church will not enlighten us." The church is saying, "the ministry will not enlighten us." The ministry is crying, "Peace—take care." We are altogether covered in gross darkness. We appeal to you for light. Send us facts—send us kind remonstrance and manly reasoning. We are perishing for lack of truth. We have been lulled to sleep by the guilty apologist.

A letter from a Post Master in Virginia, to the editor of "Human Rights," dated August 15, 1835, contains the following:—

> I have received two numbers of Human Rights, and one of The Emancipator. I have read and loaned them, had them returned, and loaned again. I can see no unsoundness in the arguments there advanced—and until I can see some evil in your publications, I shall distribute all you send to this office. It is certainly high time this subject was examined, and viewed in its proper light. I know these publications will displease those who hold their fellow men in bondage: but reason, truth and justice are on your side—and why should you seek the good will of any who do evil?
>
> I would be pleased to have a copy of the last Report of the Am. Anti-Slavery Society, if convenient, and some of your other pamphlets, which you have to distribute gratis. I will read and use them to the best advantage.

A gentleman of Middlesex County, Mass. whose house is one of my New England homes, told me that he had very recently met with a slaveholder from the South, who, during a warm discussion on the subject of slavery, made the following acknowledgment: "The worst of it is, *we have fanatics among ourselves,* and we don't know what to do with them, for they are *increasing fast,* and are sustained in their opposition to slavery by the Abolitionists of the North."

A Baptist clergyman whom I met in Worcester County, Mass., a few months since, told me that his brother-in-law, a lawyer of New Orleans, who had recently paid him a visit, took up the Report of the Massachusetts Anti-Slavery Society, and read it with great interest. He then inquired, whether the principles set forth in that document were Anti-Slavery principles. Upon being informed that they were, he expressed his entire approbation of them, and full conviction that they would prevail as soon as the South understood them; for, said he, they are the principles of truth and justice, and must finally triumph. This gentleman requested to be furnished with some of our publications, and carried them to the South with him.

There certainly can be no doubt to a reflecting and candid mind, as to what will and *must* be the result of Anti-Slavery operations. Hear now the opinion of one of the leading political papers in Charleston, South Carolina, the Southern Patriot.

> While agitation is *permitted* in Congress, there is *no security for the South.* While discussion is *allowed* in that body, year after year, in relation to slavery and its incidents, the rights of property at the South *must, in the lapse of a short period, be undermined.* It is the weapon of all who expect to work out *great changes in public opinion.* It was the instrument by which O'CONNELL gradually shook the fabric of popular prejudice in England on the Catholic question. His sole instrument was agitation, both in Parliament and out of it. His constant counsel to his followers was, agitate! agitate! They did agitate. They happily carried the question of Catholic rights.
>
> Agitation may be successfully employed for a bad as well as good cause. What was the weapon of the English abolitionists?—Agitation. Regard the question of the abolition of the slave trade when first brought into Parliament—behold the influence of PITT and the tory party beating down its advocates by an overwhelming majority! Look at the question of abolition itself, twenty years after, and you see WILBERFORCE and his adherents carrying the question itself of *abolition of slavery,* by a majority as triumphant! How was all this accomplished?—By agitation in Parliament! It was on this ample theatre that the abolitionists worked their fatal spells. It was on this wide stage of discussion that they spoke to the people of England in that voice of fanaticism, which, at length, found an echo that suited their purposes. It was through the debates, which circulated by means of the press throughout every corner of the realm, that they carried that question to its extremest borders, to the hamlet of every peasant in the empire. Can it then be expected, if we give the American abolitionists the same advantage of that wide field of debate which Congress affords, that the *same results* will not follow? The local legislatures are limited theatres of action. Their debates are comparatively obscure. These

are not read by the people at large. Allow the agitators a great political centre, like that of Washington—*permit* them to address their voice of fanatical violence to the whole American people, through their diffusive press, and they want no greater advantage. They have a MORAL LEVER BY WHICH THEY CAN MOVE A WORLD OF OPINION.

The course of the southern States is therefore marked out by a pencil of light. They should obtain additional guarantees against *the discussion of slavery in Congress, in any manner, or in any of its forms, as it exists in the United States.* This is the only means that promises success in removing agitation. We have said that this is the accepted time. When we look at the spread of opinion on this subject in some of the eastern States—in Vermont, Massachusetts and Connecticut—what are we to expect in a few years, in the middle States, should discussion proceed in Congress? These States are yet uninfected, in any considerable degree, by the fanatical spirit. *They may not remain so after a lapse of five years.* If they are animated by a true spirit of patriotism—by a genuine love for the Union, they should, and could with effect, interpose to stay this *moral* pestilence. Their voice in this matter would be influential. New York and Pennsylvania are intermediate between the South and East in position and in physical strength.

Samuel L. Gould, a minister of the Baptist denomination, writing to the Secretary of the American Anti-Slavery Society, from Fayette Country, Pennsylvania, in 4th month, 1836, says:—

The Smithfield Anti-Slavery Society, [on the border of Virginia] has among its members, several residents of Virginia. Its President has been a slaveholder, and until recently, was a distinguished citizen of Virginia, the High Sheriff of Rockingham County. Having become convinced of the wickedness of slaveholding, a little more than a year ago he purchased an estate in Pennsylvania, and removed to it, his colored men accompanying him. He now employs them as hired laborers.

I may mention, in this connection, an Alabama slaveholder, a lawyer named Smith, who emancipated his slaves, I think about twenty in number, a few months since. He was the brother-in-law of William Allan of Huntsville, who was in 1834, president of the Lane Seminary Anti-Slavery Society, and subsequently an agent of the American Anti-Slavery Society, and who had for years previous been in kind and faithful correspondence with him on the subject of slavery.

Henry P. Thompson, a student of Lane Seminary, and a slaveholder at the time of the Anti-Slavery discussion in that Institution, was convinced by it, went to Kentucky, and emancipated his slaves.

Arthur Thome, an elder in the Presbyterian Church, Augusta, Kentucky, emancipated his slaves, fourteen in number, about two years since. J. G. Birney, speaking of him in the Philanthropist, says:—

> For a long time he had been a professor of religion, but had not, till the doctrines of abolition were embraced by his son on the discussion of the subject at Lane Seminary, given to the subject more attention than was usual among slaveholding professors at the time. At first he thought his son was deranged—and that his intended trip to New York, to speak at the anniversary of the American Anti-Slavery Society, was evidence of it. He sought him (as we have heard,) on the steamboat, which was to convey him up the Ohio river, that he might stop him from going. Something, however, prevented his seeing his son before his departure, and there was no detention.
>
> The truth bore on the mind of Mr. T. till it produced its proper fruit—and he now says, that he is confident no other doctrine but that of the SIN of slaveholding, connected with an *immediate* breaking off from it, will influence the slaveholder to do justice.

I see by the late Washington papers, that one of my South Carolina cousins, Robert Barnwell Rhett, the late Attorney General of the State, has come up to my help on this point, with his characteristic chivalry; [howbeit "he meaneth not so, neither doth his heart think so."] In his late address to his Congressional Constituents, he says:—

> Who that knows anything of human affairs, but must be sensible that the subject of abolition may be approached in a thousand

> ways, without direct legislation? By perpetual discussion, agitation and threats, accompanied with the real or imaginary power to perform, *there will be need of no other action than words to shake the confidence of men in the safety and continuance of the institution of slavery, and its value and existence will be destroyed.* These are all the weapons the abolitionist desires to be allowed to use to accomplish his purpose. When Congress moves, it will be the last act in the drama; and it will be prepared to enforce its legislation. To acknowledge the right, or to tolerate the act of interference at all with this institution, is to give it up—to abandon it entirely; and, as this must be the consummation of any interference, the sooner it is reached the better. The South must hold this institution, not amidst alarm and molestation, but in peace—perfect peace, from the interference or agitation of others; or, I repeat it, she *will*—she *can*—hold it not at all. * * * There is no one so weak, but he must perceive that, whilst the spirit of abolition in the North is increasing, slavery in the South, in all the frontier States, is decreasing.

Farther, I may add the names of J. G. Birney of Alabama, John Thompson and a person named Meux, Jassamine County, Kentucky, J. M. Buchanan, Professor in Center College, Kentucky, Andrew Shannon, a Presbyterian minister in Shelbyville, Kentucky, Samuel Taylor, a Presbyterian minister of Nicholasville, Kentucky, Peter Dunn of Mercer County, Kentucky, a person named Doake in Tennessee, another named Carr in North Carolina, another named Harndon in Virginia—with a number of others, the particulars of whose cases I have not now by me, all of whom were slaveholders four years since, and were induced to emancipate their slaves through the influence of Anti-Slavery discussions and periodicals.

The Democrat, a political paper published at Rochester, New York, contained the following in the summer of 1835.

> On Saturday last, many of our citizens had an opportunity of witnessing a noble scene. On board the boat William Henry, then lying at the Exchange street wharf, were TEN SLAVES, or those who had recently been such, and several free persons of color. The master, a gentleman of more than seventy years of age, accompanied

> them. His residence was in Powhattan County, seventy miles below Richmond, Virginia. He was on his way to Buffalo, near which place he intends purchasing a large farm, where his "people," as he calls them, are to be settled. The above named gentleman was led to sacrifice much of this world's lucre, besides some $5000 of *human "property,"* by becoming convinced of the sinfulness of his practice while reading *Anti-Slavery publications.*

A letter now lies before me from an elder of a religious denomination in the far South-West, who was converted to Abolition sentiments by Anti-Slavery publications sent to him from the city of New York, and who has already emancipated his slaves, ten in number. The writer says, "my hopes are revived when I read of the progress of the cause in the Eastern States, and of the increase of Anti-Slavery Societies. My soul glows with gratitude to God for his mercy to the down-trodden slaves, in raising up for them in these days of savage cruelty, hundreds who, fearless of consequences, are standing up for the entire abolition of slavery, whom, though unseen, I dearly love. O! how it would delight me to listen to the public addresses of some of these dear friends."

Hear, too, the reason assigned by James Smylie, a Presbyterian minister of the Amite Presbytery, Mississippi, for writing a book in 1836, to prove that slavery is a divine institution.

> From his intercourse with religious societies of *all* denominations in Mississippi and Louisiana, he was aware that the Abolition maxim, viz: that *Slavery is in itself sinful, had gained on and entwined itself among the religious and conscientious scruples of many* in the community, so far as to render them *unhappy.* The eye of the mind, resting on Slavery itself as a *corrupt fountain,* from which, of necessity, *nothing but corrupt* streams could flow, was *incessantly* employed in search of some plan by which, with safety, the fountain could, in some future time, be *entirely* dried up.' An illustration of this important acknowledgement, will be found in the following fact, extracted from the Herald of Freedom: "A young gentleman who has been residing in South Carolina, says our movements (Abolitionists) are producing the best effects upon the South, *rousing the consciences of Slaveholders,* while the slaves seem to be impressed as a body with the idea,

that help is coming—that an interest is felt for them, and plans devising for their relief somewhere—which keeps them quiet. He says it is not uncommon for ministers and good people to make confession like this. One, riding with him, broke forth, 'O, I fear that the groans and wails from our slaves enter into the ear of the Lord of Sabaoth. I am distressed on this subject: my *conscience* will let me have no peace. I go to bed, but not to sleep. I walk my room in agony, and resolve that I will never hold slaves another day; but in the morning, my heart, like Pharaoh's, is hardened.'"

In the autumn of 1835, an influential minister in one of the most southern States, (who only one year before had stoutly defended slavery, and vehemently insisted that northern abolitionists were producing unmixed and irremediable evil at the South,) wrote to the Corresponding Secretary of one of our State Anti-Slavery Societies who had furnished him with Anti-Slavery publications, avowing his conversion to Abolition sentiments, and praying that Anti-Slavery Societies might persevere in their efforts, and increase them. Among other expressions of strong feeling the letter contained the following:

I am greatly surprised that I should in any form have been the apologist of a system so full of deadly poison to all holiness and benevolence as slavery, the concocted essence of fraud, selfishness, and cold-hearted tyranny, and the fruitful parent of unnumbered evils, both to the oppressor and the oppressed, THE ONE THOUSANDTH PART OF WHICH HAS NEVER BEEN BROUGHT TO LIGHT.

Do you ask why this change, after residing in a slave country for twenty years? You remember the lines of Pope, beginning:

Vice is a monster, of so frightful mien
As to be hated, needs but to be seen,
But seen too oft, *familiar* with her face;
We first endure, then pity, then *embrace*.

I had become so familiar with the loathsome features of slavery, that they *ceased to offend*—besides, I had become a *southern man* in all my feelings, and it is a part of our *creed* to defend slavery.

About two years since, Arthur and Lewis Tappan received a letter from a Virginian slaveholder, who held nearly one hundred slaves, and whose conscience had been greatly roused to the sin of slavery. In the letter, he avowed his determination to absolve himself from the guilt of slaveholding, declaring that he "had rather be a wood cutter or a coal heaver, than to *remain in the midst of slavery.*"

An intelligent gentleman, a lawyer and a citizen of the District of Columbia, has just written a letter to a gentleman of New York city, from which I give thee the following extract:

> The proceedings in Congress at this session have had the effect, I think, to rouse the attention of the public in all quarters, to the subject of slavery; and that, of itself, I think is a good: and it is in my opinion the chief present good that is to grow out of it. Discussion of some sort takes place, and the real foundation on which the system rests, cannot but be brought more or less into view. My hope is, that men who *denounce* now, will at length *reason.* That is what is wanted—reasoning, reflection, and a true perception of the basis on which slavery is founded.

The foregoing are but a few of the facts and testimonies in the possession of Abolitionists, showing that their discussions, periodicals, petitions, arguments, appeals and societies, have extensively moved, and are still mightily moving the slaveholding States—*for good.* Did time and space permit, I might, by a little painstaking, procure many more. Before passing from this part of the subject, I must record my amazement at the clamors of many of the opponents of Abolitionists, from whom better things might indeed be hoped. What slaveholders have you convinced? they demand. Whom have you made Abolitionists? Give us their names and places of abode. Now, those who incessantly stun us with such unreasonable clamor, know full well, that to give the public the names and residences of such persons, would be in most instances to surrender them to butchery. But be it known to the North and to the South, we have names of scores of citizens of the slaveholding states, many of them slaveholders, who are in constant correspondence with us, persons who feel so deeply on the subject as to implore us to persevere in our efforts, and not to be dismayed by Southern threats nor disheartend by Northern cavils and heartlessness. Yea more, these persons have committed to us the custody even of their lives, thus encountering imminent peril that they might cheer us onward in our work. Shall we betray their trust, or put them in jeopardy? Judge thou.

Now let me ask, when in former years Anti-Slavery tracts, with our doctrines, could be circulated at the South? The fact is, there were *none* to be circulated there; our principle of repentance is quite new. But I can tell thee of two facts, which it is probable thou "hast not been informed of." In the year 1809, the steward of a vessel, a colored man, carried some Abolition pamphlets to Charleston. Immediately on his arrival, he was informed against, and would have been tried for his life, had he not promised to leave the State, never to return. Was South Carolina willing to receive abolition pamphlets *then?* Again, in 1820, my sister carried some pamphlets there—"Thoughts on Slavery," issued by the Society of Friends, and therefore *not* very incendiary, thou mayest be assured; and yet she was informed some time afterwards, that had it not been for the influence of our family, she would have been imprisoned; for she, too, was accused of giving one of them to a slave; just as Abolitionists have been falsely charged with sending their papers to the enslaved. What she did give away, she was *obliged* to give *privately.* Was Charleston ready to receive Abolition pamphlets *then?* Or when? please to tell me. I say that *more,* far more Anti-Slavery tracts, &c. are *now* read in the South, than ever were at any former period. As to Colonization tracts, I know they have circulated at the South; but what of that, when Southerners believed that Colonization had *no* connection with the overthrow of Slavery? Colonization papers, &c. are not Abolition papers.

As to preachers, let me assure thee, that they *never* have dared to preach on the subject of slavery in my native city, so far as my knowledge extends. Ah! I for some years sat under two *northern* ministers, but never did I hear them preach in public, or speak in private, on the *sin* of slavery. O! the *deep,* DEEP injury which such unfaithful ministers have inflicted on the South! It is well known that our young men have, to a great extent, been educated in Northern Theological Seminaries. With what principles were *their* minds imbued? What kind of religion did the *North* prepare them to preach? A slaveholding religion—and multitudes of them became slaveholders. Such was one of my *northern* pastors. And yet thou tellest me, the North has nothing to do with slavery at the South—is *not* guilty, &c. &c. "Their own clergy," thou sayest, "either entirely hold their peace, or become the defenders of a system they once lamented, and attempted to bring to an end." Do name to me one of those valiant defenders of slavery, who formerly lamented over the system, and attempted to bring it to an end. "What is his name, or what is his son's name, if thou canst tell?" Strange indeed, if, because *we* advocate the truth, others should begin to hate it; or because we expose sin, they should turn round and defend what once they lamented over! Is this in accordance with "the known laws of mind," where principle is deeply rooted in the heart?

And then thou closest these assertions *without proof*, with the triumphant exclamation, "This is the record of experience, as to the tendencies of abolitionism, as thus far developed. The South is just now in that state of high exasperation, at the sense of wanton injury and *impertinent interference*, which makes the influence of truth and reason most useless and powerless." Hadst thou been better informed as to the real tendencies of abolitionism on the South, this assertion also might have been spared. Again I repeat, the *South* does not tell us so. Read the subjoined extract of a letter now lying before me from a correspondent in a *Southern* State. "12 or 15 at this place believe that *all* men are born free and equal, that *prejudice against color is a disgrace to the man who feels it*, that such a feeling is without foundation in reason or scripture, and ought to be abandoned *immediately*, that slavery is a *malum in se*, yea, a *heinous crime* in the sight of God, to be repented *of without delay*." Read also the following, extracted from the Marietta Gazette: 'A citizen of one of the free states, not many months ago, observed to a distinguished southerner, that the operations of the abolitionists were impeding the cause of emancipation—or to that effect. "Sir," said the Southerner, "You are mistaken. Depend upon it, these agitations have put the slaveholders to very serious thinking." These, then, are the effects which Abolitionism is producing on some at the South. That others are exasperated, I do not deny. Hear what Bolling of Virginia said in 1832, in the Legislature of that State: "It has long been the pleasure of those who are wedded to the system of slavery, to brand *all* its opponents with opprobrious epithets; to represent them as enemies to order, as persons desirous of tearing up the foundation of society thereby endeavoring to brand them with infamy in order to avert from them the public ear." Here then we find a Southern Legislator acknowledging that *all* the opponents of Slavery have ever excited the same exasperation in those who are "wedded to the system." Who is to be blamed? Is *this* any cause of discouragement? That we have succeeded in rousing the North to reflection, thou art thyself a living proof; for let me ask, what it was that set *thee* to such serious thinking, as to induce *thee* to write a *book* on the Slave Question?

Thy friend in haste,

A. E. GRIMKÉ.

LETTER X.

"The Tendency of the Age Towards Emancipation" Produced by Abolition Doctrines.

DEAR FRIEND: Thou sayest, "that this evil (Slavery,) is at no distant period to come to an end, is the unanimous opinion of all who either notice the tendencies of the age, or believe in the prophecies of the Bible." But how can this be true, if Abolitionists have indeed rolled back the car of Emancipation? If our measures really tend to this result, how can this evil come to an end at no distant period? Colonizationists tell us, if it had not been for our interference, they could have done a vast deal better than they have done; and the American Unionists say, that we have paralyzed their efforts, so that they can do nothing; and yet "the tendencies of the age" are crowding forward Emancipation. Now, what has produced this tendency? Surely every reflecting person must acknowledge, that Colonization cannot effect the work of Abolition. The American Union is doing nothing; and Abolitionists are pursuing a course which "will tend to bring slavery to an end, *if at all*, at the *most distant* period,"—then do tell me, how the tendencies of the age can possibly lean towards Emancipation! Perhaps I shall be told, that the movements of Great Britain in the West Indies created this tendency. Ah! but this is a *foreign influence*, more so even than Northern influence; and if the North is "a foreign community," as thou expressly stylest it, and can on *that account* produce *no* influence on the South, how can the doings of England affect her?

Now I believe with thee, that the tendencies of the age are toward Emancipation; but I contend that nothing but free discussion has produced this tendency—"the present agitation of the subject" is in fact *the thing* which is producing this happy tendency. Now let us turn to the South, and ask her eagle-eyed politicians what *they* are most afraid of. Read their answer in their desperate struggles to fetter the press and gag the mouths of—*whom?*—Colonizationists? Why no—*they* talk colonization *themselves*, and are not at all afraid that the expatriation of a few hundreds or thousands in 20 years will ever drain the country of its millions of slaves, where they are now increasing at the rate of 70,000 every year. The American Unionists? O no! the South has not deemed them worthy of any notice! Pray, then, *whose* mouths are slaveholders so fiercely striving to seal in silence? Why the mouths of Abolitionists, to be sure—even our infant school children know this. Strange indeed, when the labors of these men are actually rolling back the car of Emancipation for one or two centuries! Why, the South ought to pour out her treasure, to support Anti-Slavery agents, and print Anti-Slavery papers and pamphlets, and do all she can to aid us in *rolling back* Emancipation. Pray, write *her a book*, and tell her she has been very needlessly alarmed at our doings, and advise her to send us a few thousand dollars: her money would be very acceptable in these hard times, and we would take it as the wages due to the unpaid laborers, though we would never admit the donors to membership with us. How dost thou think *she* would receive *such a book?* Just try it, I entreat thee.

Thou seemest to think that the North has *no right* to rebuke the South, and assumest the ground that Abolitionists are the enemies of the South. We say, we have the right, and mean to exercise it. I believe that every northern Legislature has a right, and ought to use the right, to send a solemn remonstrance to every southern Legislature on the subject of slavery. Just as much right as the South has to send up a remonstrance against our free presses, free pens, and free tongues. Let the North follow her example; but, instead of asking her to enslave her subjects, entreat her to *free* them. The South may pretend *now*, that we have no right to interfere, because it suits her convenience to say so; but a few years ago, (1820,) we find that our Vice President, R. M. Johnson, in his speech on the Missouri question, was amazed at the "cold insensibility, the eternal apathy towards the slaves in the District of Columbia," which was exhibited by *northern* men, "though they had occular demonstration continually" before them of the abominations of slavery. *Then* the South wondered *we did not interfere with slavery*—and *now* she says we have no right to interfere.

I find, on the 57th p. a false assertion with regard to Abolitionists. After showing the folly of our rejecting the worldly doctrine of expediency, so excellent in thy view, thou then sayest that we say, the reason why we do not go to the South is, that we should be murdered. Now, if there are any half-hearted Abolitionists, who are thus recreant to the high and holy principle of "Duty is ours, and events are God's," then I must leave such to explain their own inconsistences; but that this is the reason assigned by the Society, as a body, I never have seen nor believed. So far from it, that I have invariably heard those who understood the principles of the Anti-Slavery Society best, *deny* that it was a duty to go to the South, *not* because they would be killed, but because the *North was guilty*, and therefore ought to be labored with *first*. They took exactly the same view of the subject, which was taken by the southern friend of mine to whom I have already alluded. "Until til northern women, (said she,) do their duty on the subject of slavery, *southern* women cannot be expected to do theirs." I therefore utterly deny this charge. Such may be the opinion of a few, but it is not and cannot be proved to be a principle of action in the Anti-Slavery Society. The fact is, we need no excuse for not going to the South, so long as the North is as deeply involved in the guilt of slavery as she is, and as blind to her duty.

One word with regard to these remarks: "Before the Abolition movements commenced, both northern and southern men expressed their views freely at the South." This, also, I deny, because, as a southerner, *I know* that *I* never could express my views freely on the abominations of slavery, without exciting anger, even in professors of religion. It is true, "the *dangers, evils* and *mischiefs* of slavery" could be, and were discussed at the South and the North. Yes, we might talk as much as we pleased about *these*, as long as we viewed slavery as a *misfortune* to the *slaveholder*, and talked of "the dangers, evils and mischiefs of slavery" to *him*, and pitied *him* for having had such a "sad inheritance entailed upon him." But could any man or woman ever "express their views freely" on the SIN of slavery at the South? I say, never! Could they express their views freely as to the dangers, mischiefs and evils of slavery to the *poor suffering slave?* No, never! It was only whilst the *slaveholder* was regarded as *an unfortunate sufferer*, and sympathized with *as such*, that he was willing to talk, and be talked to, on this "delicate subject." Hence we find, that as soon as *he* is addressed as a *guilty oppressor*, why then he is in a phrenzy of passion. As soon as we set before him the dangers, and evils, and mischiefs of slavery to *the down-trodden victims of his oppression*, O then! the slaveholder storms and raves like a maniac. Now look at this view of the subject: as a southerner, I know it is the only correct one.

With regard to the discussion of "the subject of slavery, in the legislative halls of the South," if thou hast read these debates, thou certainly must know that they did not touch on the SIN of slavery at all; they were wholly confined to "the dangers, evils and mischiefs of slavery" to the *unfortunate slaveholder*. What did the discussion in the Virginia legislature result in? In the *rejection of every* plan of emancipation, and in the passage of an act which they believed would give additional permanency to the institution, whilst it divested it of its dangers, by removing the free people of color to Liberia; for which purpose they voted $20,000, but took very good care to provide, "that no slave to be thereafter emancipated should have the benefit of the appropriation," so fearful were they, lest masters might avail themselves of this scheme of expatriation to manumit their slaves. The Maryland scheme is altogether based on the principle of banishment and oppression. The colored people were to be "got rid of," for the benefit of their lordly oppressors—*not* set free from the noble principles of justice and mercy to *them*. If Abolitionists have put a stop to all *such* discussions of slavery, I, for one, do most heartily rejoice at it. The fact is, the South is enraged, because we have exposed her horrible hypocrisy to the world. We have torn off the mask, and brought to light the hidden things of darkness.

To prove to thee that the South, as a body, never was prepared for emancipation, I might detail historical facts, which are stubborn things; but I have not the time to go into this subject that would be necessary. I will, therefore, give a few extracts from documents published by the old Abolition Societies, whose principle was gradualism. In 1803, in the report of the Delaware Society, I find the following statement:—"The general temper and opinion of the opulent in this state, is either *opposed* to the generous principles of emancipation to the people of color, or indifferent to the success of the work." In 1804, when a Committee was appointed to draft a memorial to the Legislature of North Carolina, we find the following sentiment expressed in their Report:—"They believe that public opinion in that state is *exceedingly hostile to the abolition of slavery;* and *every* attempt towards emancipation is regarded with an indignant and jealous eye; that at present, the inhabitants of that State consider the preservation of their lives, and all they hold dear on earth, as depending on the continuance of slavery, and are even riveting *more firmly* the fetters of oppression." "They believe that great difficulty would attend the presentation of an address to the public, and that, if presented, it would not be read." The address was, however, issued, and in it we find this complaint—"Many *aspersions* have been cast upon the advocates of the freedom of the blacks, by malicious and interested men." In 1805, in the Report of the Alexandria Society, District of Columbia, they say—"There is rather a disposition to *increase* the measure of affliction already appointed to the poor deserted African:" and complain of the decline of the Society, for which they assign several reasons, one of which is, "the admission of slaveholders into fellowship at its formation." Several of the Reports state, that they fully learned the impolicy of *this* measure, by the violent opposition which these slaveholding members made to their efforts for emancipation. Just as well might a Temperance Society admit a practical drunkard into their ranks, as for an Abolition Society to admit a slaveholder to membership.

In 1806, the Report of the Pennsylvania Society says—"We believe the true reason, why ostensible and public measures are not pursued by the advocates of abolition in the southern states, will be found in the pretty general impression, that it would not, *under existing circumstances*, and in the *present temper of the public mind*, be expedient and useful." The Wilmington Report "laments that the people of South Carolina *continue opposed* to our cause"—and in 1809, the Report of this same Society says, "We regret most sincerely the difficulty we labor under in establishing corresponding agents in the southern states, on whose fidelity and integrity we can firmly rely." In 1816, the Delaware Society makes the following confession—"When we look back at the bright prospects which opened on this cause within the last 20 years, and recur to the joyful feelings excited by the just anticipations of speedy success in this conflict with cruelty and wrong, we cannot but feel the pressure of that gloom which is the consequence of *disappointment and defeat*." In 1826, we find the North Carolina Report acknowledging that "the *gentlest* attempt to agitate the subject, or the *slightest hint* at the work of emancipation, is sufficient to call forth their *indignant resentment*, as if their dearest rights were invaded."

How, then, can our opponents say, that the cause of emancipation has been *rolled back* by *us?* We ask, when was it ever *forward?* As a southerner, I repeat my solemn conviction, from *my own experience*, and from all I can learn from historical facts, and the reports of the Gradual Emancipation Societies of this country, and the scope of the debates which took place in the Kentucky, Virginia and Maryland Legislatures, that it *never was* forward. If the tendencies of the age are towards emancipation, they are tendencies peculiar to this age in the United States, and have been brought about by free discussion, and in accordance, too, with the *known laws of mind;* for collision of mind as naturally produces light, as the striking of the flint and the steel produces fire. *Free discussion is this collision*, and the results are visible in the light which is breaking forth in every city, town and village, and spreading over the hills and valleys, through the whole length and breadth of our land. Yes! it has already reached "the dark valley of the shadow of death" in the South; and in a few brief years, He who said, "Let there be light," will gather this moral effulgence into a focal point, and beneath its burning rays, the heart of the slaveholder, and the chains of the slave, will melt like wax before the orb of day.

Let us, then, take heed lest we be found fighting against God while standing idle in the market place, or endeavoring to keep other laborers out of the field now already white to the harvest.

Thy Friend,

A. E. GRIMKÉ.

LETTER XI.

The Sphere of Woman and Man as Moral Beings the Same.

Brookline, Mass. 8th month, 28th, 1837.

DEAR FRIEND: I come now to that part of thy book, which is, of all others, the most important to the women of this country; thy "general views in relation to the place woman is appointed to fill by the dispensations of heaven." I shall quote paragraphs from thy book, offer my objections to them, and then throw before thee my own views.

Thou sayest, "Heaven has appointed to one sex the *superior*, and to the other the *subordinate* station, and this without any reference to the character or conduct of either." This is an assertion without proof. Thou further sayest, that "it was designed that the mode of gaining influence and exercising power should be *altogether different and peculiar.*" Does the Bible teach this? "Peace on earth, and good will to men, is the character of all the rights and privileges, the influence and the power of *woman.*" Indeed! Did our Holy Redeemer preach the doctrines of *peace to our sex* only? "A *man* may act on Society by the collision of intellect, in public debate; *he* may urge his measures by a sense of shame, by fear and by personal interest; *he* may coerce by the combination of public sentiment; *he* may drive by physical force, and *he* does *not* overstep the boundaries of his sphere." Did Jesus, then, give a different rule of action to men and women? Did he tell his disciples, when he sent them out to preach the gospel, that man might appeal to the fear, and shame, and interest of those he addressed, and coerce by public sentiment, and drive by physical force? "But (that) all the power and all the conquests that are lawful to *woman* are those only which appeal to the kindly, generous, peaceful and benevolent principles?" If so, I should come to a very different conclusion from the one at which thou hast arrived: I should suppose that *woman was the superior*, and *man the subordinate being*, inasmuch as moral power is immeasurably superior to "physical force."

"Woman is to win every thing by peace and love; by making *herself* so much respected, &c. that to yield to *her* opinions, and to gratify *her* wishes, will be the free-will offering of the heart." This principle may do as the rule of action to the fashionable belle, whose idol is *herself;* whose every attitude and smile are designed to win the admiration of others to *herself;* and who enjoys, with exquisite delight, the double-refined incense of flattery which is offered to *her* vanity, by yielding to *her* opinions, and gratifying *her* wishes, because they are *hers.* But to the humble Christian, who feels that it is *truth* which she seeks to recommend to others, *truth* which she wants them to esteem and love, and not herself, this subtle principle must be rejected with holy indignation. Suppose she could win thousands to her opinions, and govern them by her wishes, how much nearer would they be to Jesus Christ, if she presents no higher motive, and points to no higher leader?

"But this is all to be accomplished in the domestic circle." Indeed! "Who made thee a ruler and a judge over all?" I read in the Bible, that Miriam, and Deborah, and Huldah, were called to fill *public stations* in Church and State. I find Anna, the prophetess, speaking in the temple "unto all them that looked for redemption in Jerusalem." During his ministry on earth, I see women following him from town to town, in the most public manner; I hear the woman of Samaria, on her return to the city, telling the *men* to come and see a man who had told her all things that ever she did. I see them even standing on Mount Calvary, around his cross, in the most exposed situation; but He never *rebuked* them; He never told them it was unbecoming *their sphere in life* to mingle in the crowds which followed his footsteps. Then, again, I see the cloven tongues of fire resting on each of the heads of the one hundred and twenty disciples, some of whom were *women*; yea, I hear *them preaching* on the day of Pentecost to the multitudes who witnessed the outpouring of the spirit on that glorious occasion; for, unless *women* as well as men received the Holy Ghost, and *prophesied*, what did Peter mean by telling them, "This is *that* which was spoken by the prophet Joel: And it shall come to pass in the last days, said *God*, I will pour out my spirit upon *all* flesh: and your sons and your *daughters shall prophesy*. . . . And on my servants and on my *handmaidens,* I will pour out in those days of my spirit; and *they shall prophesy*." This is the plain matter of fact, as Clark and Scott, Stratton and Locke, all allow. Mine is no "private interpretation," no mere sectarian view.

I find, too, that Philip had four daughters which did *prophesy;* and what is still more convincing, I read in the xi. of I. Corinthians, some particular directions from the Apostle Paul, as to *how* women were to pray and prophesy in the assemblies of the people—*not* in the domestic circle. On examination, too, it appears that the very same word, *Diakonos*, which, when applied to Phœbe, Romans xvi. 1, is translated *servant*, when applied to Tychicus, Ephesians vi. 21, is rendered *minister.* Ecclesiastical History informs us, that this same Phœbe was preeminently useful, as a minister in the Church, and that female ministers suffered martyrdom in the first ages of Christianity. And what,

I ask, does the Apostle mean when he says in Phillipians iv. 3.—"Help those women who labored with me in the gospel"? Did these holy women of old perform all their gospel labors in "the domestic and social circle"? I trow not.

Thou sayest, "the moment woman begins to feel the promptings of ambition, or the thirst for power, her ægis of defence is gone." Can man, then, retain his ægis when he indulges these guilty passions? Is it woman only who suffers this loss?

"All the generous promptings of chivalry, all the poetry of romantic gallantry, depend upon woman's retaining her place as *dependent* and *defenceless*, and making no claims, and maintaining no rights, but what are the gifts of honor, rectitude and love."

I cannot refrain from pronouncing this sentiment as beneath the dignity of any woman who names the name of Christ. No woman, who understands her dignity as a moral, intellectual, and accountable being, cares aught for any attention or any protection, vouchsafed by "the promptings of chivalry, and the poetry of romantic gallantry"? Such a one loathes such littleness, and turns with disgust from all such silly insipidities. Her noble nature is insulted by such paltry, sickening adulation, and she will not stoop to drink the foul waters of so turbid a stream. If all this sinful foolery is to be withdrawn from our sex, with all my heart I say, *the sooner the better.* Yea, I say more, no woman who lives up to the true glory of her womanhood, will ever be treated with such *practical contempt*. Every man, when in the presence of true moral greatness, "will find an influence thrown around him," which will utterly forbid the exercise of "the poetry of romantic gallantry."

What dost thou mean by woman's retaining her place as defenceless and dependent? Did our Heavenly Father furnish man with any offensive or defensive weapons? Was *he* created any less defenceless than *she* was? Are they not equally defenceless, equally dependent on Him? What did Jesus say to his disciples, when he commissioned them to preach the gospel?—"Behold, I send you forth as SHEEP in the midst of wolves; be ye wise as serpents, and *harmless* as *doves*." What more could he have said to women?

Again, she must "make no claims, and maintain no rights, but what are the gifts of honor, rectitude and love." From whom does woman receive her *rights?* From God, or from man? What dost thou mean by saying, her rights are the *gifts* of honor, rectitude and love? One would really suppose that man, as her lord and master, was the gracious giver of her rights, and that these rights were bestowed upon her by "the promptings of chivalry, and the poetry of romantic gallantry,"—out of the abundance of his honor, rectitude and love. Now, if I understand the real state of the case, woman's rights are not the gifts of man—no! nor the *gifts* of God. His gifts to her may be recalled at his good pleasure—but her *rights* are an integral part of her moral being; they cannot be withdrawn; they must live with her forever. Her rights lie at the foundation of all her duties; and, so long as the divine commands are binding upon her, so long must her rights continue.

"A woman may seek the aid of co-operation and combination among her own sex, to assist her in her appropriate offices of piety, charity," &c. *Appropriate* offices! Ah! here is the great difficulty. What are they? Who can point them out? Who has ever attempted to draw a line of separation between the duties of men and women, as *moral* beings, without committing the grossest inconsistencies on the one hand, or running into the most arrant absurdities on the other?

"Whatever, in any measure, throws a woman into the attitude of a combatant, either for herself or others—whatever binds her in a party conflict—whatever obliges her in any way to exert coercive influences, throws her out of her appropriate sphere." If, by a *combatant*, thou meanest one who "drives by *physical force*," then I say, *man* has no more right to appear as *such* a combatant than woman; for all the pacific precepts of the gospel were given to *him*, as well as to her. If, by a *party conflict*, thou meanest a struggle for power, either civil or ecclesiastical, a thirst for the praise and the honor of man, why, then I would ask, is this the proper sphere of *any* moral, accountable being, man or woman? If, by *coercive influences*, thou meanest the use of force or of fear, such as slaveholders and warriors employ, then, I repeat, that *man* has no more right to exert these than *woman*. All such influences are repudiated by the precepts and examples of Christ, and his apostles; so that, after all, this appropriate sphere of woman is *just as appropriate to man.* These "general principles are correct," if thou wilt only permit them to be of *general application.*

Thou sayest that the propriety of woman's coming forward as a suppliant for a portion of her sex who are bound in cruel bondage, depends entirely on its *probable results.* I thought the disciples of Jesus were to walk by *faith, not* by sight. Did Abraham reason as to the *probable results* of his offering up Isaac? No! or he could not have raised his hand against the life of his son; because in Isaac, he had been told, his seed should be called,—that seed in whom all the nations of the earth were to be blessed. O! when shall we learn that God is wiser than man—that his ways are higher than our ways, his thoughts than our thoughts—and that "obedience is better than sacrifice, and to hearken than the fat of rams?" If we are always to *reason* on the *probable results* of performing our duty, I wonder what our Master meant by telling his disciples, that they must become like *little children.* I used to think he designed to inculcate the necessity of walking by faith, in childlike simplicity, docility and humility. But if we are to *reason* as to the *probable results* of obeying the injunctions to plead for the widow and the fatherless, and to deliver the spoiled out of the hand of the oppressor, &c., then I do not know what he meant to teach.

According to what thou sayest, the women of this country are not to be governed by principles of duty, but by the effect their petitions produce on the members of Congress, and by the opinions of these men. If they deem them "obtrusive, indecorous, and unwise," they must not be sent. If *thou* canst consent to exchange the precepts of the Bible for the opinions of *such a body of men* as now sit on the destinies of this nation, I cannot. What is this but *obeying man* rather than God, and seeking the *praise of man* rather than of God? As to our petitions increasing the evils of slavery, this is merely an opinion, the correctness or incorrectness of which remains to be proved. When I hear Senator Preston of South Carolina, saying, that "he regarded the concerted movement upon the District of Columbia as an attempt to storm the gates of the citadel—as throwing the bridge over the moat"—and declaring that "the South must resist the *danger* in its inception, or it would *soon become irresistible*"—I feel confident that petitions will effect the work of emancipation, *thy* opinion to the contrary notwithstanding. And when I hear Francis W. Pickens, from the same State, saying in a speech delivered in Congress—"Mr. Speaker, we cannot mistake all these things. The truth is, the moral power of the world is against us. It is idle to disguise it. We must, sooner or later, meet the great issue that is to be made on this subject. Deeply connected with this, is the movement to be made on the District of Columbia. If the power be asserted in Congress to interfere here, or any approach be made toward that end, *it will give a shock to our institutions* and the country, the consequences of which no man can foretell. Sir, as well might you grapple with iron grasp into the very heart and vitals of South Carolina, as to touch this subject here." When I hear these things from the lips of keen-eyed politicians of the South, northern apologies for not interfering with the subject of slavery, "lest it should increase, rather than diminish the evils it is wished to remove" affect me little.

Another objection to woman's petitions is, that they may "tend to bring females, as petitioners and partisans, into every political measure that may tend to injure and oppress their sex." As to their ever becoming partisans, i. e. sacrificing principles to power or interest, I reprobate this under all circumstances, and in *both* sexes. But I trust my sisters may always be permitted to *petition* for a redress of grievances. Why not? The right of petition is the only political right that women have: why not let them exercise it whenever they are aggrieved? Our fathers waged a bloody conflict with England, because *they* were taxed without being represented. This is just what unmarried women of property now are. *They* were not willing to be governed by laws which *they* had no voice in making; but this is the way in which women are governed in this Republic. If, then, *we* are taxed without being represented, and governed by laws *we* have no voice in framing, then, surely, we ought to be permitted at least to remonstrate against "every political measure that may tend to injure and oppress our sex in various parts of the nation, and under the various public measures that may hereafter be enforced." Why not? Art thou afraid to trust the women of this country with discretionary power as to petitioning? Is there not sound principle and common sense enough among them, to regulate the exercise of this right? I believe they will always use it wisely. I am not afraid to trust my sisters—not I.

Thou sayest, "In this country, petitions to Congress, in reference to official duties of legislators, seem, IN ALL CASES, to fall entirely without the sphere of female duty. Men are the proper persons to make appeals to the rulers whom they appoint," &c. Here I entirely dissent from thee. The fact that women are denied the right of voting for members of Congress, is but a poor reason why they should also be deprived of the right of petition. If their numbers are counted to swell the number of Representatives in our State and National Legislatures, the *very least* that can be done is to give them the right of petition in all cases whatsoever; and without any abridgement. If not, they are mere slaves, known only through their masters.

In my next, I shall throw out my own views with regard to "the appropriate sphere of woman"—and for the present, subscribe myself,

Thy Friend,

A. E. GRIMKÉ.

LETTER XII.

Human Rights Not Founded on Sex.

East Boylston, Mass. 10th mo. 2d, 1837.

DEAR FRIEND: In my last, I made a sort of running commentary upon thy views of the appropriate sphere of woman, with something like a promise, that in my next, I would give thee my own.

The investigation of the rights of the slave has led me to a better understanding of my own. I have found the Anti-Slavery cause to be the high school of morals in our land—the school in which *human rights* are more fully investigated, and better understood and taught, than in any other. Here a great fundamental principle is uplifted and illuminated, and from this central light, rays innumerable stream all around. Human beings have *rights*, because they are *moral* beings: the rights of *all* men grow out of their moral nature; and as all men have the same moral nature, they have essentially the same rights. These rights may be wrested from the slave, but they cannot be alienated: his title to himself is as perfect *now,* as is that of Lyman Beecher: it is stamped on his moral being, and is, like it, imperishable. Now if rights are founded in the nature of our moral being, then the *mere circumstance of sex* does not give to man higher rights and responsibilities, than to woman. To suppose that it does, would be to deny the self-evident truth, that the "physical constitution is the mere instrument of the moral nature." To suppose that it does, would be to break up utterly the relations, of the two natures, and to reverse their functions, exalting the animal nature into a monarch, and humbling the moral into a slave; making the former a proprietor, and the latter its property. When human beings are regarded as *moral* beings, *sex*, instead of being enthroned upon the summit, administering upon rights and responsibilities, sinks into insignificance and nothingness. My doctrine then is, that whatever it is morally right for man to do, it is morally right for woman to do. Our duties originate, not from difference of sex, but from the diversity of our relations in life, the various gifts and talents committed to our care, and the different eras in which we live.

This regulation of duty by the mere circumstance of sex, rather than by the fundamental principle of moral being, has led to all that multifarious train of evils flowing out of the antichristian doctrine of masculine and feminine virtues. By this doctrine, man has been converted into the warrior, and clothed with sternness, and those other kindred qualities, which in common estimation belong to his character as a *man;* whilst woman has been taught to lean upon an arm of flesh, to sit as a doll arrayed in "gold, and pearls, and costly array," to be admired for her personal charms, and caressed and humored like a spoiled child, or converted into a mere drudge to suit the convenience of her lord and master. Thus have all the diversified relations of life been filled with "confusion and every evil work." This principle has given to man a charter for the exercise of tyranny and selfishness, pride and arrogance, lust and brutal violence. It has robbed woman of essential rights, the right to think and speak and act on all great moral questions, just as men think and speak and act; the right to share their responsibilities, perils and toils; the right to fulfil the great end of her being, as a moral, intellectual and immortal creature, and of glorifying God in her body and her spirit which are His. Hitherto, instead of being a help meet to man, in the highest, noblest sense of the term, as a companion, a co-worker, an equal; she has been a mere appendage of his being, an instrument of his convenience and pleasure, the pretty toy with which he wiled away his leisure moments, or the pet animal whom he humored into playfulness and submission. Woman, instead of being regarded as the equal of man, has uniformly been looked down upon as his inferior, a mere gift to fill up the measure of his happiness. In "the poetry of romantic gallantry," it is true, she has been called "the last *best* gift of God to man;" but I believe I speak forth the words of truth and soberness when I affirm, that woman never was given to man. She was created, like him, in the image of God, and crowned with glory and honor; created only a little lower than the angels,—not, as is almost universally assumed, a little lower than man; on her brow, as well as on his, was placed the "diadem of beauty," and in her hand the sceptre of universal dominion. Gen: i. 27, 28. "The last *best gift* of God to man!" Where is the scripture warrant for this "rhetorical flourish, this splendid absurdity?" Let us examine the account of her creation. "And the rib which the Lord God had taken from man, made he a woman, and brought her unto the man." Not as a gift—for Adam immediately recognized her *as a part of himself*—("this is now bone of my bone, and flesh of my flesh")—a companion and equal, not one hair's breadth beneath him in the majesty and glory of her moral being; not placed under his authority as a *subject*, but by his side, on the same platform of human rights, under the government of God only. This idea of woman's being "the last best gift of God to man," however pretty it may sound to the ears of those who love to discourse upon "the poetry of romantic gallantry, and the generous promptings of chivalry," has nevertheless been the means of sinking her from an *end* into a mere *means*—of turning her into an *appendage* to man, instead of recognizing her as *a part of man*—of destroying her individuality, and rights, and responsibilities, and merging her moral being in that of man. Instead of *Jehovah* being *her* king, *her* lawgiver, and *her* judge, she has been taken out of the exalted scale of existence in which He placed her, and subjected to the despotic control of man.

I have often been amused at the vain efforts made to define the rights and responsibilities of immortal beings as *men* and *women*. No one has yet found out just *where* the line of separation between them should be drawn, and for this simple reason, that no one knows just how far below man woman is, whether she be a head shorter in her moral responsibilities, or head and shoulders, or the full length of his noble stature, below him, i. e. under his feet. Confusion, uncertainty, and great inconsistencies, must exist on this point, so long as woman is regarded in the least degree inferior to man; but place her where her Maker placed her, on the same high level of human rights with man, side by side with him, and difficulties vanish, the mountains of perplexity flow down at the presence of this grand equalizing principle. Measure her rights and duties by the unerring standard of *moral being*, not by the false weights and measures of a mere circumstance of her human existence, and then the truth will be self-evident, that whatever it is *morally* right for a man to do, it is *morally* right for a woman to do. I recognize no rights but *human* rights—I know nothing of men's rights and women's rights; for in Christ Jesus, there is neither male nor female. It is my solemn conviction, that, until this principle of equality is recognised and embodied in practice, the church can do nothing effectual for the permanent reformation of the world. Woman was the first transgressor, and the first victim of power. In all heathen nations, she has been the slave of man, and Christian nations have never acknowledged her rights. Nay more, no Christian denomination or Society has ever acknowledged them on the broad basis of humanity. I know that in some denominations, she is permitted to preach the gospel; not from a conviction of her rights, nor upon the ground of her equality as a *human being*, but of her equality in spiritual gifts—for we find that woman, even in these Societies, is allowed no voice in framing the Discipline by which she is to be governed. Now, I believe it is woman's right to have a voice in all the laws and regulations by which she is to be *governed*, whether in Church or State; and that the present arrangements of society, on these points, are *a violation of human rights, a rank usurpation of power,* a violent seizure and confiscation of what is sacredly and inalienably hers—thus inflicting upon woman outrageous wrongs, working mischief incalculable in the social circle, and in its influence on the world producing only evil, and that continually. *If* Ecclesiastical and Civil governments are ordained of God, *then* I contend that woman has just as much right to sit in solemn counsel in Conventions, Conferences, Associations and General Assemblies, as man—just as much right to it upon the throne of England, or in the Presidential chair of the United States.

Dost thou ask me, if I would wish to see woman engaged in the contention and strife of sectarian controversy, or in the intrigues of political partizans? I say no! never—never. I rejoice that she does not stand on the same platform which man now occupies in these respects; but I mourn, also, that he should thus prostitute his higher nature, and vilely cast away his birthright. I prize the purity of *his* character as highly as I do that of hers. As a moral being, *whatever it is morally wrong for her to do, it is morally wrong for him to do.* The fallacious doctrine of male and female virtues has well nigh ruined all that is morally great and lovely in his character: he has been quite as deep a sufferer by it as woman, though mostly in different respects and by other processes. As my time is engrossed by the pressing responsibilities of daily public duty, I have no leisure for that minute detail which would be required for the illustration and defence of these principles. Thou wilt find a wide field opened before thee, in the investigation of which, I doubt not, thou wilt be instructed. Enter this field, and explore it: thou wilt find in it a hid treasure, more precious than rubies—a fund, a mine of principles, as new as they are great and glorious.

Thou sayest, "'an ignorant, a narrow-minded, or a stupid woman, cannot feel nor understand the rationality, the propriety, or the beauty of this relation"—i.e. subordination to man. Now, verily, it does appear to me, that nothing but a narrow-minded view of the subject of human rights and responsibilities can induce any one to believe in *this subordination to a fallible* being. Sure I am, that the signs of the times clearly indicate a vast and rapid change in public sentiment, on this subject. Sure I am that she is not to be, as she has been, "*a mere second-hand agent*" in the regeneration of a fallen world, but the acknowledged equal and co-worker with man in this glorious work. Not that "she will carry her measures by tormenting when she cannot please, or by petulant complaints or obtrusive interference, in matters which are out of her sphere, and which she cannot comprehend." But just in proportion as her moral and intellectual capacities become enlarged, she will rise higher and higher in the scale of creation, until she reaches that elevation prepared for her by her Maker, and upon whose summit she was originally stationed, only "a little lower than the angels." Then will it be seen that nothing which concerns the well-being of mankind is either beyond her sphere, or above her comprehension: *Then* will it be seen "that America will be distinguished above all other nations for well educated women, and for the influence they will exert on the general interests of society."

But I must close with recommending to thy perusal, my sister's Letters on the Province of Woman, published in the New England Spectator, and republished by Isaac Knapp of Boston. As she has taken up this subject so fully, I have only glanced at it. That thou and all my country-women may better understand the true dignity of woman, is the sincere desire of

Thy Friend,

A. E. GRIMKÉ.

LETTER XIII.

Miscellaneous Remarks,—Conclusion.

Holliston, Mass. 10th month, 23d, 1837.

MY DEAR FRIEND: I resume my pen, to gather up a few fragments of thy Essay, that have not yet been noticed, and in love to bid thee farewell.

Thou appearest to think, that it is peculiarly the duty of *women* to educate the little children of this nation. But why, I would ask—why are they any more bound to engage in this sacred employment, than men? I believe, that as soon as the rights of women are understood, our brethren will see and feel that it is their duty to co-operate with us, in this high and holy vocation, of training up little children in the way they should go. And the very fact of their mingling in intercourse with such guileless and gentle spirits, will tend to soften down the asperities of their characters, and clothe them with the noblest and sublimest Christian virtues. I know that this work is deemed beneath the dignity of man; but how great the error! I once heard a man, who had labored extensively among children, say, "I never feel so near heaven, as when I am teaching these little ones." He was right; and I trust the time is coming, when the occupation of an instructor to children will be deemed the most honorable of human employment. If it is drudgery to teach these little ones, then it is the duty of men to bear a part of that burthen; if it is a privilege and an honor, then we generously invite them to share that honor and privilege with us.

I know some noble instances of this union of principles and employment, and am fully settled in the belief, that abolition doctrines are pre-eminently calculated to qualify men and women to become faithful and efficient teachers. *They alone* teach fully the doctrine of human rights; and to know and appreciate these, is an indispensable prerequisite to the wisely successful performance of the duties of a teacher. The right understanding of these will qualify her to teach the fundamental, but unfashionable doctrine, that "God is no respecter of persons," and that he that despiseth the colored man, because he is "guilty of a skin not colored like our own," reproacheth his Maker for having given him that ebon hue. I consider it absolutely indispensable, that this truth should be sedulously instilled into the mind of every child in our republic. I know of *no* moral truth of greater importance at the present crisis. Those teachers, who are not prepared to teach *this in all its fullness,* are deficient in one of the most sterling elements of moral character, and are false to the holy trust committed to them, and utterly unfit to train up the children of *this* generation. So far from urging the deficiency of teachers in this country, as a reason why women should keep out of the anti-slavery excitement, I would say to my sisters, if you wish to become preeminently qualified for the discharge of your arduous duties, come into the abolition ranks, enter this high school of morals, and drink from the deep fountains of philanthropy and Christian equality, whence the waters of healing are welling forth over wide desert wastes, and making glad the city of our God. Intellectual endowments are *good*, but a high standard of moral principle is *better*, is *essential*. As a nation, we have too long educated the *mind*, and left the *heart* a moral waste. We have fully and fearfully illustrated the truth of the Apostle's declaration: "Knowledge puffeth up." We have indeed been puffed up, vaunting ourselves in our mental endowments and national greatness. But we are beginning to realize, that it is "Righteousness which exalteth a nation."

Thou sayest, when a woman is asked to sign a petition, or join an Anti-Slavery Society, it is "for the purpose of contributing her measure of influence to keep up agitation in Congress, to promote the excitement of the North against the iniquities of the South, to coerce the South by fear, shame, anger, and a sense of odium, to do what she is determined not to do." Indeed! Are these the only motives presented to the daughters of America, for laboring in the glorious cause of Human Rights? Let us examine them. 1. "To keep up agitation in Congress." Yes—for I can adopt this language of Moore of Virginia, in the Legislature of the State, in 1832: "I should regret at all times the existence of any unnecessary excitement in the country on any subject; but I confess, I see no reason to lament that which may have arisen on the present occasion. It is often necessary that there should be some excitement among the people, to induce them to turn their attention to questions deeply affecting the welfare of the Commonwealth; and *there never can arise any subject more worthy their attention, than that of the abolition of slavery*." 2. "To promote the excitement of the North against the iniquities of the South." Yes, and against her own sinful copartnership in those iniquities. I believe the discussion of Human Rights at the North has already been of incalculable advantage to this country. It is producing the happiest influence upon the minds and hearts of those who are engaged in it; just such results as Thomas Clarkson tells us, were produced in England by the agitation of the subject there. Says he, "Of the immense advantages of this contest, I know not how to speak. Indeed, the very agitation of the question, which it involved, has been highly important. Never was the heart of man so expanded; never were its generous sympathies so generally and so perseveringly excited. These sympathies, thus called into existence, have been useful preservatives of national virtue." I, therefore, wish very much to promote the Anti-Slavery excitement at the North, because I believe it will prove a useful preservative of national virtue. 3. "To coerce the South by fear, shame, anger, and a sense of odium." It is true, that I feel the imminent danger of the South so much, that I would fain "save them with fear, pulling them out of the fire;" for, if they ever are saved, they will indeed be "as a brand plucked out of the burning." Nor do I see any thing wrong in influencing slaveholders by a feeling of shame and odium, as well as by a sense of guilt. Why may not abolitionists speak some things *to their shame*, as the Apostle did to the Corinthians? As to anger, it is no design of ours to excite so wicked a passion. We cannot help it, if, in rejecting the truth, they become angry. Could Stephen help the anger of the Jews, when "they gnashed upon him with their teeth"?

But I had thought the principal motives urged by abolitionists were not these; but that they endeavored to excite men and women to active exertion,—first, to cleanse *their own* hands of the sin of slavery, and secondly, to save the South, if possible, and the North, at any rate, from the impending judgments of heaven. The result of their mission in this country, cannot in the least affect the validity of that mission. Like Noah, they may preach in vain; if so, the destruction of the South can no more be attributed to them, than the destruction of the antediluvian world to him. "In vain," did I say? Oh no! The discussion of the rights of the slave has opened the way for the discussion of *other rights*, and the ultimate result will most certainly be, "the breaking of *every* yoke," the letting the oppressed of *every* grade and description go free,—an emancipation far more glorious than any the world has ever yet seen,—an introduction into that "liberty wherewith Christ hath made his people free."

I will now say a few words on thy remarks about Esther. Thou sayest, "When a woman is placed in similar circumstances, where death to herself and all her nation is one alternative, and there is nothing worse to fear, but something to hope as the other alternative, then she may safely follow such an example." In this sentence, thou hast conceded every thing I could wish, and proved beyond dispute just what I adduced this text to prove in my Appeal. I will explain myself. Look at the condition of our country—Church and State deeply involved in the enormous crime of slavery: ah! more—claiming the sacred volume, as our charter for the collar and chain. What then can we expect, but that the vials of divine wrath will be poured out upon a nation of oppressors and hypocrites? for we are loud in our professions of civil and ecclesiastical liberty. Now, as a Southerner, I know that reflecting slaveholders expect their peculiar institution to be overthrown in blood. Read the opinion of Moore of Virginia, as expressed by him in the House of Delegates in 1832:—"What must be the ultimate consequence of retaining the slaves amongst us? The answer to this enquiry is both obvious and appalling. It is, that *the time will come, and at no distant day, when we shall be involved in all the horrors of a servile war*, which will not end until both sides have suffered much, until the land shall everywhere be red with blood, and until the slaves or the whites are totally exterminated. If there be any truth in history, and if the time has not arrived when causes have ceased to produce their legitimate results, the dreadful catastrophe in which I have predicted that our slave system must result, if persisted in, *is as inevitable as any event which has already transpired.*"

Here, then, is one alternative, and just as tremendous an alternative as that which was presented to the Queen of Persia. "There is *nothing worse* to fear" for the South, let the results of abolition efforts be what they may, whilst 'there is something to hope as the other alternative;' because if she will receive the truth in the love of it, she may repent and be saved. So that, after all, according to thy own reasoning, the women of America "may safely follow such an example."

After endeavoring to show that woman has no moral right to exercise the right of petition for the dumb and stricken slave; no business to join, in any way, in the excitement which anti-slavery principles are producing in our country; no business to join abolition societies, &c. &c.; thou professest to tell our sisters what they are to do, in order to bring the system of slavery to an end. And now, my dear friend, what does all that thou hast said in many pages, amount to? Why, that women are to exert their influence in private life, to allay the excitement which exists on this subject, and to quench the flame of sympathy in the hearts of their fathers, husbands, brothers and sons. Fatal delusion! Will Christian women heed such advice?

Hast thou ever asked thyself, what the slave would think of thy book, if he could read it? Dost thou know that, from the beginning to the end, not a word of compassion for *him* has fallen from thy pen? Recall, I pray, the memory of the hours which thou spent in writing it! Was the paper once moistened by the tear of pity? Did thy heart once swell with deep sympathy for thy sister *in bonds?* Did it once ascend to God in broken accents for the deliverance of the captive? Didst thou ever ask thyself, what the free man of color would think of it? Is it such an exhibition of slavery and prejudice, as will call down *his* blessing upon thy head? Hast thou thought of *these* things? or carest thou not for the blessings and the prayers of these our suffering brethren? Consider, I entreat, the reception given to thy book by the apologists of slavery. What meaneth that loud acclaim with which they hail it? Oh, listen and weep, and let thy repentings be kindled together, and speedily bring forth, I beseech thee, fruits meet for repentance, and henceforth show thyself faithful to Christ and his bleeding representative the slave.

I greatly fear that thy book might have been written just as well, hadst thou not had the heart of a woman. It bespeaks a superior intellect, but paralyzed and spell-bound by the sorcery of a worldly-minded expediency. Where, oh where, in its pages, are the outpourings of a soul overwhelmed with a sense of the heinous crimes of our nation, and the necessity of immediate repentance? Farewell! Perhaps on a dying bed thou mayest vainly wish that "*Miss Beecher on the Slave Question*" might perish with the mouldering hand which penned its cold and heartless pages. But I forbear, and in deep sadness of heart, but in tender love though I thus speak, I bid thee again, Farewell. Forgive me, if I have wronged thee, and pray for her who still feels like

Thy sister in the bonds of a common sisterhood,

A. E. GRIMKÉ.

P. S. Since preparing the foregoing letters for the press, I have been informed by a Bookseller in Providence, that some of thy books had been sent to him to sell last summer, and that one afternoon a number of southerners entered his store whilst they were lying on the counter. An elderly lady took up one of them and after turning over the pages for some time, she threw it down and remarked, here is a book written by the daughter of a northern dough face, to apologize for our southern institutions—but for my part, I have a thousand times more respect for the Abolitionists, who openly denounce the system of slavery, than for those people, who in order to please us, cloak their real sentiments under such a garb as this. This southern lady, I have no doubt, expressed the sentiments of thousands of the most respectable slaveholders in our country—and thus, they will tell the North in bitter reproach for their sinful subserviency, after the lapse of a few brief years, when interest no longer padlocks their lips. At present the South feels that she must at least *appear* to thank her northern apologists.

A. E. G.

ADDRESS TO THE MASSACHUSETTS LEGISLATURE, FEBRUARY 21, 1838

MR. CHAIRMAN—

More than 2000 years have rolled their dark and bloody waters down the rocky, winding channel of Time into the broad ocean of Eternity, since woman's voice was heard in the palace of an eastern monarch, and woman's petition achieved the salvation of millions of her race from the edge of the sword. The Queen of Persia,—if Queen she might be called, who was but the mistress of her voluptuous lord,—trained as she had been in the secret abominations of an oriental harem, had studied too deeply the character of Ahasuerus not to know that the sympathies of his heart could not be reached, except through the medium of his sensual appetites. Hence we find her arrayed in royal apparel, and standing in the inner court of the King's house, hoping by her personal charms to win the favor of her lord. And after the golden sceptre had been held out, and the inquiry was made, "What wilt thou, Queen Esther, and what is thy request? it shall be given thee to the half of the kingdom"—even then she dared not ask either for her own life, or that of her people. She *felt* that if her mission of mercy was to be successful, *his* animal propensities must be still more powerfully wrought upon—the luxurious feast must be prepared, the banquet of wine must be served up, and the favorable moment must be seized when, gorged with gluttony and intoxication, the king's heart was fit to be operated upon by the pathetic appeal, "If *I* have found favor in thy sight, O King, and if it please the King, let *my* life be given at my petition, and *my* people at my request." It was thus, through personal charms, and sensual gratification, and individual influence, that the Queen of Persia obtained the precious boon she craved,—her own life, and the life of her beloved people. Mr. Chairman, it is my privilege to stand before you on a similar mission of life and love; but I thank God that we live in an age of the world too enlightened and too moral to admit of the adoption of the same *means* to obtain as holy an end. I feel that it would be an insult to this Committee, were I to attempt to win their favor by arraying my person in gold, and silver, and costly apparel, or by inviting them to partake of the luxurious feast, or the banquet of wine. I understand the spirit of the age too well to believe that *you* could be moved by such sensual means—means as unworthy of you, as they would be beneath the dignity of the cause of humanity. Yes, I feel that if you are reached at all, it will not be by me, but by the truths I shall endeavor to present to your understandings and your hearts. The heart of the eastern despot was reached through the lowest propensities of his animal nature, by personal influence; yours, I know, cannot be reached but through the loftier sentiments of the intellectual and moral feelings.

I stand before you as a citizen, on behalf of the 20,000 women of Massachusetts, whose names are enrolled on petitions which have been submitted to the Legislature, of which you are the organ. These petitions relate to the great and solemn subject of American slavery,—a subject fraught with the deepest interest to this republic, whether we regard it in its political, moral, or religious aspects. And because it is a *political* subject, it has often been tauntingly said, that *women* had nothing to do with it. Are we aliens, because we are *women*? Are we bereft of citizenship, because we are the mothers, wives and daughters of a mighty people? Have women *no* country—*no* interests staked in public weal—no liabilities in common peril—no partnership in a nation's guilt and shame? Let the history of the world answer these queries. Read the denunciations of Jehovah against the follies and crimes of Israel's daughters. Trace the influence of woman as a courtezan and a mistress in the destinies of nations, both ancient and modern, and see her wielding her power too often to debase and destroy, rather than to elevate and save. It is often said that women rule the world, through their influence over men. If so, then may we well hide our faces in the dust, and cover ourselves with sackcloth and ashes. It has not been by moral power and intellectual, but through the baser passions of man.—*This* dominion of women *must* be resigned—the sooner the better; "in the age which is approaching, she should be something *more*—she should be a *citizen*; and this title, which demands an increase of knowledge and of reflection, opens before her a new empire." I hold, Mr. Chairman, that American women have to do with this subject, not only because it is moral and religious, but because it is *political,* inasmuch as we are citizens of this republic, and as such, *our* honor, happiness, and well being, are bound up in its politics, government and laws.

I stand before you as a southerner, exiled from the land of my birth, by the sound of the lash, and the piteous cry of the slave. I stand before you as a repentant slaveholder. I stand before you as a moral being, endowed with precious and inalienable rights, which are correlative with solemn duties and high responsibilities; and as a moral being I feel that I owe it to the suffering slave, and to the deluded master, to my country and the world, to do all that I can to overturn a system of complicated crimes, built up upon the broken hearts and prostrate bodies of my countrymen in chains, and cemented by the blood and sweat and tears of my sisters in bonds.

(The orator then proceeded to discuss the merits of the petitions.)